Bridalveil Falls, west of Highlands, in winter.

W9-ABY-902

Whitewater Falls, near Brevard, the highest waterfall east of the Mississippi.

Tweetsie Railroad, between Boone and Blowing Rock.

The awesome beauty of Roan Mountain and nearby balds.

Stone Mountain as seen from the meadow at the foot of the mountain.

The mile-high swinging bridge at Grandfather Mountain.

Chimney Rock and Lake Lure.

Waterfalls along the Horsepasture River.

Kayaking on the North Carolina/Tennessee border.

Trail of Faith monument at Valdese.

Mabry Mill, across the border in Virginia.

Historic Old Burke County Courthouse.

Downtown old and new Asheville.

Rhododendron Gardens at Roan Mountain.

Thomas Wolfe house, miniature version, at Maggie.

Interior of St. Mary's Church at Beaver Creek (West Jefferson).

Angel from the shop of Tom Wolfe's father in Asheville.
The angel is in the Hendersonville Cemetery.

Jomeokee, at Pilot Mountain State Park.

Rainbow Falls on Horsepasture River near Brevard.

The Last Supper fresco at Holy Trinity Church in Glendale Springs.

All Souls Cathedral at Biltmore Village.

100

Practically Perfect Places
in the North Carolina Mountains

by
Robert L. Williams

Southeastern
Publishing Corp.
Dallas, North Carolina

All opinions expressed in this book are those of the author, who visited every destination described in this book at least one time and, in many instances, a dozen times. The author did not receive any remuneration of any sort while traveling to or while at the destinations included in this volume. No one representing any of the destinations in any way paid or provided considerations in exchange for inclusion in this book.

During the preparation of this book every reasonable effort was made to insure accuracy. These efforts included personal visits to the destinations and, when feasible, interviews with spokespersons representing the destinations. Neither the author nor the publisher assumes any legal responsibility for any incidents arising from the use of the book, photographs, or information provided.

Library of Congress Cataloging-in-Publication Data

Williams, Robert L., 1932-

100 Practically Perfect Places in the North Carolina Mountains; photographs by the author; cover design by Kathy Holbrook.

(Practically Perfect Places series)

ISBN 1-893330-CO-1

Library of Congress Catalog Card Number pending.

1. Driving tours-North Carolina-Guidebooks. 2. Walking tours-North Carolina-Guidebooks. 3. History-North Carolina-Guidebooks. 4. Travel Education-North Carolina-Guidebooks.

Published by Southeastern Publishing Corporation
Printed in the United States of America

ACKNOWLEDGMENTS

During the writing of this book, I encountered numerous persons who provided assistance in countless ways. One of these, Dean Carpenter, provided enthusiastic and unqualified support from the moment the idea of this book was mentioned until the completion of the project. Deborah Page of the Spangler Branch of the Cleveland County Memorial Library and Jo Anne Owens of the Cleveland County Memorial Library's central offices provided great assistance again and again by answering questions, making suggestions, and providing direction to the overall plan of this book.

Karen Searle, Blue Ridge Regional Manager at the Eastern National office of the Blue Ridge Agency in Asheville, read the proposal and examined the table of contents and outline and made several suggestions that improved this book immeasurably. Eastern National is a private non-profit organization that provides Blue Ridge Parkway-related educational products and services in 12 Blue Ridge Parkway Visitor Centers, and proceeds from retail sales are donated to support the many educational, research, and conservation programs in National Parks, with particular emphasis on the Blue Ridge Parkway. For her help, and for the goals and aims of the agency, I am immensely grateful.

Allan Rogers of the South Mountains State Park and Joe Sox at Crowders Mountain State Park provided superb assistance.

The personnel at the State of North Carolina Division of Tourism, Film and Sports Development cheerfully answered questions and made suggestions leading to the improvement of this book.

Joyce Paulin and Barbara Wright read the manuscript and made valuable suggestions, and, during the long process in which this book labored toward completion, both provided enthusiasm and evaluations that were appreciated and valued.

Chris Robbins and the staff of Tweetsie Railroad in Blowing Rock, Hugh Morton at Grandfather Mountain, the management and staff at Chimney Rock Park, and the personnel at the Great Smoky Mountains Railroad provided enormous help.

And, because there are so many superlative people who have made this book possible and also relatively easy, and because I can never remember them individually, I wish to thank them collectively.

Finally, I thank God for having made the North Carolina mountains.

RLW

DEDICATION

This book is dedicated, with love and respect, to people everywhere who love the mountains of North Carolina the way my family and I love the peaks and valleys of the Tar Heel State, and especially to all the Special Ones who have believed in and supported this work all the way, from inception to publication--and beyond: to Jackie, Anna, and Adrian Carpenter and, as always, to Elizabeth and Robert, who daily give more than anyone could ask or deserve.

100 PRACTICALLY PERFECT PLACES
IN WESTERN NORTH CAROLINA

Perfect destinations for North Carolina travelers may be impossible to find, but in the Tar Heel State's mountains there are dozens of attractions that are practically perfect. This book describes one hundred of these remarkable sites: the ten most fascinating sites (in the author's opinion) in ten areas. A practically perfect place has many characteristics, among them beauty, proximity, ease of travel, low costs, aesthetics, historical significance, educational value, and fascination in general with the rich wonders of this unparalleled state.

This book includes visits to very special waterfalls, superb towns and cities, mountain peaks, lakes and streams, educational attractions and museums, churches (selected for history and beauty of architecture rather than theology), private homes of larger-than-life characters, graveyards (the resting places of such figures as Zeb Vance, Tom Wolfe, O. Henry, Tom Dula, Laura Foster, Chief Junaluska, and other important personalities), and superb stop-off points on the Blue Ridge Parkway.

There are also great outdoor experiences described in detail, as well as some of the finest scenic drives anywhere. This book is an introduction to North Carolina for the many fortunate travelers who visit this fantastic area for the first time, and, for those of us who proudly call North Carolina home, it is a joyous return to the splendid history, remarkable heritage, and matchless beauty of the Old North State.

100 PRACTICALLY PERFECT PLACES
in the North Carolina Mountains

Introduction

Perfect places are hard, if not impossible, to find; practically perfect places, on the other hand, abound in North Carolina, and you can find them with the help of a good road map and sound advice, which can be found in this book.

What is a practically perfect place? For starters, it is one that you can locate without great difficulty. It isn't perfect or even practically perfect if you get lost for half a day and find the place only at the end of your trip, when it's too late to enjoy it. This book gets you there efficiently. Directions begin at one of four major arteries in this state: Interstate 40, the Blue Ridge Parkway, Interstate 85, and Interstate 26.

A practically perfect place is one that, once there, you can enjoy to the fullest and in a variety of ways. Some people take delight in great hikes, while others enjoy a rewarding drive of several miles across mountain ridges and through secluded valleys and alongside whitewater rivers. Others revel in picnics, in gorgeous sunsets, in beds of wild flowers in bloom.

Some travelers (or armchair travelers, for that matter) enjoy good food, interesting restaurants, antique shops, craft and folk art shops, music, and antiquity. Many celebrate the history and culture of an area, while still others look for the perfect photograph for an on-going and endless collection.

One great American pastime is simply driving through the lanes and main streets of town, past the historic sections of villages largely neglected by Time, or mingling among colorful people whose lives are historical studies in themselves.

This book offers suggestions in these areas, too.

Still confused as to what a practically perfect place is? It's a location or scene of nearly perfect physical, emotional, or intellectual beauty, one where you can study nature, the Past, the Present, or the lives that have inspired us or made our lives richer. This beauty can be found in the friendly folks who are proud of home town or countryside or pristine wildernesses, in the beauty that creates a wonderland of peaks, clouds, blossoms, and antiquity, and in the celebration of exhilarating outdoor experiences.

A practically perfect place is one where you can spend a day, a weekend, or an entire vacation and find that the views remain constantly fresh and exciting and that each hour and each activity can blend so smoothly with the preceding and with the subsequent that there is never a sensation of time, place, or urgency.

And it doesn't hurt much if these places, with very few exceptions, are free, or nearly free. Some attractions that cost a little more are included because they are special places that will remain in your memory or heart and provide, as Wordsworth said, "life and food for future years."

That's essentially what this book is about: places where entire families, church groups, carloads of friends, or the lone individual in search of the next adventure can visit, explore, and remember with the warmth and delight generated by an old sweater and a bed of coals in the fireplace on a cold rainy night. This book offers a chance to re-visit old friends, whose beauty and enchantment never grow old, and to make new friends who will widen your horizons and add immeasurably to your life.

The poet John Donne speaks of lovers who are separated by space only and who are emotionally connected by a love that is as gold to airy thinness beat. That's the effect the mountains of North Carolina have on me. Wherever I am, I am never disconnected from them, just as I am never far removed from the Past. I do not know about the Future: the Present is far too great for me to devote much time to what is around the next corner.

Over the years I have been to and enjoyed the visits that I describe in this book. From the day I bought my first car (over half a century ago!) to the present time, I have been an ardent traveler in North Carolina. I have also visited locations in Africa, Germany, Italy, Austria, and other parts of the distant world. My work (the greatest career I can imagine!) has taken me to Canada, to New Mexico-the aptly named Land of Enchantment, Arizona, Colorado, Oklahoma, Arkansas, Texas, and other states west of the Mississippi.

I have also traveled much without ever leaving the Carolinas except for brief forays into Georgia, Tennessee, Virginia, and South Carolina. Incidentally, if you have missed out on these wonderful neighbors of ours, you have omitted a superlative part of your travel education. But don't worry. The plan for this series of books is to include the Practically Perfect Places in the North Carolina Piedmont, then the Coastal area, and these will be followed by similar treatments of the states mentioned above. The project will continue as long as there are states to explore and time and energy on the part of the writer.

As a result of my travels to this point I have written travel articles for the *Charlotte Obsersver*, the old *Charlotte News*, *Blue Ridge Country*, *Backwoods Home Magazine*, *Our State Magazine* and dozens of other leading magazines and newspapers as well as for several book companies. After thirty years of writing (and after thirty-something in book count and thousands of newspaper and magazine pieces), I have never found any place on earth that I love as much as I love North Carolina, and I don't plan to stop writing or traveling as long as there is some great place I have not seen, some travel work I have not written, or some place I want to visit again for the pure joy of the experience.

For now, you are invited to join me in your quest to enjoy North Carolina more than ever. Follow me to places where you can learn about the lives of distinguished men and women and children; where you can eat the best hamburgers in the entire world; where you can savor (unless you are squeamish) a meal of buffalo, alligator, pheasant, and rattle-snake-all on the same platter, or the best of more traditional meals; where you can hike if you wish, swim if the inclination strikes, picnic when you are hungry, enjoy strolls through gorgeous gardens, study wild life, learn about military encounters, and return to your home economically un-harmed and spiritually, emotionally, and intellectually enriched.

In this book you will find detailed directions that lead you to the destinations. Each brief chapter (there are 100 of them) also lists nearby attractions, so that you can visit several of the sites on one visit. Facilities are listed for each site, so that you can make your plans accordingly. The listing includes campgrounds, picnic areas, parking spaces, public tele-phones, restrooms, and other necessary or desirable appointments.

For each site you will read a thumbnail sketch of why the destination is important or rewarding, followed by a brief mention of the special attractions that you do not want to miss in the excitement of your trip. The final part of each chapter consists of ways in which you can make the most of your visit.

You will note that admission prices, where applicable, are provided, as are mailing addresses and telephone numbers of the attractions. I know from the outset that prices, addresses, and numbers will change, but I feel that it is better that you have some notion of the cost of a visit than to be shocked speechless after you have driven long miles to an attraction. At one attraction, not listed in this book, I saw a mother of four children pay for tickets, and I saw the look of horror when she real-ized that the total cost-almost $200 - was enough to wreck the rest of the plans for the family vacation. I think you ought to know before you have to face a shortened trip or disappointed children.

You also will note several repetitions in this book. The reason for the brief duplicated material is that you might not have read-or remembered-the details provided in a previous or subsequent trip description, and the intention is to keep you from having to flip frantically through the book in seach of a fact I can have at your fingertips.

A final note: A noted personality years ago was asked what wish he would most want to come true. He responded that he wanted to read Count Leo Tolstoy's "War and Peace" again-for the first time.

So it is with me. My greatest wish would be to be able to experience the wonders and beauties of the mountains of North Carolina every week-for the first time!

The trips start whenever you are ready; they go wherever you want them to take you; they last as long as you like; and they end only when you call a halt (a temporary one, I sincerely hope!) to the journey. You need comparatively little: a few dollars, a spirit of adventure, a little spare time, and some means of transportation.

Plus, of course, this book.

We do the rest.

The awesome beauty of Roan Mountain.

SECTION 1: THE BEST OF THE MOUNTAINS
TRIP 1: ROAN MOUNTAIN
THE SPLENDOR OF THE RHODODENDRON GARDENS

LOCATION:

Roan Mountain is on the North Carolina-Tennessee border. The easiest way to get there from the central part of North Carolina is to exit I-40 onto US 226 at Marion and follow US 226 to intersect with NC 261 at Bakersville. From there look for State Road 1348 (Roan Mountain Road) and follow it to the parking lot at Roan Mountain.

NEARBY ATTRACTIONS:

From Roan Mountain you are a short and highly scenic drive from Mount Mitchell, Beech Mountain, Linville Falls, Little Switzerland, Valle Crucis, and Blowing Rock.

HOURS OF OPERATION:

There are no gates, and the area is open all day every day, without exception. In winter be alert for bad weather, however.

ADMISSION:

There were no admission charges of any sort for many years, but in 1997 ticket gates were established, and now you must pay $3 per vehicle in order to see the rhododendron gardens. However, this admission price is small indeed for the beauty that is yours for the fee. Call 828-682-6146 for area information.

FACILITIES:

There are hiking trails ranging from short and easy to long and strenuous, picnic areas, restrooms, overlooks, self-guiding nature trails that are handicap accessible, and photo opportunities that are almost unlimited.

WHAT'S THE STORY?

Roan Mountain is one of the beauty spots of North Carolina and, indeed, the United States. The terrific Catawba rhododendron natural gardens are incomparably beautiful in early to mid-June.

SPECIAL ATTRACTIONS:

Other than the gardens, the best parts of the Roan Mountain area are the majestic mountains seen from various points along the Cloudland Trail and the beautiful balds. The view from the peaks is staggering.

MAKING THE MOST OF YOUR VISIT:

Standing in the midst of the Pisgah National Forest, Roan Mountain rises 6,285 feet above sea level. If you happen to be there in mid-June, you will see some of the most glorious floral spectacles anywhere on the continent as the thousands of laurel and rhododendron blossoms appear. If you are there in the early spring you can see, again, literally thousands of wild flowers blooming along the trails and in the fields adjacent to trails.

In the autumn you are treated to another display of nature's best as the fall wild flowers bloom. One aspect of autumn beauty is that the fall flowers tend to hold their beauty as if it is suspended in time. The blossoms extend their lives to the very last breath of autumn, before the deadly chill of winter arrives. Any other time you are there you will find whatever beauty the season has in store. The best times to visit Roan Mountain are whatever time you can be there, but if you are looking for a time of year, choose May, early June, or October.

Despite the lack of flowers or rhododendron blossoms, the late fall and early spring seasons exhibit a stark magnificence that has its own radiance, even on gloomy days. Some would argue that on the heavy, overcast days the mountains are at their majestic peak because of the very starkness that anywhere else might be construed as gloom. Even in the dead of winter, the mountain is a place of splendor. And the simple truth is that you can see more landscape, more valleys and distant peaks, in the fall and winter months than at any other time.

Whatever time you are there, plan to be outside. Keep in mind that the high altitude will produce chilly weather that, when coupled with gusty winds, will make you happy you brought along a jacket. As with most mountain terrain, the Roan Mountain climate is such that in mid-summer you can expect thunderstorms and rain in the early afternoons. Go prepared.

In order to enjoy the mountain to the fullest, make the hike up the 800-foot rise near Carvers Gap, or cross the road and hike the gentle and incredibly beautiful balds that offer the finest in walking, sauntering, or bona fide back-pack hiking. In fact, one segment of the Appalachian Trail crosses the mountain, and you can enjoy as much of the trail as you wish to tackle.

The climb up Roan Mountain, while it looks strenuous, is in fact very easy. The 800-foot rise is a gradual slope, and the area near the top is handicap accessible, so that virtually any of the visitors (and there are thousands each year) can enjoy any of the glorious offerings.

At the top of Roan Mountain you will find gentle trails that are wide, spacious, and fun to walk. Try the Cloudland Trail first.

If you cannot make the mile-long hike, you can drive on up the mountain to the final parking lot. Near the parking area you can walk to an overlook that provides an astonishing view of the valley just across the Tennessee border. You can see farmhouses, pastures, tiny communities, and the rolling hills beyond Roan. The small town of Roan Mountain lies just across the border.

When you see the sign for the Rhododendron Gardens, do not stop at this point. Enjoy the evergreen forest and its beauty first, and stop at the gardens on your return.

Picnic tables are available near the end of the mile-long walk, which now is surrounded by a hardwood forest of hickory, ash, and oak. Remember that from the last parking lot the walk is only half a mile.

The terrain near the end of the trail is rocky and the footing is uncertain, so be sure to wear good walking shoes and to take your time. The overlook mentioned above is worth all of the effort you put into the walk. The actual overlook is large enough to hold more than a dozen persons at a time.

The handicap-accessible rhododendron gardens are found near the information boards and comfort stations. Here you will see three loops of paved trails that link with each other so that you can travel all three loops without having to backtrack a great deal (although the beauty of the place is such that backtracking can be a delight because you get to see the beauty a second time).

Here you will find one loop that is easy to negotiate by persons in wheelchairs. As you explore the three loops, you will be reminded of the mazes once popular on large private estates. You will find yourself in a land that is thickly populated by the rhododendron growth, and you are virtually shut off from the rest of the world. Even when the peak blossom season has passed, you will find the gardens are still places of rewarding beauty.

One great aspect of the lower trail is the self-guided nature trail. At one small overlook you are privileged to enjoy what appears to be an endless thicket of rhododendron. Nowhere is the ground visible because of the dense foliage.

Next comes an even greater (if such is possible) experience for the hiker. Try Round Bald and some of the other balds that you will find directly across the highway from Roan Mountain. You will find yourself climbing a total of more than 5,000 feet within a short time.

A note should be made here of the actual elevation. You will not hike a mile higher than the elevation at Carvers Gap. Instead you will travel up and down from bald to bald, and if you hike down a hill half a mile and then half a mile back up the hill, you have ascended (and descended) a total of one mile, even though you are at the same sea level elevation.

But don't think in terms of distance but instead in terms of time. If you hike two hours across the balds, you will need two more hours for the return trip. The balds can be hypnotizing in a sense, because you reach the crest of one bald and see another ahead of you, one that is equally beautiful, and there is a great temptation to keep on walking. Do so, if your energy and time will permit, but do keep in mind that crossing the balds after dark is not enjoyable. Allow abundant time to return.

You are actually on the Appalachian Trail during this part of your visit to Roan Mountain and surrounding terrain. Some of the walk or hike can be very strenuous, so keep your own physical condition in mind as you walk.

At Carvers Gap you are at 5,512 feet above sea level. Just across the road from Roan Mountain is an old-fashioned stile of the sort that once was common in rural areas. The stile is made up of four logs on each side of the fence, and the logs are used as an easy means of crossing the fence. On the other side of the stile is a number of steps that extend more than half way to the top of the bald. The actual treads of the steps are also made of sun-bleached logs.

You will see paths leading alongside the logs. The paths were made by hikers who were impatient with the pace required by the logs so the visitors made their own pathway. What the hikers did not-and do not-realize is that the logs were placed where they are in an effort to prevent erosion and further damage to the pathway up the hill to the bald.

Please stay on the log steps. Here at Roan Mountain and in numerous other mountain areas (beach areas as well) the terrain is very fragile, and careless use of an environmentally tenuous area can cause irreparable damage. Future generations will thank you for your concern and interest in protecting the fragile ecology of Roan Mountain and other locations.

Past the stile you will see an information board that is fastened to the fence rails. Read the sign and you will see that the Roan Highlands shelter is almost three miles away. If you walk to the shelter, remember that you have a three-mile return trek awaiting you. This translates into close to two hours of steady mountain walking, unless you are in good physical shape.

Pause often as you climb the Round Bald slopes. Look back at the beautiful formation of Roan Mountain. When you reach the higher elevations, you have superb views of low-lying areas. You are advised to stay on the clearly marked trail. Don't take short-cuts. The trail is the best footing on the bald, and if you leave the trail you may find yourself in soggy terrain or among rocky sections where the footing is treacherous. As you walk, notice how the light, the shadows, and the highlights of the peaks and valleys around you change every five to ten minutes.

The colors on the mountainside vary greatly from season to season, and you can visit Roan Mountain almost weekly and find a seemingly new trail to hike or new beauties to admire. You will also find that the animal life varies almost as much as does the flora in a span of a month or so. Blueberry bushes that are only tiny shrubs in the spring will be full-fruited plants in late summer, and these berries serve as food for the countless birds and other creatures that enjoy these delicacies.

Deer are abundant on Roan Mountain, and you have the best chance to see them early and late. In summer groundhogs are active, particularly just before dark.

In the warm months wild flowers dot the hillside, and in fall the changing leaves create an indescribable beauty. And when the trees are bare and the sky is dark, Roan Mountain is always and eternally beautiful and amazing.

You may wish to avoid the trails across the series of balds after heavy rains or prolonged dampness caused by snowfalls. The trails are wet and sticky, and the damage to your shoes and your temperament is minor compared to the damage to the ecology. Take along enough clothing to stay warm, but dress in layers in the event you become too warm from exertion.

Carrying along a camera is always a good idea. For best results in all kinds of lighting use a 200 ASA film. Anything slower may not be adequate for existing light conditions, and faster film often does not produce exact color hues.

One strong recommendation: carry along a pocket-sized note pad or notebook and an extra pen or so. Pause to jot down your impressions and ideas for later reference. Date your entries so that you can find comparable conditions for later trips, if your trip was particularly enjoyable.

Don't dig up vegetation, and don't damage the beauty of this excellent spot. Remember the visitors code: Take photographs and memories only, and leave behind nothing but your footprints.

View from the Top of Mount Mitchell

SECTION 1: THE BEST OF THE MOUNTAINS
TRIP 2: MOUNT MITCHELL
THE TOP OF THE CAROLINA WORLD

LOCATION:

Mount Mitchell is 35 miles north of Asheville via the Blue Ridge Parkway. The easiest way to reach the state park from I-40 is to exit from the Interstate highway onto the Blue Ridge Parkway on the eastern outskirts of Asheville. Follow the Parkway north 35 miles to the signs directing you to the parking area near the top of Mount Mitchell.

NEARBY ATTRACTIONS:

Mount Mitchell is within easy driving distance of Craggy Gardens, Asheville, Old Fort, Lake Tahoma, and Lake James. You are also near Crabtree Meadows, the North Carolina Arboretum, and the home of Zeb Vance, one of the most colorful personalities in the history of North Carolina.

HOURS OF OPERATION:

Hours vary, depending upon seasons, but the usual time of operation is from 8 a.m. until 5 or 6 p.m., later in summer. The North Carolina parks generally observe the following hours: from November through February, 8 a.m. until 6 p.m.; during March and October, from 8 a.m. until 7 p.m.; during April, May, and September, from 8 a.m. until 8 p.m.; during June, July, and August, from 8 a.m. until 9 p.m. Mount Mitchell State Park may be closed in winter because of snow, ice, or other hazardous weather. If you have questions, call before making the trip.

ADMISSION:

There are no admission fees.

FACILITIES:

At Mount Mitchell State Park you will find comfort stations, a picnic area, concession stand, public telephone, restaurant, park office, a mountain museum, and exceptional hiking trails as well as an observation tower.

WHAT'S THE STORY?

Mount Mitchell State Park is the site of the highest mountain east of the Mississippi River. At 6,684 feet above sea level, Mount Mitchell is not only the highest mountain in the east but also one of the most rugged and most beautiful.

SPECIAL ATTRACTIONS:

At the top of the mountain you will find, in addition to the museum and tower, information plaques atop the observation tower identifying points of interest. The distance and nearby peaks are named, and you can pick out landmarks in all directions. You can also visit the grave of Dr. Elisha Mitchell. There are bridle trails as well as hiking opportunities.

MAKING THE MOST OF YOUR VISIT:

When you think of the mountains of North Carolina there is a tendency to lump all the ranges into an all-encompassing term: the Great Smokies, or the Blue Ridge, and sometimes even the Appalachians. But there are several ranges, major and small, such as the Blue Ridge, the Smokies, South Mountains, the Uwharries, the Black Mountains, the Balsams, the Nantahalas, and the once-majestic but now erosion-worn Crowders Mountain areas. You can also add the Sauratown Mountains in the Mount Airy region.

Even born-and-bred North Carolinians are sometimes shocked to learn that the Tar Heel State boasts more than 40 peaks with elevations greater than 6,000 feet. Eighty peaks range in height from 5,000 to 6,000 feet, and several hundred peaks rise 4,000 to 5,000 feet above sea level.

Much confusion has arisen because of the several ranges and their highest peaks. The highest peak in the Great Smokies, for instance, is Clingman's Dome; however, despite a heated debate that lasted for several months, Mount Mitchell remains the peak that exceeds all others in altitude in the East.

The story behind the man whose name will forever be linked with the mountain is a tragic one. After having explored the peak on a number of occasions, Dr. Elisha Mitchell, a professor who was the inspiration for countless hundreds of students, returned to the Black Mountains in 1857. On Saturday, June 27, Mitchell told his son, daughter, and friends that he was going to walk across the mountain to visit with his friend, Big Tom Wilson, legendary explorer of the mountains. Mitchell planned to be back with his party within two days.

By July 1 Dr. Mitchell had not returned, and word had come from Big Tom Wilson that Mitchell had not arrived at Wilson's home. Immediately a search party that included Zebulon Vance, known as one of the greatest orators in North Carolina history as well as governor of the state, Civil War officer, and politician, went in search of the missing professor.

For those who do not know the higher mountains, summer there is not always marked by high temperatures; in fact, when August days bring sweltering heat throughout most of the state, it can be chilly if not cold atop the mountains. And on the July days when the search party scoured the mountain for Mitchell the high temperatures were in the low forties.

By July 6 there were 80 men taking part in the search, and some of the skilled mountain men made their way down Sugar Camp Creek to the 40-foot cataract and the 14-foot deep plunge pool at the base of the falls. There they found the body of Dr. Elisha Mitchell lying at the bottom of the pool.

Zeb Vance later described Dr. Mitchell as good, great, wise, pure of heart, instructor of youth, disciple of knowledge, and as a friend to science and virtue. This is high praise indeed coming, as it did, from a man who brooked little foolishness and insipidity. This same Zeb Vance once confessed to whipping a young man with whom he had engaged in a running animosity, and Vance offered as his only defense, "I couldn't help it; he was so cussed ugly."

Dr. Mitchell's body was carried out of the dense forest and was subsequently buried in the graveyard of the Presbyterian church in Asheville, but less than a year later the body was exhumed and hauled to the top of Mount Mitchell where the remains of the much-admired man were laid to rest at the peak of the mountain. The stories insist that oxen pulled a sled holding the body until the terrain became so rough that the oxen could no longer negotiate the mountainside.

Then several of the mountain men hoisted the coffin to their shoulders and carried the body to the peak. This act is again high praise, because Dr. Mitchell, although he was a college and university professor, never lost contact with the men who made the mountains their homes.

In the years prior to his death Dr. Mitchell had been a professor of science at the University of North Carolina. As part of his early work he had used mathematical computations and barometric pressure to determine that Mount Mitchell was 6,476 feet high. In 1844 he revised his estimate and concluded that the peak was actually 6,672 feet high.

While still not exact, it is remarkable that Mitchell was within 12 feet of the precise elevation of the mountain. One of Mitchell's students, incidentally, was Thomas Clingman, who was later to become a United States senator. Clingman insisted that Mitchell had erred and that the peak was actually 6,941 feet above sea level. What followed was, often, a low-key controversy between professor and student.

The undercurrent of professional competition eventually was laid to rest when the determination was made of the exact height of the mountain. In the briefest sense, Mitchell won.

Later, Governor Locke Craig (1860-1924) succeeded in having the mountain preserved as a state park. In 1915 Mount Mitchell State Park became the first such park in North Carolina history. When you arrive at the park and at the peak, you will find 1,677 acres of awesome and terrifyingly beautiful mountain terrain. As you enter the park, you will drive parallel to one of the hiking and bridle trails. On your left will be Mount Gibbes (elevation 6,250 feet), and on the way to the top of the mountain you will see on your right Mount Hallback (elevation 6,300 feet). At the top you will find a parking lot and facilities that are handicap accessible. From the parking lot you have a wide choice of directions you may wish to take.

You may not be aware that, according to scientific reports, Mount Mitchell and the surrounding peaks were once much higher than they are today. To cite a more extreme instance from within the same state, it is said that Crowders Mountain in Gaston County, today only a brave hill, was once higher than are the present-day Rocky Mountains. The Black Mountains have managed to retain greater altitude than many other mountains have because of the igneous and metamorphic rock composing much of the mountain. The rock has resisted the ravages of wind, rain, ice, and other erosive agents so that the mountain has survived, largely, while others have virtually disappeared.

In the Black Mountains there are six peaks that are among the ten highest east of the Mississippi. However, you may be surprised to learn just how short, in terms of distance, the entire range is. Unlike the Great Smokies, which extend for scores of miles, the Black Mountains are only 15 miles long.

The major waterway running through the Black Mountains is the South Toe River. Legend holds that the river was named for an Indian princess, Estatoe, who fell in love with a brave from another tribe. Rather than see her marry outside her own tribe, Estatoe's own people murdered the young woman's suitor. Unwilling to face life without her lover, Estatoe drowned herself in the river, which was from that time called Estatoe River. The white men who came into the territory shortened the name to the Toe River.

The legend, like most legends, may be taken with the grain of salt that usually accompanies folk lore. For instance, there are those who question whether Indian tribes ever had princesses among them. The same story, it should be added, has surfaced in other locations. To provide two illustrations, in the northeast mountains of Georgia there is a burial mound near Cleveland and Helen, and a similar story is associated with the Cherokees who lived there. The woman leaped from a cliff in the Georgia story, and in Tucumcari, New Mexico, the same story is told with only minor changes. At Connestee Falls, near Brevard, another Indian maiden took drastic steps, in this case feigning her death after her lover proved untrue, and in South Carolina yet another Native American maiden, Princess Issaqueena, felt the need to end her own life because of conflicts in life styles and values.

But don't waste time and sleep worrying about the truth of the legends. Enjoy them for what they are, and believe them if you find the stories meaningful. And enjoy your trip to the rugged mountain area where the story allegedly occurred.

A visit to Mount Mitchell is in many ways like a quick trip to Canada, with climate, plant life, and much animal life similar to that enjoyed by our northern neighbors. The park is inhabited by numerous deer, wild turkeys, grouse, black bears, foxes, skunks, bobcats, and other animal life that adapts readily to alpine climate. You will be in good company.

If you are amazed by the plant life, you will not be the first to be so astounded. In 1787 French botanist Andre Michaux collected more than 2,500 specimens of trees, shrubs, flowers, and other plants from the Black Mountains. John Fraser, native of England, also explored the area and studied plant life. It was in his honor that the most popular tree of the Black Mountains bears its current name: the Fraser fir.

Today the plant life abundant on Mount Mitchell includes oak, hickory, maple, fire cherry, and various evergreens. Wild flowers are abundant.

Of all the wonders of this incredible mountain range, though, one of the most remarkable is that you are able to visit it at all. By the early part of this century the demands for more lumber led to the exploitative logging of the range. Some of the slopes were almost totally barren of tree growth when the logging operations ceased.

The battle to save the trees of Mount Mitchell did not end, however, when logging ceased. Today the problem may be even more dangerous than the axe and saw had been in a previous time.

The problem facing the trees of the Black Mountains has not been identified with certainty, but one of the likely culprits is air pollution. It has been estimated that destruction of Fraser firs and spruce trees has increased by 30 per cent, and while air pollution had not been found guilty of all of the destruction, there has long been a correlation between abnormal rates of tree deaths and the presence of acid-borne air.

Eight out of every ten days, literature available at the park notes, Mount Mitchell is surrounded by fog and clouds as acidic as vinegar. You can see entire stands of dead trees as you drive up the Parkway toward Mount Mitchell, and park officials point out that setting aside natural resources is not enough: we must find better ways to protect the environment.

There are also insects that are injecting their toxins into the trees and preventing the trees from receiving nourishment enough to retain health and strength.

During your visit you may decide to take a hike and see for yourself what is happening atop Mount Mitchell. You will be less than pleased in some areas and delighted in others. The sight of dead or dying trees is disheartening, but the awareness of stands of beautiful and healthy trees can and should be inspiration to us to cooperate in every way to keep the park green.

The first hike, a short one, should be to the observation tower. Pause at the grave site of Dr. Elisha Mitchell before you ascend the tower to enjoy the panoramic view afforded you. You will see the inscription at his final resting place: "Here lies in the hope of blessed resurrection the body of Rev. Elisha Mitchell, D. D., who after being for thirty-nine years a professor in the University of North Carolina lost his life in the scientific exploration of the mountain, in the sixty-fourth year of his age-June 27, 1857."

For a longer (and completely delightful) hike, start at the top of the mountain and walk to Mount Tom, the mountain named for legendary mountaineer Tom Wilson, friend of Dr. Mitchell.

When you stand on Mount Mitchell and look toward Big Tom, you may be discouraged by the distance and obvious difficulties of the hike. But rest assured that the trek is really not at all difficult. Nor is it long and arduous.

Mount Tom, or Big Tom, is 6,558 feet above sea level. Not far away is Mount Craig, appropriately named for Locke Craig, who lived from 1860 until 1924 and who was governor of North Carolina from 1913 to 1917. The two peaks are sometimes referred to as the Black Brothers because of the dark soil, rocks, and trees that are subdued in their coloration.

Along the way pause to consider some of the legends and folk tales about some of the vegetation. The balsam fir produces an oil that is used for cementing lenses together, in art work, and in medicines. The resin allegedly cures hoarseness and sore throats. You can almost smell the balsam before you see it: the aroma is a rich, deep, and highly pleasant smell.

The sap of the Fraser fir is said to be efficacious in the treatment of rheumatism, dysentery, and open wounds of all kinds. The red spruce, which is primarily used for lumber, is also used to make musical instruments, and the small boughs can be boiled in water to produce what is called "spruce beer."

If you wish to camp, there is a nine-family campground open from May 1 through October 31 (and it can be truly frigid during these months, particularly in the first and last stages of the camping season! You can see icicles hanging from ledges in the middle of the afternoon, and at night there is always a danger of hypothermia-in the daylight hours, too-so dress properly!). The sites each have a grill and a picnic table. Restrooms are nearby, but there are no showers or hot water. A camping fee of $12 per day for each site is charged. Call (828) 675-4611 for more details. Hypothermia is mentioned here not to frighten you but to warn you that the danger is a very real one. Hypothermia can hit in warm weather as well as during the depths of winter. It can occur readily in weather as warm as 41 degrees Fahrenheit, and often the temperature at Mount Mitchell falls below that point.

All that is necessary is for body temperature to drop by as little as five degrees. When the body temperature drops as much as 10 degrees below normal, the survival rate drops dramatically. Stay warm, and treat any slurring of speech, uncontrollable shivering, weakness, and impaired judgment as signs of possible hypothermia.

Remember that one type of clothing retains its insulating properties even when soaking wet: wool. Cotton does not have this ability, so you may wish to wear wool clothing if you are going to be exposed to the weather for considerable periods of time.

Pack-in camping here is free for those who wish to leave their cars and cares in the parking lot and backpack into the forest to the Commissary Ridge shelters. You must, however, register your trip on the forms provided at the trailheads near the parking area, or you can also register at the park office.

Mile-High Swinging Bridge at Grandfather Mountain.

SECTION 1: THE BEST OF THE MOUNTAINS
TRIP 3: GRANDFATHER MOUNTAIN
THE MARVEL OF A MOUNTAINSIDE SAVED

LOCATION:

One mile off Blue Ridge Parkway at Linville on US 221 you will see the entrance to Grandfather Mountain. To get to the park, leave the Parkway at Milepost 305 and drive north. Almost immediately you will see the entrance to Grandfather Mountain on the right. There is a ticket booth just off the highway. Pay here and drive ahead to the various points of interest.

NEARBY ATTRACTIONS:

Nearby are Linville Caverns, Linville Gorge, Linville Falls, Blue Ridge Parkway, Tanawha Trail, Price Lake, Blowing Rock, Boone, Linn Cove Viaduct, and Moses Cone mansion, to the east. Or you can drive west to Little Switzerland, Crabtree Meadows, Craggy Gardens, and Asheville.

HOURS OF OPERATION:

The park is open all year from 8 a.m. until 5-6 p.m. in fall and winter; 7 p.m. in summer.

ADMISSION:

Admission fees are $9 for adults, $5 for children, $4.50 for special hiking permits. You may stay as long as the park is open, and the picnic tables and all other facilities and attractions are free for public use, once you have paid your entry fee.

FACILITIES:

Hiking trails, comfort stations, restaurant, gift shop, picnic tables, snack bar, and public telephones are available and convenient. Among the other central attractions are the animal habitats and the famous Mile-High Swinging Bridge.

WHAT'S THE STORY?

Grandfather Mountain is one of the true miracle stories of North Carolina's mountain history. In addition to numerous wild animal exhibits and other natural beauties, there is the prestige of the mountain's having been named by the United Nations as a nature preserve of global importance.

SPECIAL ATTRACTIONS:

Grandfather Mountain features the highest swinging bridge in the United States, natural habitats for bears, deer, otters, cougars, woodchucks, and eagles, hiking trails, nature museum, gift shop, and educational displays. Grandfather is also the highest peak in the Blue Ridge Mountains, with an elevation of 5,694 feet above sea level. One point of special interest is the photo gallery depicting major celebrities from around the nation who have been guests at Grandfather Mountain. This portrait gallery is almost an American Hall of Fame, with some of the noted personalities from the worlds of politics, sports, theology, and entertainment.

MAKING THE MOST OF YOUR VISIT:

The major problem facing the Grandfather Mountain visitor is finding the will power to leave. This site is indeed a marvel of a mountain, not only for its incredible rugged beauty and the vast panoramic views from the foot or the top but for all the superb habitats for animals and for the exceptional concern for the ecology of the mountain.

When you arrive at the gate, you will see first a paved and steep, winding road leading up the mountain. As you start the drive to the top, you will see magnificent views of the major part of the mountain. If you are interested in stopping to shoot a few photos, this is a good place to start.

The first major stop is at the visitors center and museum of nature. There is plenty of parking space available, and while you are stopped you have a series of activities and attractions to enjoy. Try the museum first and familiarize yourself with the story of the mountain.

You will learn that the mountain, despite its rugged and formidable appearance, is a fragile piece of history and biology, and for this reason there are rigid regulations concerning the use of hiking trails and campfires. One careless act can cause irreparable damage to one of nature's wonders, and the rules are for one purpose only: to protect the mountain so that everyone can enjoy its rich heritage.

Inside the museum you can learn, in addition to the story of Grandfather Mountain, the legend of Mildred the Bear and her celebrity status at the mountain. For many years Mildred and her cubs were among the most notable attractions at the mountain, and her death was mourned nationally. Leading newspapers across the country carried her obituary notice.

There are other bears living in the natural habitat, and you can watch them to your heart's content or, if you wish, you can feed them snacks available at the nearby concession stand. As a rule, there will always be adult bears and, a few feet farther down the trail, a habitat for cubs. At almost any time in the warmer months you can see an array of both adult and cub bruins.

One of the most popular attractions to visit is the deer park where you can watch mature deer as well as fawns as they graze and forage among the trees and waterway. Inside the deer habitat you will also find groundhogs and squirrels, among other animal attractions. These animals are so accustomed to people that they will virtually pose for you.

To the left of the deer habitat you can see the cougar or panther habitat. Here you will see full-grown panthers, sometimes known as mountain lions or pumas, prowling among the forested area or lying in the sun atop the huge boulders. Here, as in the rest of the park, you will see immaculately clean environments for the animals, which are obviously healthy and surrounded by the best of living conditions.

To the left of the cougar lair you will see the eagles in their environment. These majestic birds are not in captivity. They suffered injuries in the wild and live at the Grandfather Mountain habitat because they cannot survive in nature. Do not feel concern because the birds are on public display: if they were not in a habitat such as the one here, they would without doubt have perished.

Near the cougar habitat you will also see one of the new and totally fascinating displays: the otter habitat. Here these agile and playful creatures are a miniature three-ring circus as they clown and cavort to the delight of the spectators. Ask one of the habitat staff when the next chunk of ice will be placed in the pool. It is an astonishing show of aquatic skills to watch the otters as they cavort with the block of ice.

When you have concluded your visit to the animal habitats, you can drive on up the mountain to the Mile-High Swinging Bridge that is one of the most popular attractions in the state. The swinging bridge extends from the gift shop and parking area to a rocky crag more than a hundred feet away.

As you climb the steps to the bridge, you will see a marker in the pavement that denotes the exact height at that point: one mile, to the foot. As you cross the bridge, you can see for miles and miles in all directions. On the other side of the bridge you can make your way across weather-scarred rocks to several vantage points that offer scenery unparalleled in the East.

There are no guard rails along the rocky peak, and you are cautioned to use your best judgment and to watch your step at all times. Be particularly alert if there are children along. This is not to say that the area is dangerous; it is merely a statement that a mistake in footing here can be deadly serious.

Wherever you stop, no matter what time of year, you will find yourself face-to-face with nature's beauty. In May the lady's slipper and trillium, among other wild flowers, are in bloom. In late May and into late June the red rhododendron, laurel, and flame azalea are at their peaks. From the first of July until past the middle of the month the white rhododendron is in bloom. From August until the first killing frost there will be other flowers in bloom along the drive and along hiking trails.

If you are interested in getting out farther into nature, try the hiking trails of Grandfather Mountain. Before you start, be sure to check with mountain personnel for registration and ticket information.

When you have exhausted the points of interest (without exhausting yourself first), you can try your hand at hiking some of the finest trails in the South. Before you start on a trail, be certain that you have an abundant supply of water, food, and warm clothing. Keep in mind that your body needs water in winter just as it does in summer. Food that produces energy over the long haul is often better than the quick-energy candy bars. One of the best foods to carry in a pack is a supply of apples, dried or fresh, and/or nuts. These foods are easily digested, filled with nutrients, and easy to carry. When you are finished with an apple or a pocketful of peanuts, you do not have bulky containers to carry out of the forest. But please do not litter the trails!

When you are hiking, you will be subjected, perhaps, to high winds (which may reach near 100 miles an hour at times on the top of Grandfather during storms), moderate temperatures in summer, and below-zero readings in winter. You can also encounter heavy snowfalls, drenching rains, thunder and lightning, sleet, and, when the weather is right, even a bear. Rattlesnakes are not terribly uncommon in the higher elevations.

You could try Grandfather Trail, which is rugged and rather strenuous from the outset. The footing is rocky and uncertain. The trail weaves, dips, and climbs. Shortly after you start the trail you will reach a rope stretched from top to bottom of a climb to assist hikers in making their way up or down the incline.

At the half-mile mark you will reach a spur trail called the Underwood Trail. You have the option of taking this trail, which is far easier, or hiking the regular Grandfather Trail.

Grandfather Trail leads to MacRae Peak (elevation 5,939) and to Attic Window Peak (elevation 5,949). At MacRae Peak you will reach the ladders that are needed to ascend and descend the sheer cliffs.

The first campsite is at mile 1.2, and the second is at the mile and one-half point. No fires are permitted at this site.

A little past two miles you reach a fork in the trail where Calloway Trail leads to the left. The trail to the right now becomes the Daniel Boone Scout Trail. There are two campsites at the fork in the trail and a third and fourth are located within one-fifth of a mile.

Along the way you will pass Calloway Gap (elevation 5,600) on your right, and at 0.3 mile you will reach Calloway Peak (elevation 5,964). At 0.4 of the Daniel Boone Scout Trail you will reach an overlook above the Linn Cove Viaduct, one of the most unusual engineering feats along the Blue Ridge Parkway.

It is this viaduct and its corresponding story that help to make Grandfather a miracle, or at least a marvel, of a mountain. For years the Blue Ridge Parkway temporarily ended and tourists had to drive along a rough, curving, and generally irritating highway.

The reason for the temporary end of the Parkway was that Mr. Hugh Morton, exceptional photographer and owner of Grandfather Mountain, refused to sell the land so that the construction firms could ravage the exquisitely beautiful mountain and destroy much of the delicate natural balance. Later, a settlement was reached, and Morton won. And the entire nation won as well.

Today travelers can drive almost literally on the side of the mountain along a viaduct which has been labeled a masterpiece of engineering and construction. No damage was done to the beauty or ecology of the mountain, and the result of Morton's determined effort to protect Grand-father resulted in one of the remarkable and beautiful segments of the Parkway.

When you drive along the Viaduct, keep in mind that the mountainside, under less concerned and capable supervision, could have been damaged beyond belief.

Near Grandfather Mountain you can reach the Tanawha Trail, which parallels the Blue Ridge Parkway. You can hike the Tanawha Trail, one of the greatest trails anywhere. Later in this book you will find a complete trip to the Tanawha Trail. Half a mile along the way you will reach a spur trail leading to the Boone Fork parking area.

At the top of Mount Pisgah.

SECTION 1: THE BEST OF THE MOUNTAINS
TRIP 4: MOUNT PISGAH
LIFT UP YOUR EYES AND BEHOLD

LOCATION:
Drive 30 miles south of Asheville via the Blue Ridge Parkway south, or 18 miles north of Brevard on NC 276, then onto the Parkway north. The parking lot is at Milepost 408.5.

NEARBY ATTRACTIONS:
Within easy driving distance are Asheville, Brevard, Sliding Rock, Grave-yard Fields, Devil's Courthouse, Whitewater Falls, Looking Glass Falls, and the Cradle of Forestry.

HOURS OF OPERATION:
The area is open all day every day, year round.

ADMISSION:
There are no fees at any time for anything.

FACILITIES:
There are no facilities on Mount Pisgah, but within a short walk or

drive there are overnight accommodations, store, service station, restaurant, and gift shop, as well as long and superb hiking trails and picnic tables.

WHAT'S THE STORY?

Mount Pisgah is one of the highest peaks (5,721 feet above sea level) in the southwestern part of North Carolina. The huge mountain was once part of one of the largest private estates in the United States.

If you want to get a better idea of the extent of the wealth of the man who owned the immense tracts of land in western North Carolina, here is a sampling. Lawrence Brown of Georgia State University has calculated the Vanderbilt holdings by comparing the total wealth with that of computer magnate Bill Gates, whose wealth is estimated in excess of $40 billion. Vanderbilt, when he died, had an estate worth $105 million.

But what was the comparative buying power of the wealth of the two men? Or, put another way, how much would Vanderbilt's millions be worth in today's economy?

Brown's calculations are that at the end of 1997 the wealth of Vanderbilt would have earned 10 per cent, compounded annually, which is what the stock market has done on an annual basis for the past 121 years.

By the end of 1997 Vanderbilt's $105 million would have exploded to $10.7 trillion. And Vanderbilt would have been worth 267 times what Bill Gates is worth. For every dollar in the $40 billion in the Gates fortune Vanderbilt would have had almost 268 bucks. From his vast fortune, Vanderbilt paid day laborers who worked on his famed mansion the sum of 50 cents per day-about a nickel an hour for a 10-hour day.

MAKING THE MOST OF YOUR VISIT:

First, before you drive to the area, get out a copy of the Old Testament and read the Biblical story associated with Mount Pisgah. You will find that Mount Pisgah is a mountain ridge east of the north end of the Dead Sea. In Deuteronomy 3:27 you will read that Moses was ordered to climb to the top of Mount Pisgah and to "...lift up your eyes westward and northward and southward and eastward, and behold it with your eyes; for you shall not go over this Jordan."

Incidentally, Moses would have had a harder time climbing the North Carolina version of Mount Pisgah than he did in scaling the ridge near Nebo. The Biblical Pisgah in Jordan is only 2,644 feet high. The Tar Heel mountain is more than twice as high as the one described in the Bible. Keep in mind, though, that you will have the advantage of a ready-made trail leading from the parking lot on the Parkway near the inn to the top.

There are several good reasons to make this trip. The first is to see the terrain and derive some notion of how incredibly huge the estate was before so much of the land was given to the American government and, by extension, to the people of this country.

George Vanderbilt, buying land in small parcels and large, eventually owned 125,000 acres. That amount of land is equal to more than 193 square miles, which is larger than some countries. The Biltmore Estate was once larger than Barbados, Liechtenstein, Granada, Monaco, and 11 other countries.

When you stand atop Mount Pisgah and look toward Asheville (and realize that the Vanderbilt estate covered a great portion of the land between the city and the mountain), you can entertain an idea of the magnitude of the Vanderbilt holdings. Later a total of 100,000 acres of the land was given to this country, and it became Pisgah National Forest.

A second (and better) reason for climbing Mount Pisgah is to enjoy the awesome view. On a clear day, you can see, perhaps not forever, but for countless miles in all directions. You can see the towns and communities nearby, dozens of other peaks, valleys, and 360 degrees of magnificence.

Third, you can enjoy the foliage in autumn, the song birds and accipiters throughout nearly all of the year, the profusion of wild flowers growing along the trail, the bizarre designs carved into the rock surfaces by wind and rain and other forces of nature, the stark and fearsome beauty of the denuded trees in winter, and the cool, refreshing breezes on the hottest summer days.

A fourth, and excellent, reason for the climb is to see if you can make it. It is a tough hike, not for the enfeebled or those with significant physical problems. However, 80-year olds make the climb, as do people on crutches and with a variety of minor (or major) debilitations. Do not attempt the climb if you have serious concerns about your health. You can enjoy the mount by observing it from below or from some of the vantage points around the area.

The fifth reason for making the trip is that if you arrive from Asheville, you can enjoy the tunnels along the Parkway and the marvelous scenery along the way. If you arrive from Brevard, you can enjoy the terrific waterfalls and the river that runs alongside the highway for much of the drive.

The original estate, complete with the house near Asheville, was, in the early part of the 20th century, almost beyond the comprehension of most people. Vanderbilt at age 16 bought a sailboat and earned money by shipping produce and passengers between Staten Island and New York City. At the time of his death, in 1877, he had amassed a fortune conservatively estimated at more than $100 million. Consider this vast amount of money in terms of the buying power of the dollar in 1877 (roughly, some economists have said, 40 times greater buying power than in the late 1990s) and you can derive some idea of just how much the man was worth. As late as 1930, more than half a century after Vanderbilt managed to accumulate such an unfathomable amount of money, it was still possible, for example, to buy a great pair of shoes for as little as $3. A pound of steak sold for less than ten cents a pound, as did a pound of cheese. A hot dog or hamburger sold in cafes for a nickel each, and you could buy a wonderfully comfortable house for less than $10,000.

George Washington Vanderbilt, grandson of Commodore Vanderbilt, came for a visit to North Carolina in the mid-1880s. He loved the area around Asheville so much that he rode through the hills around the city until he found a vantage point from which he had an outstanding view of all the countryside around the spot. He bought the land for his retreat home, the Biltmore House, and then continued to purchase parcels of land until, at the time of his death, he owned all of what is presently Pisgah National Forest and still had 25,000 acres of land in addition.

Part of the property owned by Vanderbilt included the peak known today as Mount Pisgah. Vanderbilt himself had a hunting lodge built near Mount Pisgah, and trails were blazed through the mountains so that it was possible for horse traffic to reach the lodge.

After Vanderbilt's death in 1914, land was deeded to the United States government, and that land was to mark the beginning of the Pisgah National Forest. More land was sold, and the estate dwindled to about 8,000 acres. The sold land became, in part, the city of Biltmore Forest, sections of the Blue Ridge Parkway, and parts of I-26 and I-40.

When you arrive at Mount Pisgah, you will find a picnic area (and quite a beautiful one) on the western side of the Parkway and two parking areas within easy walking distance of the start of the Mount Pisgah trail. The Mount Pisgah parking lot is located on the left, if you are driving south, shortly before you reach the Mount Pisgah Inn. If the parking lot is filled, there is another parking lot across the parkway and south 300 yards. At the second parking lot there are rest rooms and picnic tables.

As you start the hike and pass the sign warning that the trail ahead is strenuous, you will climb along a nearly flat trail for almost half a mile and then you will instantly start to see why the trail is labeled as strenuous. The climb, gradual at first, increases in difficulty and does not relent until you are at the top of Mount Pisgah. In the early stretches of the trail the forest is essentially hardwood (oak, ash, hickory, and an assortment of low-growing trees and shrubs). On a warm autumn afternoon you can hear the unceasing sounds of squirrels, ground squirrels, or chipmunks, and songbirds in the low-growing shrubs along the trail. You may see cardinals, towhees, brown thrashers, mockingbirds, wrens, and other common birds.

One of the unusual animals in the woods is the red squirrel which, according to students of nature, is a rarity in that it kills and eats live prey. It is believed that the red squirrel may attack and devour as many as 200 birds in a year.

The largest animals common to the forest in this area are probably the white-tailed deer, an agile animal that can leap 8 feet vertically, 30 feet horizontally, and attain a speed of 30 miles per hour when frightened. Black bears, however, can be found in nearly all mountain areas. They have even visited downtown parts of such distant cities as Shelby, in Cleveland County, roughly only 50 miles from Charlotte.

As you begin the steep climb, the trail, which narrows to a single-file corridor through the walls of rhododendron, rises more than 700 feet within one mile. The rocks that compose the trail surface cause the footing to become more difficult, and you will find one minor problem that could enlarge to that of a full-scale difficulty. The incessant hikers' boots pulverize the fallen leaves until the fragments are reduced to tiny balls of dry vegetation. As you step on these, they tend to roll, like incredibly small ball bearings. The rocks then become slippery and difficult to negotiate. If you should slip and fall onto the jagged and uneven rocks, you could receive a serious injury.

Do not try to hike up the Mount Pisgah trail in anything less than good hiking boots or comfortable shoes with good soles. Stay away from leather soles. Dress, as usual, in layers so that you can remove excess clothing when the exertion of the climb causes your body temperature to rise.

At the top, when you finally reach it, you will see that the vegetation has changed from hardwood forest to rhododendron and laurel, and the thickets along the trail are at points almost impenetrable. The trail moves along the southern slope and works upward at a seemingly slow rate. Near the top the trail switches back to a northerly direction and you can see the television tower that was erected many years ago atop the mountain.

At the very top you emerge from a rhododendron "hell," or thicket, and reach a platform overlook. From this vantage point you have a 360-degree panoramic view of the entire countryside. It is much cooler at the top of the mountain than it was at the parking lot, and you are advised to wear warmer clothing if you plan to spend any time at the top. In warmer months it is also advisable to carry along rain gear, because thunderstorms on an almost daily basis sweep across the mountains. Be careful that you are not caught atop the mountain in a thunderstorm. The peak, the huge tower, and the bare rock surface at the top combine to make the location highly undesirable during lightning storms. If you see a storm developing, leave the overlook and the peak as quickly as you can and start toward lower elevations. Once you are into the thick growth along the trail you will be relatively safer.

On most hikes you can assume that you will travel much faster downhill then you did going uphill. This trail may be the reverse. For this reason you should not linger at the top too late and let darkness catch you on the trail.

You may want to try some of the gentler hikes while you are in the area. Buck Springs Trail is a good one, but you will need a second car at the exit on NC 276, the highway to Brevard.

You can find the trailhead behind the Pisgah Inn, and from that point you can walk in a southerly direction through a great forested area, cross a number of small streams, none of which will constitute even a minor problem, and generally follow the Blue Ridge Parkway to the juncture of Parkway and US 76. You emerge from the forest on the highway, where there is a small parking area for second cars. There is a full treatment of this trail elsewhere in this book.

Your other option is to hike the trail both ways. The trail is, one-way, 6.4 miles, and the vertical rise is 2,600 feet. The trail is moderate in terms of difficulty, and it is easier if you start at the Pisgah Inn rather than on US 76.

Rocky overlook at Devil's Courthouse

SECTION 1: THE BEST OF THE MOUNTAINS
TRIP 5: DEVIL'S COURTHOUSE
THE LAIR OF JUDACULLAH

LOCATION:
From the junction of I-40 and the Blue Ridge Parkway in Asheville, drive 40 miles south of Asheville on the Blue Ridge Parkway at Milepost 422.4

NEARBY ATTRACTIONS:
Brevard, numerous waterfalls, hiking trails, Graveyard Fields, Mount Pisgah Inn, Mount Pisgah, Asheville, Shining Rock Wilderness Area, and Sliding Rock Recreation Area are all within easy driving distances.

HOURS OF OPERATION:
The area is open all the time, day or night, year round.

ADMISSION:
There are no fees of any sort at any time.

FACILITIES:

There are no facilities or conveniences other than parking space. Closest comfort station is across the highway at the Shining Rock Wilderness Area parking lot. It's just you and the mountain-and sometimes the weather-and perhaps Judacullah!

WHAT'S THE STORY?

Devil's Courthouse was thought by the Cherokee Native Americans to be the home of Judacullah, the one-eyed monster-god who sat in judgment of the deeds of the Cherokees. The view from the top is exemplary.

SPECIAL ATTRACTIONS:

Many songbirds, flowering shrubs, smaller animals, hawks, owls, wildflowers, occasional deer, and some of the best scenery in the nation are yours for the asking-and for exertion needed to climb the mountain. The view from the top is unparalleled.

MAKING THE MOST OF YOUR VISIT:

This short walk of 1.6 miles round trip is one of the most gruelling in the area in that it is a constant climb, with no relief except at the bottom and top. But because the trip is so short, you can make it easily if you are in reasonably good shape physically. But here is a minor problem of interpretation. You may be in good enough shape to walk around the block a dozen times, but the ascent of the Devil's Courthouse trail is not a gentle walk: every step is uphill until you reach the top, and the slope is very steep in places.

To give you another viewpoint, consider that the total hike up the mountain is .8 mile, but the vertical rise over this short hike is 1,400 feet. But do not be discouraged. There are no time limits set for your trip, and there are benches spaced up the entire trip so that you can sit and rest nearly any time you find yourself getting winded.

You can find people of all ages on the trail, and it is not truly rare to see people in their seventies and eighties on the slope. Sixty-year olds are commonplace.

What you will see at the top is worth all the sweat and aching muscles you will bring back from the top. The entire walk should take you a little more than an hour, minimum. You may, however, be tempted to extend the pleasure to several hours because the view from the top is so great, the air is so pure and bracing, and the exhilaration of the walk is on a par with a spiritual experience. This is an easy place to fall in love with, and any time I am asked to name my favorite location in North Carolina, Devil's Courthouse is tied with about 600 other superb places. It is truly terrific.

If you find yourself over-tired, use the benches. The trip is meant to be a pleasure, not punishment. If you wish to rest every five minutes, it's your choice.

And while you are resting you are not missing anything. In fact, you may be gaining. Some of the younger visitors gallop all the way to the top and make you, unless you are one of them, have cause to remember other days when exhaustion was only a word in some dictionary. In the inexhaustible joy of youth, the only truly tiresome experience is that of sitting still.

But while others are galloping, you may be catching your breath and waiting for your galloping pulse to slow down a bit. While you are doing so you will likely see some of the antics of the many chipmunks in the area or catch sight of some wildflower that you would have missed in your irrepressible energy and your eagerness to get to the top. You may glimpse the joy of what the poet (in this case, Wordsworth) meant when he wrote, "A violet by a mossy stone, half hidden from the eye; fair as a star, when only one is shining in the sky."

You will see violets galore, as well as dozens of other kinds of flowers, in warm weather. The bushes are filled with the feathered flurry of activity and the air is filled with the songs of the birds. So why not pause and enjoy every moment of the walk?

As you arrive at the parking area, you will find Devil's Courthouse on the left side of the Parkway as you drive south. You will arrive almost immediately after you pass through a tunnel shortly after you leave Graveyard Fields. Prepare to turn left as you emerge from the tunnel.

If you cannot make the climb for whatever reason, you can walk around the parking lot or simply sit in your car and enjoy the sight of the rugged mountain with the clouds or dense fog surrounding the peak. On almost any day, weather permitting, you can see hardy souls silhouetted against the sky as they stand atop the highest crags on the mountainside.

If you do feel like a hike, walk up the right side of the Parkway (as you head north). Follow the paved path into the forest. Instantly you can sense the reasons the Cherokee Indians considered the mountain to be the sanctuary of Judacullah. The mountain, particularly when it is fog-shrouded, is awesome, even frightening.

As you climb, think of the sign at the east edge of the parking lot. The Department of Interior sign reads: "The Balsam Range is rich in legendary superstitions and to the Indians these mountains assumed mysterious shapes and forms. Here at Devil's Courthouse his Satanic majesty was believed to have sat in judgment of all who were lacking in courage or had strayed from a strict code of virtue. Cherokee superstitions coupled many natural phenomena with the mysterious spirits that peopled the area."

You can see how the mountain would inspire superstition. As you walk, observe the many types of hardwood trees and shrubs. If the weather is warm, listen for the sounds of distant thunder. If you hear a storm approaching, cut your visit short and head back to the shelter of your automobile. This advice holds for any and all visits you make along mountain crests where the peaks expose you to the elements.

The trail, as you start up, is wide enough for two or three people to walk side by side. As you climb past the one-third point the pathway narrows slightly until by the time you reach the peak it is a single-file trail.

A host of creatures call the mountain home. There are snakes on the mountain, but they tend to be more afraid of you than you should be of them. Still, do not stick your hands into cracks and crannies where you cannot see what you are about to touch. In cooler weather the snakes are not a problem, and in warm spring and fall days you may see one occasionally as it suns itself on a rock.

If you brought your camera along (make it a point to take it with you on all walks of this sort, if you enjoy photography) you will have many wonderful opportunities to snap great shots along the ridge and rock outcropping that you are approaching.

Devil's Courthouse, like most higher elevations, changes color as clouds, sunlight, fog, and changing light conditions lend a variety of hues and shades to the rocks and trees.

The best months of the year to hike up Devil's Courthouse are late April, May, October, and early November; best time of day is early morning. If you plan to hike in late afternoon, be certain to allow enough time to descend from the peak while there is still adequate light.

When you near the top the terrain levels off and you can walk easily for about the length of a football field. By easily I mean that you are not climbing. You will work your way among rocks and boulders, among laurel and rhododendron and other bushes and shrubs.

When you emerge onto the peak itself, you will find a protective wall to prevent spectators from coming too close to the ledge, and around the wall you will find plaques that help you to identify the peaks seen in the distance.

You will have nearly a 360-degree panoramic view of the entire area, and you can see into South Carolina, Georgia, and Tennessee. You can also climb onto the rocks for varying views of the mountains and valleys before you, but you should keep in mind at all times that you should exert the greatest care toward your own safety. Some of the rocks are in safe terrain, and the footing is good. Others are not. Stay well back of the ledges.

If you want to photograph the walled-off portion of the peak, climb the rocks on the east side of the peak and gain an added 30 feet. In this way, your camera lens can take in the overlook as well as the rest of the scene.

You will find that the clearest views are found in the cooler months, and you can climb Devil's Courthouse virtually any time that the Blue Ridge Parkway is open to traffic. However, it is far better to avoid extremes in climate, whether winter or summer, and in winter the wind chill factor can greatly interfere with the joys of the climb.

Plan to spend time atop the peak. Rest on the rocks or in the shade, and enjoy the changing hues in the valleys below as clouds darken the glens and coves. And allow your meditations to include thanks for such a mountain, such a highway as the Blue Ridge Parkway, for a state like North Carolina, and for a nation that values its scenic wonders.

Colonel Ferguson's Grave at Kings Mountain

SECTION 1: THE BEST OF THE MOUNTAINS
TRIP 6: KINGS MOUNTAIN NATIONAL MILITARY PARK
THE HILL THAT BECAME A PINNACLE

LOCATION:

From I-85 between Gastonia and Shelby take Exit 8 onto NC/SC 161 and follow this highway six miles into the Kings Mountain National Battleground.

NEARBY ATTRACTIONS:

Kings Mountain State Park (South Carolina), Schiele Museum in Gastonia, Stowe Botanical Gardens in Belmont, C. Grier Beam Truck Museum in Cherryville, Crowders Mountain State Park, Cherryville Historical Museum, and Kings Mountain Fire Museum are all within a one-hour drive of the National Battleground.

HOURS OF OPERATION:

The park is open year round from 9 a.m. until 5 p.m. Closed on Thanksgiving, Christmas, and New Year's Day. Kings Mountain State Park hours are, April-October, 7 a.m. until 9 p.m.; November-March, 8 a.m. until 6 p.m.

ADMISSION:

Kings Mountain National Military Park is free at all times; Kings Mountain State Park charges $2 for a parking fee for automobiles and motorcycles and $7 per day for multi-passenger vehicles carrying 15 passengers.

FACILITIES:

At Kings Mountain National Military Park there are picnic tables and shelters, bookstore, restrooms, park interpreters, visitors center, 18-minute movie, and 1.5 mile hiking trail around the battleground. At the South Carolina Kings Mountain State Park there are picnic tables, shelters, campground, store, living history farm, nature/history programs, equestrian facilities, hiking trails, swimming, and boating. Group camping facilities are available.

For details contact Kings Mountain National Military Park, P. O. Box 40, Kings Mountain, NC 28086. Call (864) 936-7921 during office hours. Kings Mountain State Park, 1277 Park Road, Blacksburg, SC 27902. Call (803) 222-3209 between 11 a.m. and noon and 4 p. m. and 5 p. m.

WHAT'S THE STORY?

The battle of Kings Mountain in 1780 pitted hundreds of Americans against Colonel Patrick Ferguson (whose rank was that of major before the battle; he died never knowing that he had been promoted to the rank of colonel), who was the only non-American in the entire battle. Somehow the raw and ill-equipped Patriots managed to win a devastating victory and hastened the end of the American Revolution.

SPECIAL ATTRACTIONS:

At the National Military Park there are monuments erected in tribute to courageous fighters, and a huge cairn marks the grave of Colonel Ferguson and a woman who was killed shortly after Ferguson fell in battle. At Kings Mountain State Park there is an 1840s homestead complete with barn, cotton gin, blacksmith shop, livestock, carpenter's shop, garden.

MAKING THE MOST OF YOUR VISIT:

Kings Mountain, the Hill that became a Pinnacle, is not a mountain and did not belong to the king. And it is not in western North Carolina. It is not in North Carolina at all, but it is only a 10 minute drive from one of North Carolina's busiest highways, and the city of Kings Mountain itself is in the Tar Heel State-and in the western part of it.

Kings Mountain may be only a hill, but that hill became one of the most important sites in the Revolutionary War. The Battle of Kings Mountain, some scholars say, was the key to American forces in the South.

You will find the hill-mountain on the border of North and South Carolina. Rising only about 60 feet above a plain which in turn is about 800 feet above sea level, the modest mountain at its peak is only about 600 yards long and 70 feet wide at one end and 120 at the other. The elevation took its name, not from British royalty, but from an early settler.

What the mountain lacks in altitude and geographic majesty, however, it makes up for in military importance and in its role in the history of the United States. For it was here, on October 7, 1780, that the battle took place that was later described by Thomas Jefferson as a "memorable victory," that was "the joyful annunciation of that turn of the tide of success, which terminated the Revolutionary War with the seal of independence."

To set the scene for the battle, Charleston had fallen to the British, whose plan was to march through North Carolina and on to Virginia, where the war would end with a British victory. Hundreds and thousands of American men flocked to join what they believed to be the winning side.

At the Charleston rout, the British captured 5,500 Patriot troops (including seven generals and 290 other officers) and took control of much-needed weapons and supplies. Later, "Bloody" Tarleton met and destroyed a detachment of Virginia Continentals near the border of the Carolinas. "Not a man escaped," wrote Dr. Robert Brownfield, a surgeon with the Continental forces. "Not a man was spared...."

Near Camden, General Horatio Gates' army suffered a devastating defeat and Gates fled for his life almost as soon as the battle started. The British seemed to be in a headlong rush toward victory.

Major Ferguson, attempting to intimidate the Over-Mountain Men and their supporters, whom he referred to as "hellish banditti," sent advance warning that if they did not lay down their arms he would "march his army over the mountains, hang their leaders, and lay their country waste with fire and sword."

The troops under the command of Major Patrick Ferguson were marching from Gilbert Town toward Charlotte, where Cornwallis had set up headquarters, when the Over-Mountain Men under the able leadership of Charles McDowell, Isaac Shelby, John Sevier, Benjamin Cleveland, and others, followed in Ferguson's footsteps. The Mountain Men were relatively inexperienced in battles of any sort, and their equipment was basic at best. But they had a fiery desire for independence and freedom. They marched through snow, rain, and fog, and, often weak from hunger and worn from seemingly endless days on the trails, they caught

Ferguson's men at Kings Mountain and the fight began. Major Ferguson was as a soldier a formidable adversary, but he and his troops had no chance.

The Patriots had more than freedom on their minds; they also were determined to extract their measure of revenge for the way "Bloody" Tarleton had massacred American Patriots earlier. One of the witnesses to the Waxhaws battle reported that as every Patriot was lying helplessly upon the ground, Tarleton's men bayoneted each soldier, no matter how badly wounded, who showed any sign of life.

It is small wonder that in the Battle of Kings Mountain when the British begged for quarter the Patriots refused to stop the battle and yelled to other Patriots to give the enemy "Tarleton's Quarter," a reference to the Waxhaws massacre.

After prolonged brutal fighting, Patriot soldiers saw what they had dreamed of seeing: Ferguson, astride a beautiful horse and blowing the silver whistles he used for issuing directives, rode frantically across the ridge before he and his few remaining officers met Sevier's men.

Shots rang out, and half a dozen bullets struck the British commander, who fell from the saddle. Patriot soldiers laid Ferguson on a blanket and carried him to a tree, out of the line of fire. Within minutes Ferguson was dead, and shortly afterwards his officers and men asked for quarter.

"Damn you," Colonel Shelby yelled at them, "if you want quarter, throw down your arms!"

When the ghastly battle ended, there were corpses strewn like fallen logs over the slopes. The revolutionary forces had killed 225 of Ferguson's men, wounded 163, and had taken 716 as prisoner. Later nine more were charged with war crimes and were "swung-off" from the limbs of huge trees, prompting a patriot soldier to observe that he wished all the trees of the forest bore such fruit.

Among the victims of the battle was Virginia Sal, who was described as a camp follower, one of two red-haired women who accompanied Ferguson. The other woman, ironically, was also named Virginia-Virginia Paul. And to triple the irony, Colonel William Campbell, who devised the plan of attack that led to the overwhelming victory by the American Patriots, was from Virginia. Virginia Paul, the other red-head, was seen riding a horse across the field of battle. Witnesses reported that she had an almost nonchalant attitude, as if in shock or out of touch with reality.

Virginia Sal, so the story goes, was buried with Colonel Ferguson in a grave not far from where Ferguson fell. The bodies of the other soldiers were hastily buried under logs, leaves, limbs, and rocks. For weeks afterward wolves, wild hogs, vultures, and other creatures of carrion feasted on the remains. How many British fought and died in the Battle of Kings Mountain? Only one: Colonel Ferguson. The other soldiers were local or regional men who chose to be loyal to the King.

Why did Ferguson choose to fight at Kings Mountain? Many scholars have offered the thesis that Ferguson knew that Kings Mountain had several springs and small streams to provide water necessary for men and animals.

Why was the battle so important? The morale factor is inestimable. Untold hundreds of men who had chosen to remain loyal to the crown changed their minds and moved to the side of the Patriots. When the common man realized that backwoodsmen with little or no training could not only fight with but defeat the best soldiers England had to offer, the American Cause became stronger at once and independence became a fact, not an idea.

Kings Mountain today is the site of two exceptionally varied and beautiful parks, existing back to back. At the Kings Mountain National Military Park start your tour with a trip to the visitors center and watch the short film about the Battle of Kings Mountain. There is no charge for the film, which is shown on the half-hour during the regular park hours.

Outside the visitors center a self-guiding trail leads around the ridge of Kings Mountain. Trail markers describe the events that took place at each location.

If you have time for the half-hour walk, leave the visitors center and follow the loop trail to the right. As you follow the paved trail you will see sites where several leaders died. Near the end of the trail you will see the Hoover Monument marking the spot where President Herbert Hoover in 1931 addressed a gathering of 75,000 people who hiked through the forest to meet at the summit of the mountain. A three-minute walk past the Hoover Monument is the United States Monument honoring the men who fought at Kings Mountain.

Then, almost as a shock, you will see the marking showing where Colonel Ferguson was fatally wounded, and the huge monument with the cairn marking the final resting place of Ferguson and Virginia Sal.

At this point the reality of the entire battle scene hits hardest as you realize that here neighbors and relatives fought each other over the principle that all people are created free and equal. Here the modest hill became a towering peak.

You can find overnight accommodations and restaurants in nearby Gastonia, Shelby, Kings Mountain, and Gaffney.

Hanging Rock near Winston-Salem

SECTION 1: THE BEST OF THE MOUNTAINS
TRIP 7: HANGING ROCK STATE PARK
A MOUNTAIN AWAY FROM THE MOUNTAINS

LOCATION:
Hanging Rock State Park is located four miles northwest of Danbury. One easy way to get to the park from I-40 is to follow I-77 to Exit 85, which is the old CCC Camp Road. Stay on this road until you intersect with NC 262. Stay on NC 262 through the town of Pilot Mountain and intersect with NC 66. Follow this road for 25 miles to Moore's Springs Road (State Road 1001) and follow the road to the entrance to Hanging Rock State Park.

NEARBY ATTRACTIONS:
Pilot Mountain, town and mountain, Horne Creek Living Historical Farm, Mount Airy, Winston-Salem and Old Salem, Sauratown Mountains, and Historic Bethabara are located within easy driving distance of Hanging Rock.

HOURS OF OPERATION:

The Hanging Rock State Park is open from 8 a.m. until 6 p. m. during November and through the end of February; from 8 a. m. until 7 p. m. in March and October; from 8 a.m. until 8 p.m. during April, May, and September; and from 8 a.m. until 9 p.m. June through August.

ADMISSION:

There are no admission fees charged for entrance into Hanging Rock State Park. There are fees to camp, swim, or fish in the developed sites.

FACILITIES:

Camp sites, hiking trails, picnic tables and shelters, restrooms, vacation cabins, boat ramp for canoes and other small craft, boat rentals, swimming area, fishing lake, dressing rooms, snack bar, lounge, interpretive programs, public telephone are all within easy access on the park grounds.

WHAT'S THE STORY?

Hanging Rock State Park is one of the most varied areas for public recreation in North Carolina. One of the main attractions is the Hanging Rock mountain itself. Many of the facilities were built by Civilian Conservation Corps workers between 1935 and 1942, and the bathhouse has been designated as a National Historic Landmark.

SPECIAL ATTRACTIONS:

In addition to the Hanging Rock itself, you can hike or drive (part of the way, at least) to a series of very fine waterfalls, caves, and natural landmarks. There is an observation tower from which you can enjoy a splendid view for miles and miles, and you can also enjoy rock climbing as well as other outdoor activities.

MAKING THE MOST OF YOUR VISIT:

Start enjoying Hanging Rock long before you arrive at the state park itself. The drive along I-77 is surprisingly scenic and enjoyable, and from the time you leave the uncrowded Interstate highway and drive along the rural roads, you will see essentially flat land that averages 800 feet above sea level. Tiny and ancient farmhouses, crops in fields, and livestock, plus the occasional sight of a deer or fox along the road can add immeasurably to the bucolic experience.

As you approach Hanging Rock State Park you will see the Sauratown Mountains, which, although not as high as mountains in the western part of the state, give the impression of being much taller than they really are because of the nearly level land surrounding the peaks. If you have traveled to the West, you have noticed that the Rocky Mountains, which are twice as high as mountains in North Carolina, do not appear to be so terribly large because the peaks jut up from a plateau that is already 6,000 feet high-almost as high as Mount Mitchell. The Sauratown Mountains, with their peaks reaching from 1,700 to 2,500 feet above sea level, produce the same type of effect.

In fact, the Sauratown Mountains were once majestic and tall, until millions of years of wind, rain, snow, and other natural forces eroded the once-mighty peaks. Only the quartzite, a compact granular rock composed of quartz essentially, prevented the final erosion of the Sauratowns.

These mountains, which are often called "the mountains away from the mountains" because of their separation from the Blue Ridge range, were once the home of the Saura Indians. The Indians are long since departed, but the mountains remain for the enjoyment of visitors to Hanging Rock State Park.

As you enter the 6,192-acre park, you will see Indian Creek running parallel to the road. One of the hiking trails, Indian Creek Trail, follows the stream bed along part of the creek. When you are inside the park, you have a variety of choices as to how best to spend your time and energies.

If you are looking for a picnic area, you will find one if you stay to the left as you drive along Hanging Rock Road. You will also find restrooms near the picnic tables. Your after-lunch activity might well be a hike up the Hanging Rock Trail to the rock itself. The trail to the top is 1.2 miles and is rated as moderate. This author's opinion is that the trail is more strenuous than it is moderate. The reason is that the walk, which is easy at the first and near the end, is a constant climb, with level ground rare and welcome. If you are not in reasonably good shape, the trek may tax your endurance severely.

But the rewards far outweigh the tribulations. You can make the walk, even if you are out of shape, if you take your time and stop frequently to enjoy your surroundings. At the top you will be treated to some excellent scenery and exhilarating fresh air and sense of solitude. You and the hawks, vultures, and ravens, as well as the songbirds and small animal life, will share experiences that will become some of your fondest recollections.

If mountain climbing is not your taste at the moment, you may find the waterfall trips to be perfect. The falls at Hanging Rock are not stupendous in terms of volume or height, but they are some of the best in this part of the state.

To see the two best waterfalls in the least amount of time, return to the lower parking area and take the trail along Indian Creek. During part of the short walk of little more than an easy mile, you will pass the picnic tables and restrooms and enter the forest. At .2 mile you will intersect with the famous Mountains-to-Sea Trail. Stay on the combined trails until you reach a T-intersection. At this point you have walked .3 mile.

You will see a spur leading off to the right and you can follow it .1 mile to Hidden Falls. To see the falls completely you must approach the rather high ledge and look over into the shallow ravine. Hidden Falls can be seen and photographed readily from this point. Be advised that Indian Creek in dry months is not a raging torrent. Instead, it is a gentle and modest-sized creek wandering through the forest. The falls are not enormously high, but they are interesting and attractive.

While you are in the vicinity you can view Window Falls. If you return to the intersection you will see the sign directing you to Window Falls. The sign will be on your left. Follow the trail to a series of steps cut into the slope and walk along a rocky and rough but easy surface. Within one mile of total hiking (and within a short jaunt from the T-intersection) you will cross a huge rock and on your right you can see a rock wall with a three-foot hole in it. This natural hole is the "window" through which you can see the small waterfall.

You can return to your car and drive to the park entrance on SR 1001 and leave the park temporarily. Intersect with SR 1489 (the Piedmont Springs Road) off to your left. Take this road until you reach NC 8/89. Turn left and then take SR 1482 down to a parking area on the banks of the Dan River.

Here you will find a small boat ramp where you can launch a canoe, tube, or other small craft, such as a kayak. The current moves steadily but not swiftly, and this is a nearly perfect stream for floating and fishing. The Dan River has a reputation for having large numbers of smallmouth bass, catfish, perch, and other panfish indigenous to the area. You need no special permits to canoe or kayak, but you must have a valid North Carolina fishing license if you plan to catch a mess of fish for your supper.

If you want to camp, you can enjoy the campground at Hanging Rock State Park. There are 73 campsites available on a first-come first-served basis. In the family campground you will find a fire pit and grill at each site. Tent pads are also available at each of the sites.

The campground is near both parking lots and not far from the lake. Vacation cabins are also nearby. There is room here for your camping trailer, too. Other services provided include wash houses, hot showers, and laundry sinks.

There is a fee charged for using the campgrounds. Call the park office (336) 593-8480 for details.

There is a group camping area near the entrance to the park where eight campsites are available on a reservation basis. Pit toilets and drinking water are the only services provided other than a fire pit and picnic table.

Near the family campground you will see six rustic family vacation cabins. Each cabin is fully equipped and ready for use. The two-bedroom cabins will sleep six people. There are also kitchen and a living room. You can rent these cabins in the spring and fall by the night, with a two-night minimum rental fee. The summer rentals are by the week only. Again, call the park office for rental fees and for details about reservations.

While you are at Hanging Rock you may want to fish in the 12-acre lake. Private boats are not permitted, but you may rent canoes or row-boats at the boathouse during the summer. A fishing license is required at the lake, too. The swimming area is also located at the lake. On the shore are the bathhouse, snack bar, and lounge.

For those wanting more hiking than the casual walks described above, you may wish to try the full-length hiking trails at the park. You will find over 18 miles of woodland trails. You also have a choice of lengths. The shortest hike is .2 mile and the longest is 4.2 miles. The difficulty of the trails ranges from easy to moderate to difficult or strenuous.

Some of the hiking trails may also be used as bridle trails. Hikers may use any of the trails designated as bridle trails.

If you have not found enough entertainment and activities at this point, you can try your hand at rock climbing. But this is not a sport for amateurs. Climb only with experienced people. The two areas for climb-ing are the two miles of rock cliffs known as Cook's Wall and Moore's Wall. You will find cliffs up to 400 feet in height.

The face of Stone Mountain.

SECTION 1: THE BEST OF THE MOUNTAINS
TRIP 8: STONE MOUNTAIN
A VISIT TO A PLUTON PARADISE

LOCATION:

Stone Mountain dominates the area near Roaring Gap. From I-40 exit onto I-77 at Statesville and from I-77 onto US 21 near Elkin. Drive north to the intersection with State Road 1002. Follow SR 1002 to the John P. Frank Parkway and from there to the entrance to Stone Mountain State Park.

NEARBY ATTRACTIONS:

Stone Mountain is within easy driving distance of Doughton Park, one of the true beauty spots along the Blue Ridge Parkway and, for that matter, anywhere in the state or in the South. From Stone Mountain you are also within range of Sparta, Jefferson, Mount Jefferson, and the towns of Elkin and Wilkesboro.

HOURS OF OPERATION:

Stone Mountain State Park is open November through February from 8 a.m. until 6 p.m.; in March and October from 8 a.m. until 7 p.m.; in April, May, and September from 8 a.m. until 8 p.m.; from June through August from 8 a.m. until 9 p.m.

ADMISSION:

No admission fees are charged. There is a fee for family or group camping.

FACILITIES:

Restrooms, public telephones, abundant parking, park office, and handicap accessible areas are handy, and if you want physical activity, you can have all you can handle here.

WHAT'S THE STORY?

To the surprise of many people, North Carolina does indeed have its own Stone Mountain, not to be confused in any way with the mountain by the same name in Georgia. The Tar Heel version of Stone Mountain is an absolute delight, and if you have not yet made your visit, you don't know what a joy you have missed. The best times to visit this mountain are anytime the park is open. Here, on a monadnock millions of years old, you have the best of mountain views and experiences, and there are dozens of wonderful ways to have a great time.

SPECIAL ATTRACTIONS:

First, there is the Mountain, which is one of the true wonders of this part of the world. After the mountain there are waterfalls, hiking trails, picnic grounds, group and family camping, trout fishing, nature study, and rock climbing.

MAKING THE MOST OF YOUR VISIT:

Starting with a disclaimer of sorts, I have enjoyed the best of the mountains in Germany, Austria, Italy, and other Alpine areas, as well as the mountains of Colorado, New Mexico, Vermont, Canada, New Hampshire, Maine, Georgia, South Carolina, and other parts of the country. The Rockies are incredible, as are the Alps. But I have never found a better place than western North Carolina. A partial listing of the elements of this state that I love without reservation would fill a large volume. So I admit more than a degree of prejudice when I write about my home state. And in a strict sense Stone Mountain is not in western North Carolina, but it is indeed in the mountains.

I am reminded of a long-time resident of the Rowan County area who once visited a rather large nearby lake for the first time. Later, when asked about the size of it, he replied, "Well, if the ocean's any bigger, it's a whopper!"

Parallels exist. In my view, if Heaven is significantly better than the mountains of North Carolina, it's a more terrific place than I could begin to imagine!

As to Stone Mountain in particular, there are several reasons the mountain is more than ordinarily super-special. First, the huge stone monument to Nature's beauty is isolated, like Hanging Rock and Pilot Mountain, from the rest of the Blue Ridge chain; therefore, the height of the mountain is awesome. The actual height above sea level is 2,305 feet, but it appears higher. From the base of the mountain to the top the distance is the equivalent in height to a 60-story building.

The 300-million year-old mountain itself is about four miles in circumference and the park area is about 25 square miles. The huge rock is classified as a pluton. The term is derived from the Latin *Pluto*, which is a reference to the Greek and Roman god who ruled over the underworld, or Hades.

The derivation of the word is interestingly similar to the origin of the mountain. Pluto himself was the son of Cronus and Rhea, and brother to Zeus and Poseidon. The brothers overthrew their father and then cast lots for the kingdoms of heaven, hell, and the sea, with Pluto winning (?) the infernal regions. One would hate to see what he received if he had lost. But there in Hades he ruled with pitiless power; flattery and praise were to him nothing, and sacrifice was useless. He was, however, moved by the music of Orpheus.

Stone Mountain, in no way to be considered the equivalent of Hades (far to the contrary, it is a heavenly place, comparatively speaking), was formed by the volcanic action that forced molten lava from far beneath the earth's surface, and the intense heat created destroyed all forms of life in the area. Plutonic rocks are characterized by slow cooling after great pressure occurs.

Keep Pluto in mind as you visit Stone Mountain. Remember, too, that Orpheus was a musician so divine that even the wild beasts, rocks, trees, and rivers were thrilled by his music. When his wife, Eurydice, died, Orpheus begged Pluto and associates to restore her to life. Moved by his music, they relented, with the stipulation that when Eurydice returned to life she must always walk behind Orpheus and that he must never turn around or look back.

As you explore this vast remnant of molten rock, you may be reminded of the legend of Pluto, or you may simply prefer to take a stroll around the park and, in particular, up the mountain and across it. If you have a poetic streak in you, there may be more than a suggestion of the Orphic lute in the song of the wind as it moves through the trees atop Stone Mountain, a music so soothing that even the trees and rocks and rivers (in this case, Big Sandy Creek) can be moved by it. Or it may be only a gentle cooling sensation on a hot day.

At any rate, don't look back. You need to keep your footing as sure and certain as possible, if you try the climb up to the top of the mountain.

And it is not necessary to be a poet to love Stone Mountain, but it can help to have a lyrical inclination.

Second, while most mountains in this area are covered with trees, grass, shrubs, or all of the previous, Stone Mountain is in many huge areas totally devoid of any large or noticeable plant life. There are trees at the bottom and top, and some hardy ones manage to survive on the precipitous slopes, but for the most part the mountain presents the visual impression of being one enormous and magnificent boulder.

Third, despite the apparent barren austerity, Stone Mountain has an amazing variety of plant and animal life. There are white-tail deer, beavers, gray and red foxes, turtles, snakes of several sorts, bobcats, and raccoons. Bird life includes ravens or crows, pileated woodpeckers (often called the raincrow by the older rural folks), wild turkeys, ruffed grouse, scarlet tanagers, vultures, hawks, brown thrashers, whippoorwills, and many smaller birds. The streams are populated by several species of trout, and frogs, toads, and salamanders. In the plant domain there are chestnut oaks, white pines, scarlet oaks, red maples, hickories, black oaks, cedars, and other trees in the medium-sized range.

Shrubs include laurel, rhododendron, and blueberry. You will see an abundance of wild flowers that somehow find rootholds and nourishment in the seemingly sterile environment. Ferns in many areas grow in profusion. One of the interesting plants is the famed "butterfly bush," a plant which attracts butterflies by the dozens or even hundreds. If you are lucky you can see one of the plants while you are on a summertime visit, and the plant may be literally covered with beautiful butterflies.

While at Stone Mountain you will want to climb to the top of the gray hump. In order to do so you can start at either end. Start at the picnic area and walk south to a large meadow filled with wild flowers and high grass in summer (and at times with deer as they graze contentedly in the solitude of Stone Mountain when the tourists and visitors are absent).

From the meadow you can see Stone Mountain in all its awesome glory. You can follow the well-worn footpaths to the north end of the monadnock and start the climb upward, or you can head for the south end of the hump and take the straighter but often breath-taking trail. You will make your way through a thick rhododendron and mixed hardwood forest and emerge at the base of the mountain. Take a few more steps and you can see the spectacular waterfall that plummets 200 feet down the mountainside.

The waterfall has gone by a variety of names in the past: Deer Falls, Twin Falls, Sandy Creek Cascades, Beauty Falls, and Stone Mountain Falls. All of the names are appropriate for reasons which follow.

Legend holds that when early settlers moved into the area the families each took turns at searching the shallow plunge pool at the base of the falls for deer that lost their footing and went over the falls. Fresh meat was at a premium at that time, and finding a dead or fatally wounded deer virtually in your back yard was much easier than tracking one through the mountainside. There are no records as to how many deer actually died at the falls, but one fact is abundantly clear: while it is probable that deer died in the falls, it is known that some human beings have died there. So here is a warning you should heed!

Do not try to wade across the creek as it pours over the rocky face of Stone Mountain. Do not wade even in the shallow water at the side of the creek. The danger is not in the depth of the water but in the treacherously slick rocks which offer no footing at all. If you should slip, the drop is a long one, and the bottom of the fall is atop a heap of rocks.

The Twin Falls name came, logically, because there are really two waterfalls, as such, rather than one.

Sandy Creek Cascades is, or was, a good name because the creek that flows over the rock is called Big Sandy, and the waterfall is actually more of a cascade than a true waterfall. A cascade slides over sloped rocks, while a true waterfall drops in a free fall from the top to the plunge pool. Middle Falls, deep in the forest below Stone Mountain Falls, is an example of a true waterfall in that the water falls 25 feet in an uninter-rupted drop.

Beauty Falls was a superb name. All you need to do is take one look at the waterfall and you can see why is was once so-named.

Finally, Stone Mountain Falls is an obvious name.

The trail at the waterfall leads straight up the mountain-in the form of a series of flights of steps. Count them as you climb and you will see that there are 289 steps in the trail. As you climb you will be within a few feet of the water-close enough that you will be hit by spray and mist.

At the top you can wander around the nearly flat rock and enjoy a magnificent view, but do not wander down the slope and away from the trail. It is incredibly easy to descend to a point where you cannot safely return and the only other option is to fall the equivalent of the 60-story building previously mentioned.

The trail will take you all the way across the top of the stone hump. At the north end the descent is gradual, easy, and dry. If you want more hiking, you can take the trails to Wolf Rock and to Cedar Rock. Follow the trails all the way to the summit and again enjoy a rewarding view.

Stone Mountain is a rock-climber's paradise, if this is your preference of recreation. But climb, always, with an experienced person and be cer-tain that your equipment is in excellent shape. You should also be in excellent shape, for rock climbing is a tough, often brutal, and always gruelling sport. There are thirteen trails leading up the rock face and you have a choice of hard, harder, or hardest. If you don't want to climb the rocks, you can sit on a bench in the meadow and watch others.

Stone Mountain streams are inhabited by rainbow, brown, and brook trout. There are 17 miles of trout streams available, and before you start to fish you must familiarize yourself with the rules and regulations. There are streams where only single-hook artificial lures may be used; others are catch-and-release waters.

For family campers there are 37 campsites available on a first-come first-served basis. As with all state parks, there is a fee for camping ($12 per day). At the family sites there are tent pads, tables, grills, a dump station for RVs, drinking water, hot showers, and laundry tubs.

Two group campsites are also available, but these must be reserved. A fee is also charged. The group sites offer only tables, fireplaces, and pit toilets.

Stone Mountain has it all: beauty, elevation, clean air, trout streams, camp grounds, nature study, hiking, photo opportunities, rock climbing, animals and birds to observe, wild flowers and lush vegetation, and, above all, an imposing joy that will be, as the poet Wordsworth put it (and you read earlier), "life and food for future years."

Overlook view of Jomeokee.

SECTION 1: THE BEST OF THE MOUNTAINS
TRIP 9: PILOT MOUNTAIN STATE PARK
VISITING THE HAWKS OF JOMEOKEE

LOCATION:
Pilot Mountain State Park is located near the small town of Pilot Mountain, which can be reached via NC 268 off I-77 at exit 85. You are now on the CCC Camp Road, which will lead you into Pilot Mountain. Intersect with US 52 south and within five miles you will reach the entrance to Pilot Mountain State Park.

NEARBY ATTRACTIONS:
While you are in the vicinity of Pilot Mountain State Park you can expand your trip into a mini-vacation and make side trips to Winston-Salem, particularly to Old Salem, and to Hanging Rock State Park, Horne Creek Living Historical Farm, the city of Elkin, to Stone Mountain, and to Doughton Park.

HOURS OF OPERATION:

The park is open from November through February: 8 a.m. until 6 p.m.; during March and October: 8 a.m. until 7 p. m.; during April, May, and September: 8 a.m. until 8 p.m.; and from June through August: 8 a.m. until 9 p.m.

ADMISSION:

No admission fees are charged.

FACILITIES:

There are picnic tables, restrooms, campgrounds, canoe launch, canoe access sites to the Yadkin River, horse trailer parking, auto parking, drinking water, public telephone, firewood on sale, and camping areas. Most facilities are handicap accessible.

WHAT'S THE STORY?

Pilot Mountain was known to the Indians who inhabited the area centuries ago as Jomeokee, or Great Guide or Pilot. The 3,703-acre state park area includes the famous Pilot Mountain peak as well as 17 miles of hiking trails and the Horne Creek Living Historical Farm.

MAKING THE MOST OF YOUR VISIT

The Pilot Mountain peak itself is the star of the show. This 1,400 foot peak is, like other pinnacles in the area, the remnants of once mighty mountains and was once a part of the Sauratown range.

The story is a long one: some scholars have estimated that the developmental period of Pilot Mountain was about one billion years. The story is that at one time the entire Piedmont area, extending from the Hudson River area of New York to central Alabama, a total distance of about 1,000 miles, was submerged under the Iapetus Sea. Silt, sand, and clay, over a period of countless years, washed into the sea and thick layers of sediment accumulated. As pressure and heat acted upon the sediment, a form of rock known as quartzite was formed.

Continued pressure forced the rocks higher and higher, and soon they projected thousands of feet above the Piedmont plain. The Sauratown Mountains now consist of three peaks-Hanging Rock, Pilot Mountain, and Sauratown Mountain-which resisted the erosive forces of nature well enough that they exist today, although in diminished form, while the rest of the area fell away to rolling hills and farmland.

If you wish to identify the three peaks, the middle one is Sauratown Mountain and the one farthest east is Hanging Rock. The one closest to the Blue Ridge Mountains and the one that is the site of Jomeokee is, of course, Pilot Mountain.

It was the Saura Native Americans who gave the 1,400-foot peak of Pilot Mountain the name "Jomeokee." The more aggressive Cherokee

Indians moved into the region and forced the 2,000 Sauras out and finally into the mists of history. The earliest European people into the area were the Moravians who maintained an uneasy relationship with the Native American Cherokees, who allied with the British.

As Native Americans and white settlers traveled in and out of the territory, they used the tall pinnacle as a landmark that could be seen for many miles. The Great Guide is still a remarkable and highly prominent feature of the three-peak landscape, and if you look 30 miles to the west from Jomeokee you will see the Blue Ridge Mountains.

In 1751 Joshua Fry and Peter Jefferson, the latter the father of Thomas Jefferson, mapped the area. The elder Jefferson also made visits to the area of what is now Mount Jefferson. In more recent times Pilot Mountain was a commercial establishment, and it was not until 1968 that concerned citizens spurred a movement to raise money and convert Pilot Mountain and other acreage into a state park. This dream became a reality in 1970 when land along the Yadkin River was added to the initial purchase and enlarged Pilot Mountain State Park to its present 3,703 acres.

When you arrive at the park, the first activity might well be a quick walk to the overlook or observation tower near Jomeokee. You stand close enough to the peak, which is 2,420 feet above sea level, that you can see the erosion marks on the rock pinnacle. Keep in mind that the peak itself is 1,400 feet higher than the surrounding area, and the elevation above sea level is greater. The Yadkin River valley is slightly more than 1,000 feet above sea level.

If you are there when the hawks are migrating, you can spend hours watching the kettles of hawks percolating. The term *kettle* is used because the hawks tend to move up and down inside the loose formation in what some have described as a bubbling effect. Others have seen the formation and its movement as being more like a gentle whirlwind or whirlpool effect. Whatever you wish to call it, the spectacle is an interesting one.

On a good day you can see 40 to 60 hawks in a single kettle as they make their way southward to the Gulf of Mexico area where they will winter. In an age when pollution and man's carelessness with nature have reduced some wildlife to dangerously low levels, it is rewarding to see so many hawks that have survived.

You will also see, if you are there at migrating time, highly serious bird watchers who spend the entire day, or most of it, with a note pad in hand. They count the hawks and record their findings. They are concerned with the numbers of hawks because the population of accipiters, particularly regarding such birds as the peregrine falcon, are important to the overall ecology of the area and to the balance of nature, which is at times precarious.

If the hawks are not present, you can still enjoy the sight of ravens or an occasional vulture soaring over Jomeokee. When you have devoted sufficient time to the pinnacle from a distance, you may want to take a brief walk along the floor of what was once a sea. Beside the observation platform there is a short and rather easy trail that descends into the underbrush and toward Jomeokee.

The .8 mile trail leads you completely around the pinnacle, and you can see for yourself the marks made on the rock as the ancient seawaters carved fascinating and almost mysterious designs in the quartzite monadnock.

You can walk completely around the Big Pinnacle, as the peak is called, and return to the starting point. There are many more trails to hike, if you want more physical exercise. The 11 trails include hikes of one-tenth of a mile up to more than five miles.

The Little Pinnacle Trail is the shortest, and the longest is the Corridor Trail. It may also be the trail with the greatest variety of terrain, vegetation, and wild life.

The easiest trail is, again, the Little Pinnacle Trail. The hardest is either the Mountain Trail or the Ledge Spring Trail.

At Pilot Mountain State Park you can enjoy family camping or canoe camping. In the family campground you have restrooms and drinking water, in addition to a tent pad, table, and grill. There are 49 camp sites available on a first-come first-served basis.

For canoe campers, you can drift or paddle down the Yadkin River and stop at the larger of the two islands alongside the old railroad. Here are two camp sites and nothing else but river water and island vegetation and wild life. There are no facilities of any sort on the islands.

The larger island is a 45-acre stretch of land, and the small one is one-third the size of the first. You can approach the two islands by foot along the Bean Shoals Trail. You will need to drive to State Road 2072, the Hauser Road, and then take the park road into the forest and drive to the circular parking lot at the end of the road. You will pass picnic tables and camp sites along the way.

If horseback riding is your primary interest, there are some excellent bridle trails in the area, and if your visit is to be a brief one, you have a choice of good picnic tables within easy reach of the parking lots.

Animal life includes white tail deer, red and gray foxes, woodchucks or ground hogs (whose story is an interesting one and well worth researching, particularly as the ground hog relates to the Christmas story), opossums, squirrels, hawks, owls, vultures, ravens, pileated woodpeckers, brown thrashers, mockingbirds, wrens, and a huge variety of other songbirds.

Wild flowers abound in the park, and you can find them beside trails in almost any part of the park territory. Flowering shrubs and huge trees provide a huge amount of vegetation. You can find laurel, rhododendron, blueberries, oaks, pines, and other taller trees as well as honeysuckle, grape vines, and, to your dismay, poison ivy.

Beware, too, of the laurel and rhododendron sap, which in some areas was used by Native Americans as a poison. You will perhaps encounter several kinds of snakes as you walk the trails. Among the possibilities are the copperheads and rattlers, but these reptiles prefer not to have human encounters, and they will give you room unless you molest and frighten them. Whether you are hiking at Pilot Mountain or anywhere else where rattlers may be found, remember that the rattlesnake does not always emit the warning rattle or buzz. The rattler, like many other reptiles, will twitch its tail nervously when it senses danger, but the snake does not need to rattle when it is stalking a mouse or bird.

Do not let the possible presence of snakes prevent you from enjoying the outdoors life. Your chances of seeing a venomous snake are slim, and even if you see one, there is small chance that you will have a real confrontation. Be aware of their presence, just as you are aware of the presence of poison oak, ivy, sumac, ticks, mosquitoes, and stinging insects. Take normal precautions and exert reasonable care.

When you have examined Pilot Mountain and are ready to move on, drive down to Horne Creek Historical Farm. Here you will find a farmstead, complete with house, gardens, animals, tools, and other objects and activities typical of the 1900-era farms. You can enjoy a hands-on experience on weekends. If you prefer a group tour or educational programs, call (919) 325-2298.

Fishermen visiting Pilot Mountain will not be able to fish for trout, but there are catfish, perch, crappie, and other panfish in the nearby Yadkin River.

And, if you are looking for another mountain area located within a state park, you have another one within a short drive. I strongly recommend state parks for several excellent reasons: they are uniformly clean, organized, and highly educational. Rangers and park workers are well-informed, courteous, and eager to help visitors have a great time; the parks charge no admission fees, and camping and other costs are minimal. You have protection, rules and regulations that are enforced to guarantee that all visitors have an opportunity to engage in healthful and meaningful outdoor sports and activities.

Best of all, in one sense, is that the state park lands are often the best territories you could find anywhere in the region. The parks became parks because there were important ecological and scenic elements present. It was these characteristics that prompted interested citizen groups to form and campaign to save the beauty and the environment, and the state parks remain true to the original reasons for saving the land.

At state parks you have a great variety of educational and recreational opportunities. You can often swim, fish, hike, ride horseback, rock climb, camp, enjoy programs and presentations, observe wild life, picnic, boat, sight-see, photograph, and learn the history of an area. They are among the best bargains in the entire state of North Carolina which is, and you can ask anyone who travels extensively, one of the richest locations anywhere in the United States for varied and rewarding outdoor enjoyment.

The nearby state park is Mount Jefferson, and while you are there you can check out the New River State Park as well.

On the trails at Mount Jefferson.

SECTION 1: THE BEST OF THE MOUNTAINS
TRIP 10: MOUNT JEFFERSON STATE PARK
THE DARK BEAUTY OF A NATIONAL LANDMARK

LOCATION:

As you approach the town of Jefferson in the northwest corner of North Carolina, at 1.5 miles south of Jefferson, via US 221 (which exits off Interstate 40), watch for the Mount Jefferson Road, which leads off the highway to the park office, information center, and picnic grounds.

NEARBY ATTRACTIONS:

New River State Park, Doughton Park, Glendale Springs and Jefferson (home of the world-famous Church of the Frescoes and St. Mary's Church, where other frescoes were created by Ben Long, arguably the finest fresco artist in the world today), Blue Ridge Parkway, and the cheese factory in the West Jefferson area are all within easy driving distance.

HOURS OF OPERATION:

Regular hours of operation are November through February, 8 a.m.

until 6 p.m.; March and October, 8 a.m. until 7 p.m.; April, May, September, 8 a.m. until 8 p. m.; June through August, 8 a.m. until 9 p.m.

ADMISSION:

There are no admission charges at the park.

FACILITIES:

Picnic tables, parking area, rest rooms are available at the park, and much of the area is handicap accessible.

WHAT'S THE STORY?

Mount Jefferson is popular and significant in terms of its history, the natural wonders not just on the mountain but in the valleys around the mountain, its educational offerings, and its beauty.

MAKING THE MOST OF YOUR VISIT:

Plan to visit New River State Park while you are in the vicinity of Mount Jefferson. The two are so close together that you can drive from one to the other in a matter of minutes, and the contrast between the two areas is fascinating. And, despite the differences, the two parks and geographic areas have more in common than most people would suspect.

Atop Mount Jefferson there are educational displays that describe in considerable detail the geological history of the region. One of the startling assertions is that about 300 million years ago the African and North American continents were in much closer proximity: they may have been, the plaques state, at one time even connected before the gigantic land masses drifted apart. Consider that if the continents had been one land mass, then the relationship between two rivers, the Nile and the New River, might have been dramatically close.

The New River, despite its name, is not new at all. It is, in fact, believed to be the second-oldest river in the entire world. Only the Nile is older. The implications are interesting, to say the least.

One of the reasons the two state parks should be seen within a similar time frame is that when you look at Mount Jefferson, which rises 4,900 feet above sea level, and then look at the valley of the New River, you can imagine that once the mountain range was lofty and majestic, but when the river began to carve away at the softer substances in the mountains, only the hardest or most durable compositions resisted the erosion.

When you visit the New River State Park and Mount Jefferson State Park, you will find that both of the geologic landmarks contain trails that can be hiked easily in only a matter of hours. You can, in fact, walk the educational trails at a very casual pace and learn a great deal about the mountains of North Carolina while you enjoy the sights along the trails.

You may want to visit New River State Park first, so that you can see and enjoy the stream that has flowed in essentially the same channel for millions of years. You will learn that the river existed long before the mountains erupted to their early heights. Like the Nile, the New River flows north.

Because of the age of the river, it is logical to assume that civilizations along the river would also reach back into the most ancient times. Artifacts unearthed in the area indicate that Native American tribes, including Cherokees, Shawnees, Creeks, and Canawhays, alternately occupied the area. Some of the Native Americans were present as early as 10,000 years ago.

Wild life in the area at that time included elk, white tail deer, bison, beaver, bear, fox, raccoon, mink, otter, and many other creatures, large and small. With the exceptions of the elk and bison, the majority of these animals are still residents of the New River and Mount Jefferson territory.

The river was named Wood's River at first, the label having been derived from the name of Colonel Abraham Wood, who traded with the Indians in the middle of the 17th century. The present name was applied by Peter Jefferson, father of Thomas Jefferson, who explored the territory in 1749 as he surveyed the boundary lines separating North Carolina and Virginia.

Several years ago the New River was in great danger of being destroyed, in a sense, as a power company applied for permission to dam the river to create reservoirs. Citizens groups formed and protested vehemently that the river should remain unspoiled and free, and in 1975 the North Carolina General Assembly designated a long stretch of the river as a State Scenic River.

Because of the determined efforts of men and women who loved the river and wanted it spared from commercial exploitation, the river was protected and a state park was formed.

There are several other points where you can launch canoes. There are several bridges that cross the river and most of these are suitable canoe launch locations.

When you have familiarized yourself with the New River area and when you have enjoyed the canoeing or simply walking along the shores of the New River, you may drive a few minutes to the parking area of the Mount Jefferson State Park. Here you will find few facilities in terms of camping or outdoor living. The mountain is a celebration of a natural monument, a link to the ancient world, a permanent reminder of beauty and strength and at the same time to the fragility of parts of the natural world.

There are picnic facilities, restrooms, grills, and drinking water, in addition to hiking trails. It is these trails that are the major attraction at the mountain, other than the peak itself. The main trail climbs to a North Carolina Forest Service lookout tower, a second trail leads along the ridge to Luther's Rock Overlook, and the final walk includes a trip along the Rhododendron Trail, a self-guiding nature walk. You can hike all of the three trails in two hours and still have plenty of time to pause and read the informative material posted along the trails.

The park was officially named Mount Jefferson State Park in 1955 and covers 541 acres, making it one of the smallest parks in the state in terms of land area. The park is located in Ashe County midway between the towns of Jefferson and West Jefferson. The mountain itself rises for 1,600 feet above the surrounding territory and can be viewed for miles around. The mountains in this area, like other peaks in the region, are remnants of once-high mountains created ages earlier.

Dr. Elisha Mitchell, when he completed a visit to the peak in 1827, noted that the area was "an ocean of mountains." The mountain has been described as a naturalist's paradise. The wooded terrain includes a variety of evergreen and hardwood trees, flowering shrubs, and the ubiquitous wildflowers, all of which vary at different elevations of the mountain. The lower elevations are populated with sugar maple, red maple, black locust, mountain ash, white ash, mountain maple, bigtooth aspen, hickory, poplar, yellow birch, basswood, chestnut oak, white oak, white pine, and many northern red oak varieties. The upper areas include chestnut oak, purple rhododendron, and mountain laurel. Other vegetation includes serviceberry, bush honeysuckle, flame azalea, and dogwoods.

In 1975 the National Park Service named Mount Jefferson Park a Natural National Landmark because of its interesting and unusual plant varieties. The wildflowers along the trails include wild iris, jack-in-the-pulpit, galax, wood lilacs, white beebalm, false lily-of-the-valley, wild azalea, and dutchman's breeches.

A variety of wildlife, including chipmunks, red and gray squirrels, deer, woodchucks, and, on occasion, red and gray foxes, may be seen.

From the picnic area you can take the main trail to the summit of the mountain. The trail splits, leading right to Luther's Rock Overlook, or left to the lookout tower.

The tower trail itself is a well-established path. On clear days you can see peaks in three states: North Carolina, Virginia, and Tennessee. One of the outstanding peaks is Whitetop Mountain in Virginia.

From the lookout tower, walk .2 mile southeast and you will reach an information display entitled "As Time Goes By." In the display the growth rings of a tree-trunk section are labeled with important events and dates. The time table includes an 1827 date that marks Dr. Mitchell's visit. At that time he wrote that he had never seen anything more beautiful than the view from the top. Other dates are the establishment of other state parks including Mount Mitchell, the first in 1915, and the latest date of 1991, the 75th anniversary of the state park system.

Within another tenth of a mile to Luther's Rock Overlook you have an excellent view of the New River. This view is a great reminder of the relationship of the mountain and the river.

On the Rhododendron Trail, the park service provides booklets that are numbered to point out most important elements of the peak and valley and key points concerning the history of the region.

One grim reminder of the fragility of nature can be found in the information pertinent to the fate of the noblest giant of the forest, the American chestnut, that was destroyed when the blight hit. Now, only dead tree trunks remain of the great forest. The best ray of hope lies in the young sprouts that have emerged from the old root systems.

While the prognosis is not unbridled enthusiasm, you can keep in mind that on the border of Cleveland and Rutherford counties to the south there are at least two nearly full-grown chestnut trees that have somehow resisted the blight. In fact, the trees were once infected but managed to recover and regain their original health. Forest workers are making efforts to find ways to cross-pollinate the trees with young trees and perhaps find a way to render the chestnut tree immune to the blight.

If this dream becomes a reality, one of the finest dreams of the American naturalist will be realized, and millions of North Carolinians will rejoice in the promise of the resurrection of the great tree whose blossoms once made the mountainsides look as if they were covered in snow.

And that is the thought to take with you as you leave Mount Jefferson and this part of the book. The next section takes you to a new type of exploration, that of the best of the waterfalls in the mountains of the Tar Heel state.

High Shoals Falls at South Mountains State Park.

SECTION 2: THE BEST OF THE WATERFALLS
TRIP 1: SOUTH MOUNTAINS STATE PARK
HIGH SHOALS FALLS-AND MORE

LOCATION:

As before, using Interstate 40 as a starting point, exit I-40 onto NC 18 in Morganton and drive south toward Shelby. Halfway between the two cities you will see signs directing you to South Mountains State Park. Follow the signs to old NC 18 and stay on the old highway until you reach Ward Gap Road. Turn right and head west for three miles. The last part of the road is gravel but it is in good shape all year. Drive slowly, however, because the gravel will cause you to skid if you must brake sharply.

NEARBY ATTRACTIONS:

In addition to the towns mentioned above, you are within an easy drive to Kings Mountain National Military Park, Kings Mountain State Park (both across the South Carolina border), the C. Grier Beam Truck Museum and the Cherryville History Museum (both in Cherryville), the Waldensian Museum in Valdese, and Lake James State Park.

HOURS OF OPERATION:

The park is open from 8 a.m. every morning until 6 p.m. November through February; 7 p.m. March and October; 8 p. m. in April, May, and September; 9 p. m. June through August.

ADMISSION:

No admission fees are charged at any time. There are small fees for camping, but no fees are charged for picnicking, hiking, or use of park facilities. Camping fees at this writing are $8 per night per campsite. Call 828-433-4772 for more information.

FACILITIES:

The park has picnic tables, grills, rest rooms, pit toilets for backcountry recreation, and parking lots that tend to become crowded on summer weekends.

WHAT'S THE STORY?

The South Mountains are among the best-kept secrets in North Carolina. While most travelers head for the Great Smokies or the Blue Ridge Parkway (fine destinations, in all respects) until recently very few stopped by the South Mountains range. But with the expansion of the state park in acreage and the improvement of roads and facilities, more tourists are finding this uncrowded and almost pristine pure mountain retreat, which is almost isolated from main roads. Once you arrive you will find one of the best waterfalls in the foothills.

SPECIAL ATTRACTIONS:

The best views are those of High Shoals Falls and the Upper Falls. The Jacob's Fork River is unusually beautiful throughout the entire park area, and Shinny Creek (pronounced as if it were *Shiny*) has some highly attractive cascades and smaller falls.

MAKING THE MOST OF YOUR VISIT:

The first order of business is to see the waterfalls. This is one of the sites where you must walk at least one mile into the forest to see the falls, and, of course, another mile back out. The trail to the falls is rather rugged at times, but for the most part you will have little difficulty if you are in reasonably good shape and can handle brief steep climbs. On a fairly regular basis people in their sixties, seventies, and even eighties make the hike and suffer no ill effects. You will reach several flights of steps cut into the hillside or composed of native rock. Some of these steps can be tiring if you are not in good shape.

The keys to the hike, if you are hesitant, are simple: good shoes, appropriate clothing (depending upon the season and the weather), good attitude, and plenty of time. Do not rush the walk if you want to enjoy a trouble-free outing.

The walk itself is a wonderful one. The best times to visit the High Shoals Falls are in winter, spring, and fall, and the best times of day are mornings. Plan to arrive about the time the park gates open. Take along a picnic lunch and leave it in the trunk of your car while you make the hike. It is better not to start the hike immediately after eating, unless you eat a very light meal. You do not need to worry about carrying water or other outdoor gear except rain wear if the weather is unsettled.

Plan for about half an hour or slightly more to make the walk to the falls. From the parking lot across the clearing from the park office, you will see a wide and paved trail leading into the forest at the west end of the parking lot. Follow the trail past the restroom area and along the banks of the Jacob's Fork River. You will enjoy taking your time and observing the cascades, rapids, and frothing water as you walk. There are dozens of places where you may wish to stop and enjoy a prolonged view of the river.

Within a few minutes (less than 10) you will reach a bridge that crosses Shinny Creek. Cross the bridge and continue along the well-marked path. The river will always be on your left as you go into the forest deeper and deeper, until you cross the first bridge over the river.

The footbridges are in themselves neat and picturesque. Pause in the middle of the bridge and enjoy both the upstream and downstream views of the river. You left the paved area near the restrooms, but the path remains hard and virtually dry all the way. As you cross the final bridge you will notice that the path is now narrow and crooked.

Soon you will be entering a part of the walk where the huge boulders are on both sides of the trail as well as in the middle of the river, and you will climb rather steeply as you head for a destination near the top of the mountain.

You can hear the waterfall several minutes before you reach the falls. When you reach the top of the last ridge you can see ahead of you an overlook that has been built out over the water. From this overlook, which has a high rail around it for safety, you have a flawless look at the waterfall and the pool at the bottom.

If you will watch carefully, you can see the trout swimming in the deep pool. If you arrive on a cold day you will have the added treat of seeing ice formations along the sides of the rock walls at the edges of the falls.

The volume of the waterfall, which is about 80 feet high, will vary considerably, depending upon the amount of rainfall over the past days. In the drought of summer, usually the end of July and the first of August, the flow is diminished greatly, but throughout most of the year there is a moderate to good volume to the falls.

The High Shoals Falls are, technically, a cascade, because the water remains in contact with the stone-faced cliff all the way down the slide. But the rock face is so steep, almost vertical, that the spectacle can rightfully be called a waterfall.

Years ago you could see the Upper Falls by hiking up a long and steep roadbed to a point above the falls, and this hike would be in addition to the one you just made. But the park personnel have constructed a set of steps leading up the steep ridge to the left of the High Shoals overlook. These steps will take you within five minutes to the Upper Falls, which, in the opinion of many, are more beautiful, although not as high, than the High Shoals falls. The new trail adds greatly to the trip.

At High Shoals Falls you will see a narrow ribbon of water perhaps eight to 10 feet wide as it crashes down the side of the mountain. At the Upper Falls you will see two distinct sets of falls, one 50 feet above the other. The higher of the two falls under normal rainfall conditions is split into two separate falls, each only four or five feet high. There is a huge rock in the middle of the falls, and the waterfall is separated by the rock.

At the lower part of the Upper Falls the waterfall itself is about 15 feet wide and the falling water descends over the eight-foot boulders from two and even three directions. On the left, as you face upstream, the water falls straight downward, while on the extreme right the water cascades at an angle away from the center of the stream and then reverses itself and descends back toward the middle of the river.

Below the falls about 30 feet there is a rock that extends 25 feet into the stream, and you can walk out onto the rock, which is wide and gently humped, and enjoy the best possible view of the falls. Just watch your footing, because only a short distance below you there is the drop-off for the higher waterfall. Exert great caution the entire time you are there.

The rocks themselves are worth a trip. As you look upstream you can see cleft rocks that separated as neatly as split oak wood. It's hard (for me, at least) not to think of Robert Frost's poem "Two Tramps in Mud Time," in which the poet writes, about another topic, "Good blocks of beech it was I split, as big around as the chopping block/ And each piece I squarely hit fell splinterless as the cloven rock."

On the left side of the river you will see a deep growth of evergreen trees, and on the lower right there are clumps of laurel and rhododendron. On the far right you will see hardwood trees mixed with evergreens.

The water is as clear as glass, and you can see the pebbles on the bottom as if they were on dry land. It is not much of an exaggeration (and maybe none at all) to say that if someone had dropped a quarter into the river it would not only be a simple matter to spot it but you could tell which side of the coin was facing upwards.

You can follow Jacob's Fork River upstream from the Upper Falls and see countless trout pools. One particularly productive trout area is called the Shades of Death (and sometimes Shadows of Death). Here the trees and shrubs are so thick that the sun can penetrate the overhead foliage only with difficulty. Dyed-in-the-wool trout fishermen insist that this is the best fishing in the entire area.

If you are interested in trout fishing, the river from the Shinny Creek bridge down to the parking lot is a stocked stream that provides excellent fishing opportunities for the younger members of the family. There are regulations governing the types of bait and hooks that can be used in the more than 14 miles of trout waters inside the park, and you should determine what you can or cannot use before starting to fish. Most of the streams are in the Wild Trout waters and two miles of streams are classified as delayed harvest streams.

Wild life in the park includes whitetail deer, woodchucks, opossums, squirrels, foxes, hawks, owls, and a variety of snakes, all but two of them harmless. An occasional bear may wander about the forest in late spring and early summer. The two poisonous snakes are the timber rattler and the copperhead. These snakes are relatively abundant and are protected by park regulations. You can avoid them by making your visit during cold weather. If you visit during warm weather, wear protective boots. Take no chances. While I have hiked in the park on numerous occasions and have never seen a poisonous snake, you may see three or four on your visit, but this is unlikely if you stay on the trails.

Songbirds of many varieties make their homes in the South Mountains, and you will see a number of them at almost any time of the year in daylight hours. Wildflowers are also abundant in the park, not just on the river but along the trails.

If you want to do more strenuous hiking, there are many miles of good trails near the waterfalls. The Fox Trail is 4.2 miles long and crosses the southern third of the park from east to west. The Upper Falls Trail is 1.9 miles, and the Little River Falls Trail is 3.1 miles. You can pick up a trail map and select trails that you can combine into almost any length hike that you prefer.

The Dogwood Trail, which is 2.5 miles long, leads along the park boundary and to Benn Knob, the highest peak in the park, with an elevation of 2,894 feet above sea level. The Lower CCC Road leads along the western boundary of the park and is 5.6 miles in length.

If you want overnight camping, there are primitive family campgrounds with 11 sites. There are 14 pack-in camp sites. There are modest fees for use of the camp sites.

For horseback-riding enthusiasts there are 29 miles of horse trails. Horse-trailer parking is on the north side of the park entrance road or on Raven Rock Road. Bike trails are available also. In short, you have over 7,000 acres of woodland in which to walk, ride, and enjoy yourself.

The streams in which you can fish originate on the park and mountain land, and these are rated as Class A streams, which means that there is no purer water to be found.

Do not drink the water, although it is Class A. Carry your own drinking water along with you.

The next trip is to the highest waterfall (by nearly all estimates) in the state and east of the Mississippi. We're going to Whitewater Falls, one of the finest scenic areas in the South.

Whitewater Falls near Brevard.

SECTION 2: THE BEST OF THE WATERFALLS
TRIP 2: WHITEWATER FALLS
THE AWESOME BEAUTY OF THE BEST

LOCATION:

Drive on US 64 south of Brevard to Sapphire and then turn left on NC 281. Drive 8.2 miles on NC 281 (sometimes called Whitewater Road) and then turn left into Forest Service parking lot. Follow the clearly marked and paved path to the falls.

NEARBY ATTRACTIONS:

The terrific city of Brevard is nearby, as are Highlands, Dry Falls, Bridal Veil Falls, and Cullasaja Falls, all on US 64. The South Carolina version of Whitewater Falls is only a few minutes' drive across the border.

HOURS OF OPERATION:

There are no gates, and the waterfall is accessible 24 hours a day, 365 days a year.

ADMISSION:

Until recently no fees at any time were charged, but recently a $2 fee has been initiated.

FACILITIES:

There are restrooms (which are closed during winter months), and paved trails part of the way. There are no picnic tables or other amenities.

WHAT'S THE STORY?

The attraction of the Whitewater Falls area is simple and yet exhilarating as you walk across a parking area and then look into the gorge where the highest waterfall in the eastern United States roars over the rock ledges and crashes to the rocks in the bottom of the gorge. The sight is awesome every month, every visible hour of the day.

SPECIAL ATTRACTIONS:

The Whitewater River flows through farmland and forest, and it cuts and forces its way over, around, and through rocks and other impediments until it leaps over the ledges and falls 411 feet into the gorge and then flows and falls into South Carolina where it drops another 400 feet. The combined falls are without doubt the highest in the East. Surrounding the waterfall are the dense forests of the Nantahala Forest, which are worth a long visit, as well.

MAKING THE MOST OF YOUR VISIT:

There are two exceptional ways to visit Whitewater Falls. The first is to observe the falls from the overlook area. The second is to climb up the rocky trail to the top of the falls, and then to descend into the gorge to the bottom of the falls.

Perhaps the most astonishing part of the spectacular waterfall is that *you* own it. You and all the other United States taxpayers, that is. The waterfall is for the most part on federal land, and as part of the Nantahala Forest is owned by the Forest Service (and taxpayers) and is under the management of the Highlands Ranger District.

When you arrive and start toward the gorge, you will see signs warning you that thus far X-number of persons have lost their lives by climbing out on rocks in an effort to get a better view or a little larger thrill and then losing their footing. A fall from the rock cliffs is likely to be a fatal one, and you should take the warning seriously.

On your walk to the falls you can catch glimpses through the trees of Lake Jocassee in South Carolina. The view is obviously better when the leaves are off the trees.

Enjoy the waterfall, but do not take foolhardy chances. You can see the entire waterfall from the overlook or other vantage points on the trail. There is no reason to cross under the barrier in order to get a better look. You cannot improve on the one you already have.

If you wish to photograph the falls and get as much as you possibly can of the scene into the picture, you can follow the steep and somewhat slippery trail off to the right of the first overlook. Descend-carefully-about 100 feet and then 300 feet and you will come to an opening in the trees. From your vantage point, if you have a 35-80mm lens for your camera, you can take in essentially all of the beauty while capturing the best details of the scene.

One special caution is that you may find that this trail is chained off. If so, do not go under or around the chain. Respect the admonitions represented by the barricade.

If you have time, energy, and stamina, and if you are in good physical condition, you may wish to walk (or climb) all the way to the base of the falls, unless the trail is closed off. The trail is a series of steps cut into the side of the mountain, and they can be easy to descend and severely difficult to climb. You may recall the steps at Stone Mountain that lead alongside the waterfall or cascade. These steps are worse in several ways. First, the trail is often wet and slippery, and then the steps are at an uncomfortable height for some people. There are 400 of them, and you will find that the trip back up the steep slope is considerably harder than the trip down.

If you go into the gorge, you will find some superb trout fishing there, largely because many people who like to fish do not like such a strenuous climb to get to and out of the fishing area. In some of the deeper pools you will find some of the largest and most beautiful trout you are likely to see in the Carolina mountain areas.

When you are ready to climb out of the gorge, leave in plenty of time to stop and rest along the way, unless, again, you are in excellent physical condition. If the weather is unsettled, leave for the top extra early rather than allow yourself to be caught in a storm at the bottom of the gorge. You might want to take along a supply of water and little else. Excess baggage is seldom if ever welcome, and on the climb out of the gorge you will be grateful for everything you did not take in with you.

You will find it difficult to leave Whitewater Falls, whether in North or South Carolina, but when you do, this author promises you another waterfall that is, if not as high, a match for any other waterfall in the state for awe-inspiring beauty. Because you are already in the vicinity, your next trip could handily be to Dry Falls or to the Horsepasture River waterfalls, both of which are spectacular experiences. There, at either destination, you will find that Dry Falls is anything but dry and that the Horsepasture River offers not one but a series of terrific waterfalls. Each of the locations features one of the most powerful rivers in western North Carolina, and the waterfalls are an experience you are not likely to forget.

Dry Falls near Highlands.

SECTION 2: THE BEST OF THE WATERFALLS
TRIP 3: DRY FALLS
STAYING DRY INSIDE A WATERFALL

LOCATION:

Dry Falls can be found five minutes west of Highlands, on US 64. Watch for signs on the left side of the road. Dry Falls site is a five-minute (or shorter) walk from parking lot.

NEARBY ATTRACTIONS:

Within a half-hour drive of Highlands you will pass six superb waterfalls (and actually drive under one of them, if you wish). You are within easy driving distance of Brevard, Franklin, and Dillard, Georgia, home of one of the finest family restaurants in the South, perhaps in the world.

HOURS OF OPERATION:

Dry Falls area is open 24 hours a day every day of the year.

ADMISSION:

There are no fees of any sort.

FACILITIES:

There are restrooms only.

WHAT'S THE STORY?

Dry Falls is one of the most picturesque waterfalls in North Carolina. Not as high as Whitewater Falls, it has great volume and timeless beauty. And when you leave the waterfall, you have just begin the trip. The entire Cullasaja Gorge is spectacular.

SPECIAL ATTRACTIONS:

The forest teems with wild life, including deer and bear, and the stream is home of trout. The gorge itself is one of the few that you can travel totally by car and enjoy good highways. The nearby Bridal Veil Falls is one of the few that you can drive under.

MAKING THE MOST OF YOUR VISIT:

As with many trips, you will benefit more from the visit if you will spend a few minutes in getting familiar with what it is you are going to see. A brief digression: several years ago I made a tour of the House of Seven Gables in Salem, Massachusetts. On the tour there was a man who complained about everything we saw, and it was only when the trip had concluded that he realized that there had indeed been a book written about the house. At that point he wanted to make the tour again. His wife didn't!

The point is obvious. If the man had known what he was going to see, he could have perhaps read the Hawthorne novel and thus prepared himself to enjoy the house tour.

Before you reach Highlands you will see a sign directing you to Whiteside Mountain. If you feel up to a hike, you can make the tour of the mountain (about a three-mile trip) and perhaps get to see the Kilroy-was-here scrawling on the rock cliff. The writing was done, apparently, by the Spaniards under the command of De Soto as the Spanish government financed explorations through the high country of the South during the gold frenzy of an earlier day.

Before you make the Dry Falls trip, take a little time to study maps and do a little reading, if only in this book. As you approach Highlands from the Brevard direction, if you will drive slowly and glance into the deep forests from time to time, you will see several waterfalls surrounded by the trees. The streams are not large and the falls are not high, but the falls and cascades are delightful. Later, as you drive through Highlands on US 64 west, you will see a road sign directing you to NC 106 south. If you take the road you will leave North Carolina within two miles and enter the Peach State. (Don't be misled. Georgia does not lead the nation in the production of peaches. In fact, according to one published report, one county in South Carolina produces more peaches than does the entire state of Georgia. But who cares, other than peach growers? Ty Cobb is still the Georgia Peach, and Georgia is a wonderful neighbor!) As you near the border between the two states, you will see a sign directing you to a waterfall. Unless you have plenty of time and feel energetic, do not make the visit. You must drive down a long and curving unpaved road and then make a rather long walk to the falls.

As you enter Georgia, before you reach Dillard you will see on your left a beautiful waterfall on the side of the mountain. You can enjoy the falls from the comfort of your car. In dry seasons the falls diminish greatly and are best after a heavy rain.

Drive on into the tiny Georgia town of Dillard for one of the best meals you will ever have. At the evening meal the fare may include but not be limited to prime rib, baked chicken, fried chicken, flounder filets, barbecued chicken, and other entrees, and you have a family style serving of numerous vegetables, salads, and desserts. It's an all-you-can-eat arrangement, and the cost of the meal in the evening is under $15 per person. At lunch the cost is somewhat less, but the offerings are not as sumptuous.

In Dillard you will find some great antique and gift shops. The back road of the town is the scene of some of the best shops. You can also spend the night at the Dillard House, which is one of the oldest restaurants and inns in the area.

As you continue on US 64 west past Highlands, you will pass the dam that forms the impoundment known as Lake Sequayah. You can stop by the roadside and enjoy the beauty of the lake. With the Cullasaja River on your left, if you watch carefully, parking on the roadside when you can do so safely, you can see a series of nearly 20 smaller waterfalls, ranging in height from six feet to nearly 50 feet. These first falls are the Kalakaleskies.

Then, on the right, you will see Bridal Veil Falls which, in dry weather, can be a disappointing trickle. During wet seasons the falls can be terrific as the stream flows out of the forest and then cascades and falls over the immense rocks. Behind the falls there is a huge grotto-like area large enough for you to drive your car under. It is a treat to see the water falling on your left (as you head west) and the rock walls on your right. At one point the highway curved to the waterfall area, but now the highway passes several feet from the falls. The area near the falls is still paved, however, and you can safely drive under Bridal Veil Falls.

If you can travel safely, the best time to see Bridal Veil Falls is during a vicious cold snap. The icicles hanging from the rocks and the spray freezing on nearby trees combine to produce one of the most beautiful pictures imaginable. At times the icicle part of the scene is eight to 10 feet wide, and the stream adds another six feet to the display.

It is uncertain how high the falls and cascade combined are, but the waterfall itself is about 40 feet high, and the cascade above the waterfall appears to be at least 100 feet.

Drive five more minutes or less and you will see the sign directing you to Dry Falls. You will not be disappointed in what you see. Park in the paved space and follow an easy and wide path into the forest. You will parallel the highway for a very short walk and then curve to your left. You can hear the awesome roaring of the waterfall long before you arrive.

When you round the curve in the path and start to descend the long series of steps, you will see Dry Falls. The waterfall is not dry at any time; in fact, the volume of the huge waterfall is great even in the driest weather.

The reason for the name of the waterfall becomes evident when you reach the falls. You will see that you can walk behind the falls and remain perfectly dry. There is room for two dozen people to move around comfortably behind the waterfall.

If you can visit Dry Falls during the coldest weather, or even after a snowfall, you will enjoy a vision of beauty that you will remember forever. There is a soothing and healing power in the sight of the waterfall, surrounded by snow-covered trees and fringed by the ice-covered fence and underbrush, that will serve you long after the ice and snow have melted and the seasons have changed a dozen times.

When you leave Dry Falls and continue your drive west, you will see other waterfalls and cascades in the gorge. These include Raven's Cliff Falls, Quarry Falls, and Cullasaja Falls, all of which are impressively beautiful and ranging in height from 60 to 200 feet, including the entire cascade. As you emerge from the gorge you will see one of the most beautiful sights along the entire river. You may need to drive past the final waterfall and find a place to turn around. Then drive back until you see the falls and then park on the right side of the road as you drive east. Here you can derive the fullest enjoyment from the sight of the awesome and powerful Cullasaja Falls.

While you are in the mood for more beautiful waterfalls, your next trip is along the Horsepasture River. This adventure is one of the trips where you must park and leave your car to take a short but worthwhile walk through the forest. You will find the falls along the river to be memorable.

Horsepasture River Waterfall near Brevard.

SECTION 2: THE BEST OF THE WATERFALLS
TRIP 4: HORSEPASTURE RIVER
FIVE FANTASTIC FALLS

LOCATION:

When you are at Whitewater Falls, you are also very close to the Horsepasture River and five astonishing waterfalls. Starting in Brevard, follow US 276 and US 64 south through Rosman, Lake Toxaway, and to Sapphire. When you reach the NC 281 junction (the Whitewater Falls Road) turn right and drive about two miles until you cross the bridge over the Horsepasture River. Near the bridge you will see a metal guard rail with room for cars to park along the highway. You will see signs of ample use. This is your cue to park the car and start the short hike.

NEARBY ATTRACTIONS:

In addition to Brevard, Whitewater Falls, and Lake Toxaway, you are within easy driving distance of Highlands, Franklin, the Blue Ridge Parkway, Looking Glass Falls, the Cradle of Forestry, Sliding Rock, Devil's

87

Courthouse, Mount Pisgah, and Graveyard Fields. You are also near the Shining Rock Wilderness area.

HOURS OF OPERATION:

On the Horsepasture River trail there are no gates or posted hours. You may hike the trail anytime you wish and stay as late as you wish.

ADMISSION:

There are no admission charges.

FACILITIES:

You are on your own. There are no restrooms, camping areas (formal, that is: people can and do camp in the wild), picnic grounds, or stores of any sort. It is you and the river and the wilderness.

WHAT'S THE STORY?

In the 1980s a power and electric company made efforts to buy the land where the Horsepasture River flows. The plan was to cut the timber and build a dam for hydroelectric power, but such a program would have obliterated one of the most beautiful and healthy forests in the South and at the same time destroyed the beauty of the series of waterfalls.

Happily, many persons with clout and influence organized a campaign to save the Horsepasture River, the forest, and the falls. Joined by environmentalists, the group managed to put a temporary halt to the planned ravaging of the land, and quickly the federal government stepped in, and when the final deal had been completed, the government designated the river as part of the National Wild and Scenic River program.

The result is that today you can visit the 400-acre river and forest site and enjoy the woods, the river, and the great series of waterfalls.

SPECIAL ATTRACTIONS:

While the entire area is one of superlative beauty, the most magnetic scenes are those of the waterfalls, which range in type from cascades to pure waterfalls. The Waterfall Trail leads you to five terrific falls and through some magnificent and unspoiled territory.

MAKING THE MOST OF YOUR VISIT:

When you reach the parking area alongside the highway, step over the metal guard rail and prepare to descend a very steep hill that in wet weather can be treacherous. While the hill is only 20 feet or so high, it is in places a tangle of briars, vines, and snags of wood buried in the underbrush. But if you will look carefully you will see paths made by visitors to the river and trail. There are perhaps half a dozen of these trails leading down the steep slope. Almost as soon as you reach the forest, which is only 50 to 100 feet away, you are on the trail to the waterfalls.

The trail is easy, and if you follow it to its terminus, you will hike 3.1 miles. In order to make the walk, stop and enjoy the falls, and savor the wild flowers and dense vegetation along the trail. Plan to devote three full hours.

If, however, you want to see only the first three or four waterfalls, you can cut the walk and the time needed in half. The vertical rise for the entire trip is slightly more than 1,200 feet, but if you make only the first half of the hike the total vertical rise will be little more than 500 feet. For the most part the hike is really very easy, with only half a dozen of the more difficult sections that last only 100 feet or slightly more. You will reach the first waterfall in five minutes. This is Drift Falls, where the river slides gently over a huge dome-shaped rock and down into a deep and wide pool. In the next few minutes you will reach Umbrella Falls (bear in mind that some of the falls have a variety of names) and Rainbow Falls. This last waterfall is by far the most spectacular on the entire trail. Here the river pours over a 100-foot cliff and crashes to the rocks below, and on sunny days the mist rises, catches the light of the sun, and a series of rainbows will form. At times you can see two, three, or even more rainbows in almost any direction.

You may want to stop your walk at this point. The final of the waterfalls is Stairstep Falls, which can take you a long and rather difficult hour to reach. Often the trail is muddy from the streams that trickle across it, and the hiking gets considerably tougher.

After a heavy rain the volume of water creates a deafening roar and a spray that will soak you 200 yards away, especially if there is a wind blowing in your direction. This is true only at Rainbow Falls, so plan your clothing accordingly.

With some of the other falls you can edge your way down to the water's edge and get some great photos. You can do the same at Rainbow Falls if the weather has not been rainy in recent days. But no matter what the weather, the beauty of the falls remains superb, and the trip is an unforgettable one.

Looking Glass Falls north of Brevard.

SECTION 2: THE BEST OF THE WATERFALLS
TRIP 5: LOOKING GLASS FALLS
CURB SERVICE BEAUTY

LOCATION:

From Brevard, drive north on US 276; from the Blue Ridge Parkway drive south, turning onto US 276 just south of Mount Pisgah. You will find the waterfall just beside the road.

NEARBY ATTRACTIONS:

Within easy driving distance from Looking Glass Falls are Brevard, Hendersonville, Flat Rock, Sliding Rock, Blue Ridge Parkway, Cradle of Forestry, and several other waterfalls.

HOURS OF OPERATION:

The waterfall is located beside the highway and there is no gate. You can view the falls any time of day, any day of the year.

ADMISSION:

In the late 1990s, according to newspaper reports, a $2 admission fee will be charged.

FACILITIES:

There are no facilities of any sort. Two minutes away at Sliding Rock there are rest rooms and drinking water. Also nearby are picnic tables, camp grounds, and public telephones.

WHAT'S THE STORY?

Looking Glass Rock is one of the most popular scenic areas caught among literally dozens of other attractions. This waterfall can be enjoyed from the car, from the overlook, or from the shore of Looking Glass Creek. An even better way to enjoy it is wading or swimming in the icy water on a blistering hot August afternoon.

SPECIAL ATTRACTIONS:

The sight of a 60-foot high waterfall that roars over a lofty rock ledge and then crashes into a beautiful plunge pool at the base of one of the most awe-inspiring mountains in the area must rank as the special attraction. However, in the nearby streams and forests you can find brook, rainbow, and brown trout, deer, hawks, bobcats, raccoons, vultures, wild turkeys, grouse, quail, and occasionally a black bear. A short drive away you can visit the fish hatchery, and the Cradle of Forestry is the first forestry school in the United States. Rock climbing on Looking Glass Rock is one of the popular area sports.

MAKING THE MOST OF YOUR VISIT:

The most obvious way to enjoy your visit is to leave Brevard and travel to the US 64/276 intersection and turn left. Drive about nine miles, past the ranger station, until you reach the parking area for Looking Glass Falls. The waterfall is named for the huge 3,969-foot high mountain which, when the sun strikes the moist surface of the huge rock dome, reflects sunlight like a mirror.

When you arrive at the falls and walk down to the creek, you will feel the mist and spray from the waterfall while you are still 30 feet away. The perfect time to visit the scene is after a huge snow or deep freeze. At these times the pool, the creek, and the falls are perfect pictures of idyllic and pristine beauty.

You will have the waterfall all to yourself, or nearly so, on a raw winter day. In summer, particularly on weekends, you may have trouble finding a place to park. If the weather is hot, you might wish to yield to the temptation to let the creek waters cool you down. Swimming and wading are permitted, but there are no life guards.

If you want to try the very popular hiking trail that is named after the mountain and rock, from the Pisgah Ranger Station drive 3.5 miles toward the Parkway until you reach the junction with the Davidson River Road (Forest Service Road 475). Turn left on FR 475 and drive .5 mile west to the parking area which is on the right side of the road. The trail head is located near the parking lot.

The hike is 3.1 miles long and is rated as moderate to strenuous. You will climb almost 1,500 feet as you make your way up the sometimes steep trail. Bear in mind that the trail length is one-way. You must walk another 3.1 miles back to your car, but the trip down is much easier than the climb. The roughest part of the trail occurs shortly after you start, so do not give up when you encounter the steep trail. It gets better.

You may see, on the north, northwest, and south faces of the huge rock that is Looking Glass Rock, insect-sized forms making their way up the rock face. These are the rock climbers who arrive in large numbers to test the ascents.

When you reach the top, you will see quickly that the dome is not railed. In this and other respects the dome is somewhat similar to Stone Mountain, particularly in that as you stand on the dome you have the sensation of being on a flat surface. But the dome slopes, perhaps more than you realize until you are in difficulty. When the rock is wet, it is slippery. Do not go near the slopes. It is easy to pass the point of no return.

When you leave Looking Glass Falls you may wish to try the Sliding Rock Recreational Area. Here you can participate or simply observe as hardy water-lovers sit down in the frigid water and let the current carry them with ever-increasing speed down a 60-foot slope that terminates with a splash in the deep pool at the base of the slide. Sliding Rock is only a two-minute drive past Looking Glass Falls, on the way to the Blue Ridge Parkway.

If you want to watch, you can drive into the parking area and then follow the paved walk down to the overlook below the plunge pool. Here is a good place to photograph sliders or simply to revel in their pleasure.

But you can try the slide yourself, if you wish. There are dressing rooms between the parking lot and the overlook, and you can change into proper attire.

If dry-land entertainment is more to your liking, you can drive back toward Brevard and stop at the Cradle of Forestry. This is a marvelous place to visit and is fully described in a later part of this book.

Crabtree Falls near Asheville.

SECTION 2: THE BEST OF THE WATERFALLS
TRIP 6: CRABTREE FALLS
A MOUNTAIN BEAUTY AND AN ISOLATED DELIGHT

LOCATION:

Crabtree Meadows Campground is located at Milepost 340 on the Blue Ridge Parkway. Crabtree Falls is at the end of a mile-long trail (two miles, round trip) on Crabtree Creek.

NEARBY ATTRACTIONS:

It is an easy drive to Craggy Gardens, Little Switzerland, Asheville, Folk Arts Center, and Western North Carolina Center.

HOURS OF OPERATION:

The trail to the waterfall is open all the time, 365 days each year. There are no barricades or gates.

ADMISSION:

There is no fee to hike to the waterfall, but if you plan to camp, you must pay a small fee of $10 per day.

FACILITIES:

At the Crabtree Meadows you will find picnic tables, a camp store, restrooms, campgrounds, drinking water, showers, RV and camper space, and gift shop.

WHAT'S THE STORY?

The Crabtree Meadows area once was part of a huge growth of crabtrees, often known better as crab apple trees. This small tree, known as *Malus coronaria*, bears beautiful red-and-white blossoms in early spring and, later, small, incredibly tart apples that are as a rule 1.5 inches in diameter. These crabapples are used widely in ornamental ways and some-times in making jellies. The small apples differ from the traditional apple in more ways than taste: they cling to the trees until mid-winter, unless strong winds and storms rip them away. You can pick them after freezing weather arrives, and they are often as flavorful in their dehydrated state as they are in their peak ripeness.

These crabtrees are likely cross-results of orchard apple trees that once grew nearby. You can still see an occasional apple tree growing along Parkway territory.

SPECIAL ATTRACTIONS:

The primary attraction is the waterfall. You will also find blooming shrubs, such as rhododendron and laurel, numerous wild flowers, and such animals as white tail deer, foxes, hawks, owls, bobcats, opossums, raccoons, and a wide variety of songbirds. The campground is one of the most delightful of all the recreational areas along the Parkway.

MAKING THE MOST OF YOUR VISIT:

First of all, make the walk to the waterfall. Park in the designated spaces inside the Crabtree Meadows area and follow signs to the west end of the campground. Smell the smoke from dozens of campfires as you walk, and listen to the wind in the upper reaches of the huge trees. Listen, too, for the sounds of birds and small four-footed animals in the underbrush. Chipmunks, squirrels, and groundhogs can be seen often.

To prepare for the walk, wear good shoes and appropriate clothing. You will be gone for an hour or so, and if you depart in late afternoon the air may be chilly at the bottom of the hill and at the base of the waterfall. Be prepared for spray and mist that carry a considerable distance.

Do not over-dress in warm weather: you may be cool as you start down the trail to the falls, but you will work up a sweat as you climb the hill back to the parking area. In July and August you can expect rain and perhaps thunderstorms.

You can take the steep way down to the falls and have the longer but less strenuous trail back up, or you can reverse the direction. You can also return the way you went down, if that is your preference. The advantage to taking both trail sections is that you get a better chance to see more scenery.

If you make the hike early in the morning you have a much better chance of seeing a deer, particularly if you make the trip shortly after sunrise. Your next best chance is at dusk, although you do not want to be caught after dark on the trail, which is hard enough to negotiate in daylight hours.

A word about trail difficulty: the hike is rated as moderate, and it is very easy going down the short way. Your only problem is losing your footing by moving too rapidly. You will reach a series of steps and small bridges over trickles of streams feeding into Crabtree Creek. The distance from the trailhead to the falls is .8 mile.

The elevation at the top of the trail is 3,735 feet. Along the hike you will experience a vertical rise of 1,920 feet. The waterfall is 60 feet high and is exceptionally beautiful. The best spot from which to photograph the waterfall is on the wood bridge leading across Crabtree Creek about 50 feet below the falls.

Crabtree Meadows is a 250-acre recreation area that borders part of the Pisgah National Forest. The loop trail continues past the falls and starts up the hill on the other side. Earlier you learned that the trail is moderate to strenuous. To amplify that comment, an easy trail is one that the person in reasonably good shape can walk without pausing to rest and without experiencing any real difficulty. A moderate trail means a trail longer in length, steeper, and with footing more difficult. A strenuous trail is one that is usually much longer, steeper, and difficult. You may need to stop and rest often on a strenuous trail.

The Crabtree Falls Trail is not really long (2.4 miles for the round trip) and never really steep or difficult. But the climb to the parking lot, while not steep or difficult, is totally unrelenting. You climb constantly for 1.4 miles, and you may need either rest time or a slower pace if you are not in the best of shape.

Some people find the stone steps to be tiring, because of the height. At one section you will find 22 steps followed by 24 more shortly. These are not really a problem. There will be a rocky section to cover from the last stone steps to the falls.

Along the return half of the loop you will pass, in season, through growths of wild orchids, trillium, great laurel, mountain laurel, and a wide range of ferns.

The return of the loop involves climbing many stone steps; these are set in soil and are well maintained. As soon as you cross the viewing bridge at the falls, you find the path leads to 22 rock steps followed by an acute turn and nine steps more. Another 0.4 mile from the falls will bring you to 11 stone steps with a handrail. The trail continues at this point with a rock wall along the edge of the path before reaching another series of 12 stone steps.

Continuing the upward hike you will cross, via a rustic footbridge, Crabtree Creek and a series of smaller rills that feed the creek. The creek is at 0.6 mile from the falls; wildflowers are at 0.8 mile from the falls.

This trail is one that may be crowded, particularly on weekends. This is partly because of the proximity of the campground to the hiking trail (the return half of the loop actually leads through part of the camping area) and partly because of the popularity of the Blue Ridge Parkway. During nearly any time of the year except deepest winter you will often find two dozen or more hikers on the trail.

If you want a calmer time, hike to the falls during the week, rather than on a weekend. Try hiking in the morning rather than in the afternoon. On a seasonal basis, spring is less crowded than the summer and fall months. Late autumn is also a good time to be on the trail.

Linville Falls near Parkway.

SECTION 2: THE BEST OF THE WATERFALLS
TRIP 7: LINVILLE FALLS
FOUR VIEWS OF EESEEOH

LOCATION:

Follow the Blue Ridge Parkway to Milepost 316.3 and then turn south of the spur road where the signs point to Linville Gorge Recreation Area. Drive two miles to the parking area at the ranger office. The trail to the falls leads off to the right as you head south.

NEARBY ATTRACTIONS:

From the ranger office you are within walking distance of Dugger's Creek Loop Trail, to the Plunge Basin Overlook Trail, to Linville Gorge Wilderness trails, to Little Switzerland, and to Spruce Pine and the North Carolina Mineral Museum. You are also within easy driving distance of Grandfather Mountain and the Price Lake/Blowing Rock area.

HOURS OF OPERATION:

The Ranger office closes at five p. m. or six p. m., but the trails leading to the falls and into Linville Gorge are always open. Office hours are contingent upon seasons and weather.

ADMISSION:

There are no admission charges, unless you decide to camp. There is a fee of $10 per day for camping in the area.

FACILITIES:

Here you will find restrooms, drinking water, picnic tables, abundant parking, self-guiding trails.

WHAT'S THE STORY?

Linville Gorge and Linville Falls are among the most-visited sites along the Blue Ridge Parkway corridor. Here you can enjoy great views of spectacular waterfalls, terrific points of view from which to enjoy Linville Gorge, and nature trails that lead into primitive and superb natural environments. In 1952 John D. Rockefeller, Jr., donated more than 7,000 acres of wilderness land to the American government, and other land acquisitions have swelled the total amount of land to more than 11,000 acres.

SPECIAL ATTRACTIONS:

After you enjoy your time at the waterfalls, you can climb a trail to Wiseman's View from which you have a great look at the falls from a higher elevation. You can enjoy the sight, if you are lucky, of deer drinking from the Linville River, trout fishermen trying their luck and skills, raccoons, hawks, owls, and bobcats, to mention only a few of the many varieties of animal life in the gorge area. There are also black bears in the gorge. Linville Caverns are within an easy drive, as well.

MAKING THE MOST OF YOUR VISIT:

As with all trips, this one is made more special if you take the time to learn about the territory and its past. In the case of Linville Falls and Linville Gorge, the area is named after the William Linville family. The Linvilles, John and his son, along with a companion named John Williams, were camping along the Linville River when Indians attacked the sleeping men. Both of the Linvilles were killed and Williams was wounded.

Later, settlers moved into the territory but few remained because, in spite of the fact that the wilderness and river were beautiful beyond description, the land was so rugged that eking a living from the forest and the rare open meadows was difficult if not impossible. Only the hardiest remained. During the period of the Civil War an iron works was established upstream from the falls for the purpose of manufacturing rifles from the South. During World War II military personnel trained by climbing the cliffs of the gorge. Prior to World War II the Rockefeller family bought the area and kept it until 1951.

You can see Linville Falls the easy way and the harder ways. For those who do not wish to walk a considerable distance, there are a paved parking lot and well-maintained paths to a location very near the falls.

For those who want to enjoy a hearty walk of a mile or two (up to about 15 miles if you are really energetic) you can walk along the wide and only moderately strenuous trail leading to the west side of the gorge and to a series of overlooks with views so great you will not believe what you are seeing.

And what you are seeing, in addition to the falls, is the "Eeseeoh," a Cherokee word that reportedly means "river of many cliffs." You will see that the description is an accurate one, for the gorge, said to be the wildest east of the Mississippi, descends about 2,000 feet in elevation before the river reaches Lake James. As the river sweeps downward, the swift current takes with it debris, particles from rocks, and smaller rocks from the shoreline. With each passing day (or minute, for that matter) the river imperceptibly but inexorably widens and deepens the gorge, already millions of years old. As you climb, you will rise 880 feet from the parking lot level.

It is estimated that half a billion years ago the area known today as Linville Gorge lay at the bottom of a sea. The sand grains, buried deep under layers of several types of rocks, were cemented into sandstone.

As centuries passed, the rock beds were pushed up and "folded," and the sandstone recrystallized into denser rock, which is called today Erwin quartzite. The name comes from Erwin, Tennessee, where the formation was studied decades ago.

At Linville Falls one enormous rock "fold" tipped so far that it broke and pushed older rock beds on top of the quartzite. Erosion then cut through the older rocks, leaving "windows" through which the quartzite is exposed. The cliffs were left after the river cut its way through the softer rock beds.

The Linville Gorge Trail, 1.4 miles in length, leads from the mountains above the gorge to the river itself. The trail ends 0.1 mile downstream from the Lower Falls, the highest waterfall on the Linville River.

To get to the trailheads for the Plunge Basin Overlook Trail and the Linville Gorge Waterfall Trail, walk to the east, past the headquarters building, and follow the trail into the forest. At the first junction follow the right-hand trail 0.3 mile to a second set of signs. At this point the trail forks. The Plunge Basin Overlook Trail leads straight ahead, while the Linville Gorge Waterfall Trail turns sharply to the left and follows the rise of the mountain upward for a short distance.

Continue straight ahead for 0.6 mile to reach the Plunge Basin Overlook. At the overlook you will have a superb view of Lower Falls as the water plunges into the basin. If you climb down the slope to the river you will reach a barricade. Do not attempt to go under, over, or around it. Follow the trail to the left of the barrier and descend sharply.

Through a series of switchbacks the trail winds gently from the steps to an incredible rock cliff, which is hundreds of feet long and over 100 feet high. The trail descends until you reach a portion of the trail that is almost completely rock surface. Shortly you will be on the shore of the river. You can walk upstream a short distance to a river-level view of the Lower or Linville Falls.

As you walk through the enormous forest on your way back to the headquarters building, notice the size of some of the trees. It is said that the hemlocks in the gorge represent the largest virgin forest of this species known to exist on earth today.

So you have a choice of seeing the falls from above or from below-or both. There are four trails around Linville Falls, and you can hike all of them easily in one afternoon.

You also have two waterfalls to enjoy. The Upper Falls are not as high as the Lower Falls, but, although the volume is the same, you will see the water funneled into narrow rock-bound passageways creating horrifying roars. The height of the Upper Falls is about 20 feet or slightly less, while the Lower Falls height is 40 feet.

Over the years I have found that the best time to visit Linville Falls is whenever you have a tankful of gas for your car and some free time. The only really bad times are when there is a heavy snow on the ground, when temperatures are frigid, or when heavy rains have made footing slippery and hiking unenjoyable.

You will find the greatest crowds during summer and fall week-ends and the smallest number of visitors during week-days in winter. The 50,000 people who visit Linville Falls each year often return time after time. When you make the trip you will know why the site is so popular. And you will understand why lovers of waterfalls go back again and again.

One segment of the Cascades on the Parkway.

SECTION 2: THE BEST OF THE WATERFALLS
TRIP 8: THE CASCADES
A WATERFALL WITHOUT END

LOCATION:
At the E.B. Jeffress Park on the Blue Ridge Parkway, Milepost 272, you will find a waterfall relatively small in volume but astonishing in its dramatic effect.

NEARBY ATTRACTIONS:
Doughton Park, Stone Mountain, New River State Park, and Mount Jefferson State Park are all within easy driving distance.

HOURS OF OPERATION:
There are no gates, and the park is open 24 hours each day, 365 days of the year.

ADMISSION:
There are no fees of any sort.

FACILITIES:

At the park you will find restrooms, picnic tables, and drinking water.

WHAT'S THE STORY?

The "waterfall without end" is a stream that cascades, falls, shoots, and plunges down an entire mountainside. The small stream, to judge from appearances, could never generate a great enough volume to create more than a trickle, but you will be left in amazement when you see the results of gravity acting upon water.

SPECIAL ATTRACTIONS:

The major attraction is Falls Creek and the exciting and rewarding cascades and waterfalls, and a close second is the delightful trail that leads to the cascades. Along the trail are information markers offering an instant education concerning mountain life and lore. A third attraction is the short walk to the Jesse Brown rustic cabin and the site of Cool Spring Baptist Church. A later chapter describes this church and cabin.

MAKING THE MOST OF YOUR VISIT:

Start with the easy walk part-way down the mountainside to the Cascades. The entire distance, round trip, is 2.2 miles, and the terrain is so easy that you can make it without difficulty even if you are not in fighting shape. If you are in walking shape, you have a remarkably pleasant stroll ahead of you. You will need about 1.5 hours to make the trip at a casual pace and return to the parking lot.

You will experience a vertical rise of 600 feet, but if this seems strenuous for the distance, remember that total vertical rise means any change in elevation, whether up or down. So you can count the 300-foot descent as the same as the ascent. That means that you actually face a climb of 300 feet, the length of the playing area of a football field, minus end zones.

You will see spectacular scenery along the way, and at the same time you will enjoy American mountain heritage and learn a great deal about the forest and the inhabitants therein. The major animals that live in the forest include the white tail deer, which only a short time ago was found primarily in the higher elevations and along the coast but which now has enjoyed a fantastic increase in population and is now found nearly all over the state, even inside some towns and cities, or at least in the outskirts of the towns.

Other animals include raccoons, skunks, opossums, rabbits, squirrels, chipmunks, woodchucks, a variety of snakes (mostly harmless-but still exert caution!), lizards, song birds of many species, hawks, owls, and foxes. You actually have a better chance of seeing the larger animals as you drive to the park, but while you are walking, particularly early and late, if you are silent you may enjoy the experience of spotting some of the forest creatures.

The Cascades, which await you after a short walk, are formed by Falls Creek which slides down the rocky face of the mountain at a very comfortable pace, and it is joined by several smaller tributaries in the form of rills, brooks, and spring branches. Then, all at once, it seems, the creek flows more rapidly down the slope as a fairly large stream.

On the mountain Falls Creek begins a journey that takes it to the valley below, where it joins the Yadkin River, which in turn flows into the Pee Dee River and finally into the Atlantic Ocean at Winyah Bay, South Carolina.

As you walk, stop and enjoy the information signs posted along the path. Of special interest is dog hobble, which, you will read, is an attractive evergreen matting vine that grows in a hopeless tangle, rather like honeysuckle. The tangled growth is named, according to the sign, because a bear hound, loping along with its nose to the ground and being preoccupied with the bear's scent, would plunge into the thicket or low growth and become hopelessly entangled or "hobbled" by the foliage and thus become helpless prey to the angered bear.

You will see huge stands of tulip poplar or yellow poplar, which in rare instances can reach a height of 200 feet but averages 100 feet in height and has a trunk diameter of up to 12 feet but averages four feet. This majestic tree produces 12-inch square logs as long as 60 feet, usually without knotholes or blemishes of any significance.

The wood of the green tulip poplar is soft, easily cut, and extremely heavy until cured, at which time it is light and still easy to cut. Eventually it cures into a very hard wood suitable for all types of building projects. Log cabins made of these giant trees have lasted for more than 200 years in the South as long as the cured wood is kept dry.

This tree is sometimes called catface poplar because, when the log is cut straight across, the heartwood often has a dark shape that closely resembles the head and ears of a cat. The tree lives as long as 300 years, and in warm weather it produces beautiful flowers resembling tulips. These "tulips" range in color from light green to orange and are two inches high.

You will also see fine examples of hickory, black cherry, white pine, chestnut, black walnut, basswood, butternut, and serviceberry trees. If you do not know a pine from an oak, you can still enjoy the trees because they are identified not only by name but with a short description of their major functions and uses.

The black locust is an interesting tree in that its roots are hosts to nitrogen-fixing bacteria, and the tree, instead of robbing the soil of nutrients, actually enriches the dirt. And the tree is wonderfully decay-resistant and is used as fence posts, railroad ties, and utility-pole arms.

Seeds of the black locust, like those of the tulip poplar, are commonly eaten by quail, deer, and rabbits. The roots, leaves, and bark are poisonous to man, however, and should not be ingested or chewed.

Witch hazel is another tree common to the trail. The witch hazel is noted for its use in making camp brooms and tooth brushes (for old-timers) as well as for its highly aromatic odor. The leaves and twigs of the shrub or small tree are used as additives to rubbing alcohol, and small twigs on a campfire produce a delightful aroma. So resistant is the tree to wilting that it was for years recommended by the United States Army for use in camouflage.

When you start down the slope, you will start the trail beside the rest rooms and water fountain. The pathway separates within 0.2 mile. You may take either trail, because they join before your reach the Cascades. I recommend taking one trail down and the other on the way back so that you can see more terrain and learn more about the area. The left direction will lead you along a gentle slope and beside a small stream that constantly grows larger, even without visible streamlets joining it.

You will cross rustic and unique footbridges as you hike into the dark woods where the laurel and rhododendron block out the sun, and almost as soon as you cross the bridges you will hear the roar of the cascades. When you reach the patch of dog hobble on the left, you are almost at the top of the waterfall.

The trail then curves sharply and you will descend a long series of steps to a point where the trail divides. The right spur will lead you to an overlook so close to the water that you will be sprayed by mist on a windy day. You can see the overlook, which is only 40 feet from the trail division. You will stop along a high wall. Do not attempt to climb the wall or sit on it. Be warned that a number of people have ventured out onto the slight rocks and have fallen to their deaths. If you look down the stream to the places where the water leaps from one immense rock surface to another, seemingly in an endless manner, you can readily understand how a fall could be fatal. A person would fall for hundreds of feet unless he luckily clutched and held to a tree root or limb. Don't take the chance.

When you return to the major trail, you can descend another 100 feet to get another delightful view of the waterfall. You can see the falls above and below you, and in either direction is a superb experience.

Connestee Falls near Brevard.

SECTION 2: THE BEST OF THE WATERFALLS
TRIP 9: CONNESTEE FALLS
DOUBLE YOUR PLEASURE

LOCATION:

This incredible double falls (at least from one perspective) is located just off US 276 about six miles south of Brevard.

NEARBY ATTRACTIONS:

The superb city of Brevard is the closest town, but other towns and cities within easy driving distance include Cashiers, Hendersonville, Highlands, Asheville, Sapphire, Flat Rock, and a series of tiny but nice towns and communities. You are also within a short drive of Whitewater Falls, Looking Glass Falls, Sliding Rock, Cradle of Forestry, Blue Ridge Parkway, Graveyard Fields, Devil's Courthouse, and Mount Pisgah.

HOURS OF OPERATION:

The waterfall path is open all day every day.

ADMISSION:

No admission is charged.

FACILITIES:

There are no immediate facilities, other than picnic tables and fireplaces, but nearby are all the accommodations you need.

WHAT'S THE STORY?

Here is yet another waterfall and ledge from which an Indian princess leaped because of a broken heart. In this case it was the beautiful maiden Connestee who, pining away because her husband, a man of European descent, deserted her to return to his own people. The woeful and distraught maiden leaped into the gorge near the waterfall where she and her beloved had rested happily during their courtship. The full story, in brief, is that the white man was wounded by a war party of the Cherokees, and the man was brought to the Indian village as a captive. While he recovered from his wounds, his nurse and faithful companion was the Princess Connestee, and when the two fell in love the father of the princess, Chief Wahilla, gave the two permission to marry. This story, whether factual or apocryphal, has counterparts in other North Carolina legends, as well as in Georgia and as far away as Tucumcari, New Mexico.

MAKING THE MOST OF YOUR VISIT:

The two waterfalls known as Connestee Falls are 110 feet high and enormously beautiful. (That is two falls of 110 feet each, and a combined height of 220 feet.) To get to the falls, once you have driven six miles south of Brevard on US 276, you must leave the car in a parking lot just off the highway. Watch your odometer as you leave Brevard, and be ready to pull off as soon as you see the sign directing you to the parking lot.

You will make a short walk (five minutes or so) to the high point of the falls on Carson Creek. You can walk another short distance down an incline to an overlook from which you can see the two separate (or combined, depending upon your point of view) waterfalls. The second waterfall is created by Batson Creek as it rushes down the mountainside and over the ledge.

You can move via a third short walkway down to the base of the falls where you can get a great view of the entire set of falls. This is one of the locations from which you can take your photos. The overlook is another good spot for photos.

You can picnic, photograph, and enjoy the natural beauty of the area. The waterfalls are beautiful and rewarding any time of the year and any time of the day.

Remember, however, that the waterfalls are on private property, and you are the guests (if uninvited) of the owners. Respect the property and the rules and regulations, and please do not litter or in any other way deface or mar the trail, falls, or parking lot.

Elk River Falls near Roan Mountain.

SECTION 2: THE BEST OF THE WATERFALLS
TRIP 10: ELK RIVER FALLS
A HIDDEN JEWEL ON A SECLUDED STREAM

LOCATION:

Two miles north of Elk Park just off the Elk River Road you will find this picturesque waterfall. In order to reach Elk Falls, drive north of Morganton (this is one easy way from the central part of the area; there are other ways from various directions) on NC 181. Follow Highway 181 until it junctions with NC 194 north of the Blue Ridge Parkway.

If you approach via the Parkway, you can exit onto NC 181 and stay on the highway until you reach Newland. Continue north to the tiny town of Elk Park. At this point the driving gets slightly tricky.

As you pass through the main part of town, you will need to be alert for the turn-off to the falls. There is no easily visible sign, so you should watch for the Old Mill Road, which turns off at a sharp angle to the right. Drive about .4 mile and then turn left onto Elk River Road, which is State Road 1305.

Within about two miles the pavement ends, but do not become discouraged. The gravel road, which admittedly is uncertain in very wet weather, is usually reliable. Drive two slow miles on the gravel road until you see the sign on the right that directs you to Elk Falls.

NEARBY ATTRACTIONS:

At Elk Falls you are within convenient driving distance of Banner Elk, Roan Mountain, Beech Mountain, Sugar Mountain, Seven Devils, Boone, and other small but attractive towns and cities.

HOURS OF OPERATION:

The falls are open to the public all day every day of the year.

ADMISSION:

There is no admission charge.

FACILITIES:

There are no facilities available at the falls, but in nearby Elk Park you can find sandwiches and modest meals, and in the surrounding towns you can find accommodations of all sorts.

WHAT'S THE STORY?

This part of the river is designated for day use only. While it is public property, you are restricted in what you can do there. There is a picnic area, and you can find a short hiking trail of about a quarter of a mile to the falls.

The river is delightfully beautiful from the time you reach it until you arrive at the falls. The stream meanders through meadows and forests, and you are never far from the water. At the parking area you can hear the falls as soon as you leave the car, and as you start the short walk through the woods you will see an access area from which you can see from the top of the falls a pool of incredible beauty.

Warning: do not venture too close to the edge of the rocks. In damp weather (and the mist from the falls may keep the area moist much of the time) the rocks are dangerously slippery.

Hike the remainder of the way to the bottom of the falls. The easy-to-follow trail leads across a narrow ridge of rock to a point just below the falls. Again, the rocky ridge, which is only a few feet wide at its widest point, may be slick. Wear appropriate shoes and exert caution as you move forward.

You will notice that the rocky ridge is a narrow peninsula that juts into the stream, and on both sides of you there is water of varying depths and frigid temperatures. You can stand or sit on the rocky ridge and enjoy the falls to your heart's content. This is a perfect spot from which to photograph the waterfall.

The best time to photograph the waterfall is on a cloudy day. On a sunny day you should arrive at the falls by mid-morning.

Best times of the year to photograph the falls are in the spring and early summer when flowering shrubs are in full bloom or in the fall when the leaves are changing. On a hot day, there is a wonderful chill in the air at the waterfall, and on a cold day you should dress warmly. Carry along rain gear because the spray from the falls can dampen your clothing if not your spirits.

Be particularly cautious during flooding periods. The river is modest-sized, and the shoreline is low in places, making it easy for the water to overflow the banks of the river.

But during good weather, this is one of the most beautiful spots in the entire state. Just remember that there are no restroom or toilet facilities, and the only available water is from the tiny streams feeding the river and from the Elk River itself.

Courthouse in Brevard.

SECTION 3: THE BEST TOWNS AND CITIES
TRIP 1: BREVARD
THE CITY AMONG THE WATERFALLS

LOCATION:

Brevard, one of the nicest cities anywhere in the state or in the South (the entire country?) presents downtown beauty and fascination and is the doorway to the southwestern part of North Carolina. It is located near the South Carolina line and is within a short drive to the Georgia line. Brevard is within an hour's drive from Asheville by either NC 191 and NC 280 or by US 64 from Charlotte, 123 miles away. Driving time from Charlotte is 2.5 to three hours.

NEARBY ATTRACTIONS:

Brevard is amazingly near attractions of all sorts. You are an easy and short drive from the famed Cradle of Forestry, Mount Pisgah, Graveyard Fields, Devil's Courthouse, Shining Rock Wilderness Area, Hendersonville, Flat Rock, hiking trails galore, campgrounds, trout streams, and some of the best waterfalls in the South. Farther to the west you can reach the town of Highlands, which is only a ten-minute drive from the Georgia State Line and the town of Dillard, noted for its many antique stores and particularly for the Dillard House, one of the finest family-style restaurants anywhere. If you drive back toward Hendersonville you can reach Holmes Educational Forest, a delight for children and adults alike.

HOURS OF OPERATION:

Most of the stores in Brevard are open from 9 a.m. until 5 p. m. or slightly later. Restaurants are open from 7 a.m. until 9 p.m. or later, depending upon the type of restaurant and the meals served. Some shops are open as late as 9 p.m.

FACILITIES:

In Brevard or surrounding Transylvania County you can find recreational outlets of all sorts, hospitals, libraries, book stores, golf courses, canoeing and kayaking opportunities, arts studios and crafts stores, equestrian opportunities, the nationally and world-famous music festival, excellent colleges, rock climbing, swimming, wildlife education center, summer camps, square dancing, inns, churches, and museums, among many other attractions.

WHAT'S THE STORY?

Brevard, like many western North Carolina towns and cities, has it all. Situated in a county that shares the name of the home of the most famous vampire of all time-Dracula!-Brevard and the surrounding Transylvania County offer unparalleled beauty, superb opportunities for pleasures of all types. This city of 6,000 (and the county of 27,000) persons has been listed regularly among the best towns and cities in which to live in the United States. The standard of living is high, education is exemplary, crime is low, and the weather is exceptional.

Per capita income is about $20,000 annually, and the median age is slightly over 40 years. Average rainfall is 68 inches, and the average daily temperature in January is about 43 degrees, while the average daily maximum temperature in July is nearly 72 degrees. The town is spotlessly clean, and the air and water are clean.

SPECIAL ATTRACTIONS:

Within the town limits of Brevard, or only slightly beyond, you can visit majestic homes like Silvermont, a wildlife education center, beautiful mountain lakes, and special mountains. Downtown Brevard is a treat for shoppers, and the area inside and outside the town is a photographer's dream. The Jim Bob Tinsley Museum and Research Center is a delight and a pure fascination for students of mountain and western culture and art.

MAKING THE MOST OF YOUR VISIT:

If you haven't visited the fabulous waterfalls just outside Brevard, you may wish to start your visit by seeing Whitewater Falls and the other well-known cataracts and cascades nearby. See the section of this book on waterfalls for details. If you have already seen the falls, now it is time to see Brevard. Drive into town first and motor around the main streets and back streets to see some beautiful homes, churches, and civic buildings. The old courthouse in the center of town is highly attractive as well as unusual.

Two special places to visit are the Silvermont estate and the Jim Bob Tinsley Museum, which is one of the finest surprises you will get in a small-town museum. It's a great place to visit.

The Silvermont mansion is four blocks east of the courthouse on East Main Street. This is the former home of industrialist Joseph Silversteen and his family. The Silversteens-Joseph and his wife Elizabeth-moved to Brevard from Pennsylvania in 1902 and built the 33-room colonial revival house and lived there until the mid-twentieth century. The house is described in more detail in another part of this book: the section on the best of the mountain homes.

For many, the real surprise and delight in Brevard is the fairly new Jim Bob Tinsley Museum and Research Center, which is located at 20 West Jordan Street.

Opened in 1994, the Jim Bob Tinsley Museum contains many of the personal mementos of Jim Bob himself, a former educator, a nationally recognized author, photographer, and entertainer.

For those who do not know about him, Jim Bob, first of all, wrote the definitive book on waterfalls in Transylvania County, and for years he led treks into the wilderness to see falls that the typical person never dreams of seeing. Even now Tinsley leads an occasional trek into the mountains. But much of the time he can be found downtown in Brevard and often in the museum.

Tinsley has donated to the museum for the enjoyment of the public and historians such items as the rare Gillespie long gun made by the Gillespie brothers in 1800, cowboy collectibles, Native American artifacts, and even a mountain lion rug.

Of special interest are the many photos of Tinsley with some of his favorite movie stars, singers, and other entertainers. The books written by Tinsley include "He Was Singin' This Song" and "For a Cowboy Has to Sing." The forewords to these books were written by Gene Autry, Roy Rogers, and Dale Evans.

The museum is packed with other items of interest to anyone who cares about the mountains and the West. Among the items are recast Remington bronzes and original John Hampton works. The artist's "Turning the Leaders" won the gold award at the Phoenix Museum Art Show in 1991.

If this isn't enough, there are the puma room, the historic saddle collection, the Totem Lodge Chair, an antique horn chair, and branding irons. The museum and research center, which includes Tinsley's books and his research documentation, is open from 10 a.m. until 4 p.m. Tuesday through Saturday. There is the Museum Gift Shop with the same hours. The non-profit museum has no admission charge but donations are accepted. For more information call (828) 884-2347.

If you want to see the oldest frame house standing in western North Carolina, drive a few miles outside Brevard on NC 280 to the community of Pisgah Forest. Here you will find the Allison-Deaver House, built in the 1790s. Very large by standards of mountain houses at this time, the Allison-Deaver house has 2,200 square feet. There is a front porch that extends along the entire width of the house, and above it there is a balcony of the same size. Five columns from the porch support the balcony, and five more columns support the roof covering the two areas.

The first part of the house was built by Benjamin Allison, and in 1834 William Deaver, one of the founding fathers of the forested land known today as Transylvania County, bought the house. The story persists that during the Civil War James Deaver, son of William, was a captain in the Confederate Army, and a mob of bandits came to the house in search of him. When the elder Deaver opened the door, the men, thinking him to be James, shot him dead without a word.

The mixed Greek Revival and Federal style house, saved from demolition by the Transylvania County Historic Society, is listed on the National Register of Historic Places.

If you want to get away from the town and city life, try one or more of the wildlife study areas near Brevard. One of the best possibilities is the Holmes Educational Forest outside town on US 64 toward Hendersonville, or east. This is one of six educational forests managed by the State of North Carolina. Here you will find on the 235-acre tract of forest land exhibits, trails, and other teaching tools designed to promote an understanding of the importantance of forests in our lives.

You will also find picnic grounds and a campground, as well as drinking water and restrooms.

Children will especially enjoy the talking trees on the .5 mile walk which features recorded messages in various trees that have a story to tell about the forest. Among informative facts given are the history of the area, the background of the trees themselves, and their individual roles in ecology.

You can walk four other trails of varying length. Check the maps at the exhibit boards for exact mileage. No bikes or horses are permitted on the trails-only hikers.

If groups are interested, members can enjoy ranger-conducted programs on forest management and protection. For campers, there are camping areas with pit toilets and cold showers. There are no fees for the use of the campground, but you must contact rangers in order to reserve sites.

To get to the Holmes Educational State Forest, drive on US 64 toward Hendersonville until you reach Penrose, and then turn right onto Crab Creek Road. Six miles later you will reach the turn-off to the forest, which is on the right side of the road and is very easy to miss unless you watch carefully.

The forest is open Tuesday through Friday from 9 a.m. until 5 p. m. and on weekends from 11 a.m. until 8 p.m. For more details call (828) 692-0100.

This is only the beginning. You can secure a map of the city and county and follow your own instincts to enjoy dining out at the wide range of restaurants and then embark on a shopping trip around the town.

At the Brevard Music Center you can enjoy classical, pop, Broadway musical, and opera presentations. Performers range from Mitch Miller to Dudley Moore and, until his recent death, Buffalo Bob Smith of earlier TV fame, as well as classical performers. For information call (828) 884-2019.

Downtown Asheville.

SECTION 3: THE BEST TOWNS AND CITIES
TRIP 2: ASHEVILLE
THE ANGEL ON THE PORCH

LOCATION:
Asheville has the travel advantage of being at the junction of Interstate 26 and Interstate 40, two of the main thoroughfares in western North Carolina. Distance-wise, this mountain city is 115 miles from Charlotte, 74 miles from Hickory, and it is within easy driving distance from Greenville or Spartanburg in South Carolina, Knoxville, Durham, Winston-Salem, and such smaller towns and cities as Morganton, Chimney Rock, Shelby, and Marion.

NEARBY ATTRACTIONS:
Asheville is only a five-minute drive from the Blue Ridge Parkway and is close to Mount Pisgah, Brevard, Craggy Gardens, Mount Mitchell State Park, the Weaverville home of Zebulon Vance, Crabtree Meadows (on the Parkway), the Museum of North Carolina Minerals, Flat Rock, and Hendersonville.

HOURS OF OPERATION:
Most of the museums and other attractions are open from 9 a.m. until 5 or 6 p.m. Restaurants remain open in many instances until 9 p. m. and later. Hours for shops range from 8 a.m. until 9 p.m. although some close at 6 p.m.

ADMISSION:
Most of the attractions charge a modest admission fee, with $5 or $6 (or less) being common. Many attractions, such as the Folk Art Center, are free.

FACILITIES:
In and around Asheville you can find almost anything you want in the way of recreation, amusement, and needs. There are hiking trails, horse trails, bike trails, campgrounds, bed-and-breakfast inns, museums of natural science, kids' attractions, exceptional walking tours, great restaurants, astonishing architecture, a very strong sense of literature, nature centers, hospitals, churches of almost every denomination, and whatever else can be found in a city that is both large and small at the same time.

WHAT'S THE STORY?
According to the Asheville Chamber of Commerce, when the town's first settlers had established a tiny community, the price of land was about $2 for a half-acre lot. John Adams was President of the United States,

and Asheville was merely a stopping place for the drovers who herded their livestock, including hogs, turkeys, and cattle, to the coast. In this scenic area where the Blue Ridge and Great Smoky mountains meet, the town born in 1797 began to grow until it reached its present-day population of 67,000 residents, with a total of 192,000 in Buncombe County.

Outside Magazine rated Asheville as one of the top cities "where you don't have to give up good living to live a good life." The magazine rated Asheville as the third best city in terms of location, job opportunities, cultural attractions, and outdoor activities. *Vacation Magazine* rated Asheville as one of its top 10 getaway destinations.

More art deco architecture, the Chamber of Commerce reports, from the 1920s and 1930s can be found in Asheville than in any other southeastern city except Miami Beach. The Chocolate Fetish shop was rated by the Los Angeles *Times* as making the nation's best chocolate truffles.

Grove Park Inn was rated by the readers of *Family Circle Magazine* as one of the top family resorts in the nation. At this luxurious attractions novelist F. Scott Fitzgerald was often a guest, as were many of the nation's celebrities. President Franklin Delano Roosevelt appreciated Asheville deeply, and Mary Pickford, Douglas Fairbanks, and other movie stars frequented the area.

So do other people from all walks of life. More motorists exit and enter the nation's most popular scenic highway, the Blue Ridge Parkway, in Asheville than at any other point along the entire 470 miles of the Parkway.

The list goes on and on. And Asheville truly deserves all the accolades that have been heaped upon the city. If you do not visit any other city in western North Carolina, be certain to include a lengthy trip to Asheville. In fact, more than one visit is almost a requirement. You will not see more than a fraction of what the city has to offer if you can spend only a few hours.

SPECIAL ATTRACTIONS:
While you are in the Asheville area, you should be sure to see and enjoy several key points of interest. These include the Thomas Wolfe Memorial, the house that the noted author used as the backdrop of his first and most powerful novel: *Look Homeward, Angel.* Wolfe was preoccupied with angels, and the marble angel that stood at his father's workshop has been a point of interest for all Wolfe fans. Wolfe, who spent his early years in Asheville and was buried there after dying at a tragically young age, wrote about the angel not only in his initial novel but in some of his other works, including "Angel on the Porch."

Other special attractions include the Western North Carolina Nature

Center, the Folk Art Center, the city's art-deco City Hall, the Health Adventure at Pack Place, the Colburn Gem and Mineral Museum, Asheville's Art Museum, historic Richmond Hill, and, to be as brief as possible, the streets and shops of Asheville are all tourist attractions and memorable experiences.

MAKING THE MOST OF YOUR VISIT:

If you can't stay for at least a week, you cannot see all there is to see in Asheville (and, indeed, a week would only allow you to make a start!), but if you can spare only a few hours, here are some of the places to visit.

You can start with the North Carolina Arboretum, located near I-26 and I-40 at the edge of the Pisgah National Forest. This 424-acre attraction has a Visitor Education Center, a state-of-the-art greenhouse complex, gardens, a loop trail, and a series of on-going programs. Some of the special points of interest include the Plants of Promise Garden, a Quilt Garden, Stream Garden, and Spring Garden.

With the completion of the connecting spur from the Blue Ridge Parkway, the number of visitors to the arboretum is expected to surpass one million visitors each year. A former director for the National Arboretum in Washington, DC, has said that the arboretum in Asheville will be one of the finest in the entire nation.

There is no admission fee, and the arboretum is open from 8 a.m. until 9 p.m. seven days a week. The Visitors Center is open from 8 a.m. until 5 p.m. For more details call (828) 665-2492.

A second stop is at 48 Spruce Street where you will find the Thomas Wolfe Memorial, the boyhood home of Wolfe and the center of his most famous novel. If you can possibly find time to do so, read *Look Homeward, Angel* before making the visit. If not, at least read a brief biography of Wolfe so that you will be more receptive to the details you receive by the expert guides or interpreters at the site. Admission to the Wolfe Memorial is $1 for adults and $.50 for children. Hours are from 9 a.m. until 5 p.m. Monday through Saturday during the months of April through October and on Sunday from 1 p.m. until 5 p.m. Then from November 1 through March 31 hours are 10 a.m. until 4 p.m. from Tuesday until Saturday and on Sunday from 1 p.m. until 4 p.m.

Fire damaged the house severely just before publication date of this book, and the house will be closed until renovations and reconstruction can be completed.

If you want to try the downtown walking tour, you can walk 1.6 miles (or shorter distances) along the entire trail. You can hike the Gilded Trail (.5 mile and marked with a feather), the Frontier Period (.2 mile and marked with a horseshoe), the Times of Thomas Wolfe (.4 miles and marked with an angel), the Era of Civic Pride (.2 miles and marked with a courthouse symbol), or the Age of Diversity Trail (.3 miles and marked with an eagle).

The Gilded Age Trail leads you from the square to the Zeb Vance monument, down Patton Avenue, to the place where famed short story writer O. Henry (William Sidney Porter) lived and at times wrote, to the Dhurmor Building with its carved frieze with its mythological characters, to the art-deco architectural style of the S & W Cafeteria location. You will see Wall Street where E.W. Grove and others constructed hotels and Flat Iron Building.

The tour ends with the Basilica of Saint Lawrence with one of the largest elliptical domes in America.

The other tours lead you through similarly interesting and often elaborate parts of downtown Asheville. You can hike as few or as many as you wish.

If you wish to see a truly elaborate, luxurious, beautiful, and fascinating mansion, drive to Richmond Hill to see the house that was built by former ambassador and congressman Richmond Pearson (the house was designed by James G. Hill). The Queen Anne mansion had, as an example of its completeness, no fewer than 10 master fireplaces. This house is featured in the section on the best mountain homes.

If you drive to the heart of downtown Asheville you will find Pack Place, and inside there are museums for every taste. One that the kids will love is the Health Adventure. For art lovers there is the Asheville Art Museum. Rockhounds and gem lovers will find what they want to see in the Colburn Gem and Mineral Museum. Then there is the YMI Cultural Center and the Diana Wortham Theatre for those with a taste for live drama and/or African American art, culture, and history.

The Colburn Gem and Mineral Museum features an amazing array of minerals and gems from around the world. There is a 229-carat cut blue topaz and a 376 pound aquamarine crystal. One of the most unusual gems is hiddenite, one of the rare precious stones of the world, one that is found predominantly in the area of Hiddenite in Alexander County, near Taylorsville.

One amazing sight is that of a rock that actually bends. Pack Place is open Tuesday through Saturday from 10 a.m. until 5 p.m. and from Sunday from 1 p.m. until 5 p.m. For information call (828) 254-7162.

The Asheville Art Museum, also located in Pack Place, dates back to 1948 when local artists formed an association devoted to the visual arts. The Pack Place location is the museum's fifth home, and here it occupies three floors that are devoted to classrooms and galleries for the art works.

In recent years the New York Metropolitan Museum of Art lent 56 color prints to the Art Museum. The works depict America in the worst stages of the Great Depression. Call (828) 253-3227 for more details.

If the kids are restless and tired of museums, take them to yet another type of museum, but one they are guaranteed to love. This is the Health Adventure in Pack Place. Here children (and their parents) will learn more than you thought possible in such a short time. They (and you) will learn about nearly every aspect of the human body, from giant teeth to a talking glass lady and a skeleton that rides a bicycle. You can even touch a five-foot brain.

And while you are examining the brain you can test your own brainpower at the creativity tables. Or you can travel 60,000 miles via a life-sized model to see the journey of the blood.

If you prefer, you can visit the NutriSpace Gallery to see how much fat, sugar, and fiber is in your diet. At the Miracle of Life Gallery you learn about heredity, and you can see photos of life before birth.

If that isn't enough, you have cowboys, pirates, and giant strawberries in an area where children under age 8 can put on a puppet show, dress up in a variety of ways, slide down a giant tongue, or be the captain of their own boat.

Hours are the same as for the other museums in Pack Place. Call (828) 254-6373 for more information.

This is only a beginning. For the complete story you can drive to Asheville and learn what else is offered. Be sure to visit the great restaurants and bookstores in this super city.

Old Depot in Hendersonville.

SECTION 4: THE BEST TOWNS AND CITIES
TRIP 3: HENDERSONVILLE
A TOWN FOR ALL SEASONS

LOCATION:

Hendersonville, in addition to having an almost perfect climate, is also located nearly perfectly. Almost on the cross-roads of Interstate 26 and US 64, the city is easily accessible from all directions. It is also located near some of the finest attractions in western North Carolina. To reach Hendersonville from South Carolina, take I-26 north of Spartanburg, or you can follow US 25 north of the Greenville-Spartanburg area. From Asheville, take I-26 off I-40 straight into the Hendersonville area. From Brevard take US 64 west, and from the Rutherfordton-Lake Lure area follow US 64 west.

NEARBY ATTRACTIONS:

Hendersonville is close to Chimney Rock, Asheville, Flat Rock (with the Carl Sandburg house and the Flat Rock Playhouse and its superlative dramas and musicals), Brevard (with dozens-actually hundreds-of water-falls within a short drive), the tiny but delightful town of Highlands, and the Blue Ridge Parkway, to name only a few of the area delights. You are also very close to Holmes Educational State Forest, which is a great place for the young ones in the family, as well as for the adults.

HOURS OF OPERATION:

Most of the town's restaurants are open for lunch and dinner, with some serving breakfast. City businesses and shops are open during regular business hours. The antique shops are open, for the most part, Monday through Saturday from 10 a. m. until 5 or 6 p. m. Some few are open Sunday afternoon. Most of the clothing stores operate from 9:30 a.m. or 10 a.m. until 5, 5:30, or 6 p.m. Arts and crafts shops are typically open from 9 or 9:30 a.m. until 5 p.m. Monday through Saturday.

FACILITIES:

Hendersonville has all the activities you would expect to find in a much larger city, but without the problems of big-city traffic and conges-tion. There are arts and cultural activities, civic groups, a large number of churches (many of them beautiful and unique), hospital, medical facili-ties, and generally fine transportation system. The Hendersonville Airport (near the Blue Ridge Community College campus) offers charter service to larger airports as well as a flight school and plane maintenance. The highway system to Hendersonville is excellent and includes the Blue Ridge Parkway (nearby), I-26, I-40 not far away, US 25, US 64, and US 176. Greyhound Bus Lines serve the area daily. The bus station is located at 330 Seventh Avenue East. Call the bus station at 828-693-1201. In addi-tion, there are five in-town taxi services.

WHAT'S THE STORY?

In addition to being a wonderfully beautiful, clean, and quiet city (with one of the greatest main streets you are likely to find), Hendersonville is further blessed with a fantastic climate, with summer temperatures averaging 71 degrees and winter days averaging 41 degrees. Winters are nippy but generally mild, with about 20 inches of snowfall or less. Spring and autumn are gorgeous and as close to perfect as weather gets.

Henderson County and Hendersonville were named for Leonard Henderson, chief justice of the North Carolina Supreme Court. For de-cades the area was part of the hunting grounds of the Cherokee Indians, and shortly after the Revolutionary War William Mills explored the terri-tory and received one of the early land grants. Mills River and Mills Gap are two geographic landmarks named by Mills.

The altitude of Henderson County ranges from 1,400 feet to more than 5,000 feet, and Hendersonville is about 2,200 feet above sea level.

Roads in the county are good, and the traffic flow generally is easy to handle. The greatest congestion comes in spring and fall and on weekends.

SPECIAL ATTRACTIONS:

One site that is excellent for outdoor recreation is the Holmes Educational State Forest, described earlier. There are good picnic grounds for the family meal, and after eating you can take short or long hikes and learn a great deal about the forest and about the trees individually and collectively.

For another great stop, try Piggy's restaurant at 102 Duncan Hill Road. Call (828) 692-1995 for information. But before you go, be alerted to the fact that you are heading for what is probably the best hamburger you ever ate in your life.

And while the food is good, the ambiance is remarkable. You can study the walls and the ceilings and learn a great deal more than you would have believed possible. The decorations are more than words can describe. When you have eaten (and there is a great deal more than burgers) step next door for some of the best ice cream you ever tasted. Hours at Piggy's are 11 a.m. until 7 p.m. Monday through Saturday.

For other good places to eat, drive around town and pick a dining spot. This town of 9,000 has more than three dozen places to eat, and most of them are truly good. Best of all, the food prepared in the hometown restaurants is among the best in the state.

There are many other delightful attractions, a sampling of which will be described in the following section.

MAKING THE MOST OF YOUR VISIT:

The first stop in Hendersonville is Main Street, which is one of the most attractive thoroughfares in North Carolina. This long, serpentine, and impeccably neat street curves its way through the town. Flowers bloom from dozens of planters, and trees provide shade and beauty for the shopper or visitor.

This is the street that, in the 1890s, was laid out so wide that horses and wagons and carriages could turn around easily. The logic behind the street was that the traffic between the city of Asheville and the Piedmont would bring commerce and profit to the town that occupied the terrain that was once part of the old Judge Mitchell King's estate and some of the land of Colonel James Brittain and John Johnson.

On this winding street you can enjoy music, street dancing on Friday nights in summer, clothing shops, restaurants, and book and gift stores. The old courthouse was constructed in 1904-05 in a Classical Revival style, and the golden dome was topped with a statue of Justice, sans blindfold.

If you need to shop for food, the Curb Market behind the courthouse (on the corner of North Church Street and Second Avenue) offers home-grown produce, dairy products, baked goods, hand-made crafts, walking sticks, wood crafts, rugs, dolls, and pickles and relishes. The Curb Market is non-profit, and one of the restrictions is that all of the occupants of the 130-plus selling spaces must be residents of Henderson County and the arts and crafts and produce must be made or grown in Henderson County.

At the Hendersonville Depot, located between US 65 and 7th Avenue (you will see the railroad tracks as you enter town from an east-west direction), you will find a tastefully restored and decorated depot built first in 1879 and replaced in 1902. Inside the depot there is the Apple Valley Model Railroad consisting of a 420-foot square foot layout and 500 feet of track and more than 100 track switches. The trains chug through miniature versions of Hendersonville, Asheville, Brevard, and Saluda, including the nationally known Saluda Grade, the steepest mainline railroad grade in the United States. There are also mountains, waterfalls, lakes, and the scenic tunnels.

The depot is open to the public all year on Wednesday from noon until 3 p.m. and on Saturdays from 9 a.m. until noon.

Visit the Historic Johnson Farm four miles north of the city on NC 191 (Haywood Road) across from the Rugby Middle School. This farm was once a 19th century tobacco farm that evolved into a tourist attractions in the early years of the 20th century. The farm is owned today by Henderson County Public Schools and now operates as a heritage education center and farm museum.

You can visit the 1870-era brick farm house, a boarding house out of the 1920s, a museum in a barn, 10 outbuildings, two nature trails, and 15 acres of farmland and forest. Guided tours are available May through October and November through April. The farm is open to the public on Tuesday through Saturday from 10 a.m. until 4 p.m. and on Sunday from 1 p.m. until 4 p.m. (during the May-October season). The second season hours are Wednesday through Saturday from 10 a.m. until 2 p.m.

There is an admission charge of $3 for adults and $1.50 for students. Pre-schoolers are admitted free. Group rates are available. Call (828) 891-6585 or (828) 697-4733. This is a non-profit organization.

For an unexpected treat, drive to the Hendersonville Airport at 1340 Gilbert Street. Here you will find an array of historic and award-winning airplanes, including a 1930 Curtis Robin, a 1944 North American Texan, and a dozen other rare and historic planes. The Western North Carolina

Air Museum is open, weather permitting, each Wednesday, Saturday, and Sunday from noon until 6 p.m. There is no admission charge. For details call (800) 828-4244 or (828) 693-9708.

And this is just the beginning. Throughout the year there are nationally known celebrations, such as the Apple Festival on Labor Day weekend, Coon Dog Festival the first Saturday after July 4, Fourth of July Celebration at Jackson Park, Farm City Day on the first weekend in October, a Civil War reenactment on the first weekend after Labor Day, the Western North Carolina Air Show on Memorial Day weekend, the Johnson Farm Festival the last Saturday in April, and a number of others.

Outside town there are camps, wilderness areas, and fishing and hiking opportunities. Hendersonville may be the Apple Capital of the South, but it's a peach of a city!

Bridal Veil Falls west of Highlands.

SECTION 3: THE BEST OF THE TOWNS AND CITIES
TRIP 4: HIGHLANDS
THE GATEWAY TO THE WATERFALL HIGHWAY

LOCATION:

Highlands is neither near nor far. From Asheville and I-40 you can be in Highlands in about two hours. From Brevard the driving time is one hour. From Greenville, South Carolina, you will need about two hours to reach Highlands. From Highlands you are about 15 minutes from Dillard, Georgia. Closest neighbors, in addition to the ones already mentioned, to the town of Highlands are Cashiers, Sapphire, Franklin, Cullasaja, and Sky Valley.

NEARBY ATTRACTIONS:

Once you reach Highlands you are within easy driving distance of Dry Falls, Bridal Veil Falls, Whitewater Falls, Glen Falls, and Horsepasture River Falls, including Umbrella, Rainbow, and others. You are very close to the Black Rock State Park in Georgia and to Mountain City, Georgia, home of the famous Foxfire Museum (and the Foxfire books). One nearby peak of major interest is Whiteside Mountain, five miles east of Highlands on US 64.

HOURS OF OPERATION:

Most Highlands stores and shops are open from 9 a.m. until 5 p.m. There are no gates to any of the waterfalls and these are open whenever you can get there. For best photo and sightseeing opportunities, however, you should be at Whitewater Falls before lunch. Restaurants are open for lunch at about 11:30 a.m. and open for dinner until 9 p.m.

ADMISSION:

Most of the destinations described in this chapter do not charge for admission. Call for details before you leave home.

FACILITIES:

At Dry Falls and Whitewater Falls there are restrooms, but the Whitewater facilities are closed during the winter months. There are restrooms at the Foxfire Museum and at Black Rock State Park in Georgia, where there are also campgrounds, picnic tables, shelters, and a visitor center.

WHAT'S THE STORY?

Highlands is, like many of the mountain communities, a small town and a large one. In the winter the year-round population is about 3,000, while in the summer the influx of tourists and folks with summer homes in the area results in a town with 20,000 people who are there for the same reasons you are: to enjoy one of the most beautiful towns in North Carolina and certainly a town with one of the best summer climates you can find.

SPECIAL ATTRACTIONS:

One of the finest summer attractions of the area is the Highlands Playhouse, which has been in operation for more than half a century. Dramatic productions of all sorts are staged for the entertainment and enlightenment of the audience. Call (828) 526-3415 for details.

The Bascom-Louise Gallery presents exhibits and art events during the summer or tourist season, and the Center for Life Enrichment offers entertainment and education in formats ranging from cabaret performances to information presentations. Call (828) 526-4949 for the Bascom-Louise Gallery and (828) 526-9381 for the Center for Life Enrichment.

The Highlands Chamber Music Festival (828) 526-9060 offers classical or chamber music each summer, and the Highlands Forum presents political and economic lectures and discussions on topics of national and international significance. Call the Highlands Chamber of Commerce at

(828) 526-2112 for details.

MAKING THE MOST OF YOUR VISIT:

If you plan to spend a day or a week at Highlands, you will want to sample some of the food offered there and nearby. You can dine sumptuously or simply, and the variety in such a small town is astonishing. The Dunfergot offers pizza, subs, salads, lasagna, and similar foods that you can enjoy while watching a movie in the dining theatre. The Fireside Inn is a family-style restaurant serving three meals a day. The Frog and Owl Kitchen is a mountain bistro experience, and the Highlander Restaurant serves three meals a day in a family-style offering. Other restaurants offer steaks, sea food, veal, lamb, barbecue, and nearly any other dish available in restaurants in larger cities. Nick's is a favorite of numerous tourists as well as local residents, and it is not unusual to find cars from several states in the parking lot on a given night.

Your first stop might well be at one of the several unique waterfalls near this town that is tucked among the crags, peaks, and valleys of the mountains of western North Carolina. Along the way you might want to stop and visit in one or all of the three tiny towns nearby. In this area you can take advantage of the numerous outdoor activities offered: superb sightseeing, photography, hiking, rock climbing, kayaking, canoeing, rafting, camping, fishing, and driving.

The three towns are situated along US 64, known as the Waterfall Highway because of the large number of great waterfalls that are close enough to the road for you to enjoy them without having to hike a great distance. They are Sapphire, Lake Toxaway, and Cashiers.

Highlands, incidentally, is the highest town above sea level in North Carolina (if you discount the assertion of a ski resort village that makes the same claim) with an altitude of 4,118 feet above sea level. The Highlands area also has the greatest annual rainfall, with Macon County receiving an average of 82.41 inches per year. So if you visit in the warmer months, prepare for rain if you plan to be outdoors for prolonged periods of time.

As you drive, no matter what the season, exert caution on the curving mountain roads. Be prepared for the sudden stops of drivers ahead of you. Watch for deer and black bears ambling along the shoulders of the road.

The perfect place to start your scenic exploration of the area is along US 54 west of Highlands. Almost as soon as you leave town you will see a beautiful lake and dam, and just beyond it you will see Bridal Veil Falls, a 120-foot waterfall that pours over a ledge and then lands across a stretch of pavement. At one time you drove under the waterfall, but the road has been modified so that you don't need to do so-but you still can, if you prefer.

Two minutes from Bridal Veil Falls you will reach Dry Falls, described in the waterfalls section of this book. If you follow a short trail to the Cullasaja River you will see why the waterfall was so named. You can walk behind the falls and stay perfectly dry, except for a little spray. There is room for two dozen people behind the falls.

The Cullasaja River gorge beyond Highlands is an endless series of waterfalls of all sizes, but you can see the major falls better if you drive east from Franklin. When you reach the most awesome part of the gorge, at Cullasaja Falls, you will see a dramatic and superlative waterfall that is striking almost beyond belief: a 250-foot series of wild and turbulent cascades. For another type of travel enjoyment, drive back through Highlands on US 64 for five miles, to the Jackson and Macon County lines. Look for signs directing you to Whiteside Mountain. This mountain is reportedly one of the oldest in the world. It is also a monument to history.

Drive south on the Wildcat Ridge Road (State Road 1600) for one mile, to the sign directing you to Whiteside Mountain. Follow the arrows to the parking lot. There is a two-mile trail leading to the summit, which is 4,930 feet above sea level. From this point you have a great view of the Chattooga River, the one that was featured in the movie *Deliverance*. Along the way you see the 600-foot granite cliffs and perhaps see the first graffiti in the New World-the scratchings in the stone of the Spaniards who followed DeSoto in his search for gold before the area was settled by Europeans.

Now drive back into Highlands. If you prefer to spend the night there, you can stay at inns listed on the National Register of Historic Places.

For your final stop in Highlands, visit Highlands Nature Center on Main Street where there are educational materials and displays on the natural life around the area. The center offers classes on appreciation and understanding of the wild life, plant and animal, in the Nantahala Forest that virtually surrounds the town of Highlands.

Old Burke County Courthouse in Morganton.

SECTION 4: THE BEST TOWNS AND CITIES
TRIP 5: MORGANTON
THE BEST OF THREE WORLDS

LOCATION:

It is extremely easy to reach Morganton via Interstate 40, which slices across North Carolina in an east-west direction and from the Atlantic Ocean at Wilmington to the Great Smokies in the west. Exit I-40 onto either NC 18 or US 64 (the same stretch of road known as the Waterfall Highway farther west) and you can be in downtown Morganton within five minutes. Simply drive north.

NEARBY ATTRACTIONS:

From Morganton it is an easy drive to Asheville (one hour via I-40), Charlotte (1.5 hours by I-40 to Statesville and I-77 to Charlotte), the Blue Ridge Parkway, Lake James, Linville Falls, Table Rock, Linville Gorge, and a cluster of smaller towns with charm and historic interest. You are also close to one of the finest parks in the state: South Mountains State Park.

One of the most fascinating trips just north of Morganton is the overlook for viewing the Brown Mountain Lights, which have baffled scientists and students of nature for decades.

HOURS OF OPERATION:

Shops in Morganton keep regular business hours, from about 9 a.m. till 5 or 6 p.m. Malls stay open until 9 or 10 p.m. The town's several restaurants are open for lunch from 11 a.m. or 11:30 a.m. Many restaurants stay open during the afternoon. The ones that close are open for dinner at 5 p.m. and stay open until 9 p.m. The nearby state parks are open from 7 a.m. or 8 a.m. until, depending upon the time of year, 6, 7, 8, or 9 p.m.

ADMISSION:

There is no admission charge to the state parks, but there is a small fee for camping in the established campgrounds. There is no fee to enter Linville Gorge or the Linville Falls area, and nearly all of the attractions in Morganton are free.

FACILITIES:

You can enjoy camping at Linville Falls, in Linville Gorge (but you must have a permit), at Lake James State Park and at the South Mountains State Park. Hiking trails can be found at the state parks and Linville Gorge as well as at Table Rock, which is very close to Morganton. You can swim at Lake James State Park. There are picnic grounds at the parks and in the Linville Falls area as well as at Table Rock.

WHAT'S THE STORY?

Morganton, which is an attractive, clean, and safe city (with a low crime rate, good schools, and good economy), has been rated by Reader's Digest as one of the top places in the entire United States in which to live and rear a family. The town is in a sense on the frontier where the Piedmont plateau and the Blue Ridge Mountains meet. It's a town of culture and civic pride, with the mountains and the lakes adding other dimensions so that Morganton is truly the center of three worlds. Visitors can enjoy history, nature, water sports, and good food.

MAKING THE MOST OF YOUR VISIT:

Most weather in the area is not totally unpredictable and extreme; in fact, the weather in the North Carolina mountains is almost perfect much if not most of the time. Exceptions are mentioned only to suggest that you prepare for the unusual.

If you want a good meal at a very reasonable price, you can dine at the Uptown Restaurant, which offers freshly baked sour-dough bread as well as a variety of specials in addition to those on the basic menu. Yanni's is a good place for a sandwich and salad or a quick and good basic meal.

King Street Cafe offers more elaborate and delicious meals at a slightly higher price. It is a good idea to call for reservations for evening meals.

Morganton was established in 1784 as Morgansborough, after Revolutionary War leader Daniel Morgan. Here you will find the historic Burke County Courthouse as it has existed, with minor changes, over a century and a half. Built in 1833 to 1837, this is the only courthouse, other than the one in Raleigh, where the North Carolina Supreme Court held sessions. It is also the oldest public building west of Salisbury, North Carolina.

Inside the courthouse, located on Green Street on Courthouse Square in the center of town, you can see the Burke County Heritage Museum, which has permanent and special displays showing life as it was lived in Morganton's past. On the same floor of the courthouse you can visit the Historic Burke Foundation and get information on the Morganton Downtown National Register District.

In the Burke County Visitor Information Center you can learn about dozens of nearby historic and educational sites. Write the Center at 102 East Union Street, Courthouse Square, Morganton, NC 28655, or call (828) 433-6793 or fax at (828) 433-6715 or visit at the Web site: www.hci.net/-bcttc/ if you prefer.

In the Heritage Museum you can see a 20-minute slide show depicting area attractions and historic sites. There is no admission charge. Hours of operation are 9 a.m. until 5 p.m. Tuesday through Friday and 10 a.m. until 1 p.m. on Saturday. Call (828) 437-4104 for more details.

The Visitor Center is open at the same hours but is also open on Mondays. Inside the Center you will find hundreds of brochures and other publications to assist you in finding the best sites to visit.

You can enjoy a walking tour of Downtown Morganton. From the old courthouse walk to the north corner and then turn left. Walk west to 200 North Sterling Street to view the Alva Theatre, which opened July 4, 1929, and was the first theatre in the county to show "Talkies." The style of architecture used in the theatre includes Moorish, Baroque, and Mediterranean styles.

The Visitors Center can provide you with a map of downtown Morganton and you can use the map as your tour guide.

If you want to drive to some sites, on South King Street one block southwest of the courthouse you can see The Cedars, one of the most beautiful residences in town. This is private property, so please restrict your visit to walking or driving by. Respect the privacy and rights of the residents. A short distance away you can see Creekside, also a private residence. The Cedars, at 100 South King Street, was originally a Greek

Revival style, but in 1855 Colonel Samuel McDowell Tate remodeled it into a Second Empire style which features a three-story octagonal tower. The vestibule, at the base of the tower, is made of seven different kinds of wood. Creekside, at 825 West Union Street, is said to be one of the largest houses in Western North Carolina. It is described as "the most monumental mansion of the Piedmont."

Drive past and enjoy the architecture and landscaping of the Broughton Hospital, which is said to be the first of the Burke County structures designed by a professional architect, Samuel Sloan of Philadelphia. The hospital, praised as "a wonderful example of Victorian eclecticism," is on NC 18 as you enter Morganton from the south.

One of the top historic sites is Quaker Meadows plantation house, north of Morganton on NC 181. Just outside town, watch for St. Mary's Church Road on the right. Turn right and drive less than half a mile to the Federal style brick plantation house built by Revolutionary War leader Captain Charles McDowell. Here the Over-Mountain Men camped while plans were made for the attack on the British army headed by Colonel Patrick Ferguson, who was on his way to liaison with Lord Cornwallis. The house now belongs to the Historic Burke Foundation, which is overseeing the restoration and conversion of the house to a regional history site. The house restoration was scheduled for completion by autumn 1998.

Near the plantation house is Quaker Meadows Cemetery, the earliest identified site related to European settlement in the western part of North Carolina. Here 59 grave locations have been established, some of them dating to the pre-Revolution era. Leaving downtown Morganton, drive around the corner to West Union Street and then turn left. Drive to the outskirts of town to intersect with US 70/64 and drive west to Burkemont Avenue and turn right. Drive to Western Piedmont Community College where you can visit the Senator Sam Ervin, Jr., Library and Museum.

The first building you will reach when you drive onto the campus is the Phifer Learning Resources Center, and the Sam Ervin Library is upstairs in Room 150. The Sam Ervin Library is more than a collection of books; it is the personal library and the mementos of the man who dominated the Watergate hearings decades ago and who for 30 years practiced law in Morganton and served as state legislator and as judge in Burke County Criminal Court and in the North Carolina Supreme Court from 1948 until 1954, before he was elected to fill out the term of his late brother in the United States House of Representatives. He then was appointed to complete the term of the late Clyde R. Hoey in the United States Senate. In Congress he soon came to be considered as the leading authority on Constitutional law.

For an outdoor experience, drive south on NC 18 10 miles to the entrance to South Mountains State Park, where you will find facilities for picnicking, primitive camping, horseback riding trails, trout fishing, and miles and miles of hiking trails. One superb trail starts at the west end of the parking lot. The trail leads alongside the river for a distance, then crosses the river (there is a good footbridge) and continues up the south side of the river to High Shoals waterfall, where a railed overlook offers a perfect view of the 80-foot cataract. This waterfall is described in more detail in the section on waterfalls.

For another outdoor experience, drive north of Morganton on NC 181 approximately 10 miles to Table Rock Road. Follow this road to Table Rock Mountain. Park at the starting point of the trail that leads to the top of the mountain. Here there are restrooms, picnic tables, and hiking trails. The trail to the summit of Table Rock consists of 2.4 miles of rather hard climbing, but the view at the end of the hike makes it all worthwhile. Other trails in the vicinity lead into Linville Gorge. There are no admission fees charged.

For another treat, unlike any you are likely to find anywhere else, drive on north on NC 181 to the Brown Mountain Lights Overlook, which is only a wide pull-off on the right side of the road, and you will not see any buildings, facilities of any sort, or signs. You will see only gray boulders and a super valley below you.

This attraction is free, and there are no posted hours, but you will see only the valley and the mountains during daylight hours. On a clear night, however, particularly a crisp, cool, autumn night, you, if you are lucky, will see the Brown Mountain Lights, a natural phenomenon that has baffled the ages.

Decades ago a dedicated man of science, Thomas Alva Edison, told a local man that there were no mysteries in Nature, that all could be explained logically and scientifically. So the man, a Mr. Rinehardt, and Edison made the trek to Brown Mountain, where the two made their camp at the overlook. Hours later the mysterious lights appeared, and the friend asked Edison for the scientific and logical explanation.

"There are some things," Edison replied, "that cannot ever be explained, and we should simply enjoy them and wonder about them."

For your final stop on the tour, drive west of Morganton on I-40 to the tiny town of Nebo, and from there follow the signs to Lake James State Park where you can find swimming, hiking, boating, fishing, and nature study activities. There are no fees for hiking and enjoying the park, but if you choose to swim you will pay a very small fee.

Trail of Faith Monument in Valdese.

SECTION 4: THE BEST TOWNS AND CITIES
TRIP 6: VALDESE
THE SPIRIT OF THE TRAIL OF FAITH

LOCATION:

Again using Interstate 40 as the starting point, take Exit 112 and follow signs. You are within two minutes of downtown Valdese when you leave the interstate highway. You are also within an easy drive to Charlotte, Asheville, and other area towns and cities as well as a number of natural attractions.

NEARBY ATTRACTIONS:

In Valdese you are near Linville Falls, Linville Gorge, Table Rock, Lake James State Park, South Mountains State Park, the Blue Ridge Parkway, Asheville, Hickory, Charlotte, and, of course, Morganton, which is only a 10-minute drive away.

HOURS OF OPERATION:

Most of the area stores are open from 9 a.m. until 5 p.m.; however, some of the best attractions are open only two or three days a week or by appointment. Call ahead to be certain you will be able to see the best the town has to offer. You will find that some of the attractions are staffed with people so helpful that they will open just to accommodate you.

ADMISSION:

Nearly everything is free. You may be offered a chance to make a small donation to help defray operating costs, and you are urged to drop in a dollar or two. The staffs often are volunteer workers and the only income at the attractions is from donations.

FACILITIES:

There are picnic tables at park areas, but there are not any campgrounds in town, and you will find very few places to eat in Valdese. There are no bus services or other public transportation in the town. But there is an abundance of hospitality that can make your trip memorable.

WHAT'S THE STORY?

Within a very short drive from I-40 you can find and enjoy an exceptionally good museum, a Trail of Faith dotted with symbols of Waldensian tradition and heritage, a wonderful winery, a park complete with a working grist mill and superb waterfall, and a quiet downtown area featuring one of the most beautiful churches in the state, and the famous Old Rock School. If you are lucky you can get in a quick game of bocce, or boccie (a sport something like bowling which dates back to 5200 B.C.). You will also find a profusion of some of the warmest hospitality available anywhere. As an added pleasure, you can hear some few remaining people speak a language unlike any other: Patois.

MAKING THE MOST OF YOUR VISIT:

If you want to see and enjoy Valdese to the fullest, plan to spend the entire day. Despite its small size (2,500 to 3,000 residents) the town has an amazing number of highly interesting attractions. The first stop should be at the Waldensian Museum, at 101 Rodoret Street, SE. As you enter the downtown area you will see on the left (as you head west) the huge and incredibly beautiful Waldensian Presbyterian Church. The Waldensian Museum is across the street from the church.

Inside the museum you will be given a brief history of the Waldensian faith. You will perhaps be surprised to learn that the faith endured religious persecution as early as 400 A.D. and that the Waldensian Church of Italy is the oldest evangelical church in existence, dating to 1183. In 1532 the Waldensians became a part of the Reformation. In 1555 the first Waldensian Church was built (previously the construction of churches was prohibited). In 1848, on February 17, the Waldensians were granted (by King Carlo Alberto or Charles Albert of Sardinia) basic civil and religious liberty.

On May 29, 1893, the Waldensian settlers arrived in the area that was to become Valdese. By 1896 construction was begun on the Romanesque church. On February 16 (the day before one of the most significant anniversaries in Waldensian history) of 1974 the museum was open to the public.

The museum features ancient photos, furniture, authentic Waldensian clothing, tools, an incredible quilt depicting the history of the Waldensians, and hundreds of items that open to the visitor a glimpse of what the Waldensian heritage really is.

After you tour both floors of the museum, be sure to allow time to enjoy the exterior beauty of the building as well. Notice the superb workmanship inside and out, and the architectural splendor of the museum. The museum building complements the architecture of the church across the street.

Leaving the museum, return to Main Street and drive west to Church Street and turn right. This road will take you within a five-minute drive to the Old Colony Amphitheater where you will see the Trail of Faith. Here you will see structures symbolic of the Waldensian heritage and faith. This short cultural hike includes a sawmill (Waldensians were superb carpenters), a stone oven (the Waldensians were also exceptional stone masons and bakers), a cave symbolizing the fact that Waldensians had to meet and worship in secret (and, because Bibles were prohibited to them, they memorized the scriptures), a church (now under construction), a one-room school, and other reminders of the strong faith and the determination of the Waldensians. The amphitheater where the Old Colony players perform the outdoor pageant *From This Day Forward* each summer is located at the end of the trail.

Leaving the Trail of Faith you can continue north on Church Street to the sign directing you to McGalliard Falls park. There are shelters and an overlook affording a superb view of the 45-foot waterfall and the grist mill on the other side of McGalliard Creek. If you prefer, you can return to Church Street and start back toward town, and as you cross the bridge turn left and drive to Roy Fletcher Memorial Ball Park. You can park here and walk down a trail to the grist mill. You can also walk down to the base of the falls.

For a special treat, as you leave the park turn right on Laurel Street and then right again on Villar Lane. Follow the signs to VVV Tours, or the Villar Vintners of Valdese. Here you can enjoy a tour of the small winery and enjoy a wine-tasting.

The winery is housed in what was once a barn where hand-milked cows produced milk for family needs. You will, if you are really fortunate, meet and receive a guided tour by someone who is a direct descendant of Waldensians who has made wine nearly all his adult life.

The guide, who conducts hour-long tours and explains every detail necessary to the making of good and great wines, explains that many Waldensians did not speak English until they enrolled in public school. The guide is likely to add that he could not remember meals in his home when there was not a bottle of good red wine on the table.

"Good wine and good fellowship" are the ingredient of a happy social life, the staff members say. "When we work at the winery, we have lots of help because we rest but never take coffee breaks," Joel Dalmas will add. "My grandparents made wine, none of it any good, but they didn't throw any away." Mr. Dalmas pronounces his first name as Jo-EL.

The wines here aren't thrown away, either. They range in taste, appearance, and bouquet from sweet to very dry and in quality from great to stupendous. The extra-dry wines are likely to be the best you will ever taste in this area.

A final stop in Valdese is the local soda shop, Myra's, where the taste and the cost are the way they were years ago. This is one of the few home-town eating establishments in the area, and the ice cream, the sandwiches, and the decor are calculated to cheer up anyone who somehow left Villar Vintners in less that a joyous mood.

There are no admission fees to any of the attractions, but you should call before visiting. Hours for the Villar Vintners are 1 p.m. until 6 p.m. on Friday, Saturday, and Sunday. But you can probably get in if you call and tell them when you want to come to visit. Call (828) 879-3202.

The Waldensian Museum is open on Sundays from 3 p.m. until 5 p. m. April through October. Open by appointment any day during business hours if you will call (828) 874-2531.

Lindsay's Miniature Village in Maggie.

SECTION 3: THE BEST TOWNS AND CITIES
TRIP 7: MAGGIE
THE LEGACY OF UNCLE JACK

LOCATION:

The town of Maggie and Maggie Valley are situated in the mountains of western North Carolina between Asheville and the Great Smoky Mountains National Park. To drive to Maggie and to Maggie Valley, follow I-40 west to Asheville. Remain on I-40 until you reach the exit to US 19. Follow US 19 until you reach US 19 Alternate, and follow this highway directly into Maggie.

NEARBY ATTRACTIONS:

You are close enough to several nearby attractions and cities that you can drive to them easily. You can combine the Maggie trip with one to Asheville, the Great Smokies, Blue Ridge Parkway, Waynesville, Sylva, Dillsboro, Bryson City, Cherokee, and, if you wish to make a slightly longer trip, to Fontana Lake and Fontana Village.

HOURS OF OPERATION:

Most business and attractions are open from 9 a.m. until 5 p.m. or 6 p.m., and restaurants are usually open by 11:30 a.m. until 9 p.m. Some of the attractions are open until 8 p. m.

ADMISSION:

Maggie is unlike some of the towns and cities in this section of the book because it is one of the largely commercial enterprises. There are many attractions in the area that charge admission, and these prices vary greatly. Call the individual attractions before you start your trip so that you will know what to expect to pay when you arrive.

FACILITIES:

At Maggie and surrounding area you will find campgrounds, some of them commercial and others federal, picnic grounds, gift shops and book stores, opportunities for rafting, kayaking, tubing, canoeing, hiking, swimming, fishing, and other outdoor activities. There are also medical services nearby.

WHAT'S THE STORY?

In Maggie Valley the real question is not what is the attraction but what isn't attractive. Few small towns in the state or in the South can offer so much in such a small space. But if we must list only a few attractions, the Lindsey Miniature Village is a delight, and there is the Ghost Town in the Sky as well as the Soco Gardens Zoo, which, though small, contains a surprising number of animals one would not expect to find in the North Carolina mountains.

MAKING THE MOST OF YOUR VISIT:

First of all, you need to know why the town of Maggie received its name. After all, it could as easily have become Jonathan, Cora, or Mettie. The story is that John Sidney "Uncle Jack" Setzer in the early 1900s had to ride his horse down the mountain to the old Plott post office to get the mail for the residents of the valley, and finally Uncle Jack decided that while you may not be able to fight city hall, you can take issue with the post office.

So he wrote to Postmaster General Frank Hitchcock and asked for permission to operate a post office out of his home, and the postmaster general asked him to prove the need for one. For months Uncle Jack kept track of the mail he picked up at Plott and carried to the valley residents, and when he submitted his findings, the government authorized the post office.

But the post office had to have a name, and Uncle Jack offered Jonathan (for the creek running past his home), and Cora, Mettie, and Maggie, after his three daughters. The post office decided upon Maggie, and the post office was established.

Maggie Mae herself worked in the post office from 1904 when it was founded to 1907, when she married Ira Pylant and the two moved first to Tennessee, then to California, and finally to Texas where she died in 1979 at age 88.

When you enter Maggie, you will see the Lindsey Miniature Village on the right, shortly before you reach the major business area. The address is 250 Soco Road. The Miniature Village features, as the name suggests, a complete village on a Lilliputian scale. There are the homes of Billy Graham, Carl Sandburg, Thomas Wolfe, and other notables. The Waynesville courthouse is there, as is the main street in Asheville at the turn of the century. The Biltmore train station as it appeared in the 1890s is a delight, as is the miniature train that traverses the village and outlying territory.

More recent additions to the attraction include the Magic Castle, which is an elaborate private residence in miniature, and the back lot area of the three-acre plot now includes a mountain, a fountain, and a "magic" rock. This miniature village is the only 1/12-scale work of its type in the United States. Hours for the Miniature Village are 10 a.m. until 10 p.m. seven days a week during the season. The attraction opens in mid-April and closes at the end of October, which is essentially the close of the leaf season, which attracts hundreds of thousands of visitors to the mountains.

Admission price is $4 for adults and $2.50 for students. You can also buy food, gifts, and books at the admission area of the Miniature Village. Call for winter hours.

At the Soco Gardens Zoo, which is the only privately owned zoo in Western North Carolina, you will find bears, snow leopards, wallabies and their families, llamas, emus, alligators, coatimundi, and other mammals, plus cobras, a fer-de-lance, pythons, and dozens of huge rattlesnakes. You can take a guided tour and see at close hand venomous and non-venomous snake shows. There is also a petting zoo as well as lemurs, monkeys, and other exotic animals. Admission is $5 for adults, $3 for children ages 5-10, and children under five are admitted free as long as they are with adults rather than with a group.

Hours for the zoo are 10 a.m. until 5:30 or 6 p.m. in spring and fall (no tickets sold after 5 p.m.), and in summer the hours are 9 a.m. until 8 p.m., with no tickets sold after 6 p.m.

Just on the other side of town (there are only two sides to Maggie) you will see the entrance to the Ghost Town in the Sky where you can enjoy more than 30 rides and shows, as well as the traditional gunfights, authentic Cherokee native dances, country music, a dance hall and saloon, and the roller coaster. The season runs from May 1 through October 31. Hours are 9 a.m. until dusk. Admission prices are $17.45 for adults and $12.45 for children ages 3-10. Remember that these prices, like all others listed in this book, are correct as of the date of printing. All admission fees may change without notice. Plan to spend about 10 per cent more than list prices, and if there is no increase, then you have 10 per cent more money than you thought you'd have.

For such a small place, Maggie has a large number of good restaurants that offer a wide range of meals, from family style country cooking to seafood, steak houses, and Italian foods.

Because of the seasonal nature of some of the attractions, it is advisable to call before making the trip in the late fall. You can reach the Lindsey Miniature Village at (800) 390-9422 or (828) 926-6277. Ghost Town in the Sky is (828) 926-1140 or (800) 446-7886. Soco Gardens Zoo is (828) 926-1746. You obtain a visitor's guide by calling (800) 334-9036.

Great Smoky Mountains Railroad in Bryson City.

SECTION 3: THE BEST TOWNS AND CITIES
TRIP 8: BRYSON CITY
THE LAND OF TSALI

LOCATION:

Bryson City is a small town with an enormous outdoors arena and an abundance of opportunities for the traveler to enjoy himself to the fullest. The town is located near Cherokee, Great Smoky Mountains National Park, Dillsboro, and Fontana Lake. To drive to Bryson City, take the US 23 and 74/19 exit, near Clyde, off I-40 and drive west. You will pass through Sylva and Dillsboro before you reach Bryson City. Both of these towns are small and the traffic is not a problem except during the peak leaf season in October.

NEARBY ATTRACTIONS:

In addition to the locations listed above, Bryson City is near Fontana Village, the Cherohala Skyway, Santeelah Lake, Nantahala Lake, Franklin, and Cullowhee, all of which are worth a visit.

HOURS OF OPERATION:

Stores and shops in Bryson City are usually open from 9 a.m. until 5 p.m., and the restaurants stay open from 11:30 a.m. to, in several instances, 9 p.m. A few diners serve breakfast as well. The major attractions in the town are open at 9 a.m. and close at 8 p.m. or slightly earlier. You will not find a horde of tourist attractions, but those you will find are delightful.

ADMISSION:

Be prepared to pay several dollars for the enjoyment of the attractions and opportunities. However, these joys are not in the least over-priced. You assuredly get what you pay for, perhaps more. A family might well spend $100 or more for one excursion, but at the same time you can spend the day in Bryson City and never need to spend a dime, other than for meals and lodging.

FACILITIES:

In and around Bryson City you can find campgrounds, picnic areas, scenic rivers where you can raft, canoe, kayak, swim, wade, or simply sight-see. There are restrooms, tourism office, medical facilities, and the amenities you can expect to find in any mountain tourist town.

SPECIAL ATTRACTIONS:

The Great Smoky Mountain Railroad is the best attraction in Bryson City, and the Island Park is a delight. The rivers and streams that flow through the area are treasures in themselves. Be sure to spend some time admiring the courthouse, and take a little more time to read about the history of the town.

MAKING THE MOST OF YOUR VISIT:

When you make your visit to the area of the Great Smoky Mountains of North Carolina you enter a world that is filled with excitement and beauty: a world of peaks rising thousands of feet high, of thunderous waterfalls that crash hundreds of feet to deep plunge pools, hundreds of thousands of acres of nothing but forest land, towns and villages that offer the charm and comfort of the best metropolitan areas but with living costs from another era, and beauty unparalleled anywhere in the South.

When you explore the Bryson City and Dillsboro terrain, and when you explore surrounding areas, you will find gorges, wild and scenic rivers, and literature and arts. You will also find tons of fascinating history.

When you reach the center of town, follow signs and turn left to the Bryson City train station where the Great Smoky Mountains Railway awaits. You can also catch the railway for tours into the Nantahala Gorge or to other locales by driving back to Dillsboro, which you by-passed on the way to Bryson City. In the smaller cities within a few minutes of driving time, you can find a great deal to see and do, but the starting point should be the Great Smoky Mountain Railway, which is one of the highlights of any mountain adventure.

Take along a wide range of apparel. You will probably need a jacket on all but the warmest summer days, and in the middle of summer rainfall or thunderstorms are common on any given day, usually in the mid-afternoons.

It is easy to walk around in all of the nearby towns and cities, but you will need good, sturdy, comfortable shoes. Some of the attractions are closed on Mondays, while others remain open all week during warmer weather. Call before planning your trip. Be alert while driving in this area in spring and fall. You can leave warm temperatures in the Piedmont and encounter snow, sleet, or freezing rains in the mountains. Be particularly alert in the early mornings and late evenings.

There are many good places to eat, some of which are very expensive but most of which are incredibly reasonable. You can buy a nice lunch for as little as $4.50 in some areas and you can pay as much as $30 for an elaborate dinner. Ask locals where they eat and you can usually find a place suitable to your tastes and to your budget.

You can find delightful scenery and activities virtually anywhere you go in this part of the state, and you can spend as little or as much as you like. You can take guided tours, train rides, or you can make your own auto tours or even walking tours. For one of the best ways to get to know the Great Smokies, you can try the Great Smoky Mountains Railway, which has offices in Bryson City, Dillsboro, and Andrews.

On the Great Smoky Mountain Railway excursions, you can take a train pulled by a steam engine or a diesel engine. You also can travel from the Andrews station to Red Marble Gap, a 4.5 hour trip with a one-hour stopover at Nantahala Gorge; the Nantahala Gorge train from Bryson City on a 4.5-hour ride deep into the Nantahala Gorge, with a one-hour stop at the end of the line before you start back; a third choice is to ride from Dillsboro along the Tuckaseegee River, with a one-hour stop in Bryson City. The Bryson City-to-Nantahala Gorge trip includes crossing the trestle over Fontana Lake and a stop along the Nantahala River. Here you can eat at one of two restaurants overlooking the river where there is a steady stream not just of water but of the outdoors enthusiasts who pass by in canoes, kayaks, or rubber rafts as they make their way down the river. The two restaurants are Relia's Garden and River's End Restaurant, both of which offer good food as well as outstanding beauty around them.

The Tuckaseegee trip includes riding through the famous Cowee

Tunnel, where a large number of workers (prison laborers) died in one of the worst tragedies in the area's history. The Red Marble Gap trip features, among other things, a ride up one of the highest railroad grades in eastern America.

A fourth option is the Twilight Dinner Train, a 2.5 hour trip that includes a gourmet dinner and narrated tour. This trip passes through the famous tunnel where the flood drowned all but one or two of the convicts working in it, and you also pass the train wreck featured in the movie "The Fugitive," starring Harrison Ford. You ride alongside the river Ford swam during his escape. Entrees offered on the diner trip include turkey breast, Chateaubriand, rainbow trout, roasted rosemary hen, loin of pork, salmon filet, chicken breast, beef tenderloin, and vegetable lasagne.

On your trip you might even ride in the car featured in the James Garner-Jack Lemmon movie, "My Fellow Americans," which was filmed largely in the Bryson City area and in Asheville. It would add to your fun to watch the movie, which has some delightfully enjoyable moments, before you make the trip. By doing so you can see much of the scenery and several business establishments that are featured in the movie.

Costs of the trips, which begin in March and continue through November, vary. The Twilight Dinner Train cost is $49.95 per person; Tuckaseegee River trip is $18.95 per person for diesel engine and $23.95 for steam engine. The Nantahala Gorge ride is $19.95 per person for the diesel engine and $24,95 for the steam engine. The Red Marble Gap train trip, all diesel, is $39.95 for adults and $17.95 for children on Friday and Saturday evenings. Saturday morning trips are $21.95 for adults and $9.95 for children.

Yet another choice is the Raft 'N Rail trip in which you ride the train to Nantahala Gorge and return by a seven-mile guide-assisted river raft trip. Cost of this trip is $52.95 for adults and $42.95 for children (diesel) and $57.95 for adults and $42.95 for children on the steam engine train.

Call (800) 872-4681 for more details.

Back in Bryson City you can visit the ancient Swain County Courthouse, a 1907 Greek Revival architectural structure that dominates the town square. In front of the courthouse there is a historical marker that honors Tsali, a Cherokee who gave his life so that his family and fellow men could continue to live in the western part of the state. Devote a little research time to the Tsali story before your visit, and later you might wish to visit the Tsali Recreation Area nearby. This man deserves whatever honors we can give him and his people.

Stop by the Bryson City Island Park located on Bryson Street one block from the railway depot. As you leave the depot, turn left and drive to the end of the street to find parking spaces. Cross a 150-foot swinging bridge to the seven-acre island where you will find a hiking trail and picnic facilities and a put-in area for rafters, canoers, or kayakers. At the infamous Devil's Dip section of the water there is a slalom course for experienced whitewater paddlers.

Historically, the most famous (or infamous) resident of the island was Ironfoot, whose real name was Ralph Clark. Ironfoot wore an iron stirrup attached to his leg as a crude replacement for his missing foot. Clark died in 1915 and was buried near Bryson City.

The story behind Ironfoot's lifestyle is that he was a member of the Jesse James gang and that he lost his foot in an explosion that occurred during a train robbery. He made his way to Bryson City and lived in a small hut on the island. Once, so the stories go, he was trapped there in a flood and had to climb a tree and remain there until the waters went down, and during this time neighbors provided him with food via a wire attached to a tree. There is no fee for using the Island Park, which was once named North Carolina Park of the Year.

For more history, visit the Bryson City Cemetery. To get there, start from the courthouse and drive west on Main Street to Arlington Avenue. Drive up Arlington one mile to the turn-off to the cemetery. In the cemetery you will find the final resting places of several persons key to the life and times of Bryson City in earlier days. One of these graves is that of Fannie Everett Clancy (1884-1904), whose burial place is marked by a marble angel that some local people insist is the same angel that novelist Thomas Wolfe immortalized in his most famous novel, *Look Homeward, Angel.*

Another grave is that of William Marcus Cathey, famed as the greatest of all trout fishermen and story-teller. One of his yarns is that, he said, it was once so cold that when he hung the thermometer outside the mercury dropped so fast that it jerked the nail out of the post.

A third prominent person buried there is Horace Kephart (1862-1931) who wrote *Our Southern Highlanders* and *Camping and Woodcraft.* He was also one of the driving forces behind the establishment of the Great Smoky Mountains National Park.

This cemetery is described in detail in the section on the best mountain graveyards.

Tweetsie Railroad at Blowing Rock.

SECTION 3: THE BEST TOWNS AND CITIES
TRIP 9: BLOWING ROCK AND BOONE
THE TWIN GEMS OF THE BLUE RIDGE

LOCATION:

Boone and Blowing Rock are almost twin cities that are separated only by fifteen minutes of travel along US 321, and by an endless stream of fast food franchises, souvenir shops, and an array of tourist attractions. From I-40 in Hickory exit onto US 321 and drive north through the outskirts of Lenoir and to the crest of the Blue Ridge Mountains. You will reach Blowing Rock first (although you will by-pass the town if you don't exit US 321 and drive directly into the city). Leave Blowing Rock, head straight up US 321 north and within minutes you will be in the center of Boone.

NEARBY ATTRACTIONS:

It is easy to find a multitude of attractions near both of these towns or cities. You are near the Blue Ridge Parkway, and you will pass under it between the twin cities. You are also close to the Moses Cone mansion and to Julian Price Park, both of which can be reached easily on the Parkway. You are not far from E.B. Jeffress Park on the Parkway heading north, and you are within easy driving distance of Grandfather Mountain, Linville Falls, Linville Gorge, Valle Crucis and the Mast General Store (and Valle Crucis has much more than the store to recommend it), Mount Jefferson State Park, the New River and New River State Park, Banner Elk, and Beech Mountain.

HOURS OF OPERATION:

Most of the shops in Blowing Rock and Boone observe the traditional business schedule of 9 a.m. until 5 p.m. Most of the souvenir and gift shops or handicraft shops are open until six or seven o'clock in the evening. Restaurants are open for lunch at 11:30 a.m. and for dinner until 9 p.m. as a rule. Some of the restaurants are open for breakfast.

ADMISSION:

There is no admission fee at the Moses Cone Manor, Price Lake and Julian Price Park, the Blue Ridge Parkway, or Jeffress Park, but there is an admission fee charged at the actual site of the Blowing Rock for which the town is named and at all of the commercial attractions along the highway between Blowing Rock and Boone.

FACILITIES:

You can find campgrounds both in the commercial field and on federal property. There is excellent camping at Price Lake. There are picnic tables along the Parkway, and the Price Lake picnic area is one of the finest anywhere. There are medical treatment facilities in both Boone and Blowing Rock. Restrooms are located in nearly all of the commercial establishments and at Price Lake. Gift shops abound along the highway and in towns, and you can find a wide range of specialty foods as well as general menu fare in both towns and on the highway between them.

WHAT'S THE STORY?

Boone is considered by many to be a college town. The campus of the school formerly called Appalachian State Teachers College (now Appalachian State University, a part of the University of North Carolina system) is for many the focal point of the entire town. Blowing Rock is viewed by many as a beautiful town with a near-perfect summer climate and as the summer residence for many who live elsewhere the remainder of the year.

Founded in 1903, Appalachian State Teachers College (which did not acquire that name until later) did more to bring life and vitality to the town than virtually any other influence. It was the college (and later university status) that brought some of the most fascinating people in the

South to Boone. One such person was the late Dr. Cratis Williams, who served as director of graduate studies and also distinguished himself as one of the foremost folklore scholars in the United States.

Blowing Rock, according to published sources, was once the dream of the best-selling novelist in America at one time. Thomas Dixon, a one-time resident of Shelby, amassed a considerable fortune by writing such novels as *The Leopard's Spots, The Traitor, The Flaming Sword,* and *The Clansman,* which became the basis for one of the most famous motion pictures of all time: D. W. Griffith's *Birth of a Nation.* Dixon, a former Baptist minister who abandoned the pulpit for the lecture hall and the writer's pen, also wrote the script for Griffith's film, which became the first epic film in American history.

Dixon, who lived from 1864 until 1946, decided to invest much of his fortune into a resort area in the mountains of North Carolina. The venture did not equal Dixon's dream, partially because of the economy of the times and partially because many people had escaped the mountains and had no desire to return.

A better explanation might be that Dixon's dream was too far ahead of its time, just as his social conscience might have been too deeply immersed in the past.

MAKING THE MOST OF YOUR VISIT:

There are several highly interesting and rewarding attractions in the area, including the Ashe County Cheese Factory in nearby West Jefferson in Ashe County. You can see the cheese-making process from start to finish on a year-round basis. The drive from Boone to West Jefferson via US 221 is about 10 miles. While you are in the area you can visit the two Episcopal churches where Ben Long, a native of Statesville and one of the foremost artists in the world, created the world-famous frescoes.

The entire town of Blowing Rock is a great attraction, and you will find shopping, restaurants, and bracing climate, particularly in the late fall and early winter. Wear warm clothing if you plan to visit late in the autumn.

Between Blowing Rock and Boone you will pass under the Blue Ridge Parkway, and at this point you are only a few minutes drive south to Julian Price Park, which includes camping, picnic areas, restrooms, and a spectacularly beautiful lake.

For your dining needs, the Daniel Boone restaurant in downtown Boone, on the fringe of Appalachian State University campus, offers good food and atmosphere.

While you are in Boone, however, do not miss the Appalachian Cultural Museum. This is a must-see visit, if you have interest in mountain living, folklore, antiques, mountain music, or the racecar driving of Junior Johnson.

To get to the Appalachian Cultural Museum, if you are entering Boone via US 321, watch carefully for signs. The museum is located on University Hall Drive, so be alert for either sign. You will need to be in the right lane in order to make the turn. If you are entering by way of US 421, you will turn left off the highway leading into Boone just before you reach the campus of the university. If you miss the sign, drive on until you reach the juncture of US 421 and US 321 and turn left. The campus will then be on your right, and you will turn left onto University Hall Drive.

The museum is open Tuesday through Saturday from 10 a.m. until 5 p.m. and on Sunday from 1 until 5 p.m. Admission is $2 for adults, $1.75 for senior citizens, and $1 for younger visitors from ages 12-18. Those under 12 and all ASU students are admitted free. For more details call (828) 262-3117.

The Daniel Boone Native Gardens (828) 264-2120 are located at 591 Horn in the West Drive. Here are collections of plants in an informal garden presentation. The gardens are geared toward the education concerning and preservation of the vegetation.

Located adjacent to the Daniel Boone Gardens is the Hickory Ridge Homestead, a group of authentic cabins. The homestead is open on weekends only, except during the performances of the drama *Horn in the West*.

Just outside Blowing Rock you will find the Appalachian Heritage Museum (828) 264-2792, which is the relocated home of the founders of Appalachian State University. This attraction is a living museum-that is, inside you can see people plying the crafts and skills that were once the basis of the life of the mountain family.

Nearby is Mystery Hill, where the laws of gravity, at least from an optical illusory point of view, are repealed.

One of the most delightful commercial spots in the South is Tweetsie Railroad on the Boone-Blowing Rock Highway (US 321). Here kids (and adults) can witness Indian attacks, gunfights, dance hall shows, and other frontier activities. The train ride is fabulous, and for one ticket price you can ride as often as you like. You can, in fact, enjoy all the activities to your heart's content with the one price of admission. You will note that the staff personnel at Tweetsie are among the nicest you will ever meet.

Tweetsie hours are, on the summer schedule, 9 a.m. until 6 p.m., seven days a week. The summer schedule runs from May 16 through August 30. After August 30 the attraction is open on Friday, Saturday, and Sunday each week from September 4 until November 1. During the final days in October Tweetsie presents a Ghost Train and Halloween celebration.

Admission to Tweetsie is $16 for adults and $13 for younger members of the family, ages 3-12. Younger family members are admitted free.

Inside the town of Blowing Rock you can see one of the most beautiful of all mountain towns in the state. You see a small lake as you enter, and inside the town you can stroll along the streets and visit shops, enjoy a meal, or sightsee. The rock that gave the town the name can be seen if you will drive along US 321 and watch for signs to the attraction on the right side of the road. The Blowing Rock is a huge cliff rising 4,000 feet above sea level and overlooking a gorge 3,000 feet deep where the Johns River has over the centuries cut its path deep into the valley near the rock. Here, locals say, the snow falls "upside down." The updrafts from the valley below cause airborne objects to sail upward rather than fall into the valley. There is an overlook, observation tower, and gift shop. Hours are 9 a.m. until dusk during the months of April through October. If the spring and fall are warmer than usual, the rock may be open during the months of March and November.

Call (828) 295-7111 for more details.

Book Exchange in Flat Rock.

SECTION 3: THE BEST TOWNS AND CITIES
TRIP 10: FLAT ROCK
BROADWAY IN THE HIGH COUNTRY

LOCATION:

Flat Rock is located five miles south of Hendersonville, in Henderson County. The town is just off I-26, which can be reached off I-40 in Asheville, by I-26 near Spartanburg, just off I-85, and by US 64 between Brevard and Chimney Rock.

NEARBY ATTRACTIONS:

From Flat Rock it's an easy drive to Hendersonville and Asheville to the north, to Brevard on the west, to Chimney Rock to the east, to Saluda and Tryon to the south, and to Lake Lure just east of Chimney Rock. You are also close to the Cradle of Forestry near Brevard and to Mount Pisgah, Devil's Courthouse, and Graveyard Fields on the Blue Ridge Parkway.

ADMISSION:

Some of the nicest attractions in Flat Rock are free, and yet others cost only two or three dollars. The only relatively expensive experience is also one of the very best you will find in the entire state and worth every cent it costs for you to see the attraction.

FACILITIES:

In and around Flat Rock there are restroom facilities, picnic grounds, medical centers, hiking opportunities, great photo possibilities, camping, and fishing. You may need to drive ten minutes or even half an hour, but some of the best outdoor adventures in the state are available.

WHAT'S THE STORY?

Flat Rock was, in a sense, at the time of its birth the North Carolina mountains' answer to Charleston. It was here that many of the wealthy families from the South Carolina coast came to build their summer homes in an effort to escape the heat, the malaria, and the other problems associated with coastal living.

In more modern times, off-Broadway professional theatre, a taste of Switzerland, a strong literary presence, an apparent reconciliation with socialism and capitalism, and a welcome mat to the world emerged from the past. Flat Rock became a miniature melting pot that fused cultures, life styles, the past and the present, and philosophic and artistic outlooks without problems.

MAKING THE MOST OF YOUR VISIT:

Don't miss one of the most fascinating churches in the state of North Carolina and in the South. While you are in Flat Rock, be sure to visit the

St. John in the Wilderness church, which will be described in full detail in another part of this book. For the present, take my advice and pay a visit.

The two other best stops in town are just across the road from each other. When you enter Flat Rock off US 64, intersect with the Greenville Highway, or US 25. You will see, after you turn left off US 64 and onto US 25, the church mentioned above. When you leave the church, drive back north and proceed slowly until you see signs directing you to the Flat Rock Playhouse, which is the official State Theatre of North Carolina.

The Flat Rock Playhouse is located at 2661 US 25. Call (828) 693-0731 for details.

The Flat Rock Playhouse has delivered professional theatre to more than 3,400,000 people-and a class act it is! The casts of the dramas, comedies, and musicals are top-flight in every sense of professionalism, and the crew behind the scenes create exceptionally good stage effects, from costuming to lighting to set design.

The Flat Rock Theatre staged shows that were seen by more than 60,000 people in 1996, and the number increases each year. For more than 50 years this professional theatre has been a part of the Flat Rock scene. To date, more than 400 different shows have been staged by this veteran group of professionals.

One of the great treats offered by the Vagabond Players is the staging of "Rootabaga Stories," a truncated version of the Broadway show "The World of Carl Sandburg" and "Sandburg's Lincoln." From mid-June through mid-August these shows are presented each week free to the public.

For the other dramas in the series, admission price is $20 per person for non-musical works and $23 for musicals. There are discounts prices for students (up to age 25) and seniors for each night except the Friday and Saturday evening performances. These discounts are half-price for students and $3 off for musicals and $2 off for senior citizens 60 or over.

Shows include such outstanding hits on Broadway as "Fiddler on the Roof," "Big River," "Dr. Cook's Garden," "Bus Stop," and "Cash on Delivery." Offerings range from murder mysteries to top-budget musicals, comedies, and dramas.

Fittingly, across the street from the theatre, at 1928 Little River Road, you can visit Connemara, the home of poet, biographer, novelist, and historian Carl Sandburg, whose monumental series of volumes on the life of Abraham Lincoln is among the most-honored works in modern American literature. Call (828) 693-4178 for more details. A more detailed description of the home of Sandburg and of the poet himself can be found in another part of this book: The Best of the Private Homes

You can stroll the grounds of the Connemara estate and enjoy the forest, the lake, and the garden and barnyard activity, as well as the rest of the 240-acre working farm. The hours for the house are 9 a.m. until 5 p.m. There is no admission charge.

For the remainder of your visit you can drive or walk through the historic town and enjoy viewing some of the beautiful and old houses. Or you can stop by the book store almost across the street from St. John in the Wilderness and browse through the varied selection of bargain-priced books offered by this neat and volunteer-staffed and non-profit store.

About 300 feet from the book store you can see the art on display in the galleries where the city offices are housed. You will be able to see Flat Rock, other than the dramas and the Carl Sandburg house, in about two or three hours.

If you want to see more of the Flat Rock area, drive south on I-26 to the Saluda and Tryon exits. Tryon is one of the finest small towns in the South, and Saluda is the site of the steepest railroad grade in the United States.

In both of these towns you will find friendly people, good shops and crafts shops. There are good restaurants in the area, and the scenery is excellent. The drive along the interstate highway is exceptionally attractive.

Near Saluda you can visit the Bradley Falls area. Leave I-25 at Exit 28 onto Holbert's Cove Road and follow signs. You are approaching a 10,000-acre wilderness with hiking trails, gorges, streams, and waterfalls. Call (800) 440-7848 for more details. No admission fee is charged.

At Pearson's Falls you can visit a 268-acre nature and wildlife preserve owned and operated by the Tryon Garden Club. You can walk to the 90-foot waterfall on the property and enjoy the beauty of the area. There is a small admission fee. Call (828) 749-3031 for hours and fees.

In Tryon you can visit FENCE (Foothills Equestrian Nature Center) where you will find 300 acres of walking trails, wildlife pond, and nature programs. There is no admission fee. Call (828) 859-9021 for hours. FENCE is located at 500 Hunting Country Road.

For another version of the waterfall highways of North Carolina drive along NC 176 between Saluda and Tryon to see the Pacolet River North Carolina Scenic Byway. Call (800) 440-7848 for more details.

Western North Carolina Center in Asheville.

SECTION 4: THE BEST
(DON'T TELL THE KIDS!) EDUCATIONAL SITES
TRIP 1: WESTERN NORTH CAROLINA CENTER
FACE TO FACE WITH NATURE

LOCATION:

The Western North Carolina Nature Center is located at 75 Gashes Creek Road, Asheville. To reach the Nature Center leave Interstate 40 via Exit 53B, which will lead you to Interstate 240. From I-240 take Exit 8. You will then be on Fairview Road. Drive north toward the Swannanoa River Road. When you reach a T-intersection and traffic light, turn right. You will see Gashes Creek Road on your right. Drive around a curve, cross a bridge, and climb a steep paved hill. You will see recreational equipment as you pass through the play area. The Nature Center is on your right as you climb the hill.

NEARBY ATTRACTIONS:

Within the immediate vicinity you will be able to visit Asheville and its dozens and dozens of attractions, which include splendid museums, great architecture, terrific shops, fine restaurants, local color, historic houses, and other delights. You are also near the Blue Ridge Parkway which will lead you, to the north, to Craggy Gardens and close to the home of Zeb Vance and to Mount Mitchell State Park. To the south you will reach Mount Pisgah, the Pisgah Inn, Graveyard Fields, Devil's Court-house, and the town of Brevard. On your way from the Parkway to Brevard via US 276 you will pass Sliding Rock Recreation Area, Looking Glass Falls, the Pink Beds camping area, and the Brevard Ranger Station which is adjacent to the Cradle of Forestry.

HOURS OF OPERATION:

The Center is open from 10 a.m. until 5 p.m. seven days a week. The Nature Center is closed during the winter holidays of Thanksgiving, Christmas, and New Years Day. The admission desk closes at 4:30 p.m. and no one is admitted after that time.

ADMISSION:

Fees are $4 for adults, $3 for senior citizens (age 65 and over), $2 for youths 3-14, and free for children 2 and younger.

FACILITIES:

You will find abundant parking, handicapped and stroller parking, a gift shop, restrooms, water, and paved walks all over the outdoor part of the center. The gift shop closes at 4:30 p.m.

WHAT'S THE STORY?

At the Western North Carolina Nature Center, which is owned, managed, and maintained by Buncombe County, you will find nearly everything relative to wild life in the mountains of North Carolina. The offerings include petting zoo (which closes at 3:30 p.m.), educational farm, exhibits, and dozens of other common and uncommon specimens of wild life, both animal and vegetable, in the state.

SPECIAL ATTRACTIONS:

A hands-on area permits adults and children to see, touch, and relate to some animal life, to observe large wild animals in a spacious environment, and to have a close and personal visit with mountain lions and red wolves. The Nature Center is known far and wide for the red wolf habitat where the wolves mate and their pups are reared.

MAKING THE MOST OF YOUR VISIT:

The most important part of your visit is to allow plenty of time. There is far too much to see and enjoy to rush your trip. Allow at least two or three hours, more if time permits, to savor the pleasures of the Nature Center.

Take the time to read the information presented at the various sites.

The materials presented are stated effectively and clearly, and you can greatly increase your awareness of the topics by a close scrutiny.

Start your tour at the Main Exhibit Building, where you will be able to touch a turtle, watch insects, view honeybee wings under a microscope, and an array of other forms of life. To continue the theme later, you can go outside and visit the very special World Underground and Nocturnal Hall.

When you go outside to continue the tour of the 42-acre park, you should keep in mind that none of the animals present were caught and taken from their wild environment. All of the animals were either injured or in other ways rendered unable to survive on their own in nature. So you are not seeing beautiful animals whose freedom has been wrested from them. You are seeing animals that would in all probability be dead if left to fend for themselves.

Here is a sampling of what you will see: wolves, cougars (sometimes known as mountain lions, panthers, or pumas), bobcats, bears (black bears, not grizzlies), foxes, eagles, hawks, owls, deer, wild turkeys, snakes of several varieties, otters, cows, goats, sheep, squirrels, and turtles. If it is native to western North Carolina, it is probably represented in the Nature Center.

You may wish to see the larger wild animals first, and in order to do so you need to take the paved walk to the predator habitat (which closes at 4:30 p.m.). Here you will see some of the fiercest creatures in North Carolina wild life. Among the predators you will see, in addition to the cougars, are the gray wolves, which are huge, majestic animals, and the red wolves. The animals are fed a balanced diet, and you should not feed any animals in the entire center.

The gray wolf, which along with elk, bison, and other large animals once roamed throughout North Carolina, is no longer part of Tar Heel wildlife. The red wolf is being re-introduced to the area with varying degrees of success. The cougar has disappeared from the wild, as well, except for rare and often unverified sightings.

Other animals in the Center, such as the bobcat, can still be seen, if you are lucky enough to get a glimpse, in the wild. The deer population in western North Carolina is thriving, as is the population of raccoons, foxes, hawks, owls, otters, and many other major wildlife forms. The eagle is making a re-appearance as well.

Visit the areas of your choice at your leisure. You may wish to examine the log cabin to see how it compares with other cabins you have seen on your various tours.

If you have small children, take them to the petting zoo area and let them become acquainted with the domesticated animals there. You will see many familiar farm animals, such as the chicken, cow, and sheep, but you may also notice some unusual heritage breeds at the Charles D. Owen Educational Farm.

Notice that frequently throughout parts of your tour you will see signs that say PLEASE TOUCH. These hands-on exhibits and displays invite you and your children to get to know the materials by handling them.

As you tour, don't miss the otters. These playful and graceful animals are among nature's aquatic acrobats. You will be amazed at their speed, maneuverability, and endless energy.

If you are at the Nature Center in warm weather, be sure to spend time at the butterfly gardens, which are behind the shrub garden and are just beside the Main Exhibit Building.

In fact, don't miss any of the Center's displays. Do not be content with animals only. Spend time in the Hummingbird Garden and Songbird Garden before moving on to the Fern and Wildflower Garden. The trip to the Western North Carolina Center can open your eyes-and your children's eyes-to the wonders, the beauty, and the fragility of Nature. It is a trip you do not want to miss.

Old Train Station and Monument in Old Fort.

SECTION 4: THE BEST
(DON'T TELL THE KIDS!) EDUCATIONAL SITES
TRIP 2: MOUNTAIN GATEWAY MUSEUM
THE ORIGINS OF OLD FORT

LOCATION:

When you approach the town of Old Fort via I-40 between Marion and Asheville, leave the Interstate on Exit 73. You will drive into Old Fort on Catawba Avenue. The Mountain Gateway Museum is on the right, on Water Street.

NEARBY ATTRACTIONS:

In and around Old Fort you can find several waterfalls, notably Catawba Falls on the headwaters of the river that is only a bold creek at its origin but grows into one of the largest streams in the state. In addition, you can find three museums, a geyser, and mountain music on weekends. Nearby you can visit Asheville, Black Mountain, Mount Mitchell State Park, the Blue Ridge Parkway, Lake James, Marion, gem and mineral digging, 60 miles of trout streams, campgrounds, hiking trails, and the Museum of North Carolina Minerals.

HOURS OF OPERATION:

The Mountain Gateway Museum is open daily from 9 a.m. until 5 p.m. and on Sunday from 2 p.m. until 5 p.m.

ADMISSION:

There are no admission charges, but donations are accepted. Receptacles for donations are located inside the museum, or you can give the donation to one of the guides or interpreters.

FACILITIES:

At the museum you can find ample parking, restrooms, drinking water, gift and souvenir shop, picnic area. Handicap accessible.

WHAT'S THE STORY?

In the mid-1700s white settlers moved into the area that was to become Old Fort. Because of unrest militarily between the French and Indians and the possibility that Indian warfare might break out, General Griffith Rutherford amassed an army at Quaker Meadows near Morganton and dispatched a contingent of 500 men to Catawba Vale, where they were to erect a fort at Old Fort Plantation. The community of Catawba Vale later changed its name to Old Fort.

SPECIAL ATTRACTIONS:

Within the town of Old Fort and just outside, you can visit ancient log cabins, a man-made geyser, enjoy one of the largest collections of Native American memorabilia, arts and crafts, handiwork, shops and studios, wood carvings and wood furniture, pottery, quilts, weaving, and art works, all hand-made. For more information call the McDowell Tourism Development Authority at (800) 237-6111.

MAKING THE MOST OF YOUR VISIT:

Old Fort, site of the three museums, a geyser, several waterfalls, and some of the finest country music presentations in the state mentioned above, is perhaps best known among tourists because of the Mountain Gateway Museum.

Old Fort, because of the protection offered by the original fort, became quickly known as the Gateway to the Mountains. As the Cherokee threat abated, and because of the need for more and better forms of transportation, the railroad began to move into the mountains. By 1869 the Western North Carolina Railroad extended to the town known as Catawba Vale, later Old Fort.

Old Fort is a small mountain town, but unlike most similar towns there is a great amount of activity and a large number of varied and interesting opportunities for recreation, sight-seeing, hiking, and general enjoyment. At the Mountain Gateway Museum visitors are treated to reconstructed but authentic mountain log cabins which are open for inspection.

You can learn the history of the cabins, and, best of all, you can get a real glimpse of mountain life by examining the cabins, inside and out. You will notice the ponderous logs, each of which weighs a considerable amount. As you study the logs, imagine how hard it would be for two, three, or even four strong men to lift the logs into place and fasten them securely. Then imagine how hard it would be for a single person, working without machinery of any sort other than crude implements, to lift the logs into place. Yet in some mountain homes a lone man sometimes started with a 20-foot to 30-foot green log in the yard and there he hewed the log into a nearly perfect shape and then somehow wrestled the log up the wall and into position.

Notice how amazingly smooth the logs were shaped, and pay particular attention to how well the houses were sealed. Even the doors, shelves, mantles, and all other wood included in the basic construction were shaped by broad axe, adz, and other implements used expertly by the mountain people.

Inside the Mountain Gateway Museum, you can inspect the old instruments in the Music Room, the inside-the-museum log house (or sections of it) which once served as Siloam Presbyterian Church, the first Presbyterian church in the county. The museum includes a superior collection of early tools, home-made toys, collections of exceptional photographs from the turn of the century, and compilations of home remedies for major and minor ailments.

The history of the town and countryside are inextricably involved with each other. Catawba Vale stood near the headwaters of the Catawba River, which, along with numerous clean and clear creeks, provided abundant clear water for fishing and other needs. The adjacent forests offered deer, bear, and other wild game for food and furs. Stretches of the river were suitable for canoeing, and the rich soil provided superb gardening locations.

Near the old railroad station is the Arrowhead Monument, a tribute to the Native Americans who once owned the land that the white man's encroachment took from them. You will see the unique monument almost as soon as you leave the museum.

In Old Fort the railroad became an important part of local transportation and economy, and it is fitting that the old railroad station now serves as the Railroad Museum. Inside the railroad station building you can see furniture and other items that were once part of the operating railroad. You can see the office and its equipment as well as tools and instruments used in the operation of the railroad.

In the Old Depot Museum, located behind the Arrowhead Monument, there is a maintained railroad office from the past. Inside, in addition to the traditional furniture and equipment, there is a collection of framed newspaper front pages announcing the major news stories from the Hoover administration to the Kennedy assassination.

Across the street is Grant's Museum, which is known for its outstanding collection of Native American artifacts.

Just outside town, off Old US 70, is the area known as Round Knob, where once a hotel stood. The train made regular stops at the hotel, and one of the tourist attractions was the geyser across the tracks. Known as Andrew's Geyser, the geyser attracted many people in the older days, and today thousands of visitors make the short drive to the location and enjoy a picnic lunch only a few yards from geyser.

Call (828) 668-3143 for more details.

Woody's chair company in Spruce Pine.

SECTION 4: THE BEST
(DON'T TELL THE KIDS!) EDUCATIONAL SITES
TRIP 3: SPRUCE PINE
WHERE GRANDFATHER AND BETSY ROSS MEET

LOCATION:

It is easy to locate Spruce Pine, a nice little town that is nestled in a mountain valley just off the Blue Ridge Parkway. From I-40 the easiest way to reach the town and its many varied attractions, exit at Marion onto US 226 and drive north. From the Parkway, exit onto the US 226 ramp and drive north about five miles.

NEARBY ATTRACTIONS:

Near Spruce Pine are such attractions as the North Carolina Mineral Museum, the art school at Penland, the Estatoe River, and Little Switzerland, as well as local Parkway attractions.

HOURS OF OPERATION:

Hours for most business attractions are 8 a.m. or 9 a.m. until 5 p.m. or 6 p.m. Some of the commercial attractions are open at 9 a.m. or 10 a.m. and remain open until 6 p.m. or 7 p.m. Call the various attractions before starting the trip.

ADMISSION:

Admission prices range from free to $5 and $6 for adults and $2 to $4 for children. At some of the local mining sites you are admitted free but must pay for each bucket or barrel of dirt or ore you receive.

FACILITIES:

At some of the attractions there are no facilities of any sort, and at others you can find nearly anything you want in the line of personal comfort and needs. These will be specifically detailed later.

WHAT'S THE STORY?

At Spruce Pine and surrounding attractions you will find authentic handmade chairs, grandfather clocks, mining villages, educational institutions, and museums, some of which are an absolute delight. Many of the locations offer superb insights into history, culture, and customs of the area.

SPECIAL ATTRACTIONS:

The North Carolina Mineral Museum is always an interesting place to visit, and here you will find the history of mining in the North Carolina mountains as well as samples of minerals and precious stones found in the area. You can also see samples of the clothing worn by miners and details on the use of the major minerals once they are mined.

Other places of special interest are Twisted Laurel Gallery, where you can see a showcasing of the works of 130 artists and craftspersons from Spruce Pine and Penland.

One of the best stops is at Woody's Colonial Design Chairs on the outskirts of Spruce Pine. This stop is described in full detail later. Stroup Grandfather Clocks is another stop you will not want to miss. It is also described below.

MAKING THE MOST OF YOUR VISIT:

If you arrive from the south via US 226, the first obvious stop is at the point where you drive under the Blue Ridge Parkway. Just as you emerge from the underpass, immediately turn left into the parking lot of the North Carolina Mineral Museum. If you are traveling via the Parkway, the museum is at Milepost 331.

At the museum, in addition to the displays, you can also find the local chamber of commerce where you can find information on other points of interest in the area. There are restrooms here, and you can picnic at the south end of the museum, although the picnic space is limited. For more tables and scenic views, drive south for 10 minutes on the Parkway to a roadside picnic area or to Crabtree Falls picnic area, which has an enormous number of acres and picnic tables.

At the Mineral Museum everything is handicap accessible.

As you drive into town, when you are three miles south of Spruce Pine-that is, within two miles of the Parkway area, you will see on the left Woody's Colonial Design Chairs, which is located at 110 Dale Road. Telephone number is (828) 765-4376.

Woody's chair shop has been operated by the same family for 150 years, and the current owners, Arval and Nora Woody, are fifth-generation craftsmen in the family history.

To give you some notion of what kinds of craftspersons the Woodys are, one of their chairs is on permanent display in the American Crafts Collection at the Smithsonian in Washington, D. C. One of the Woody chairs recently sold for $10,000 at a charity auction. National Geographic's publication, *The Blue Ridge Range: the Gentle Mountains*, features the work of the Woodys.

The Woodys are also featured at the New York Museum of American Crafts and in *The Craftsman in America*. In October 1997 the Woody chair company was featured by the late Charles Kuralt on one of his television segments.

In their showroom (there is no admission charged) you can see chairs like the ones the Woodys made for the Kennedy family during the Kennedy administration and Betsy Ross chairs.

The chairs are made after the style of ancient Early American structure which incorporates no glue or nails in the weight-bearing part of the chair. Chair posts are made from air-dried wood, and the backs and ladders are also dried and then the chairs are driven together so that the fit is incredibly tight. As the chairs dry more and more, the pressure becomes greater and greater.

The chairs are hand-waxed repeatedly until there is the basic equivalent of years of waxing so that the surfaces will resist ordinary scratch and scuff marks. If you want to buy one or more of the chairs, you can get them in oak, walnut, cherry, ash, and maple.

Cost of the chairs runs from $160 per chair up to $450 or more for a rocker.

If grandfather clocks are more to your liking, you can try Stroup Grandfather Clocks, telephone (528) 765-2765 at 102 Stroup Road in Spruce Pine. You can see some of the clocks on display at Twisted Laurel Gallery at 333 Locust Avenue in Spruce Pine. This gallery is discussed in greater detail later.

Stroup Hobby Shop, home of the grandfather clocks and other types of clocks, was formed in 1949 by the Reverend Mister H. M. Stroup, upon his retirement after a life in the ministry of the Baptist Church. While intended to be a hobby, the shop soon became the scene of bustling activity as Stroup made more than 900 clocks, which have been sold and delivered across the United States.

To date, the Stroups have hand-crafted more than 2,000 clocks, including the traditional grandfather, grandmother, cove top, French colonial, table, carriage, mantel, and schoolhouse regulator clocks.

At Twisted Laurel Gallery, where works from Penland artists and other area artists are on display, along with Stroup's many clocks, business hours are from 10 a.m. until 5 p.m. Tuesday through Saturday during the April through December months. In January through March the gallery is open from 10 a.m. until 5 p.m. on Friday and Saturday only, except by appointment.

The gallery is best-known for its glass collection but also features pottery, wood, fiber art, jewelry, clocks, and paintings by area artists.

To reach the gallery from the south, follow US 226 into town and cross the intersection with US 19E. Continue on US 226 until the highway veers to the left and as you turn right you can see Locust Street to the left. Take Locust Street, and within two minutes you will be at Twisted Laurel Gallery.

Cradle of Forestry near Brevard.

172

SECTION 4: THE BEST
(DON'T TELL THE KIDS!) EDUCATIONAL SITES
TRIP 4: THE CRADLE OF FORESTRY
THE BEGINNING TO PREVENT THE END

LOCATION:

At about Milepost 415 on the Blue Ridge Parkway you will see the turn-off to the Cradle of Forestry. In a few minutes after you leave the Parkway you can be at the parking lot for the historical forestry school.

NEARBY ATTRACTIONS:

From the Cradle of Forestry you are within a short drive to Brevard, a series of waterfalls like Looking Glass Falls, Mount Pisgah and the Pisgah Inn, Graveyard Fields, Devil's Courthouse, several great hiking trails, and super campgrounds.

HOURS OF OPERATION:

The Cradle of Forestry trails have no gates, but the site buildings and offices are open from 9 a.m. until 5 p.m. Call (828) 877-3130 or (828) 877-3265 for details. The site closes November 1 and reopens each spring in mid-April.

ADMISSION:

Fees for adults are $4, with $2 admission for children ages 16 and under.

FACILITIES:

Here there are short trails, gift shop with books, post cards, craft items, and educational materials for all ages, museum area, and restrooms. The site is handicap accessible at all points.

WHAT'S THE STORY?

Essentially, this is the area where the late Mr. Vanderbilt started the first forestry school in America, with Dr. Carl A Schenck as director. Under the brilliant leadership of Schenck, the school flourished. The goals of the school were to protect and conserve forest lands while teaching students how to make the most intelligent use of the forest land.

SPECIAL ATTRACTIONS:

The tour of the Cradle of Forestry is filled with special attractions, including information points, seedling nursery, Norway spruce plantation, sawmill, logging train, trout pond, and much more.

MAKING THE MOST OF YOUR VISIT:

If you plan to make the entire tour, be prepared to walk two miles for both trips. You will experience a vertical rise of 1,000 feet along the trails, which take at least 1.5 hours for a real visit. If you are not a hiker, do not worry, because the trips are along very easy paths. At no point is the walk tiring or strenuous. Frequent stops to examine the exhibits are restful, and there are no difficult areas at all.

The two Cradle of Forestry Trails are paved, but comfortable walking shoes are always appropriate. Plan to stop and spend the appropriate time at all of the displays and exhibits. You can get a real education concerning forestry.

Before you make the walk, spend a few minutes watching the short film about the Cradle of Forestry. You will learn about how in 1892 Gifford Pinchot founded the first forestry station, and he came to be recognized as the first forester in the history of the United States. He practiced his expertise for three years before Dr. Schenck arrived from Germany.

In the exhibit room you can learn the story of forestry as you tour and enjoy the exhibits. Younger children can relate with delight to the Forest Fun exhibit featuring puppets, puzzles, and costumes. There are also touch-screen video monitors which at the touch of a finger, literally, will let you select information topics relative to conservation.

The Cradle of Forestry takes you back to the beginning of the twentieth century (and dips, in fact, a little previous to that point) and you can see in action local craftsmen who ply the same trades and skills as those at the turn of the century did. When you go on the tours you can experience the same "tips" that Dr. Schenck offered to the first people who came to learn what the Cradle had to offer.

"Come to the Fair!" was the invitation extended by Schenck to businessmen, lumbermen, educators, politicians, and civic leaders of all types. He offered them a three-day excursion through the Biltmore Estate and Pisgah Forest so that he could demonstrate the techniques and results of his forest fair.

You can in essence re-live the excursion, but in far less than three days of exploring. You will make the Forest Festival Trail and use the same tips as those extended in 1908.

Tip 1 starts you off with the message from Dr. Schenck that Gifford Pinchot had pioneered and educated and a scientific forest management program with the object of making a profit for the owner of the forest and at the same time improving the forest with a diligent program of planting and improvement cutting.

Until that time lumber companies often simply cut every usable tree and then left the area denuded and prey to erosion, tangles of undergrowth, and scrub trees. These are the "eyesores" that Schenck discusses in Tip 2. Schenck wanted to restore the old forests that had been cut or burned. He relates how he first tried planting acorns and hickory nuts, but he admits that he had not calculated how much appetite squirrels and field mice would have for his work.

There were no nurseries in that day, so Schenck started his own where he could produce his own seedlings.

At Tip 3 you can see that Schenck was not a miracle worker. His experiments with the Norway Spruce Plantation proved to be disastrous in a sense, but Schenck responded by pointing out that we can learn much from failure. He then tried planting a huge variety of trees with different spacings to learn which would grow best and survive best. Tip 4 is the Conifer Plantation.

At Tip 5 Schenck laments the status of rhododendron, which he calls "the beauty and the beast of the forest!" The beauty part is obvious to everyone who loves the blossoms of the shrub, but the beast part is obvious, too: the thick foliage and the dense clusters of the plants are sufficient to create dark and impenetrable thickets or slicks where nothing else can grow. The floor of the forest is bare under the rhododendron.

The wit of Schenck is enjoyable throughout the trip. At the Tip 6 station he points out the improvement cutting to get rid of "the fellows which were 'no good'" and permitting the "promising boys" better opportunities to enjoy the light and nourishment. He says that the forest "...is a boarding house; when some boarders are gone, those remaining have more food to eat."

At Tip 7 Schenck points out that the portable sawmill was enormously successful because, with the poor roads, it was far easier to take the mill to the trees than it was to bring the trees to the mill.

Another "beauty and beast" aspect marks Tip 8, where there is a thick carpet of dead evergreen needles covering the earth and, as Schenck says, "quieting it." He notes that one fool with one match can destroy a forest in an hour, because the debris on the ground feeds the flames so well. The same debris prevents erosion and is a "blessing to the waters" because the compost holds in the moisture and keeps the soil soft so that rainfall can enter the subsoil.

At Tip 9 you see pines killed by the pine beetle and at the same time you see new pines replacing those killed. Schenck says that only the plow and fire keep nature from her work. Tips 10 and 11 deal with forest transportation. The logging train is of considerable interest because the geared locomotive was capable of pulling heavy loads up steep grades and around sharp curves. This meant that timber previously inaccessible could be harvested and the area replanted for future generations.

Tip 12 is an old farm site, Tip 13 is a hardwood plantation, and the final stop is Tip 14, the trout pond where fingerlings of trout were later used to stock the Pisgah Forest streams.

When Dr. Schenck founded the School of Forestry (now the Cradle of Forestry), he wanted the nation to understand what can be done with forests to create the greatest mutual good for man and woodlands. The result has been, historically, a better understanding of and a better relationship with our natural forest resources.

The Forest Festival Trail is one mile; the Campus Tour Trail is 0.9 mile if you hike straight through. The Forest Festival Trail trailhead is located just outside the back door of the visitor center. A wide paved walk leads northeast into the forest.

When you complete the Forest Festival Trail, begin the Campus Tour Trail, on the east side of US 276. The first stop is the community school and church behind the visitor center and to the left. The residents of the Pink Beds community, northeast of the School of Forestry, built the church-school where Dr. Schenck occasionally preached and regularly lectured to his students on the art of forest management. After visiting the school and church, cross the highway and complete the hike by walking the remainder of the Campus Tour Trail.

The second stop is the commissary, which Dr. Schenck had built for his students and for the community at large. The building served as a post office and as a snack bar for students needing food before leaving for their day's work.

The third stop is the ranger's house, where students sometimes boarded with the ranger. Students complained that the ranger's wife, Mrs. Gillespie, was a "stomach robber" and a wretched cook who couldn't boil water.

The office of Dr. Schenck is the fourth stop. Here, he and his secretary prepared and graded tests and prepared lessons. Field equipment was stored in the loft of the barn.

The Black Forest Lodge is a fascinating structure, built by Schenck in the style of the Black Forest in Germany. Several of these lodges were built strategically throughout the forest so that rangers could be on the lookout for game poachers, illegal cutting of trees, and forest fires.

The sixth stop is the blacksmith shop, where a traveling blacksmith made repairs, sharpened tools, and did the farrier or horseshoeing and wagon-repair work.

You will see where five cabins stood. Students rented and named Hell Hole, Little Hell Hole, the Palace, Little Bohemia, and Rest for the Wicked. One of the cabins, Hell Hole, still stands, in much the same shape as it was when Dr. Schenck left the Biltmore position and took his school with him. Inside the Hell Hole you can see snakeskins, a winning poker hand which some student nailed to the wall, and a circa-1900 version of the pin-up girl.

The eighth stop is the Draw Road, which is back across US 276. This road was used by the early settlers of the Pink Beds as a travel route when they drove their cattle to the Greenville, South Carolina, markets. Some even took their animals as far away as Charleston, South Carolina.

The remainder of the hike takes you past the garden spot for the school of forestry where corn, beans, potatoes, and other staples were grown. Near the garden is the old wash place, where residents made lye soap and did their laundry.

When the loop is completed, return to the parking lot near the visitor center. In 1976 the Cradle of Forestry was designated by Congress as a National Historic Site with the mandate "to promote, demonstrate, and stimulate interest in the knowledge of the management of forest lands."

The visit demonstrates how well the Cradle of Forestry has completed its mission.

Inside the Appalachian Cultural Museum in Boone.

SECTION 4: THE BEST
(DON'T TELL THE KIDS!) EDUCATION SITES
TRIP 5: APPALACHIAN CULTURAL MUSEUM
MUSIC, CRAFTS, AND JUNIOR JOHNSON

LOCATION:

Located in the city of Boone, home of Appalachian State University, the Appalachian Cultural Museum is found just off either US 321 or US 421 in downtown Boone. If you approach from the Charlotte area, you may take NC 16 to Hickory and then follow US 321 through Lenoir and Blowing Rock. Or you may drive north on I-77 to Statesville and then take NC 115 to Wilkesboro where you junction with US 421 into Boone. You will see signs on either highway as you enter Boone.

NEARBY ATTRACTIONS:

Near Boone are the Blue Ridge Parkway, the beautiful mountain town of Blowing Rock, Julian Price Park, the famous Tweetsie Railroad, and the towns of Jefferson and West Jefferson and their nearby parks, Mount

Jefferson State Park and New River State Park.

HOURS OF OPERATION:

The museum is open on Saturday from 10 a.m. until 5 p.m. and on Sunday from 1 p.m. until 5 p.m.

ADMISSION:

Cost of admission is $2 for adults, $1.75 for senior citizens, and $1 for younger family members from ages 12-18. There is no charge for those under age 12. Appalachian State University students are also admitted at no cost.

FACILITIES:

You can find abundant parking, restrooms, drinking water here. You can buy small souvenirs and gifts.

WHAT'S THE STORY?

The Appalachian Cultural Museum, as the name implies, is a showplace depicting the culture of the region. Here you can see and hear and touch history-whether the history of mountain living, mountain music, or even race-car driving.

SPECIAL ATTRACTIONS:

The town of Boone is interesting to tour by car or by walking. The town is neat, attractive, and boasts some of the best restaurants in the area. Many of these restaurants are geared to the tastes of college students, so expect a great deal of pizza and fast foods. But the Daniel Boone Restaurant, among others, is a fine place to eat. Nearby in Jefferson you can find the Ashe County Cheese Factory where you can see the cheese-making process from start to finish on a year-round basis. The drive from Boone to West Jefferson is about 10 miles. While you are in the area you can visit the two Episcopal churches where Ben Long, a native of Statesville and one of the foremost artists in the world, created the world-famous frescoes.

While you are in the Jefferson area you can visit one of the most famous restaurants in the state: Shatley Springs, where the amount and flavor of food is legendary and where the spring water (free to everyone, as much as you want, so bring plenty of clean containers, such as plastic jugs) is not only delicious but is also said to have amazing curative powers. So efficacious is the water that several physicians from around the country prescribe the water for their patients.

MAKING THE MOST OF YOUR VISIT:

While you are in Boone, the Appalachian Cultural Museum is a must-see visit, if you have interest in mountain living, music, antiques, folklore, or the race-car driving of Junior Johnson.

The first attraction you will see is the building itself. It is a striking edifice surrounded by beautifully landscaped grounds, and you will find ample parking near the two flights of steps leading into the museum.

Once you are inside the building, follow the exhibit patterns to the right and you will make a complete circle of the many fine samples of Appalachian life. Along the way you will see ancient musical instruments, clothing, tools and equipment, and even a miniature log cabin.

As you walk you will hear mountain music of an earlier day, back when tunes were simple and saturated in emotion or fun. At the log cabin notice the detailed work. Note how logs were squared and notched at corners. If you think this is easy, even with modern tools, try it some day. Keep in mind that this cabin style was built with primitive equipment and lots of sweat.

And if you think shopping is a drudge, take a look at how the mountain people obtained their clothing, quilts, table cloths, and other fabrics. One room is filled with early looms, furniture, and all the equipment that was part of the early textile mills: the looms and other apparatus needed in the real cottage industries.

Imagine, if you can, how difficult it must have been to use an axe, an adz, a crosscut saw, and other primitive equipment with which to make dimension lumber, posts, beams, and girders. Or imagine the energy and expertise necessary for the making of shingles for the home or out-buildings. With a drawing knife and a few other rudimentary tools the competent mountaineer could make lumber that rivals the best available from the most modern methods and technology.

Earlier the music was mentioned. Pay close attention to the tunes and the skills necessary for the production of the music. The mountain ballads themselves recall an earlier day and a more distant area, because many of the ballads had their origin in Scotland, England, or other European locations. Many a mountain child grew up hearing the songs from family members or neighbors and did not realize until decades later that these same songs were part of the culture of Elizabethan England.

Then turn a corner and come face to face with Junior Johnson memorabilia. It's not a time warp, but it's a realization. This museum is a beautiful tribute to the mountain people who knew and loved the land long before the Parkway and motels and chalets became a part of the scene. It's a time we cannot afford to forget.

Mountain Farm Museum in Great Smokies.

SECTION 4: THE BEST
(DON'T TELL THE KIDS!) EDUCATIONAL SITES
TRIP 6: MOUNTAIN FARM MUSEUM
THE HOMESTEAD "MALL"

LOCATION:

There are two basic ways of getting to the Mountain Farm Museum, which is sometimes referred to as the Oconaluftee Pioneer Homestead, from the interstate highways dissecting North Carolina. From the Charlotte area take I-70 north to I-40 in Asheville. From South Carolina leave I-85 in the Spartanburg-Greenville area and take I-26 to Asheville. When you reach Asheville, intersect with the Blue Ridge Parkway and drive south on the Parkway to Milepost 469. You are at the terminus of the Parkway, and you will find the Mountain Farm Museum here.

NEARBY ATTRACTIONS:

When you reach the Mountain Farm Museum, you are within easy driving distance of the Museum of the Cherokee Indian, Arrowmont

School of Arts and Crafts, the Cherokee Cyclorama, Qualla Arts and Crafts, and the Cherokee Indian Reservation. You are also at the beginning of the Great Smoky Mountains National Park.

HOURS OF OPERATION:

The Mountain Farm Museum is always open, and the adjacent Visitor Center is open from 8 a.m. until 6 p.m.

ADMISSION:

Because of the increasing number of visitors and resulting wear-and-tear on property, many areas have begun to charge a fee for admission. At this point, however, there is no admission fee. Great Smoky Mountain National Park is the most visited park in the nation, and you will find a fantastic world here.

FACILITIES:

At the Mountain Farm Museum you will find restrooms, drinking water, abundant parking, brochures, gifts and souvenirs, maps, and directions. There are picnic tables and campgrounds nearby for those wishing to stay overnight. Fees for camping in the Great Smoky Mountains National Park are as follows: Balsam Mountain, $10 per day; Big Creek, $10 per day; Cataloochee, $10 per day; Deep Creek, $12 per day; Smokemont, $15 per day. These rates change seasonally, and you are urged to call (423) 436-1200 for more details.

WHAT'S THE STORY?

When the early settlers from Pennsylvania, Virginia, and other states arrived in the Oconaluftee River area, they faced the task of building not just a home but a homestead in the broadest sense of the word: they had to carve from the wilderness a life style that was virtually totally self-sufficient. The Mountain Farm Museum is a sample of the life style faced and endured by the early pioneers.

SPECIAL ATTRACTIONS:

In the Mountain Farm Museum itself you can see an entire pioneer homestead, which includes the house itself, woodshed, meat house, bee gum stand, chicken house, apple house, corn crib, garden, gear shed, sorghum mill, barn, pigpen, springhouse, and blacksmith shop.

MAKING THE MOST OF YOUR VISIT:

One of the qualities that makes this living demonstration of a past lifestyle so interesting is the fact that "long ago" in this sense meant only 1901. The house was built by John E. Davis in 1901 from "matched" logs. What this means is that Davis took a huge tree, ripped the trunk down the center lengthwise, and used one half of the log on each side of the house. He did this on all four walls, with the result that the logs are perfectly matched from ground to eaves.

While Davis worked on logs, his two sons (eight and four years old) took a skid or sled drawn by oxen and hunted for and hauled rocks for the chimney from the far reaches of the homestead.

Because there were no nearby trading posts or supply houses, the homestead family had to provide for all of their needs. Their work included keeping and robbing bees for honey as a staple food and for sweetener. The only source of heat for winter warmth and for cooking was firewood.

Anyone who heats his house (as we do) by cutting and splitting his own wood can appreciate the efforts that the pre-chain saw era required. Heavy snowfalls often made wood gathering difficult, and the family had to keep a supply sufficient to last through the blizzards and during sicknesses which incapacitated the homestead head of the house.

The pioneer version of the supermarket meat counter was the meat house itself where the pioneer hung from poles (to keep the small predators from attacking the meat) the hogs, bears, and deer he had killed, dressed, and cured. Vegetables were difficult to come by in winter, and the meat was often the difference between being well fed and bordering on starvation.

In other outbuildings scattered about the farmstead, you can see the old-time apple house where fresh fruit was kept through the winter in either dried, natural, or liquid form. The same was true of the corn crib and its contents.

Of special interest is the blacksmith shop where the farmer used his sparse supply of metal over and over in many forms until it was reduced to nothing. Larger pieces of iron began as hinges, pokers, fireplace hooks, horse shoes, shoes for oxen, knives, hoes, and finally the smallest pieces were converted into nails.

Only by visiting the house and outbuildings can you begin to appreciate the efforts that went into the structures. Remember, these pioneers, even though they were fairly modern, did not have the opportunity to run to the building supply store and hand over a credit card in exchange for having the lumber delivered. These hardy people had to make their own doors, furniture, and all else they used, unless they were indeed fortunate. Weather was brutal in winter, and the blizzards were merciless. Help was nowhere near for many families, and they knew better than Ralph Waldo Emerson ever could what it means to be self-reliant in nearly every sense of the word.

Old Courthouse in Hayesville.

SECTION 4: THE BEST
(DON'T TELL THE KIDS!) EDUCATIONAL SITES
TRIP 7: HAYESVILLE AND MURPHY
YOU CAN GO HOME AGAIN, BUT THE WRONG
PEOPLE COME TO THE DOOR

LOCATION:

Hayesville and Murphy are about as far west as you can go and stay in North Carolina. The two towns are only a short distance apart, and you will find the drive there to be always (or nearly always) relaxing, scenic, peaceful, and beautiful. From Hendersonville, Brevard, or Highlands, stay on US 64 all the way. You make no turns and, with few exceptions, stop for no red lights. From I-40 the easiest way to Murphy or Hayesville is to exit the interstate at Clyde and remain on US 19 all the way into Murphy.

NEARBY ATTRACTIONS:

You are reasonably close to Lake Chatuge, to the Blue Ridge Parkway, and to the Cherohala Skyway. You are also near Standing Indian recreation area and to Lake Hiwassee.

HOURS OF OPERATION:

In these two mountain towns nearly all the downtown stores close at 5 p.m. or 5:30 p.m. The museums close at 5 p.m. and are open at 9 or 10 a.m. on a seasonal basis. It is better to call before starting a trip.

ADMISSION:

Nearly everything is free.

FACILITIES:

In both towns you can find overnight accommodations, public restrooms, nearby picnic areas, and plenty of places to eat, and while you may not find many expensive restaurants you will find good home cooking and some wonderfully warm people.

WHAT'S THE STORY?

The easy answer would be to say that there isn't a story at all. A popular television sitcom enjoyed years and years of immense popularity by basing an entire series on "nothing." And that is the case with these two towns. If you found that *Seinfeld* was about nothing, you will find the same thing here. On the other hand, if you enjoyed the delightful wit, social satire, and machine-gun style of comedy on the TV show, you will find these two places, while not comedy routine locations, to be wonderfully educational and informative. You can walk the streets, talk with the residents, shop, eat out, and realize that here, as much as anywhere else in the country, you have found America.

SPECIAL ATTRACTIONS:

Most people find the Cherokee County Historical Museum and the Fields of the Woods to be highly special attractions. Both are free, and both are well worth your time.

MAKING THE MOST OF YOUR VISIT:

Folks, you may want to stop reading here, or at least you may want to skip to the end of this chapter where something of real importance is hidden away. In the early part of the chapter you will quite likely be bored to death. Warning: do not read this while operating heavy equipment. On the other hand, if you are troubled by insomnia, this may be perfect for you. Read two or three pages and call me in the morning.

To leap in without further ado, Hayesville is a place near and dear to my heart, at least in absentia. Recently I called the Hayesville Chamber of Commerce and asked for information about the town. I explained that I am a native of Hayesville, having been born there on June 19, 1932.

But, I hasten to add, here's what I said to the young lady who answered the phone: "I'm a former resident of Hayesville, and you are the first person in my home town that I have spoken to in my entire life. And I have never set foot in Hayesville."

"You lived here?" she asked, with more than a hint of doubt, "and yet you never spoke to anyone? What about your family? And how did you never set foot in our town?"

I explained that I was born in Hayesville, but my family moved away during the summer of that same year, long before I had begun to talk. Or walk.

"And you've never been back to the place where you were born?" she asked.

I confessed that I had not. During the years following my family's removal from Hayesville I had traveled to Africa, to Germany, Italy, Austria, and Canada, among other places. But in the intervening years since we moved away I had never visited my birthplace; I had never even called anyone in the town. There was no one left for me to call.

Dozens of times I planned to go, and each time something occurred to wreck my plans, or I wrecked them myself.

Finally I admitted that I was intimidated by the ghosts that were waiting for me in the house where my mother, terrified, pushed against the back door to keep the bears from the house. I was frightened at the thought of confronting my Birth, of seeing the mountain house where I was born at 3:43 on the morning of June 19--also the birthday of Garfield the Cat.

I was a Great Depression baby, and my parents expected little and received less out of life. Even when I was a teenager moving painfully toward adulthood in a flatland town, far from the delightful place where I was born (I realized how delightful much later) I saw my father leave for work before daylight in the morning and arrive home after dark in the evening. Once, when I belittled the work necessary to keep a household running, my mother roused me from bed at five in the morning and invited me to work side by side with her for one day.

She sang, my mother always sang, many of the songs from sources that I would never have dreamed possible for a woman whose formal education ended in the second grade, as we toiled at tasks that never ended. We built the morning fire, baked 100 huge biscuits, a daily requirement for feeding our large family, fried bacon and eggs, did the washing, hung out clothes, chopped wood, and I was totally exhausted before it was fully daylight.

One by one our family dropped away-father, mother, older sister, two older brothers-until my brother and I were the only ones left who had ever lived in the house in Hayesville.

Driving into that little town was one of the hardest tasks I have ever performed. I dreaded seeing the house where I first saw the light of day, because my mind threatened to explode with the memories of who and what my mother had been. It had taken me years to begin to understand the ordeal of giving birth at home, working 18 hours a day without pay, suffering broken bones and having no money to pay for a visit to the doctor, nursing small children all night through early diseases, fearing for her life while she was at home alone with the children.

A dozen years ago my oldest sister, only a short time before her death, returned to Hayesville to re-visit the house where she had grown up, and she snapped a few photos with a little camera that barely recorded an image. Just before her death she gave me the pictures-"just in case you ever want to go back home."

So a short time ago I made the drive. None of my family knew where the house was located, so my wife, our son, and I drove around and around the town. We stopped people on the street and asked them if they could identify the house from the dim photo I showed them. Wonderfully kind people offered suggestions and even drove with us to look. No one refused to try to help.

We found only one house that even vaguely resembled the one in the photo, but the house had double windows rather than single ones, and there was aluminum siding in place of the wood in the house where I was born.

Discouraged, I started to leave, then changed my mind and knocked on the door. An elderly woman, her grand-daughter, and her great-grand-daughter were in the house. They looked at the picture for a long time without speaking.

Finally the grandmother said, "This house had single windows when I bought it years ago. I had the new siding put on not long ago. That's when I added the double windows."

I asked about a huge mulberry tree that had once grown in the front year. She nodded and said, "You can see the stump when you go out-side. Look under the shrub growing there."

I asked if she had received a visit from a woman who had once lived in the house. She passed the photo back to me.

"This is your house," she said softly, nodding.

I didn't have to be told. I *knew* it was my house--the house where I took my first breath, the house I had refused to visit for 65 years.

I could almost see my mother bending over the kitchen wood stove, sewing by the yellow light of the kerosene lantern, doing the thousands of things necessary to create a real home where real people can eat and sleep and work and create warmth. I could feel her there. Sixty-five years later it was still *her* house. No amount of redecorating or painting or adding furniture could erase the fact that this was my mother's house.

It was too much. I had to leave. I was unable to speak except in grunts for nearly an hour. I had never in my life felt the presence of an unseen human being more palpably than I had inside that severely simple house in a tiny town I had dreaded to visit.

I rushed away, to nearby Murphy, desperate to leave the town be-hind, the town where I began my life but produced no memories.

But I proved, if only to myself, that it is possible to go home again. There's no pain in going back to the house.

The heartbreak comes only when you knock on the door, and the wrong people invite you inside.

Now, back to the better stuff. In Murphy you can visit the Cherokee County Historical Museum at 205 Peachtree Street. There is no admis-sion charge.Call (828) 837-6792. Here you will find the heartbreak of the Cherokee Trail of Tears, the life of the early European settlers who came to the area, and you can see a huge doll collection.

On NC 294 outside Murphy you can visit Fields of the Woods, a 200-acre Bible park that has a book store, gift shop, picnic area, gospel theater, and nature trails. The highlight of the trip may well be the Ten Com-mandments carved into stone and covering nearly an entire mountainside. This also is free. Call (828) 494-7855.

In Hayesville you can visit the ancient courthouse, stop by a museum (also free) and just walk the streets of this nice and peaceful little town.

How is this an educational area? Aside from the museums, you can see, in technicolor addition, the simple and truthful way of life in a small town in the mountains. Life was not easy for the people there in another era. It was excruciatingly hard. But the people endured, rather as a symbol of the spirit of mankind and the indomitable quality of man's spirit. Look for me on the streets. If I'm not there, I assuredly want to be.

Holmes Educational State Forest near Hendersonville.

SECTION 4: THE BEST
(DON'T TELL THE KIDS!) EDUCATIONAL SITES
TRIP 8: HOLMES EDUCATIONAL STATE FOREST
MEET THE TALKING TREES

LOCATION:

As you drive west of Hendersonville (and east of Brevard) watch for Crab Creek Road off US 64. This is also known as State Road 1127. The road can be found about 1.7 miles east of the Transylvania County line. Drive south about 9 miles and watch carefully for Holmes Educational State Forest on the right. You must be alert, or you will pass the entrance without seeing it.

NEARBY ATTRACTIONS:

You are close to the two towns mentioned above and also within easy driving distance of waterfalls near Brevard. You are also close to the Blue Ridge Parkway, Chimney Rock, and the city of Asheville. Among the best attractions north of Brevard are Looking Glass Falls, the Cradle of Forestry, and Graveyard Fields and Devil's Courthouse on the Parkway. Mount Pisgah is also very close.

HOURS OF OPERATION:

You can enjoy the educational state forest from 9 a.m. until 6 p.m. daily except Monday, and you can camp there as well, and from this standpoint the area is open 24 hours a day.

ADMISSION:

There is no admission fee for use of the picnic tables, display areas, or hiking trails.

FACILITIES:

You can enjoy the picnic tables and trails mentioned above, and you can visit a series of displays that offer educational insights into the ecology, fragility, and future of the forests of the state and of the South. There are restrooms as well.

WHAT'S THE STORY?

In other parts of this book you have seen references to the Holmes Educational State Forest, which includes 235 acres of forests of trees that are native to the foothills and also to the mountains. The information here is more detailed. At the State Forest primitive camping is available, and there are regular nature programs offered. Call (828) 692-0100 for more details.

SPECIAL ATTRACTIONS:

The favorite spots in the forest are the talking trees, which tell about themselves and about the dangers that are always facing the forests of our nation. Children typically love to hear the trees "talk" and introduce themselves to visitors.

MAKING THE MOST OF YOUR VISIT:

This is one of the nicest sites for outdoor recreation in the North Carolina mountains. The fine picnic grounds are very clean and spacious, allowing plenty of room for privacy among the shady areas. You can park near the tables and not have to carry your picnic baskets long distances. In summer it is typically nice and cool in the wooded area.

After eating you can take short or long hikes and learn a great deal about the forest and about the trees individually and collectively. The "talking trees" delight the young ones as the trees "tell" about themselves, about the area, and about the history of the forest. At the Forestry Center you and your family can learn about managed forests, conservation and ecology, and through ranger programs. You can also camp in the forest on a walk-in basis, but you must have reservations before you arrive. The forest was named for John Holmes, who had the honor of serving as the first forester in North Carolina. Holmes lived from 1868 until 1958. The state forest served as a Civilian Conservation Corps Camp in the middle of the Great Depression and did not become a state forest until 1972.

If you want to take a nice, comfortable (most of the time), and occasionally challenging trail, you might want to try the Cliffside Demonstration Trail, which is 2.8 miles long. For the greatest enjoyment, hike the trail in the crisp, cool months, such as October, late September, April, and early May. This is a fine nature-study trail that brings you into contact with many of the 125 species of flowering plants or shrubs that grow in the forest.

There are study sites spaced along the trail, and at each of these you can see and learn about many of the problems facing the forests and how you can be a part of forest ecology. You will have the chance to learn (and the kids may be surprised by this) of the vast and incredibly important roles the forests play in our daily lives.

You will see a small pond, be able to enjoy a scenic overlook, and stretch your muscles on rather steep slopes that return you eventually to the forestry center.

You can take a shorter hike, if you wish, also starting at the forestry center and returning to the starting point. This hike is .8 mile and is marked with green blazes. You will see a wide variety of trees which are identified with information markers so that you can enjoy what you are seeing and learn the importance of each forest sample. These are the trees that will talk to you and tell you about their history, use, importance, and reasons for sound ecology practices. You will also cross a small series of cascades.

Contact the rangers for information on free programs that are offered to help the general public understand the history and value of forests. You can write to the Forest Supervisor at Box 308, Route 4, Hendersonville.

If the kids have special field trips or nature study projects due at school, this can be an excellent place for them to start their studies. It's also a great place for adults to re-learn the necessary lessons about forest protection.

Scottish Tartans Museum in Franklin.

SECTION 4: THE BEST
(DON'T TELL THE KIDS!) EDUCATION SITES
TRIP 9: SCOTTISH TARTANS MUSEUM
AND HERITAGE CENTER
THERE IS NOTHING *WORN* UNDER THE KILTS

LOCATION:

The Scottish Tartans Museum and Heritage Center can be found at 95 East Main Street in Franklin, North Carolina. To get to the Center from I-40, exit I-40 at Clyde and follow US 23 and US 74 south to Sylva and Dillsboro. From there take US 23 and US 441 south to Franklin. If you want to get to Franklin from Brevard, follow US 64 west through Highlands to Franklin.

NEARBY ATTRACTIONS:

From Franklin you can drive back to Highlands and enjoy the magnificent Cullasaja Gorge, including Cullasaja Falls, or drive west to Hayesville (the birthplace of this author) and Murphy. You are very near to Standing Indian recreation area and to the superb crafts school at Brasstown. By way of US 19 out of Murphy you can drive northeast to Robbinsville and Big Santeelah Lake.

HOURS OF OPERATION:

The museum is open from 10 a.m. until 5 p.m. Monday through Saturday and on Sunday from 1 p.m. until 5 p.m.

ADMISSION:

Admission fees are quite modest, and the attractions are well worth the cost--and more! Fees for adults are $2; seniors age 55 and over pay $1, and children under 12 are admitted free. All students are admitted for $1. This museum is a nonprofit organization, and the fees are used to offset operation costs.

FACILITIES:

There are restrooms, and you will find a delightful gift shop featuring all things Scottish and unique, from books to CDs and tapes to maps and virtually anything else that has to do with the Scottish tartans and related topics.

WHAT'S THE STORY?

The Scottish Tartans Museum and Heritage Center is the only United States branch or extension of the Scottish Tartans Society in Edinburgh. Here you will find incredibly knowledgeable people who will cheerfully and enthusiastically answer all questions that relate to the Scottish Tartans.

SPECIAL ATTRACTIONS:

The Scottish historic costumes and military relics are among the thoroughly interesting exhibits inside the museum. You will also find cultural programs and weaving demonstrations.

MAKING THE MOST OF YOUR VISIT:

One of the oldest jokes in the world is that antiquated chestnut about the woman who asked the Scottish man what is worn under the kilts. The man responded, "I'm a man of few words: give me your hand."

Ask at the Scottish Tartans Museum and Heritage Center and you will receive another answer concerning what is worn under the kilts. "There is nothing *worn* under the kilts," you may well be told. "Everything works as well as it ever did."

But the museum is not a joke. It is one of the most novel and informative places you are likely to find in North Carolina and in the South or, for that matter, in the nation.

First, there is an awesome and official registry of all the publicly known tartans in Scottish background and history. If in all your ancestry there is anyone who can claim any Scottish blood, you can in all probability find your family tartan.

You will also learn immense amounts about William Wallace and Robert the Bruce and the Battle of Bannockburn. And you will learn, if you wish, the stories of Rob Roy as well as the impact of a fairly recent Mel Gibson movie on interest in all things that are Scottish. And, it goes almost without saying, if you have any interest in Robert Burns, you will find enthusiastic and complete information on the man and his poetry.

In fact, the official greeting you are likely to receive will be "Ceud Mile Failte" (or at least something that sounds very much like that) which means "A thousand welcomes."

This is not an idle phrase; it is heartfelt, and you will receive ample evidence of the sincerity of the welcome.

You will learn very quickly that Murphy's Law (You remember the essential message: Anything that can go wrong, will) had its origin in a poem by Bobby Burns entitled "To a Mouse." In the poem Burns writes, "The best-laid schemes o' mice an' men gang aft agley, an' leave us naught but grief an' pain, for promised joy!"

Don't leave the mouse at this point. Pay strong attention to the following wonderful and touching (and often true) lines: "Still thou are blest, compared wi' me! The present only toucheth thee; But och! I backward cast my e'e, on prospects drear! An' forward, though I canna see, I guess an' fear!"

If you really want to make the most of your visit, take time to read more Robert Burns poetry. Read "To a Louse" in which Burns writes, "O wad some Power the giftie gie us/ To see oursels as ithers see us!/ It wad frae monie a blunder free us, / An' foolish notion:/ What airs in dress an' gait wad lea'e us,/ An' ev'n devotion!"

Add to the list "Address to the Unco Guid, or the Rigidly Righteous," "Auld Lang Syne," (Yes, this is the man who wrote the world-famous New Years song!) and "Tam O'Shanter."

No, go all out and read tons of Bobby Burns before you make the trip. You'll find much to keep your ego in check. And if you want to see one of the first stirrings of real Democracy in the English-speaking world, try "A Man's a Man for A' That."

Read of Wallace and his efforts to make and keep Scotland free; read of Robert the Bruce. In this (and any other visit) the more you take with you, the more you will bring away with you.

But why go to all this trouble, just to visit a museum? For one thing, no other country of comparable size (Scotland is about the size of South Carolina), other than Ireland, has had such an effect on the United States. You may be shocked to learn that there are more people of Scottish blood in North Carolina than in any other country in the world, except Scotland.

You will receive an in-depth education about the male kilt and its uses. For instance, the kilt serves as an overcoat, a game bag, a blanket, and a tent, among other uses. A surprisingly large garment, the tartan is nine yards long, and, according to at least once source, it gave us the expression "the whole nine yards."

Examine the weapons on display, and keep in mind that the High-landers, faces painted blue, were among the most feared warriors in history--the Ladies from Hell. But women did not wear the male kilt. The military prowess of the Highlanders became well known in World War II and in earlier conflicts, including but not limited to the Crimean War, out of which the phrase "Thin Red Line" emerged in the poetry of Kipling and Tennyson.

While you are in the area explore the history of Franklin, which was originally known as Nikwasi Village. Ages ago the village was on the trading route from Charleston, and many of the people who came here married into Indian tribes. During one big battle the Scots in the villages could not take sides because they were related by marriage to the enemy.

Take great anticipation with you as you travel, and take away a little bit of Scotland when you leave.

Folk Art Center in Asheville.

SECTION 4: THE BEST
(DON'T TELL THE KIDS!) EDUCATIONAL SITES
TRIP 10: FOLK ART CENTER
HAND (AND EXPERTLY!) MADE IN AMERICA

LOCATION:

The Southern Highlands Craft Guild Folk Art Center can be found with incredible ease. From I-40 in Asheville exit onto the Blue Ridge Parkway and drive north. About one mile after you pass over US 70 you will see signs on the left that direct you to the Folk Art Center. If you are driving US 25 or I-26 north of the Greenville-Spartanburg area, you will intersect with the Parkway just outside Asheville. Then drive north until you see signs that direct you to the Folk Art Center.

NEARBY ATTRACTIONS:

You are so close to Mount Mitchell, Craggy Gardens, and Crabtree Meadows (and Crabtree Falls) north of Asheville that you can visit these places easily. South (and into Asheville) you can find hundreds of great places to visit, and you can drive east to the Mountain Gateway Museum or south to Hendersonville, Flat Rock, and Brevard for more recreational opportunities.

HOURS OF OPERATION:

The Folk Art Center is open daily all year round except for Thanksgiving, Christmas, and New Years Day. Hours are 9 a.m. until 5 p.m. January through March and 9 a.m.until 6 p.m. during April and through December. If the Parkway is closed, don't make the trip. Call (828) 298-7928 to verify operation hours so you won't make a fruitless trip.

ADMISSION:

There is no admission charge, but you may make donations or contributions (which are tax-deductible), if you wish.

FACILITIES:

There are restrooms, abundant parking space, and 30,000 feet of displays and crafts for sale.

WHAT'S THE STORY?

The Folk Art Center is a by-product of the Appalachian Regional Commission and the Southern Highland Handicraft Guild. The combined efforts of these organizations serve a nine-state region and offer for sale crafts made authentically by local or area craftspersons.

SPECIAL ATTRACTIONS:

The Folk Art Center periodically changes its exhibitions and inventory. The most special part of the exhibits is often the new displays, particularly the in-progress handicraft work.

MAKING THE MOST OF YOUR VISIT:

Have you tried your hand at genuine crafts work? If you have, then you have a notion of how incredibly hard it is to create some of the handicrafts that you will see in the Folk Art Center. If you have not tried it, then you should do so in order to appreciate fully the skills and talents necessary to make the many items you see on display.

For instance, have you ever tried to carve a bird in flight? For that matter, have you tried to carve a simple child's whistle? Or whimmydiddle?

The old joke (very old!) is that to carve a bear, get a huge block of wood and cut away anything that doesn't look like a bear. As you can guess, this is far more difficult than it sounds, and it sounds extremely difficult.

The key to your visit is pacing yourself. Take your time and see what there is to enjoy. There are usually large displays of regional, local, area crafts, which in turn are of local, area, regional, and national (or international) appeal.

What you will see depends upon when you are there. You may get lucky and see an incredible array of hand-crafted chairs of all sorts, and it is possible that you will see the in-progress work of the craftspeople or artists.

At almost any time you visit, you will see demonstrations of age-old crafts. The Folk Art Center, in addition to the displays, is also the home of the century-old Allanstand Craft Shop, which features the work of guild members.

The second or upper level of the Center contains museum space and guild offices and the impressive craft library. In the main display area you will regularly have the opportunity to see not only work of guild members but also traveling exhibits that are selected with an eye to the interests of members and visitors to the Center.

Among the many exhibits you will see are quilts (and these are incredibly beautiful and often marvelously intricate), rugs, pottery, baskets, floral arrangements, dolls, doll clothing, stools, picture frames, and almost anything else you can think of in the way of folk arts.

You can buy craft items that are displayed in the Center. And when you buy you can do so with the confidence that the items you purchased were not imported from a foreign country. All of the inventory of the Center is genuine craftwork of artisans who are accepted experts in the art.

The Southern Highland Handicraft Guild is funded by gifts and grants from a variety of foundations, corporations, and other institutions and from the sale of crafts in the Center.

The Gallery, Museum, and Craft Shop close several times each year for changing exhibits. Call before you go to see what will be exhibited at the time of your visit.

Tiny Caudill Cabin at Doughton Park.

SECTION FIVE: THE BEST OF THE GET-OUT-AND-GO PLACES
TRIP 1: DOUGHTON PARK
THE COURAGE OF THE CAUDILLS

LOCATION:

You can reach Doughton Park easily from I-40 by exiting at Statesville onto I-77 north. Leave I-77 in Elkin and take US 21 north toward Sparta. Shortly before you reach Sparta you will intersect with the Blue Ridge Parkway. Drive south for 15 minutes to Doughton Park. You can also leave I-40 at Statesville and take NC 115 north to Wilkesboro and then follow NC 18 north to the Blue Ridge Parkway. Drive north for 15 minutes and you will again be at Doughton Park, one of the most beautiful locations on the Parkway and in the state, in the South, and in the nation.

NEARBY ATTRACTIONS:

Within easy driving distance of Doughton Park are the towns of Jefferson and West Jefferson, Sparta, Wilkesboro, New River State Park, Stone Mountain State Park, and Mount Jefferson State Park.

HOURS OF OPERATION:

The park is open seven days a week, 24 hours a day every day of the year, unless the Parkway is closed because of bad weather. The restaurant may be closed, but the attractions is always open.

ADMISSION:

There are no admission fees charges at Doughton Park, unless you plan to camp. For campers, you must pay $10 per night. In the two camping areas there are tent sites, and trailer-RV sites.

FACILITIES:

In addition to the campgrounds, there are restrooms and picnic grounds. There are also hiking trails, trout streams in the area, and historic sites, such as the Brinegar Cabin on the north side of Doughton Park.

WHAT'S THE STORY?

Doughton Park is a 6,000 acre expanse of wilderness with only one highway, the Blue Ridge Parkway, reaching it. Named after Congressman Robert Lee Doughton, the park has 36 miles of hiking trails, superb overlooks, the historic cabin of Martin Caudill and his wife and children, and the Little Glade Mill Pond, a beautiful place to stop for quiet and serene nature study.

MAKING THE MOST OF YOUR VISIT

The Get-Out-and-Go visits are, as the name implies, sites where you are not offered only attractions that can be reached by automobile. This is a place where you can, if you wish, leave the car at the parking lot and start to explore the terrain.

The Little Glade Mill Pond may be your first stop, if you arrive from the north. Here is a small and picturesque body of water that invites people of all ages. The kids can stand at the edge of the water and see several species of fish and various other forms of wild life. If you are patient for a few minutes you may see muskrats, perhaps a beaver, even a mink gliding its way through the water. There are frogs, tadpoles, crayfish, and salamanders in the water, and in the trees beyond there are many species of song birds and birds of prey, including hawks and owls. There is a small trout stream behind the pond, and you can walk around the pond and then step into the woods to catch a glimpse of the native fish in the stream.

There are water snakes in the pond, too, but they are not likely to do more than perhaps startle you.

At the Brinegar Cabin you can make a visit into the past to enjoy the way the pioneers in the area lived. The cabin is highly authentic, as are the skills and crafts practiced by the persons at the cabin. If you are lucky you might see the actual weaving or spinning process on the earliest equipment.

Outside there is a garden where the mountain family grew its own vegetables and spices for the kitchen table.

You may notice a hiking trail leading across the ridge near the Brinegar cabin. You can take the trail south to Wildcat Rock and from there south to the end of the park, if you wish. It is a fairly long and at times strenuous trail that wanders for 7.5 miles without ever straying far from the Parkway. You will find a vertical rise of 2,160 feet if you hike the entire trail, which leads through some spectacular forests and over picturesque hills and valleys. You stand an excellent chance of seeing deer and other animals if you hike near sunrise or sunset.

If you are in excellent shape, try the trail from south to north. If you are not superbly conditioned, you may want to hike from north to south. The trail is much easier in this direction.

Drive (or walk) to Wildcat Rock (the picnic tables are located near the parking area) and park in the paved area. Climb the short flight of steps and the narrow trail to the Wildcat Rock Overlook from which you can see, almost one mile below, the cabin and small clearing where the Martin Caudill family lived.

There is a makeshift trail leading down the slope of the hill straight to the cabin. I do not suggest that you take this trail, although you may see others attempting it. This is not only a highly strenuous trek; it can also be a dangerous one.

If you want to see the cabin close-up, you can drive a few miles and try the Basin Creek Trail, which is 10.9 miles round trip. Drive south on the Parkway to the exit for NC 18 to the town of Wilkesboro. Follow this highway south for six miles to Longbottom Road (State Road 1728). Turn left and drive for four miles to State Road 1730. Take SR 1730 for three miles to a bridge over a trout stream. Here you will see a place to park and the entrance to Grassy Gap Fire Road.

If you hike this trail, you will ford the creek several times, so be prepared to carry along dry socks, to wade barefoot, or hike in soggy socks. As you hike you will pass a series of old chimneys, a millstone lying in the creek, and other evidence of a once-vital village. The houses in this area were washed away by the tragic flood of 1916. The Caudill Cabin is one of the few that survived one of the most devastating floods in the history of North Carolina.

Martin Caudill's cabin is at the end of the trail. When you reach the cabin you will see that the residence, where Caudill and his wife reared their 17 children, is little more than a hut. There are cracks in the walls and in the floor, and there is very little room inside the cabin.

You can imagine the family huddled around the tiny wood stove as the high winds and sub-zero temperatures chilled the valley and clearing where deer, bear, foxes, and other animals once roamed the forests. Or imagine the family sleeping in the tiny loft or in the family part of the structure.

Far more dramatic, in a sense, is to imagine the family as they made the trek you just completed whenever they wanted to buy or trade for flour, coffee, or other staples. Any time any member of the family wanted to visit "civilization," that person had to make the 10.9 mile hike and cross the same creek you crossed about a dozen times on your trip in.

When you have hiked to your heart's content (and legs' limits), you may wish to drive through Doughton Park in both directions near sundown. In warm weather you can see a number of woodchucks or groundhogs alongside the road.

If you don't know the story of these burrowing creatures, take a few minutes here to learn about them. You may be shocked to learn that the legend of the groundhog and his shadow has its basis in the history of the early Christian church.

First of all, the ground hog, while a rodent, is placed in the same general biological family as the squirrel. It is on February 2 that we celebrate groundhog day, and the legend is that if the woodchuck sees his shadow, there will be six more weeks of bad weather, or winter. Now, here comes the connection to Candlemas, a strong Christian tradition.

Candlemas, which is also observed on February 2, marks the occasion in which Mary, in accordance with Jewish law, went to the city of Jerusalem to be purified 40 days after giving birth to a son. At the same time she was to present Jesus to God as her first-born child.

In European culture the animal in hibernation was often the badger or the bear, and the groundhog made his appearance during this same time period. No matter what the animal, the legend was that if the bear, badger, or groundhog saw his shadow, he became frightened and returned to his burrow to wait until danger had passed. If the day was cloudy and he saw no shadow, he stayed out in the fresh air and the winter ended quickly.

And on Candlemas, an old English song became popular. The song, in part, says, "If Candlemas be fair and bright, Come, Winter, have another flight. If Candlemas bring clouds and rain, Go, Winter, and come not again."

A very clean animal, the groundhog, or woodchuck, has a neat den at the end of his burrow, but the den is elevated above the rodent's bathroom, as such. The animal is careful to leave body waste only in the predetermined location. Incidentally, when he hibernates, the groundhog's body temperature drops from 98.9 degrees to 37.4 degrees, and his heartbeat drops from an active rate of 80 beats per minute to only four or five beats per minute.

While the rodent's burrows can be a danger to horses and cattle, these same burrows allow rainfall to penetrate deeper into the ground and keep the land moist and nourishing to the plants growing there. These burrows also offer protection for rabbits in both winter and summer.

When you see the animals along the Parkway, keep in mind that there are seldom horses, cattle, or crops here, and the groundhog is simply fun to watch.

So, when you are driving around in Doughton Park, or elsewhere in the mountains, and you see the woodchuck, remember his role in the traditional Christian heritage, particularly during Candlemas. There are even parts of North Carolina where families observe groundhog day in an interesting fashion. Each person buys two types of gifts: one for other members of the family and one for himself, something he really wants but knows that no one else will buy him or her.

Part of the fun lies in opening the gifts others bought for you, but it is often more fun to see what the other family members bought for themselves as their own private gifts.

If you visit Doughton Park in winter, you will have the park nearly all to yourself. One winter day my family and I saw 18 deer, one fox, one skunk, numerous hawks, owls, and many other animals in one visit to the park.

Better yet, visit the park and hike the trails in winter and in warmer weather, and make a motor visit to the park in October and then in July. It's a fabulous trip!

Shining Rock Wilderness Area.

SECTION 5: THE BEST GET-OUT-AND-GO PLACES
TRIP 2: SHINING ROCK WILDERNESS AREA
THE GIGANTIC JEWEL OF IVESTOR GAP

LOCATION:
To drive to the Shining Rock Wilderness area, drive south from Asheville or north from the Great Smoky Mountains National Park to Blue Ridge Parkway Milepost 420. Then turn north off the Parkway onto State Road 816. Drive .7 mile until you reach a larger parking area than the one you passed at .6 mile point. You are at the entrance to the Shining Rock Wilderness Area.

NEARBY ATTRACTIONS:
Almost within a stone's throw of Shining Rock Wilderness Area are Devil's Courthouse, Graveyard Fields, and Mount Pisgah. A short drive away you can reach Great Smoky Mountains National Park, Brevard, and the Cradle of Forestry.

HOURS OF OPERATION:
The wilderness area is open 24 hours a day, 356 days a year. There are no gates.

ADMISSION:
There are no admission prices at any time.

FACILITIES:
Here you will find only restrooms, primitive camping areas, and hiking trails.

WHAT'S THE STORY?
When the Wilderness Act of 1964 was passed, Shining Rock Wilderness Area was one of the first forest lands included in the legislation. On May 7, 1964, the wilderness was named a Wild Area and consisted of 13,600 acres of unspoiled wilderness. Then in 1984 the original tract was increased to 18,500 acres, all of which are now part of the National Wilderness System.

SPECIAL ATTRACTIONS:
The greatest attractions are the immense meadows filled with native blueberries and the huge rock, an immense shining quartz gem, that gives the wilderness area its name. There are also bridle trails.

MAKING THE MOST OF YOUR VISIT:
This is a walking and sight-seeing trip that can be mixed with primitive overnight camping. The total hiking distance to the Shining Rock and back is 8.9 miles, with a vertical rise of 1,360 feet. The difficulty level is moderate, and the greatest problems are not the sharp inclines (of

which there are few) but the rocky footing that is part of the trail in several areas.

When you visit Shining Rock, you need not make the entire hike. You can mix and match hiking trails, if you prefer. When you leave the parking area and reach a barricade intended not to keep hikers out but to restrict motorized travel, you are hiking along the north slope of Black Balsam Knob.

Within a short distance you will reach a junction with the Art Loeb Trail, which is divided into several sections. The first of these is 12.3 miles in length and starts at 2,100 feet above sea level and reaches a height of 3,800 feet. The second section of the trail, which is 7.2 miles in length, starts at 3,200 feet above sea level and rises to 5,100 feet above sea level. A third section cuts through the Shining Rock vicinity and is 6.8 miles in length. You start at 5,000 feet above sea level and finish at 6,200 feet above sea level. There is much more, but these lengths are usually sufficient for most hikers.

This trail is outstanding in many respects. First, it is unquestionably beautiful, rugged, and majestic. You travel over balds (the term "bald" is given to any treeless area higher than 4,000 feet above sea level), including grassy balds and heath balds (covered with low-growing shrubs) that include fetterbush, blueberry, mountain laurel, huckleberry, dog hobble, wild flowers, and rhododendron.

The blueberries here, because of the altitude, ripen much later than do their Piedmont counterparts, which are ripe as a rule by July 4 or shortly afterward. The mountain blueberries are at their peak on Labor Day, but there are usually huge crowds of pickers in the area. If your schedule will permit, try to be on the scene by August 25.

One of the treats of the Art Loeb Trail is the hike to the top of Black Balsam. Here you are at an elevation of 6,214 feet above sea level. This is the highest peak in the Balsam Mountain portion of the Pisgah District. From the top of Black Balsam you have a 360-degree panoramic view of western North Carolina, northern Georgia and South Carolina, and eastern Tennessee.

From the Black Balsam parking area (where you left the car) to Ivestor Gap the hiking distance is 2.5 miles. If you wish you can hike on to Shining Rock rather than veer off to the Art Loeb Trail. If you want to climb Black Balsam, turn right when you reach Ivestor Gap. You can also make the choice of staying on the Shining Rock Trail or following the Art Loeb Trail in a northerly direction.

The area here is inhabited by deer, black bears, foxes, skunks, hawks, owls, and several other forms of animal life. There are also a number of species of snakes in this part of the mountains. The rattler is not a stranger to this type of terrain. You can make the hike a day trip and limit yourself to the time at your disposal, but if you decide to camp, you are asked to observe the "without a trace" admonition. This means no fire rings or campsite boundaries, except those placed there by nature. Do not leave any indications that you were ever there. And do not bury your tin cans and other debris in the forest. If you can carry the cans in full, surely you can carry them out empty. Do not cut or break trees for firewood. Instead, use deadfall that abounds.

Most areas of this type urge you not to set up a camp and remain in the same spot for several days. Spend one night and move on. In this fashion you can see far more of the beauty of Ivestor Gap, Shining Rock, and Black Balsam.

Lake at Crowders Mountain near Gastonia.

SECTION 5: THE BEST GET-OUT-AND-GO PLACES
TRIP 3: CROWDERS MOUNTAIN
THE WAKING DREAM OF ULRICK CROWDER

LOCATION:

Crowders Mountain is one of the few places in this book that are not easily reached from Interstate 40. You can get there from I-40, of course, but it is far more convenient to make the drive to Crowders Mountain State Park from I-85 between Gastonia and Kings Mountain. As you leave Gastonia on I-85 south, watch for signs directing you off to the south side of the interstate. You will turn off onto Freedom Mill Road and drive 2.5 miles before you turn right onto Sparrow Springs Road. You will see the signs directing you to the park office.

NEARBY ATTRACTIONS:

Within a short drive you can be in Gastonia, Shelby, Cherryville, Lincolnton, Charlotte, and Kings Mountain, the latter very near the Kings Mountain National Military Park. In Shelby there is a small museum in the old courthouse, and in Gastonia you can visit one of the finest museums in the South when you drive down Garrison Boulevard (off US 29 as you enter the city). The Schiele Museum of Natural History is superb. In Cherryville there is the C. Grier Beam Trucking Museum as well as the town museum housed in the old jailhouse.

HOURS OF OPERATION:

Crowders Mountain State Park is open from 8 a.m. until dusk; see other state park schedules for hours.

ADMISSION:

There is no admission fee to the park; however, if you wish to fish or camp, there is a small fee.

FACILITIES:

At the park you can find restrooms, a lake for fishing, a number of hiking trails, a park office, and opportunities for nature study and hikes led by park rangers.

WHAT'S THE STORY?

Ulrick Crowder arrived in the area that bears his name in 1846. The recipient of a vast land grant, Crowder envisioned, some scholars say, an ideal town which would consist of 36 square miles, which would make the town, to be called Ulricksburg, the largest city by far in North Carolina. Inside the city there would be one square mile dedicated to educational facilities and another square mile for government and administrative buildings. The rest of the land would be used as homesites or farms for 32 families, one square mile of land per family.

Ill health forced Crowder to abandon his scheme, and later the mountain was in danger of being strip-mined and ruined. If it had not been for civic-minded and ecology-oriented citizens in the Gaston County area, the land would be an eyesore today, rather than a beautiful park.

SPECIAL ATTRACTIONS:

The best part of the park is the mountain itself, which has high and sheer cliffs used by many rock-climbing enthusiasts. The peak is not high in the usual sense, but Crowders Mountain rises abruptly from the flatlands of the Piedmont and is one of the most impressive landscapes in this part of the state.

MAKING THE MOST OF YOUR VISIT:

Start your visit to Crowders Mountain by making a drive around the park. Signs provide clear driving directions, and you can visit the picnic area and the lake. While you are at the lake you can take a casual stroll around the impoundment and enjoy both the woods and the lake. You may also get to enjoy some of the wildlife that abounds in the park.

From the park office you can follow a trail that leads through a hardwood forest and across the paved highway and again into the woods. This trail, which is almost five miles long, will lead you to the top of Crowders Mountain.

From the top of the mountain you can see the Charlotte skyline to the east; to the west you can see the new factory that replaced the historic old Firestone Mill in Gastonia. This was the mill where members of the National Textile Workers Union tried to unionize the mill workers. The mill was also where the Communist Party made its aborted efforts to take over the nation's textiles and, eventually, the nation's transportation systems and the food production industries. The old mill was, at the time, the largest mill under one roof in the entire world.

The trail you followed is called the Rocktop Trail. Hiking time is four hours, and the vertical rise is 4,520 feet. Keep in mind that this vertical rise includes uphill and downhill parts of the trail. Otherwise, the vertical rise would be greater than the highest part of the mountain.

Incidentally, this trail can be strenuous at times, so if you are hiking in warm weather, pace yourself and take breaks if you start to feel overheated. The park is also the habitat of some snakes, a couple of which can be dangerous. There are a few rattlers, according to local naturalists, and copperheads. I must confess that in the several times when I hiked the trails I never once saw a poisonous snake, but you are nevertheless urged to take necessary precautions.

As you walk or drive around the park, you may want to take a few minutes to contemplate the efforts of local citizens and some students and faculty members at nearby Gaston College who worked tirelessly to save the mountain and eventually help to make it a part of the state park system. Their efforts are evidence that the ecologists and conservation-minded people of the state and the nation can and do make a great difference.

As you enjoy the lush forests and steep cliffs of the park, and as you appreciate the 2,551 acres of beauty, imagine what the site would be like if strip-mining had occurred. Today the park area is designated as a National Heritage Area, one that is the destination of more than 165,000 visitors annually.

Some geologists and other students of the natural world are of the opinion that Crowders Mountain is older than the Rockies and was once higher. The theory that the area was once under water is supported by the discovery of the oldest creature known to have lived in the area. The *Pentrimetes obesus*, a marine invertebrate, is thought to be 480-500 million years old. From the top of the mountain you can also see Kings Pinnacle and Kings Mountain, the latter the site of one of the decisive battles of the American Revolution.

If you still have not hiked enough, you have other trails from which to choose. There is the Backside Trail (.9 mile), the Tower Trail (2 miles), Turnback Trail (1.2 miles), Fern Nature Trail (.7 mile), and Lake Trail (1 mile).

As you hike the higher elevations, note the markings in the rock cliffs. These strange designs are seen by many as evidence that the land was once an inland sea.

Information about all trails, as well as about camping and other park information, is available at the park office.

Chimney Rock, near Lake Lure.

SECTION 5: THE BEST GET-OUT-AND-GO PLACES
TRIP 4: CHIMNEY ROCK
THE GATEWAY TO TSE-LUNGH

LOCATION:

Chimney Rock Park is one of the few commercial sites in this book, and it is included for several obvious reasons. First, the attraction is a place of sheer beauty, from start to finish of the trip. Second, the park is impeccably clean and the staff members are unfailingly courteous and helpful. Third, the cost is not exorbitant. Fourth, the uniqueness of the attraction makes it a memorable place to visit.

To reach Chimney Rock Park, you can exit I-40 in Asheville and head onto I-26. Follow I-26 south until you intersect with US 64. From this point drive east to Hickory Nut Gorge. You will see signs directing you to the park almost as soon as you cross the bridge over the Rocky Broad River and turn right.

From I-85 intersect with I-26 in the Spartanburg-Greenville area and drive north. Again, exit onto US 64. From the middle of the Piedmont, follow US 64 west from Shelby or Gastonia. Before you reach Columbus you will see an exit to the Mill Spring Road which will lead you to Lake Lure. Follow US 64 through Lake Lure and to Chimney Rock, two miles west.

NEARBY ATTRACTIONS:

Close to Chimney Rock are Lake Lure, Bat Cave, Asheville, Brevard, Rutherfordton, Hendersonville, Saluda, and Tryon-all of which are good places to visit.

HOURS OF OPERATION:

Office hours at Chimney Rock are from 8:30 a.m. until 5 p.m. Monday through Friday. Ticket office hours are 8:30 a.m. until 5 p.m. Once you have bought a ticket, you may remain in the park until 7 p.m.

ADMISSION:

Admission prices for adults are $9.95; children ages 6-15 are admitted for $5. Children under 6 are admitted free.

FACILITIES:

At the park you will find restrooms, snack bar, picnic tables, elevator service, spectacular hiking trails, gift and souvenir shop, and marvelous photo opportunities.

WHAT'S THE STORY?

Briefly (more details will be provided later), Chimney Rock Park features a 26-story elevator and a tunnel through solid rock to the elevator (with delightfully cool temperatures inside the tunnel during the hottest weather). The elevator takes you to the top of the Chimney where you can visit the observatory areas and gift shop. You can also take hiking trails around the top of the mountain, or you can take a short and pleasant hike to the bottom of Hickory Nut Falls.

SPECIAL ATTRACTIONS:

The three major attractions at the park are Hickory Nut Falls, which plummet 400 feet down the face of the almost sheer rock cliff, the trails around the top of the mountain, and the overlooks high atop the mountains. One special point from which you can enjoy a fantastic view is the top of the chimney itself which affords a fantastic look at Lake Lure and surrounding area.

MAKING THE MOST OF YOUR VISIT:

When you drive into the park, you will cross the Rocky Broad River. Old-timers say that the stream was once simply the Broad River, but an earthquake dislodged immense boulders that nearly covered the stream bed, and now the river flows around and among the huge boulders, and the stream is aptly named.

From US 64 north of the center of the village of Chimney Rock, you can look to the left (as you drive toward Bat Cave) and see the waterfall sliding down the rocky cliff. Hickory Nut Falls are fed by Fall Creek, which has its origin amid the forest and crags of the immense heap of stone called Chimney Rock Mountain.

Once you are inside the park, drive to the parking area at the base of the mountain. You can leave the car and walk back to a trail that leads through a dense hardwood forest. The trail is wide and easy, with very little vertical rise, and within half an hour you will be at the base of Hickory Nut Falls.

At the falls there are overlooks that provide you the height and vantage point to take photos of the falls, which are among the highest in the state. Although the volume is not great, except after heavy rains, the scene is always impressive and satisfying.

Return to your car and drive the rest of the way up the mountain. You will park in clear view of the monolith known as Chimney Rock. Walk into the 198-foot tunnel and enjoy the 60-degree climate inside. At the tunnel entrance the elevation is 1,965 feet above sea level.

The elevator at the end of the tunnel will take you to the Sky Lounge where you can find snacks, post cards, and an array of gifts and souvenirs. Walk through the lounge and you are on the walk toward the top of the monolith from which you can revel in the panoramic view of 75 miles of valley and mountains.

Against the side of the mountain just across from the steps up to the overlook you will find flights of steps leading up the side of the cliffs. The steps are sturdy and steep, and if you are not in good shape, plan to stop and rest occasionally.

If you are looking for an excellent photo opportunity, you will see it after you have climbed several flights of steps. There is a natural alcove from which you can see the overlook below, a highly impressive sight with the American flag extended in the ever-present breeze, and the length and breadth of Lake Lure stretched out before you.

Best times for photos are mid to late afternoon when the sun will not be in your lens. The major problem is air pollution or haze that prevents your getting a beautifully clear photo. If you make the visit in the winter months, you will escape most of the haze. October is a perfect time for your visit.

But, then, October is usually the closest you will ever come to seeing perfect days in North Carolina (although nearly any day in North Carolina is highly recommended, and most Carolina days rank high on the perfection scale). I have already admitted to being highly prejudiced in favor of the Old North State.

From the overlook and from several other vantage points you can see the village of Chimney Rock below you. The mountain that dwarfs the town is also the site of the filming of many of the scenes from the recent Hollywood epic, *The Last of the Mohicans*.

At the .7-mile point in the hike you will cross Fall (or Falls) Creek, and after you cross the footbridge over Fall (or Falls) Creek you will see several incredibly beautiful views of the falls. If you have a wide-angle lens, these are perfect spots from which to photograph the falls. At the .7-mile point you have reached the end of the Skyline Trail, and you are now on the Cliff Trail.

Soon you will reach Nature's Shower Bath where water wends its way through fissures in the rock and produces a fine mist that feels wonderful on a hot day. At .5 mile on the Cliff Trail you will see a number of astounding rock formations and a spiral staircase that leads you toward the junction of trails.

As you started the walk, you picked up a self-guiding trail pamphlet, and you can select the trail you wish to take back to the starting point. Trail spurs lead to a moonshine still, picnic tables, and small concession stands.

While you are in the area, ask some of the residents to tell you of the story of the lost gold mine. On Round Top Mountain some Englishmen reportedly discovered an incredibly rich vein of gold, but, before the men could load their sacks and make their way out of the mountain wilderness, Indians attacked the men and killed all but one of them.

That one man, according to the story, waited until the Indians were gone before he began his trek back to civilization. He left the immense cache of gold hidden among the boulders of Round Top Mountain.

Before the man could manage to organize a party to return to the site, he lost his eyesight, but he still managed to draw a map to the site, and on the map he designated the location of the gold cache.

During the Civil War a Confederate officer, a general named Collett Leventhorpe, organized a search party of 50 men who spent weeks in an unsuccessful search of the mountain. The gold is still there, the legend insists.

Incidentally, while you are on the mountainside, if you listen carefully you might hear what sounds like the rumbling of thunder. But the skies may be totally clear, and there is no sign of a storm in the area.

The story behind the ghostly thunder is that ages earlier the earthquake that caused the boulders to fall into the river also caused rock formations to slide and collapse inside some of the mountains. The locals say that the rocks are even today still folding and falling, and the rumbling sound is from inside the mountains, rather than in the skies.

The Catawba and Cherokee Indians reportedly once called the gorge "the gateway to tse-lungh": the land of tobacco. There are many other stories, including the one of the spectral battle in the heavens over Chimney Rock.

And in the area, just across the highway from Chimney Rock, the Esmeralda Inn stood for ages. At the inn, which burned a short time ago, a Civil War general named Lew Wallace lived while he put the finishing touches on the stage script for *Ben-Hur*.

General Wallace later moved west and became the first governor of New Mexico. There he was a distant neighbor to James Pinckney Henderson, a native of nearby Lincoln County, who was to become the first governor of Texas.

And, just around the mountain, Wild Bill (or Old Bill) Williams, the greatest of all the mountain men, was born. Old Bill is credited with being the first man of European descent to explore the Grand Canyon. Today, Williams, Arizona, features a statue of Williams, and Williams Fork River and Mount Williams are named after the former Baptist preacher who later married two Indian maidens and created a living legend about the greatest of all the explorers.

Rhododendron at Craggy Gardens.

SECTION 5: THE BEST GET-OUT-AND-GO PLACES
TRIP 5: CRAGGY GARDENS
NATURE'S MILE-HIGH FLORAL SPECTACULAR

LOCATION:

To reach Craggy Gardens, leave I-40 at Asheville and join the Blue Ridge Parkway. Drive north (pay attention to signs as you junction with the Parkway: some drivers have experienced slight directional orientation problems. The signs directing you to the north are accurate) to Milepost 364.5. Park at the Visitor Center and, if you need them, pick up pamphlets or ask directions from the extremely courteous and helpful staff members.

NEARBY ATTRACTIONS:

At Craggy Gardens you are within easy driving distance of Mount Mitchell State Park, the terrific city of Asheville, the Folk Art Center, Lake Tahoma, Crabtree Meadows campground and waterfall, Little Switzerland, and the Weaverville home of Zeb Vance.

HOURS OF OPERATION:

There are no gates to the rhododendron gardens, but the visitor center is open from 9 a.m. until 5 p.m.

ADMISSION:

At this writing there was no admission fee. In recent months the rhododendron gardens at Roan Mountain began to charge a small admission fee, however.

FACILITIES:

There are restrooms, visitor information sources, book store, and overlooks, nearby picnic grounds, and hiking trails.

WHAT'S THE STORY?

Craggy Gardens includes 700 acres of hiking trails, scenic views, and some of the most beautiful displays of flowering shrubs anywhere in the mountains of North Carolina. The greatest single attraction to the recreational area is the annual blooming of the rhododendron.

In mid-June to late June, depending upon the weather, the entire mountainside is one giant flower garden. Each year untold thousands of people drive to the area to enjoy the flowers, picnic, and delight in the scenery which also includes hundreds of other wild flowers and exceptional views of the mountains and valleys of the area.

SPECIAL ATTRACTIONS:

This is an easy call: the flowers, the rhododendron display, the wonderful overlooks, the mountain foliage in the autumn, and the exceptional beauty of the area are wonderful attractions. One special point of interest is the shelter at the picnic area.

MAKING THE MOST OF YOUR VISIT:

You can hike the trails if you wish, and there is beauty at any time of the year. The June blossoms make the walks far more enjoyable, and the October leaf display is another special time at Craggy Gardens. The trails here are relatively short, but because of the exceptional beauty of the terrain you may wish to extend your visit for hours.

The elevation of the flower displays is 5,220 feet. Atop Craggy Pinnacle the elevation is 5,892 feet.

For a delightful stroll, start at the south end of the parking lot at the visitor center. A nearly invisible trail leads off the very end of the parking area and into a thicket of rhododendron. In early summer this thicket is ablaze with blossoms, and in most months the soil is wet or damp because sunlight very rarely filters through the thick foliage.

Along the walk you will find information or identification markers to help you to appreciate what you are seeing. Follow the trail and its steady climb to a picnic shelter in an open area surrounded by rhododendron shrubs.

The picnic shelter is particularly interesting because it was constructed decades ago from chestnut logs. At the time of the construction, the chestnut tree dominated the forests of the Southern highlands and very nearly dominated the economy of some parts of the South. During the blossoming of the chestnut trees the entire mountainsides turned as white as if a spring snowstorm had coated the trees with beauty.

At one time, before the chestnut blight destroyed the trees, the mountain people could gather chestnuts by the sackful and sell the delicious nuts all over the country. The tree itself was so large, so durable, and so true-grained that chestnut lumber was in demand for use in furniture-making, telephone pole cross-bars, and fence posts. Some growths were so large that a single tree could yield a full boxcar-load of logs or lumber.

Today, years after most wood would have deteriorated as a result of constant exposure to dampness, wind, and sunlight, the huge chestnut timbers appear to be as sound as they were when the picnic shelter was built.

If you want to read an absolutely incredible statistic, take special note of the following: while many chestnut trees reached a height of 60 feet with a base diameter of 36 inches, the trees sometimes grew to unbelievable dimensions. According to the Encyclopedia Britannica, the world record largest chestnut tree had a girth of-are you ready for this?--200 feet! No, I can't imagine it, either. Some of the trees, scholars insist, lived as long as 2,000 years ago.

The American chestnut in modern times has been measured at 120 feet in height and ten feet in diameter. But at the turn of the 20th century a fungus disease (*Endothia parasitica*) was brought into the country from the Orient to Long Island, and within 35 years the chestnut population of the United States was essentially destroyed. So study the picnic shelter; marvel at it, and join the hosts of ecologists who now have reason to think that the chestnut tree-one that is immune to the blight--may be just over the horizon.

From the shelter climb a rhododendron-covered knoll near the end of a spur trail (which is .3 mile long) to a barrier which provides another great view of the valleys south near Asheville. The trail continues to a large picnic area on the other side of the mountain. The round trip to the picnic area is .8 mile.

On your backtrack hike, after leaving the picnic area (which has water, comfort stations, and tables) you will junction with the famed Mountains-to-Sea Trail. You can extend the walk for several miles if you wish to follow the Mountains-to-Sea Trail until it joins the Douglas Falls Trail 1.5 miles later.

Along the Mountains-to-Sea Trail you will find generally easy hiking as far as footing is concerned. The rocky trail is safe and moderately difficult, with superb vistas awaiting at many points along the way. At the union of the Mountains-to-Sea Trail and the Douglas Falls Trail you will be one mile from the Parkway.

The trail re-joins the Parkway at Milepost 363.6. From here you may hike along the Parkway back to your car or move on to Milepost 363.4, which is the overlook for Gray Beard Mountain.

Between the visitor center and Gray Beard Mountain you will find another parking area at Craggy Pinnacle. From the parking lot to the peak of Craggy Pinnacle you will hike .7 mile.

The trail to the top of Craggy Pinnacle is wide, easy, and at times steep. You climb among the rhododendron shrubs for the entire trip. At the top, you will have a splendid view in 360 degrees. You can see all of the major peaks in the entire area.

If you cannot hike the trail during the blooming of the rhododendron, you will find that the scenery is wonderful at all times of the year. Winter (if the Parkway is open) is one of the best times to hike the trail, if you pick a day when the wind chill and temperature factors are not dangerous.

Boardwalk on Tanawha Trail near Parkway.

SECTION 5: THE BEST GET-OUT-AND-GO PLACES
TRIP 6: THE TANAWHA TRAIL
IN SEARCH OF THE FABULOUS EAGLE

LOCATION:

The justly famous Tanawha Trail (the name is a Cherokee word for "fabulous hawk or eagle") parallels the Blue Ridge Parkway from the Linn Cove Viaduct beginning at Beacon Heights and extends to Price Lake. The Beacon Heights parking area is at Milepost 305.5 on the Parkway, which is near Grandfather Mountain and US 221. The other end of the trail at Price Lake is near the town of Blowing Rock and US 321. Both of these national highways can be reached easily by I-40.

NEARBY ATTRACTIONS:

When you are on the trail you are near Blowing Rock, Boone, Grandfather Mountain, Little Switzerland, Crabtree Meadows, and Mount Mitchell and Craggy Gardens, Asheville is a comfortable drive to the west.

HOURS OF OPERATION:

The trail is always open, 24 hours a day, every day of the year except on the rare occasions when the Blue Ridge Parkway is closed. The visitor centers along the Parkway are open from 9 a.m. until 5 p.m.

ADMISSION:

There is no admission fee for hiking the trail, and you do not need any special permits. All you do is show up and walk.

FACILITIES:

There are no facilities whatever on the trail, but at each end of the trail you can find water, restrooms, and information outlets. There are picnic tables at Price Lake and at some of the other nearby attractions.

WHAT'S THE STORY?

For many years the Blue Ridge Parkway ended temporarily near the Beacon Heights visitor center. And during these years the visitors to the Parkway had to drive the tediously curving US 221 from near Price Lake to near Grandfather Mountain. When the Linn Cove Viaduct (one of the engineering marvels of modern times and one that you absolutely must see) was completed and traffic could move the entire length of the Parkway, the Tanawha Trail opened shortly afterwards. This trail parallels the Parkway for 13.5 miles and has a vertical rise of 6,920 feet. Rating is moderate to strenuous.

SPECIAL ATTRACTIONS:

Along the trail you will find a totally marvelous and long boardwalk that alone is worth the hike. You also pass over a series of rustic bridges and you will see a series of creeks and waterfalls. From early spring until late autumn the wild flowers along the trail are spectacular.

MAKING THE MOST OF YOUR VISIT:

If I have to choose only one trail to hike in the mountains of North Carolina, this would be the one. The reasoning is that on the Tanawha Trail you have every imaginable type of mountain terrain that you could want to see. There are towering peaks, crags, overlooks affording fantastic views, sections that will leave you panting and others that are a cake walk.

The is one of the newer trails along the Blue Ridge Parkway, and it passes through and around a fragile and antique ecosystem, tunnels of laurel and rhododendron, glades filled with an array of wild growth, and an unusual variety of wild life.

Completed in September 1987, the Tanawha Trail runs roughly around the south border of Grandfather Mountain and ends at the juncture of the Boone Fork Trail near Price Lake, one of the most beautiful bodies of water on the Blue Ridge Parkway.

Two characteristics set the trail apart from nearly all other hiking trails in the nation. The first is that the trail starts under the world-famous Linn Cove Viaduct. When engineers finalized plans for the viaduct that clings, it appears, to the side of the mountain without becoming an actual part of it, the land was donated so that the Parkway could be completed without damaging the fragile ecosystems.

The second great part of the trail is that you can start or stop at a number of locations so that you do not have to worry about two cars or an inordinately long trek. If you have two cars in the area, you can park one at the north end of the trail and then drive in the other to the Beacon Heights Parking area.

If you have access to only one vehicle, you can hike the trail in segments and and short loops before you return to move the car further north so that you never find yourself a discouraging distance from your vehicle.

Starting from Beacon Heights, you hit the roughest part of the trail almost immediately as you struggle through a maze of enormous gray boulders that dwarf cars and trucks. For a quarter of an hour you squeeze your way among the rocks, clamber over others, and ascend a rather gruelling rise. These boulders provide narrow tunnel-like passageways as you find yourself in deep recesses that are almost caves at one moment and a few steps later you will be moving across the tops of adjacent boulders.

Within a mile the trail flattens and you can walk at a very comfortable pace as you enter a birch and beech forest. Until you reach the first major creek (Wilson's Creek) the trail is wide and almost level. At the creek you will see a nice waterfall that plummets down the mountainside with astonishing power for such a relatively small stream.

At Stack Rock, 1.2 miles from the start of the trail, you can leave the trail and follow a short spur down to the Parkway. If you have apprehensions about your endurance, it is good to leave a second car at the Stack Rock parking area so you will not have a hike ahead of you that is too taxing. As you continue north past Wilson Creek, the trail crosses a huge rock formation featuring large flat rocks and extremely easy walking.

After you cross the rock field, you will climb sharply until you reach Rough Ridge and its 200-foot long boardwalk providing a fantastic overlook view of the Linn Cove Viaduct, South Mountain, Hawks Bill Mountain, and Table Mountain. Please stay on the boardwalk for two reasons: the first is that the plant life and the soil exist so precariously that your footsteps can and will do irreparable damage. The second reason is that you expose yourself to danger when you leave the boardwalk.

Besides, why leave it? It is an absolutely unforgettable part of the trail. The walk seems to continue forever as you make your way easily among rhododendron and laurel as well as boulders and almost unbroken stretches of rocks. There are overlooks built into the boardwalk so that you can enjoy the view, stop and rest, or admire the engineering feats underlying the trail itself.

At 4.8 miles from Beacon Heights you cross the vast flat stone surface, and you will enter almost immediately a thick forest of poplar, yellow birch, and oak trees that provide welcome shade in warm months and exciting color in autumn.

Raven Rock is the next major point along the trail. You will leave the hardwood forest and enter another vast expanse of flat-topped boulders and a natural rock garden that features ferns in amazing profusion growing from the rock crevices and cascading like a small green stream down the boulders. A wide variety of wild flowers in bloom may be seen from early spring until the first killing frost in autumn, usually in early October.

Three miles from Raven Rock you enter a thicket of laurel and rhododendron that extends for almost a mile. The shrubs are in full bloom in mid-June but sometimes as early as June 1 and as late as July 10 you can find a rewarding number of blooms.

As appealing as the flowers are to the eye, do not forget that both laurel and rhododendron contain a highly toxic sap that can be fatal if ingested in significant amounts. Chewing on a twig can be sufficient to cause instant and severe illness. The Native Americans who inhabited these thicketed areas reportedly used the poisonous sap to "treat' their arrows and one group of Indians reportedly used it as a suicide potion.

Do not leave the trail at any point, except to take a departure trail to the Parkway. While the Tanawha Trail is very easy once you pass the first half-hour's walk, the terrain is very treacherous if you leave the trail. In warm months there are poisonous snakes, and the danger of falling is always present. Wild animals may occasionally be seen: living here are wild cats, skunks, an occasional bear, ground hogs, rabbits, foxes, squirrels, and several other smaller animals in abundance.

Yellow jackets and hornets can be a problem if you leave the trail. These insects are content to endure the presence of hikers along the trail but they deeply resent intrusions into their terrain. Stumbling into a hornet's nest can not only be painful; it can be deadly serious.

The Tanawha Trail is joined by the Daniel Boone Scout Trail and the Grandfather Trail 2.9 miles north of Raven Rock. You must buy a hiking permit to travel on either of these trails. After you reach the Boone Fork portion of the trail in rapid succession you will reach an old logging road, a hardwood forest, open fields where you will cross the Holloway Mountain Road, apple orchards, an old graveyard, and open pasture land.

The trail joins the Boone Fork Trail that leads into the Price Lake Campground, where the Tanawha Trail ends.

You have seven parking areas where you may leave the trail if you wish. You can start at Price Lake and work your way south, saving the most difficult part of the trail for last.

You can camp at Price Lake for $10 per night. You can also enjoy hiking, trout fishing, and canoeing at the lake.

North Carolina is one of the most beautiful states in the Union, and you are urged to leave all flowers for others and to refrain from cutting or breaking tree limbs or saplings.

Weather is unpredictable along the trail, and it is always advisable to carry along a poncho. In early spring and fall there is always the danger of an unseasonable snow storm or severe cold weather. Be prepared for these sudden changes in weather.

If you see emergency situations as you travel to the Tanawha Trail area you are urged to call 1-800-PARKWAY. If you need general Parkway information you can call (828) 259-0701.

Table Rock near Morganton.

SECTION 5: THE BEST GET-OUT-AND-GO PLACES
TRIP 7: TABLE ROCK
FROM GINGERCAKE TO TABLE ROCK

LOCATION:

From I-40 in the Hickory-Morganton area, take NC 18 north into the town of Morganton. In Morganton on Greene Street (on the east side of the Burke County Historic Courthouse) you will take NC 181 north. About 10 miles north of town you will see signs that direct you to Table Rock Mountain. The road you are looking for is Table Rock Road. If you are arriving from the Blue Ridge Parkway, take NC 181 south past Jonas Ridge. Several miles later look for the Table Rock Road on the right of NC 181.

NEARBY ATTRACTIONS:

You are close enough to Morganton, Lake James, Marion, Valdese, Linville Falls, and Linville Gorge for you to make a visit to one or more of these locations.

HOURS OF OPERATION:

There are no posted hours. The area is open all day every day, but in winter the gates may be locked and, if they are, you must park on the roadway and walk to the parking lot and then to the top of Table Rock. The roadside walk is not recommended highly; wait until the Table Rock Road is open all the way to the parking lot.

ADMISSION:

There are no fees of any sort.

FACILITIES:

You will find restrooms, a parking area, and hiking trail to the top of Table Rock.

WHAT'S THE STORY?

The total distance of the Table Rock jaunt is 2.4 miles, all of it uphill until you reach the top. At times the trail can be strenuous, and if you are not in good shape you should hike slowly and stop often for resting. There is a vertical rise of 1,640 feet, 820 of which is a fairly hard climb. The other half of the vertical rise is the still-steep walk to the bottom and to the parking lot.

SPECIAL ATTRACTIONS:

The attractions are, quite obviously, the great hike to the top of Table Rock, the great views of Linville Gorge and Linville River, and the wonderfully cool and fresh mountain air atop the 4,000-foot peak.

MAKING THE MOST OF YOUR VISIT:

The great experience here is that of climbing the trail to the mountain peak and reveling in the fantastic view and in the crisp, bracing mountain air.

You can start the enjoyment miles before you reach Table Rock, when you see the startling shape of the mountain from NC 18 south of Morganton. As you approach I-40 you can see the flat top of the table rock standing out like a giant sculpture.

As you travel northward on NC 181, after the junction with NC 18 in Morganton, on your left you will see, virtually at all times, the top of the rock, and as you round curve after curve, you will notice that the rock mountain constantly changes from a flat table-like mesa to an almost pointed peak.

Before you reach the turn-off to the rock, the peak seems to sharpen until it finally appears as an inverted ice cream cone. However, neither view reveals the total truth. The top of Table Rock is neither flat nor conical. Instead, you will find at the top immense boulders with large crevices between them, and these huge carved shapes make up the top of the mountain.

Or, if you approach from the Parkway, drive south on NC 181. You can see Table Rock from State Road 1264, also known as the Old Gingercake Road. You will be in a congested area where many retired persons as well as locals have built houses along the road, and the mountain seems unnaturally large and menacing from this point of view.

As you near Table Rock you will find that several trail heads are visible along the road, and you will see parking areas with a number of cars parked there. Do not stop at these areas. Continue until you see the signs directing you to the right, toward Table Rock.

As you near the destination, you will pass the entrance to the Outward Bound facilities. As you ascend along the paved road, you will see Table Rock looming through the trees as you round the switchbacks. At the picnic area where you start the trail you will see a sign that warns you that the trail is steep and there are dangerous rocky cliffs.

The entire climb is a steady uphill grade, without relief; however, the trail is never really extremely difficult. Most of the time it is wide, well-maintained, and weedless. Only in wet weather or sub-freezing temperatures will you encounter poor footing.

In wet weather the run-off from the mountain peak will continue to seep through the rocks and parts of the trail will be slightly muddy. In very cold weather there may be ice or snow left even several days after a storm. As you enter the parking area you will see a sign advising you that the area is a bear sanctuary. There are many deer as well in the area, and you will perhaps be startled as a grouse or covey of quail erupt from the bushes only feet from you. Don't let these sudden explosions of noise and activity startle you into losing your footing.

At the .4- mile mark you will be able to see, to your left, the Linville River gorge. In all types of clear weather the gorge is spectacularly beautiful, and from your altitude the Linville River appears to be no more than a trickle instead of a powerful river, and if the wind is still, which is rare, you can hear the roaring of the rapids along the stream.

You climb steadily through a hardwood forest, and soon you will reach a fork in the trail. One fork leads off to the left, while the other heads to the right. Take neither of these, unless you wish to hike the Little Table Rock Summit Trail or the Table Rock Gap Trail. Continue straight ahead.

When you reach the .8- mile mark, the trail veers to the right and curves sharply upward through laurel slicks and dense rhododendron thickets. There are huge rocks on both sides of you as you climb through a series of switchbacks and you close in on the summit.

When you reach the .9- mile point, you will have an awesome view of Linville Gorge, the endless peaks of the Pisgah National Forest and some of the wildest country in the United States. In winter the distant peaks are often snow-covered.

The trail is single-file width now, and you will need to step carefully. The footing is uneven and at time treacherous. You will quickly see an impressive rock formation that lends the impression of having been carved and layered throughout the ages. The base of the rock is a soft gray, almost white color, and at the top is a larger dark gray lichen-covered rock that appears to be an ingenious bit of modern architecture.

Thirty yards before you reach the summit there is another rock formation that extends across the trail in tiered manner, with one rock ledge perfectly flat and the lip extending until it hovers over the undergrowth on the opposite side of the trail.

At the peak itself you will witness huge expanses of white rock that look bleached by the wind and sun. Somehow small shrubs and wild flowers found a foothold and endured the severe changes in climate.

At this top you have a complete 360-degree panoramic view of this entire section of North Carolina. On one side of the peak you see Linville Gorge again. In the distance other valleys and ancient log roads are visible. The late afternoon sunlight adds a rich gold color to the evergreen foliage.

From another view you can see Lake James in the distance. This lake is one of the finest outdoor recreation areas in western North Carolina, and its wild beauty has caused several Hollywood motion picture companies to do their location shooting here. One of the most recent films shot in part there was *The Last of the Mohicans*.

When you have enjoyed your fill of the wild beauty, you can backtrack down to the parking lot. If you have energy left, you can cross the parking lot and follow the trail into an incredibly gorgeous hardwood forest. Try to see the forest near sundown for a wonderful display of sunlight and shadows. In the fall this bit of nature's art is particularly rewarding.

As you leave the picnic area, when you pass the gate and start the first switchback downward, you can see a superior view of Table Rock. This is a marvelous spot to photograph the peak.

Best times to visit Table Rock are in late April, May, September, and October.

For another treat, unlike any you are likely to find anywhere else, drive on north on NC 181 to the Brown Mountain Lights Overlook, which is only a wide pull-off on the right side of the road, and you will not see any buildings, facilities of any sort, or signs. You will see only gray boulders and a super valley below you.

This attraction is free, and there are no posted hours, but you will see only the valley and the mountains during daylight hours. On a clear night, however, particularly a crisp, cool, autumn night, you, if you are lucky, will see the Brown Mountain Lights, a natural phenomenon that has baffled the ages.

You read elsewhere in this book about Thomas Alva Edison's visit to the Brown Mountain Lights and how he concluded that there are some natural mysteries that we shall never solve. And many years ago there was a superb country music song about the Brown Mountain Lights. The late Tommy Faile had one of the best recordings of the song, and you would do well to listen to it, if you can find it, before making the trip.

After you hear the song, you might agree, as many people do, that the musical solution is by far the best answer yet to be advanced concerning this marvel of nature.

North Carolina Arboretum.

SECTION 5: THE BEST GET-OUT-AND-GO PLACES
TRIP 8: NORTH CAROLINA ARBORETUM
A VISIT TO A RAINBOW

LOCATION:

The North Carolina Arboretum is located near Asheville, but at present the drive to the superb oasis of mountain beauty is a little tricky. In the near future there will be an entrance off the Blue Ridge Parkway ramp in east Asheville, but for now you must follow a different route. The mailing address is 100 Frederick Law Olmsted Way, Asheville, NC 28806. Telephone number is (828) 665-2492. From Asheville and I-40 take NC 191 (Brevard Road) south to Bent Creek Ranch Road. Turn right onto this road (left if you are approaching from the Brevard area) and drive west five minutes to the Wesley Branch Road. Turn left and stay on this road until you see the entrance to the Arboretum.

NEARBY ATTRACTIONS:

In the immediate vicinity of the North Carolina Arboretum you can find great attractions in Asheville (the Thomas Wolfe Memorial, Pack Square museums, superb architecture along nearly every downtown street, and the St. Lawrence Basilica, one of the most beautiful places of worship in the state). Just outside Asheville you can visit the Folk Art Center on the Parkway, and in nearby Weaverville you can enjoy the home of Zeb Vance. South of Asheville you can visit Brevard and the many waterfalls that attract hundreds of thousands of tourists to Transylvania County, the beautiful Hendersonville Main Street, Flat Rock Playhouse, Saint John in the Wilderness church, Cradle of Forestry north of Brevard, and Mount Pisgah on the Parkway.

HOURS OF OPERATION:

The Arboretum property is open every day of the year from 7 a.m. until 9 p.m. during Daylight Savings Time hours and from 8 a.m. until 8 p.m. during Eastern Standard Time seasons. The Visitor Education Center is open from 8 a.m. until 5 p.m. each Monday through Saturday.

ADMISSION:

At this time there are no admission fees.

FACILITIES:

Nearly all of the core attractions of the Arboretum are handicap accessible. There are restrooms, trails, gardens of all sorts, identification markers on the flowers, shrubs, trees, and vines, and there is abundant parking space.

WHAT'S THE STORY?

The North Carolina Arboretum is located within the 6,300-acre Bent Creek Experimental Forest, which in turn is within the 480,000-acre Pisgah National Forest. The Arboretum itself is a 426-acre beauty spot that includes an amazing number and variety of Southern Appalachian plants.

SPECIAL ATTRACTIONS:

Nearly everything inside the Arboretum is a special and beautiful attraction. It's a matter of choice. Each week of the year offers new and different attractions, but if I had to pick one or two outstanding attractions I would choose Core Gardens (with three formal garden rooms: the Stream, the Quilt, and the Spring gardens) and the Plants of Promise Garden. But you do not have to choose favorites: you can enjoy them all.

MAKING THE MOST OF YOUR VISIT

Unlike some of the other visits in this section, you will not be hiking long miles or struggling over rocky tors in order to reach a beauty spot. These longer hikes are not only great fun but are highly therapeutic in nature, and they are amazingly good for the cardio-vascular system, if you are in sound health to start with.

But sometimes you don't have time, energy, or physical stamina to undertake a gruelling trek. Still, you can still get your share of physical exercise at the Arboretum. Although you drive to it, you have huge expanses of territory to cover by walking, if you plan to see the entire display of Nature's best.

The Arboretum, established by the North Carolina General Assembly as an inter-institutional facility of the University of North Carolina, came into existence in 1986. But as early as 1895 Frederick Law Olmsted, who was the landscape architect for the Biltmore House, proposed that the Arboretum be established on the Biltmore Estate, which at the time consisted of about 125,000 acres.

When you make your visit, take along a camera and notebook. In the spring you will enjoy tulips, daffodils, and other spring flowers surrounding the flagpole near the Entrance Plaza. Nearby are boxwoods, witch-alder, and red maples.

At the Core Gardens you will visit the Stream, Quilt, and Spring gardens. Here are columbines, jack-in-the-pulpit, bee balm, false camellia, and other flowers. The Quilt Garden is, as the name suggests, a patchwork of flowers creating a design like that of a traditional Appalachian quilt. There are more than 6,000 perennials, annuals, and bulbs planted in the area.

The camera is to record the beauty you see, and the notebook is to help you to remember the names (common and botanical) of the plants you might want to add to your own garden. Take the photos so you will remember what the plant looks like and then list the details, like names, the type of plant (an annual or a perennial, for example), how tall the plant or shrub grows, and growing conditions that are best for the plant.

While you are at the Arboretum, note the delightful chairs that are placed strategically for your convenience and comfort. These are also works of charm and beauty. Or just walk around and enjoy the shade, the colors, the aromas, and the superb planning of the gardens. It's a visit you will long remember.

Swimming hole at Graveyard Fields on Parkway.

SECTION 5: THE BEST GET-OUT-AND-GO PLACES
TRIP 9: GRAVEYARD FIELDS
THE GRAVEYARD THAT IS A PARADISE

LOCATION:

Between Mileposts 416 and 424 on the Blue Ridge Parkway about one and a half hours south of Asheville you will pass Mount Pisgah and the junction of US 276. Shortly past this junction you will see the parking area for Graveyard Fields.

NEARBY ATTRACTIONS:

Devil's Courthouse, Brevard, Mount Pisgah, Pisgah Inn, Asheville, Cradle of Forestry, waterfalls, hiking, camping, and great scenery are within a few minutes of driving.

HOURS OF OPERATION:

The area is open all day and night, every day of the year.

ADMISSION:

There are no fees of any sort.

FACILITIES:

There are no restrooms, picnic tables, or shelters.

WHAT'S THE STORY?

Graveyard Fields is a vast wilderness area one hour's drive from Asheville via the Blue Ridge Parkway south, 30 minutes from Brevard via US 276 and one hour from the superb Great Smoky Mountains National Park via Parkway south. The incredible and historic area was years ago burned completely. Today the federal land known as Graveyard Fields is lush, green, and inviting.

SPECIAL ATTRACTIONS:

Living in Graveyard Fields are a large number of deer which can be seen virtually each day near dawn and dusk. You can also enjoy, in season, picking blueberries from the thousands of bushes that populate an entire hillside. Be sure to visit the two waterfalls that are easily reached by clearly marked trails.

MAKING THE MOST OF YOUR VISIT:

If you approach Graveyard Fields from the south, watch for Milepost markers. Shortly before you reach Milepost 424 you will pass through beautiful Parkway scenery and recreational areas. On the left, just before you reach Graveyard Fields, you will see a road leading to Shining Rock Wilderness Area. You can drive a mile up the road, park, and enjoy a casual walk or an all-day hike. There are restroom facilities at the parking area. Five minutes farther on the Parkway you will see on your right a parking area for Devil's Courthouse. Here you can view the ruggedly majestic and mysterious peak from the paved parking lot or you can hike up the right side of the Parkway (heading north) along a paved walkway toward the tunnel. Just before you reach the tunnel you will see the trail leading into the dense hardwood forest. Follow the .8-mile trail to the peak. This peak is described in more detail in Section I of this book.

When you reach the Graveyard Fields parking area (on the left side of the Parkway as you head north) you can leave your vehicle and enjoy a superb view of the Yellowstone Prong valley before you. There are information boards at the edge of the parking area, and you should consult these before making your descent into the valley below. Pay particular attention to the trail maps if you plan to hike to the waterfalls.

From the parking area you can survey the 25,000 acres of near-Paradise and perhaps wonder how such an incredibly beautiful spot was labeled as a graveyard (particularly as you think of the peak called Devil's Courthouse just across the highway). The reason for the name is a rather ominous one.

On Thanksgiving Eve, 1925, a blazing inferno of unknown origin swept across the valley and consumed the high-grade timber that had until that time created one of the finest forest tracts in North Carolina. When the fire was finally extinguished, the valley was a picture of total desolation. Not only were the trees burned, but the peat that served as a nutrition source for the trees burned as well. All that was left consisted of rocks, the small river, and the charred stumps of once-enormous trees that, when bleached by the sun, wind, and rain, looked like macabre gravestones.

About 17 years later tragedy again struck Graveyard Fields, as a series of fires broke out and again destroyed the young forest growth in this valley in the Pisgah National Forest. This time the fires were the result of arson.

United States active involvement in World War II had begun only weeks earlier, and while fire-fighting personnel and local law enforcement agents speculated that the fires were purposely set by disgruntled or thrill-seeking locals, rumors persisted that the incendiary work was the result of German espionage agents bent upon disrupting timber production in the nation.

Lending some credence to the espionage theory was the fact that German U-boats operating off the coast of North Carolina were sinking scores of ships in the military movement the Germans called the Great American Turkey Shoot and the coastal area was called "Torpedo Alley." Between January 1942 and July of the same year, German U-boats sank

397 ships and killed more than 5,000 people, most of them merchant seamen or civilians.

So devastating were the torpedoes that it was reported that residents of Ocracoke Island could sit on the beach at midnight and read a newspaper by the light of the burning vessels just off the coast. The Graveyard of the Atlantic and Graveyard Fields seemed to be linked ominously by the fires at sea and the fires along the rivers and creeks.

The 1942 fires began around three o'clock on the afternoon of Sunday, April 26. By Wednesday evening the fires had destroyed over 17,000 acres of scenic timberland and hunting preserve territory. One ingredient of the forest disaster was that a series of fires broke out in strategic locations, all of which were difficult to reach or were so far apart that firefighters could not control all of the blazes within a short time.

At one point fires in Haywood County were spread across a 75-mile front that dominated three sides of the picturesque county. And while the damage to timber was significant, the potential loss of human life was even worse. The trout season had just opened, and about 75 persons had entered the forest to make their way to their favorite trout streams.

G.C. Plott, county game and fish warden, commented that when he saw the first smoke, it looked as if it were coming from a cabin chimney. "In less than 10 minutes, it (the fire) appeared to have covered two miles, it spread with such rapidity," Plott said.

The fishermen were trapped. The fires closed in around them; the flames moved so quickly that the men could not outrun the fire, and they took to the icy waters of the rivers to avoid being burned alive. Fishermen later reported that the heat was so intense that leaves floating in the streams actually caught fire and burned.

A fisherman who had taken his young son with him waded into the trout stream to avoid the flames and the falling trees. The father kept soaking a sweater in the water and covering the boy's head with it to protect him from the intense heat.

One environmental tragedy was that workers had set out 17,000 spruce seedlings on the day before the fires started. All of the young trees were destroyed.

Not far from the Graveyard Fields valley workers at a lumber camp were sleeping when fire started down the mountain from them and a high wind fed the flames as they climbed the slope. By the time the men were roused from their beds, the fire surrounded them. The cook spent the night standing in a 10,000 gallon water tank that was deep enough that the water rose to the chin of the cook, who had no choice but to stand there all night.

In the particular area the fire caused the loss of three million feet of logs that had been cut and skidded to the railroad track area.

Later, State Bureau of Investigation officers arrested two young men and charged them with setting the fires. The men stated that they wanted jobs on the fire lines but no one was needed, so they set the fires to create jobs for themselves. And while local residents were angry with the men, there was also an air of relief that the fires had not been set by German saboteurs.

In the half-century since the devastating fires, Graveyard Fields continues to show the damage by the flames. When the huge trees were destroyed, undergrowth began to appear. Fortunately, the new growth took the form of several varieties of blueberries. And today the blueberry bushes line the banks of the Yellowstone Prong River and fill the open land on the north slope.

As you enter the valley, you can leave the parking lot by way of two trails, one at either end of the lot. The most common way into the valley is by the north trail, which consists of a series of stone steps, some man-made and many natural, that wind among a thick forest of laurel and rhododendron which then gives way to tall and fruitful blueberry bushes. The trail is almost always damp and often wet, so wear comfortable and durable shoes with good soles that will provide the traction you need. Do not attempt the trail while you are wearing dress shoes.

It is a good idea, too, to carry rain gear, particularly if you are visiting in the summer months when typical afternoon and evening thunderstorms or calm rains are the rule rather than the exception. A lightweight plastic poncho works beautifully.

Remember to avoid the valley during lightning storms if you can do so. If you are caught in a storm, do not stay on the open rock surface or along the banks of the river. Neither should you take refuge under the tallest trees along the river.

If you plan to picnic in the valley, take along lightweight coolers or baskets that can be carried in and out easily. It is wise not to plan to take in grills or other cumbersome equipment. Remember not to litter or mar the pristine beauty of the valley. If you can carry food containers into the valley full, you can carry them out empty. And do not leave wrappers of aluminum foil around campfires or eating areas.

If you build a campfire, keep it enclosed by rocks in one of the fire circles you will find. Do not leave a campfire until it is completely extinguished, and do not build a roaring fire in dry or windy weather. Protect the valley as if it is yours.

Because it is.

Do not dump waste into the river and do not empty soapy dish-water into the stream. Protect it, too. It is one of the life-supporting elements of the valley.

If you want the best possible weather, make your visit in the morning rather than afternoon. There is less chance of a sudden storm in the pre-noon hours.

On Labor Day, the traditional day of picking, hundreds of blueberry lovers descend upon Graveyard Fields and begin to gather the delectable berries. People of all ages arrive via campers, RVs, automobiles, motorcycles, bikes, and on foot. They carry small and large buckets, plastic jugs, coolers, and whatever else will hold blueberries.

Some of the visitors sleep in campers in the parking lot, and others pitch tents and camp along the river. Still others lay their sleeping bags on the soft ground and rest beside campfires that wink and glow all over the valley. Nearby residents often drive up for the picking and leave at dusk.

Those wishing to get a jump on the picking arrive during the final week of August and have their choice of berries. Those who spend the nights are often treated to the sight of small herds of deer that wander from the forests nearby and feed on the berries. At dusk the several varieties of owls call back and forth to each other and gather their own food from the fields. During the day hawks can be admired as they soar over the valley. Their screams rise above the sounds of wind and water.

Visitors who brought cameras instead of blueberry buckets can find their fill of spectacular scenery. At the lower end of the valley there is a delightful waterfall that splashes into the best natural swimming pool anyone could want. In a series of cataracts and falls, the Yellowstone Prong pours over immense rocks and into the 30-foot almost round swimming hole where the water is crystal clear and teeth-clenching cold even in August. Almost every hot day hardy souls brave the chill to enjoy the swim. Others are content to make the short and easy quarter-mile hike just to sit in the sun and enjoy the spectacle.

If you want a higher and more dramatic waterfall, leave the lower falls and hike to the upper end of Graveyard Fields. At the end of the trail you will find a cascade that is more than 100 feet high. The Yellowstone Prong rushes down the tree-lined rock slope and into the valley. The waterfall is a great one, although not the highest in the area. Nor does the river have the greatest volume of all the rivers in this part of North Carolina. But the beauty is memorable, and the trip is exciting and delightful.

Do not attempt to climb the rocks alongside the falls. The rocks are slippery and in places they are "rotten." That is, they crumble easily.

There is a third waterfall northward past the swimming hole, but the trip there is rugged and strenuous. However, you can see the falls from the Parkway as you approach Graveyard Fields from the north. There is a pull-off area where you can park and enjoy the falls for as long as you like.

If you don't want to walk to the falls, you can find plenty to please you simply by sauntering along the banks of the river. You will see intricate and incredibly beautiful designs the river has carved into the solid rock over a period of centuries. There are foot bridges at the bottom of the entrance trail, so you do not need to wade the stream.

If you are interested in nature study, you can find hundreds of species of trees, flowering shrubs, and wild flowers in the valley. Best time for rhododendron or laurel blossoms is in mid-June. The wild flowers are at their best in early spring and fall.

The scenery is great during all daylight hours and from all directions. You can stand at the top, in the parking area, and enjoy a 360-degree panoramic beauty. In the valley you can look upstream at some of the finest mountain scenery imaginable, and you can find beauty in every square foot of the valley.

There are song birds galore in the valley, and at night you can see, if you are patient and lucky, raccoons. Groundhogs are numerous throughout the valley and can be seen in early morning and late evening from spring through early fall.

Buck Springs Trail near Mount Pisgah.

SECTION 5: THE BEST GET-OUT-AND-GO PLACES
TRIP 10; BUCK SPRINGS
HIKING WITH CHIPMUNKS

LOCATION:

You can reach the Buck Springs Trail by driving to Mount Pisgah on the Blue Ridge Parkway at Milepost 408.5. This is roughly an hour south of Asheville off I-40. Or, if you prefer, you can follow US 64 to Brevard and then take US 276 north of the waterfall capital of the South. You will emerge on the Parkway just five minutes or so south of Mount Pisgah. Turn right and drive to the Pisgah Inn. The hike starts there.

NEARBY ATTRACTIONS:

You are near, in addition to Brevard, Hendersonville, Flat Rock, Graveyard Fields, Devil's Courthouse, Asheville, Sliding Rock, Looking Glass Falls, and Whitewater Falls.

HOURS OF OPERATION:

The trail is open all day every day; however, there may be days in which the Parkway is closed or US 276 is difficult to drive because of snowfalls.

ADMISSION:

There are no fees of any sort.

FACILITIES:

There are no facilities, other than a clearly marked trail that leads through a delightful forest and parallels the Blue Ridge Parkway fairly closely.

WHAT'S THE STORY?

This trail is not so much a hike, in the more strenuous sense of the word, as it is a gentle and enjoyable walk that will not tire you or place you in perilous situations. If you are a beginning hiker, or if you simply wish to enjoy a rather long but easy walk, this may be perfect for you. Best times to hike or walk or saunter are mid-spring through mid-autumn. You may wish to hike in the middle of the day in cold weather and fairly early in the morning in warmer weather.

SPECIAL ATTRACTIONS:

The attractions are all special in the sense that the entire trail, which is easy to moderate, is beautiful all the way. You will stay in a deep forest the entire length of the trail, and you will not have to cross streams (except to step across small trickles) or struggle up rocky cliffs. There are numerous small animals and many songbirds along the way, as well as wildflowers in warm weather.

MAKING THE MOST OF YOUR VISIT:

The total distance of this walk is 6.4 miles, one-way; if you do not have transportation waiting for you at the end of the hike, then the walk will be 12.8 miles. There are no spurs that lead back to the Parkway, so you must either complete the trail or backtrack to the starting point.

An ideal solution is to have someone drop you off at the Pisgah Inn (do not take up parking space at the inn: it is needed for diners and overnight guests) and then drive the car to the terminus of the trail on US 276. You can see the parking area on the right side of the road as you drive north.

Another solution is to take two cars and park one at either end of the trail. The occupants of one car may park on US 276 and hike north, while the occupants of the second car leave the vehicle in the Mount Pisgah picnic area and hike south. Both of the parties will meet on the trail, and then you can simply trade cars until you reach a meeting place.

It will take you about 3.5 hours to make the hike, one-way. The vertical rise is 2,600 feet, but do not be misled. Most of the climbing is an up-and-down variety, with only gradual and gentle rises facing you. The trail is easier from north to south, so if you are in less than good shape, take the easy route.

If you have only one vehicle, let one hiker start at the Pisgah Inn and then drive the vehicle to the gravel parking area from which you can start the hike in the opposite direction. The pickup can be handled in the same manner, with the north-south hiker driving the car back to the Pisgah Inn to pick up the south-north hikers.

If you start at the Mount Pisgah parking lot, go to the southernmost point of the parking lot and look for the signs directing you to the trail. Starting from the parking lot across the Parkway, cross the Parkway and go to the parking lot. The trail head will be on your immediate right as you face east.

Follow the short trail through the rhododendron thicket to the Pisgah Inn. The trail begins at the southeast corner of the Inn. Walk to the overlook and then take the trail to the right, off the overlook.

You will have company along the entire trail, if you hike in warmer weather. You will hear high-pitched, shrill whistles, very much like the frightened call of a bird. And you will hear the leaves rustling nearby.

If you watch carefully, you will see a number of chipmunks playing among the roots and leaves and rocks. An old woodsman's maxim is that if you hear the chipmunks whistle near you, there are not likely to be any snakes nearby, If you hear the ground-squirrels whistle from a distance and there are no other hikers in the area, be alert for the presence of company, desired or otherwise, in the forest.

But do not become careless simply because the chipmunks say all is well. In any event, it is fun to see, hear, and enjoy the playful activities of these animals which are so easily tamed that you can have them eating from your hand within minutes if you are truly patient and motionless.

You can easily hike a mile in half an hour, and you can keep up this pace for the remainder of the hike. It is possible to walk faster, but this trail is filled with so many less-powerful spectacles, such as brooks creeping from between rocks, that you will not want to race through the pleasure. There are interesting rock formations, wild birds, including wild turkey, grouse, and partridge.

The forest growth in the first mile is largely rhododendron and oak, and along the trail there are rotted logs that were once the magnificent chestnut trees that were a staple growth for men, birds, deer, wild hogs, and other animals in the past.

There are several springs along the trail, usually small ones, and you are cautioned against drinking the water. Carry your own canteen rather than risk a gastrointestinal catastrophe. When you reach the 2.4-mile point, you will see a huge rock cliff on the left and about 75 feet from the trail itself. You will remain closed in from the outside world by the thick foliage as you walk. At 2.6 you will skirt a thick rhododendron thicket, and through the trees you can see a distant peak.

At 2.8 you will see another stream bed and a split-log bridge crossing the trickle. The trail widens after this point. You have made a slow descent from the Pisgah Inn down the slope, and now the pathway levels and you enter a tunnel of rhododendron growth. The trail is wide enough that two can pass abreast at this time.

The only campsite along the entire trail is located at the 3.4 mile point. The camp site is on the right and is 25 feet from the trail. Remember that overnight camping on the trails of the Blue Ridge Parkway is not permitted, so before you make any plans to over-night there you should check with rangers.

At the 4.0 mile mark you will have crossed the third and fourth dry stream bed. Soon, though, you will reach a wider stream that you can cross easily by stepping stones. The stream emerges from a huge heap of boulders and forms deep pools under the tiny shrubs.

As you emerge from the rhododendron thicket and hike for another mile, you will reach a fork in the trail, with one fork leading to the left and down a steep incline 200 feet long. The other fork leading to the right continues straight ahead.

The blazes on the trees and the sign at the fork in the trail indicates that you should take the left fork, which can be done without problems, but the right fork will lead you to the gravel parking area on US 276 where the Buck Spring Trail ends. You will leave your chipmunk friends behind at this point and as you emerge from the forest you will see the shuttle car waiting for you.

View from Cherohala Skyway.

SECTION 6: THE BEST MOUNTAIN DRIVING TOURS
TRIP 1: CHEROHALA SKYWAY
DRIVING WITH YOUR HEAD IN THE CLOUDS

LOCATION:

The Cherohala Skyway is located between Robbinsville, North Carolina, and Tellico Plains, Tennessee. The National Scenic Byway, one of only 20 in the United States, is actually a continuation of NC 143 which leads north of Robbinsville and connects with NC 28, which in turn connects Bryson City with Fontana Village and Fontana Lake. To get to the Skyway from I-40, exit I-40 west of Asheville at Clyde and follow US 19 south to the junction of NC 129 between Murphy and Bryson City. Then you will follow NC 129 into Robbinsville. Drive through town to the west side, where you will join the Cherohala Skyway.

NEARBY ATTRACTIONS:

In Robbinsville you are near the grave of Chief Junaluska, one of the most famous of all the Cherokee Native Americans. You are also within driving distance of Fontana Lake and Village. If you follow the Cherohala Skyway to its terminus at Tellico Plains in eastern Tennessee, you will pass the turn-off to Bald River Falls and Tellico Falls, both of which are spectacular in beauty.

HOURS OF OPERATION:

The Skyway is always open unless heavy snow or ice forces highway officials to close it.

ADMISSION:

There is no admission fee to the Skyway or to the grave of Junaluska or Tellico and Bald River Falls.

FACILITIES:

Along the drive you will find restrooms, drinking water, picnic tables, scenic overlooks, and hiking trails. There are no service stations or restaurants, so you must take care of these needs either before you leave Robbinsville or after you reach Tellico Plains in Tennessee. Do not drive this stretch of highway with a nearly empty gas tank. The steep climbs will cause your car to consume more gas than normal.

WHAT'S THE STORY?

This superb stretch of highway is one of the most beautiful drives in the United States and is in many ways (I never thought I'd be guilty of saying this!) a rival to the Blue Ridge Parkway. Opened in November 1996, this 50-mile trip crosses ridge after ridge at altitudes of 5,000 feet and higher, and on both sides of the road, which is free of all billboards and commercial vehicles and the other inconveniences of commercial highways; you will see majestic mountains and incredibly beautiful and wild valleys. The story of how the highway came into existence can be found below.

SPECIAL ATTRACTIONS:

The three major recommendations of this highway have already been mentioned: the waterfalls near the end and the beauty of the drive. But you have the added attractions of the Joyce Kilmer National Forest and Big Santeelah Lake.

MAKING THE MOST OF YOUR VISIT:

Travelers to western North Carolina have a terrific treat in store for them-the Cherohala Highway, known more affectionately as the Skyway-that was opened in November 1996. The Skyway, in nearly every way (except total distance) a worthy rival of the Blue Ridge Parkway, crosses the ridges and peaks of the mountains between Robbinsville and Tellico Plains, Tennessee.

The idea for the scenic highway with panoramic views in every direction started, actually, in Tellico Plains, a small town in eastern Tennessee, in 1958 when Sam Williams delivered an address to the Kiwanis Club of that city.

At the time the television series "Wagon Train" was one of the most popular shows in the country, and Williams, who had long wanted a scenic highway connecting the two states, opened his speech with a serio-comic statement that led to the dramatic and incredibly beautiful highway.

"Why don't we have a 'Wagon Train' of our own," Williams said. "We have only wagon roads here."

After the laughter subsided, serious discussions began, and before the meeting ended club members were already deep into the planning stages for fund-raising projects that would make the dream highway a reality.

The proposal, logically enough, was to use across-the-crest wagon trains to raise money, through contributions, and members and other enthusiasts immediately began to assemble the necessary ingredients. And on June 7, 1958, the first wagon train left Tellico Plains for Murphy, North Carolina.

There were 67 of the steel-tired, wooden-spoked wagons, accompanied by about 325 horseback riders making the 51-mile trip between Tellico Plains and Robbinsville and on to the city of Murphy.

The last wagon train made the trek in early July and ended the journey on July 4, 1996. The largest train to made the cross-mountain trip consisted of 125 wagons and 400 horseback riders. At the dedication about 600 people gathered to mark the event.

During the wagon train period, contributions poured in, and the first work on the highway began on January 21, 1965, with the first leg reaching from Hace Lead to Santeelah Gap. On February 22, 1965, the first contract was awarded for the Tennessee portion of the highway.

One of the major problems encountered, other than the actual physical construction of the road, resulted from the Eastern Wilderness Act of 1975, which prohibits mechanized travel in the wilderness areas, which included the Joyce Kilmer-Slick Rock areas.

Thus a new route had to be established, and the result was the highway leading from Santeelah Gap and continuing along the Unicoi crest to the Tennessee state line. The highway was open for the first tourists on October 12, 1996.

In order to travel a highway as spectacular as the Skyway, the visitor in the area might want to start with a historically significant site and conclude with one of the most gorgeous and inviting beauty spots of the South.

As you leave Robbinsville you will see portions of Santeelah Lake and part of the Joyce Kilmer National Forest. If you have seen "Nell," the Jodie Foster movie, you will recognize many scenes from the movie in both Robbinsville and in the surrounding countryside.

As you drive Highway 143 West-the Skyway-you will start at an elevation of 3,000 feet, and the road climbs steeply, with grades up to nine per cent. Within four miles you will climb to 4,000 feet, and within three more miles you will be at 5,000 feet above sea level. Within ten miles from the time you enter the Skyway you will be at 5,390 feet.

Along the way you will reach the heads of trails that lead into the valleys and to the peaks of the mountains. Stop at many of the overlooks and you can hear the roaring of unseen waterfalls in the valleys below.

If you wander along the trails, or simply park in one of the overlooks, you may be treated to the songs or appearances of a wide variety of songbirds, including the belted kingfisher, olive warbler, Canada warbler, rufous-sided towhee, indigo bunting, Eastern meadowlark, cedar waxwing, wood duck, rufous hummingbird, red-winged blackbird, and the American goldfinch.

Thirty-eight miles into the trip you will see a road turning off to the left and a sign directing you to Bald River Falls. By all means take the picturesque six-mile drive along the banks of the Tellico and Bald rivers which flowed together six miles up the narrow but paved road.

I feel no guilt whatever about relating, in a book about the beauties of North Carolina, the glories of Tennessee. Elsewhere in this book you will find trips suggested (or rather, continued) into Georgia, South Carolina, and Virginia, so why not include the fantastic state of Tennessee as well? North Carolina is very fortunate to have such incredible neighbors.

In warm months you will see canoes and kayaks shooting the mild rapids, and along the way there are many flowering shrubs and bushes and the trees seem alive with songbirds.

Then you round a bend and see-at once, with startling and dramatic energy-Bald River Falls, one of the most beautiful waterfalls you are likely to find anywhere in this part of the country.

The incredible aspect of the falls lies in the way the river flows in irregular patterns over the rocks. The main channel of the river falls to a rock ledge, while on the left side of the river (as you are facing the falls) part of the current cascades down a series of smaller falls, and then the falls seem to move in a dozen directions. On the right ledge, twenty feet from the falls, a sliver of water drops down the embankment and then disappears in the underbrush and reappears just above the surface of the water.

But this is not all of the show. Continue up the winding road another quarter of a mile and you will see the Tellico River's Baby Falls, which are picturesque enough without any embellishment, but you are also likely to be treated to the sight of kayakers going over the falls.

At times there are a dozen or more kayakers waiting in line to shoot the falls, and as the small crafts hit the water they disappear instantly, only to bob to the surface almost under the falls.

The entire drive along the Skyway requires slightly more than an hour, but most motorists are likely to stop at several of the overlooks and will stretch the drive into two hours or more.

And you will find it difficult to think of a better way to spend two hours of your life. You will leave the area in a spirit of gratitude that Sam Williams was once a fan of "Wagon Train" and that the Kiwanians of Tellico Plains had the courage, the energy, and the foresight to have the dream and start it on its way to realization.

Note: Much of the material in this chapter earlier appeared in *Our State* Magazine and is reprinted here with kind permission of Mary Ellis, editor of the magazine.

Mabry Mill on Parkway in Virginia.

Orelana Hawks Puckett cabin on Parkway in Virginia.

SECTION 6: THE BEST MOUNTAIN DRIVING TOURS
TRIP 2: CUMBERLAND KNOB AND BEYOND
"MOTHER" OF A THOUSAND INFANTS

LOCATION:

Having traveled the Blue Ridge Parkway for nearly half a century, I do not know of a single mile of the way that is not a scenic treat. But because so many other trips in this book have included sections of the Parkway, this trip is far north of the other destinations. To get to this part of the Parkway, drive to Statesville on I-40 and junction with I-77. Drive north until you junction with the Parkway. Then drive to Cumberland Knob (at Milepost 216), Fox Hunters Paradise (at Milepost 217), and points south. Then you can turn around and drive north and cross the state line and proceed into the state of Virginia, where you will see Groundhog Mountain, the Puckett Cabin, and Mabry Mill.

I realize that this is cheating in a sense, because part of this trip is in Virginia. But look at it this way: when you are on the Blue Ridge Parkway you are never cheated.

If you do not wish to backtrack, you can exit I-40 onto I-77 and then junction with US 21 and drive to Elkin and from there to the Parkway. But do not worry about backtracking. The way I see this is that you simply get to see the same beauties twice.

NEARBY ATTRACTIONS:

While you are in this area, you are close enough to Doughton Park to combine a trip there with this trip. You also have the option of including Stone Mountain State Park as well. And if you drive as far north as Mabry Mill (at about Milepost 175) you are within easy distance of Rocky Knob Visitors Center at Milepost 170. There is great scenery along the way.

HOURS OF OPERATION:

The hiking or sightseeing areas described in this chapter are open all day every day of the year, weather permitting, but the Visitors Centers usually operate from 8 a.m. or 9 a.m. until 5 p.m. Plan to be safe by arriving after nine in the morning or before five in the afternoon.

ADMISSION:

There are no admission fees at any of the attractions in this chapter; however, there is a fee if you wish to camp. At Doughton Park the camping fees are $10 nightly.

FACILITIES:

You can readily find ample parking, clean and spacious restrooms, picnic tables, scenic overlooks, hiking or walking trails, and information brochures. There are also programs that are offered by staff members at many attractions.

WHAT'S THE STORY?

The Blue Ridge Parkway runs in a north-south direction for 469 miles and connects two superlative national parks: the Great Smoky Mountains National Park in the South and the Shenandoah National Park in Virginia. In North Carolina there are 252 miles of Parkway for you to enjoy, and there are five campgrounds, eight picnic areas, two lodges, and three restaurants. There are also wonderful places to shop for books and other remembrances of your trip-or to help you plan your next trip.

The Blue Ridge Parkway may have been the brainchild of United States Senator Harry Byrd of Virginia, or it could have been the idea of Theodore Straus, a member of the Public Works Administration from Maryland. In 1933 Senator Byrd and President Franklin Roosevelt toured Civilian Conservation Corps camps in the Shenandoah Mountains of Virginia (Does anyone remember the old Clyde Moody song--"In the Shenandoah Valley of Virginia"?) and the President became excited over the prospect of extending the beauty along the mountain crests. An early concept was to extend from New England into Tennessee.

The original idea was to create a toll highway, rather like the Skyline Drive, but North Carolina Governor Ehringhaus was adamantly opposed to the idea. It took more than half a century from the time the first construction work was done in 1936 until the final link of the Parkway was completed at the Linn Cove Viaduct around Grandfather Mountain.

As you drive the Parkway, you will see signs and information posted prominently that commercial vehicles are prohibited on the Parkway. No hunting is permitted, and weapons of all recognized types are similarly prohibited. You are not permitted to dig up plants or pick flowers. Signs urge you to "leave the flowers for others to enjoy." This is wonderful advice. You are not allowed to litter or to swim or camp except in authorized areas, and you are not permitted to molest any animals (or people, for that matter) on the Parkway.

This stretch of highway is, in this writer's opinion, the closest to Heaven we can reach on this earth. To me, it is one of life's great experiences to drive any part of the Parkway, and we owe it to ourselves, our children, and those who made the Parkway possible to take the best care of it that we possibly can. Speed limits are 45 miles per hour unless otherwise posted. Observe these limits: they exist for dozens of good reasons, all having your continued health in mind.

SPECIAL ATTRACTIONS:

Cumberland Knob is a great place to stop (and it was the first Visitors Center constructed on the Parkway), and the Puckett Cabin is a wonderful educational and even aesthetic experience. One of the most scenic spots anywhere is Mabry Mill, although the Puckett Cabin and Mabry Mill are both across the Virginia line. But who cares? It's all part of the greatest country in the history of humanity and the greatest region this writer has ever experienced. It's also part of two of the finest states in the nation. After all, it's only 25 extra miles to Mabry Mill and only 10 extra miles to Groundhog Mountain.

MAKING THE MOST OF YOUR VISIT:

First of all, if your schedule and energies will permit, I strongly recommend that you drive the entire length of the Blue Ridge Parkway. The only reason this one short stretch in this chapter is suggested is that you have, as stated above, already driven part of the Parkway en route to other destinations. Until you have driven the entire highway, however, you have not seen the Blue Ridge Parkway as well as you should have.

To make the most of your visit, the time you make the trip is important. To see the rhododendron and laurel at its glorious peak, you need to be there in early June. In April you can catch the dogwoods in bloom. By the warmest portions of May the blooms on the Fraser magnolias are out. The flame azalea is at its best stages by the middle of May. But be forewarned that seasons are not all the same, and on occasions the rhododendron will have passed its peak in early June and will be gone by the time it would normally have been in its glory.

To see wildflowers of all sorts, almost any time from early April through late September is good. There is almost always some shrub or flower in bloom except during the cold weather.

When you reach Cumberland Knob Visitors Center, you are at 2,737 feet above sea level. The weather here is milder in winter and cooler in summer than you would expect. You are at Milepost 217.5 at this point.

When you drive to Mabry Mill, which is the final stop on this driving tour, you will see, during regular hours, a working grist mill with one of the finest mill ponds you will ever see--complete with ducks. You can also see a blacksmith shop, a sawmill, crafts, old-fashioned spinning wheels that are in operation, and tools of all sorts. It is a wonderful and highly educational treat to see how work was accomplished in days beyond the memory of most current visitors.

Mabry Mill was built about 1901 by a master of all trades, a man named Edwin B. Mabry, who was an accomplished chairmaker, miner, blacksmith, and farmer. He was also a superb carpenter. Edwin and Mintoria Lizzie Mabry (Edwin's wife) ran the operation until 1936. On the premises they sawed lumber, ground corn, and performed other tasks for the people of the Meadows of Dan area.

When the mill closed, it was falling into a state of severe disrepair when the National Park Service, in 1945, restored the mill and landscaped the terrain. The mill is reportedly the most photographed location on the Blue Ridge Parkway.

Before you reach Mabry Mill, you will see a small and very neat cabin, complete with a split rail fence, on the north side of the Parkway. This meticulous cabin was once the home of Mrs. Orelana Hawks Puckett, who was born there in 1837 and spent her 102 years of life here.

Mrs. Puckett was quoted as saying, "The forest was green when I was a-born and I'm green yet." At age 16 she married and she and her husband earned their living by farming a small plot of land near Groundhog Mountain, which is only a mile away.

Orelana Puckett waited until she was 50 years old before she began her real career-her calling. At an age that was in that time already advanced in years, she became a midwife, and before she had completed her work, she had devoted more than half a century to helping the expectant women in the mountains.

She helped to deliver more than 1,000 children, the last of which was born in 1939. The popular claim was that during her 52 years of midwifery she never lost a baby or a mother through her own fault.

The story is that she disregarded weather and time, and if she was needed, she went, on horseback at times, walking the rest of the time. Her fee when she started her career was $1 for each birth or, "if times was good," $6. Often there was no money at all for her, and she accepted food or other considerations in lieu of her fee.

And, to make the story better, she used the money or the food often to come to the aid of her neighbors in need. A witty, cheerful, and optimistic person, she delivered her final child, Maxwell Dale Hawks, shortly before her own death at age 102.

Stop at the cabin, enjoy the neatness and beauty, and if you feel the need to pause a moment in this fast-paced world and offer a silent prayer of thanksgiving that such women as Orelana Hawks Puckett lived, the time will not be wasted. The cabin is a superior tribute to an incredible woman.

The most tragic element of her life is that Orelana Puckett herself gave birth to 24 of her own children-and not one of them survived beyond infancy!

At nearby Groundhog mountain you will see superb examples of many kinds of rail fencing, from snake, post and rail, and buck. There is a small observation tower you can climb to gain a better view of the surrounding countryside. There are restrooms and picnic tables at Groundhog Mountain.

A noted person once said that his fondest wish was to read *War and Peace* again-for the first time. My wish is that I could see the Blue Ridge Parkway again each month-for the first time!

Mill at Cades Cove Visitors Center in Great Smokies.

SECTION 6: THE BEST MOUNTAIN DRIVING TOURS
TRIP 3: FROM NEWFOUND GAP TO
AND THROUGH CADES COVE
JOURNEY INTO ANOTHER TIME

LOCATION:

Because the trip to and through Cades Cove is so time-consuming, this trip is divided into two halves, the first of which is found below. You can, of course, hurry sufficiently to see both parts of the trip in one outing, but why hurry and miss so much spectacular scenery, not to mention the dangers to yourself and others that speed and frustration create.

To get to this part of North Carolina (and across into the eastern part of Tennessee), intersect with US 441 at the end of the Blue Ridge Parkway and drive north through the Great Smokies National Park. Along the way the highway intersects with the Cades Cove road, and together the two roads will take you into the distant past and into the world of history and early Americana. To reach US 441 drive 10 miles west of Asheville on

I-40 and then take the Clyde exit onto US 19 which will lead you to Cherokee and to US 441. Do not worry about losing your way once you are on US 441: this is the only highway through the Great Smoky Mountains National Park.

NEARBY ATTRACTIONS:

While you are in the area you can find interesting stops at Smokemont, Clingman's Dome (in warm weather), at Cherokee, Bryson City, Dillsboro, Sylva, the Cherokee Indian Reservation, and the many attractions owned and operated by Native Americans in the area.

HOURS OF OPERATION:

The two highways are open all day long every day of the year during the warmer months. For off-season information call (423) 436-1200 (offices of the Great Smoky Mountains National Park). It is better to make the telephone call to be certain that the Cades Cove road is open than it is to make the trip for nothing.

ADMISSION:

There are no admission charges for using US 441 and the Cades Cove drive.

FACILITIES:

Along US 441 and the remainder of the drive you will have a chance to enjoy a picnic, camp if you wish, take part in outdoor recreations like fishing, hiking, canoeing, and nature study. There are restrooms, information desks, travel brochures, gift shops, and visitors centers.

WHAT'S THE STORY?

US 441 and the Cades Cove drive take you through the often rugged Appalachian Mountain range considered by many to be the oldest mountains in the world. You will drive through the most visited national park in the United States, and along the way you will see some of the highest peaks east of the Mississippi, old mills, cabins of settlers, and wild life galore, including black bears, deer, wild turkeys, and many other forms of animal life.

SPECIAL ATTRACTIONS:

Cades Cove has been described as a gigantic open-air museum, a link with the past, a panorama of man's history within this wild and secluded part of the Great Smokies. Among the best stops along the way are the Clingman's Dome experience, the Cable Mill, and the historic cabins and churches.

MAKING THE MOST OF YOUR VISIT:

As you drive along US 441 you will have wonderful views of the mountain peaks and valleys. Part of the way you will see clear and beautiful streams alongside the highway. In autumn the foliage is glorious beyond words; however, at this time of year you will encounter the most crowded conditions. If you plan to visit in the fall, try to make your trip during the week rather than on weekends or holidays.

If you visit in the spring the number of visitors will be somewhat smaller, and you will have the opportunity to drive at your leisure and stop to enjoy the roadside attractions. In the summer months, especially after the public schools and colleges have closed for the spring, there are many families making the trip and camping along the way.

If I had to pick the perfect time to go, there would be three major considerations: If I wanted to camp, I'd visit after Labor Day and before May 1 in the spring. Second, if I wanted to see wild life and history unfolding before me, I'd go in April or November. For the best views of autumn leaves, the best times would be week days in October.

When you drive up US 441 to the entrance to the Cades Cove part of the Great Smoky Mountains National Park, you will be leaving North Carolina. But, as you read in the Blue Ridge Parkway chapter, it is not cheating to cross state lines. To repeat the admonition, if you did not see the roadside highway markers, you would never realize that you had left one state and entered another. Secondly, the mountains of the two states are in many ways highly similar. The park is a part of the greatest land in the history of the world, a part of the greatest region of the United States, and a section of two of the finest states east-or west-of the Mississippi. In short, don't worry about crossing a state line. Look upon it as an opportunity to add Tennessee to your list of favorite places.

Cades Cove is an 11-mile driving loop (which can also be hiked or biked, and you can rent bikes in the park) that leads you to 18 superb stops. Along the way you will visit about five mountain homesteads, three ancient churches, one nature trail, a hiking trail (optional: you need not walk a step unless you wish to do so), and some delightful roads and lanes.

Caution: In the Cades Cove area (and, indeed, in many other parts of the Great Smokies) you will see huge, black, and warm and cuddly bear cubs, often with their mother. WRONG!!! These bears, cubs or adults, are not household pets and are not to be petted at any time or under any conditions. These are wild and often fierce and dangerous animals.

Let the bears be wild animals. Do not feed them, approach them, or in any way interfere with their lifestyles. During a recent trip to Cades Cove my family and I saw a mother and her three children stop their car, leap out, and run into the woods in pursuit of a mother bear and her two cubs.

Please do not make the sometimes-fatal mistake of trying to pet cubs. Mother bears do not appreciate or tolerate this, and they are highly efficient in demonstrating their displeasure.

On a more civilized level, Cades Cove was originally inhabited by Native Americans, and in the early 1800s European descendants began to move into the cove and build cabins. These settlers came from Tennessee and North Carolina. By 1850 the population of Cades Cove was about 700; by 1860 this number had been decreased to less than half the earlier number. By 1920 the population had risen to about 500 once again.

One of the first stops is at the John Oliver Place where about 1826 the Olivers moved into the cove. Notice the log walls and the notching to cut down on the use of nails. Mud was used for chinking between logs. The small windows kept heat loss to a minimum (and, incidentally, made it difficult for wild animals to enter the house).

The fourth stop is the Primitive Baptist Church, built in 1827. The church discontinued services during the Civil War because residents were bitterly divided in their loyalties.

At the 11th stop you will visit the Cable Mill. The Cades Cove Visitors Center is open from mid-April through October. There are exhibits inside that depict mountain life. During your visits to the outbuildings note the cantilevered barn style. The John Cable Mill is one of the favorite stops on the drive.

At stop 15 you will visit the Dan Lawson Place, built in 1856 from home-made bricks, unusual materials for the time. At stop 16 you will see the Tipton Place, built in 1878. One of the last stops is the Carter Shields Cabin, and at this time you have seen one of the finest collections of log structures in the United States. And you have had a glimpse of the history, not only of men but of an entire community.

Clingmans Dome in Great Smokies.

SECTION 6: THE BEST MOUNTAIN DRIVING TOURS
TRIP 4: THE DRIVE TO CLINGMAN'S DOME
THE LAND OF EKWANULTI

LOCATION:

This is the other half of the trip through the Great Smoky Mountains Natiional Park. This drive and the incredible scenery are unforgettable experiences. This is another of the motor trips designed for those who for one reason or another cannot take part in the Get-Out-and-Go trips. This trip is a 35-mile jaunt from just northeast of Bryson City to the top of Old Smoky-in this case, Clingman's Dome. You will drive part of the way on the same highway that took you to Newfound Gap and beyond to Cades Cove.

The ideal way to make this trip, if time permits, is to drive the Blue Ridge Parkway to its end and then to exit onto US 441. Then you drive north. That's how simple it is.

If you are not traveling the Parkway, you can drive down US 19, which you can reach 10 miles or so west of Asheville off I-40. You can junction with US 441 in the city of Cherokee.

NEARBY ATTRACTIONS:

On the Parkway you will pass Graveyard Fields, the Devil's Courthouse mountain, Mount Pisgah, the Shining Rock Wilderness area, Looking Glass Falls, Sliding Rock, the Cradle of Forestry (these last three to be found on US 276 between Brevard and the Parkway), Richland Balsam (the highest point on the Parkway at 6,047 feet above sea level), and Waterrock Knob, which is 5,718 feet above sea level.

If you travel US 19 you pass through Maggie Valley and the many attractions found there. Inside the Great Smoky Mountains National Park or near the entrance you will see scores of other attractions, many of them in the Cherokee area.

HOURS OF OPERATION:

The highway through the Great Smoky Mountains National Park (and there is only one real highway) will take you to the area of Clingman's Dome, which is 6,642 feet above sea level and is the highest point in the Great Smoky Mountains National Park, and a spur road will take you to the top of the mountain-or near it. Along the way you will pass near Newfound Gap, and later you can if you wish drive to within a short distance of Mount LeConte, which is 6,593 feet above sea level. This highway is open night and day every day of the week during the warm months. It is closed in winter.

ADMISSION:

There is no admission fee or charge to use the road or to enjoy the beauty along the way.

FACILITIES:

On this trip you will have access to restrooms, visitors center, hiking trails, overlooks, campgrounds nearby, picnic tables, information centers, opportunities for hiking, fishing, and sightseeing or nature study, and some highly educational plaques or information boards.

WHAT'S THE STORY?

The Great Smoky Mountains National Park contains 520,004 acres of forest and wild land, with about 276,000 acres within the state of North Carolina. The rest is in Tennessee. The park is the largest protected land area east of the Mississippi River. The park was authorized by Congress in 1926 and in 1940 it was dedicated by President Franklin Delano Roosevelt. The park is the most visited national park in the nation, with more than ten million visitors annually.

Inside the park there are nearly 1,500 varieties of blooming or flowering plants, more than 150 species of trees, over 200 species of birds, at least 50 species of fur-bearing animals, more than two dozen species of reptiles, and more than 75 forms of piscine life, including several varieties of trout.

SPECIAL ATTRACTIONS:

If you like hiking, you will find more than 500 miles of hiking and bridle trails in North Carolina and more than 900 miles of trail in both states. The longest trail is a segment of the Appalachian Trail that runs through part of the park. You can hike the entire 69-mile stretch if you wish, and if that is not enough, there is another segment of 43 miles called the Lakeshore Trail, which provides you a perfect way to visit the Fontana Dam site. There are also short trails, 54 of them, that are classified as nature trails. These can be walked easily in a few minutes up to an hour or so.

MAKING THE MOST OF YOUR VISIT:

As soon as you enter the park, stop at the Oconaluftee Visitors Center and the next-door Mountain Farm Museum, which is described elsewhere in this book. The Oconoluftee River flows through the valley and is for miles and miles a clear, clean, and beautiful stream that you can enjoy at times from your car or from the roadside. The name of the Visitors Center, which is in turn named for the river, is derived from the Cherokee word *Ekwanulti*, which means "place by the river."

As you drive the 16-mile stretch from the Visitors Center to Newfound Gap, you will be able to enjoy panoramic views of the Oconaluftee River and some of the higher peaks in the Smokies. At Newfound Gap you are at the spot where President Roosevelt led the dedication services that officially opened the Great Smoky Mountains National Park. Newfound Gap is near a place once known as Indian Gap where horseback riders and even horse-drawn wagons could pass through the mountains in this "new-found" gap.

You will pass through hardwood forests and through mountains that range in altitude from about 3,500 feet to 4,500 feet.

On the highway from Newfound Gap to Clingman's Dome (about 24 miles) you will see a demoralizing sight: thousands of dead or dying trees, many of them of the Fraser fir variety, and the even sadder part is that no one at present seems to know how to stop the widespread destruction of the beautiful trees.

The cause of the destruction may be twofold, at least. It has been thought that acid rain caused by pollution from mills and automobiles and other by-products of the 20th century has killed many of the trees, while other deaths are attributed to the wooly aphid that kills the trees by injecting a toxin that interferes with the tree's nutrition and stability. It is not that one aphid can cause the death, but there are literally millions (and perhaps billions) of these insects in the area, after having been introduced into this country during this century.

Clingman's Dome was named for General Thomas L. Clingman, who was the final Southern survivor of the famed United States Senate in 1860, an august group considered by some historians as the greatest Senate in United States history. Clingman was a general in the Civil War, and as a soldier he ranged (fluctuated, some insist) between courageous and thoughtlessly rash.

Clingman served seven terms in the House, one term as a Whig and the other six as a Democrat. It was in 1858 that Zeb Vance decided to run for election, and he chose to oppose Clingman in the house race. It was among the first endeavors by Vance in seeking a political life, and he wound up spending many years in Congress or in the mansion of the governor.

But Clingman's day in the sun was not over. When Dr. Elisha Mitchell of the University of North Carolina announced that the mountain which bears his name was and is the highest peak east of the Mississippi, Clingman disagreed, claiming that the mountain now known as Clingman's Dome was higher.

Mitchell was dead right. He died while on a mountain trek. Clingman's Dome, is, however, one of the highest peaks east of the Mississippi, and offers an unsurpassed panoramic view.

The Tunnel to Nowhere near Bryson City

SECTION 6: THE BEST MOUNTAIN DRIVING TOURS
TRIP 5: LAKEVIEW DRIVE
THE ROAD TO NOWHERE

LOCATION:

Lakeview Drive just outside Bryson City can be reached from I-40 by taking the Clyde exit about 10 miles west of Asheville and then following US 19 through Lake Junaluska and Maggie all the way to Bryson City. In Bryson City, in the center of town you will find the courthouse, and from here you will drive north on Everett Street for three miles to the entrance to the Great Smoky Mountains National Park.

NEARBY ATTRACTIONS:

You are within easy driving distance to Dillsboro and the Great Smoky Mountains Railroad, to the superb courthouse in nearby Sylva, and to the attractions found in Cherokee. It is also an easy drive to Fontana Dam, Lake, and Village. You can drive down to Robbinsville, where you can see and drive the Cherohala Skyway just outside Robbinsville.

HOURS OF OPERATION:
The Road to Nowhere is always open, except when ice, snow, and sleet cover the highway and make driving dangerous if not impossible.

ADMISSION:
There are no admission charges.

FACILITIES:
There are no facilities. There are some hiking trails and some overlooks, but there are no other conveniences.

WHAT'S THE STORY?
The story is a simple and sad one. A road was started but never finished. You drive to a 1,200-foot tunnel, park your car, and walk into the tunnel. When you emerge on the other side, the road ends abruptly. You are, in an almost literal sense, in the middle of Nowhere.

SPECIAL ATTRACTIONS:
Along the way to nowhere, you will have some spectacular views of Fontana Lake, and you can get out and stretch your legs, or stay near the car and enjoy the views.

MAKING THE MOST OF YOUR VISIT:
It had to happen sooner or later. Throughout this book you have been presented with, to this point, about 60 places you can visit and have a great time. From this point to the end of the book you will be offered about 30 more destinations. So it was bound to happen eventually that there is nowhere else to go. You are heading for Nowhere. That's the bad news. The good news is that you have a good road on which to travel.

You are now expecting an explanation, and you are entitled to one. The Road to Nowhere started out specifically to be the road to Somewhere.

The original plan was for a 50-mile road, which was to be called the North Shore Road, to connect Bryson City and that part of the state to the Great Smoky Mountains National Park.

The road was alternately called, in addition to North Shore Drive (the north shore of Fontana Lake, in case you have been wondering), Lake View Road, Lakeshore Drive, and some other labels that are unprintable, and the odds are that not one out of 100 people in Bryson City could direct you to either of the names just above. But if you ask about the Road to Nowhere, anyone can and will tell you how to get there.

This road has for more than four decades been a controversy, a problem, a dilemma, and a riddle without a solution. When the Tennessee Valley Authority completed the surveying for the final boundary of Fontana Lake, it was obvious that the existing roads could not accommodate the traffic that would be moving into the area of the lake and the national park.

While the intrigues and confusion are bewildering, here is, at least with partial accuracy, what happened. Swain County took the necessary steps to have municipal bonds financed through the North Carolina Department of Transportation. The county had lost thousands of acres of land as part of the tax base when the dam was completed and the lake was formed.

To offset, as least in part, the loss of tax base in land that was going to become part of the national park, the TVA, the North Carolina Department of Transportation, and Swain County all agreed in 1943 that the road would be constructed.

And six miles of the road were indeed completed. You leave Bryson City and start north. Within a few minutes you are at the parking area for the Noland Creek Trail. You are five miles from Bryson City at this point, and when you get out of the car and look around you, the view is staggering, whether you look all around you at the peaks and the lush forests or at the lake below, or, if you are lucky, at the flowers in bloom or the wild turkeys, even a deer, feeding at the edge of the forest.

The remainder of the road leads to Forney Ridge (also called Tunnel Ridge) where you see the road enter the nefarious tunnel. The road enters the tunnel and then abruptly ends.

But you cannot drive through the tunnel; however, you can park nearby and walk through the tunnel. Many people do. That's one of the few recreations when you are in Nowhere.

If you feel up to it, you can make your way down to the trail near the bridge. On this Noland Creek Trail you will find places to hike, picnic, bike, and sightsee. The road continues for about six scenic miles. The hike, in case you want to walk a while, from the bridge to Fontana Lake is one mile.

There is also the Lakeshore Trail, and if you drive to the tunnel, you can park on the right side of the road and hit the trail almost instantly. This trail connects with the Appalachian Trail for a hike longer than most people want to undertake at a moment's notice.

On this trip you will see the sights, but if you use your imagination and wonder what it would have been like if the road had been completed, it's staggering to think that an immense part of the national park remains unseen to all but a few hikers.

Pearson's Falls between Tryon and Saluda.

SECTION 6: THE BEST MOUNTAIN DRIVING TOURS
TRIP 6: US 176--TRYON TO SALUDA
PACOLET RIVER SCENIC BYWAY

LOCATION:

This scenic drive is located between the mountain towns of Tryon and Saluda, and you can reach the drive from I-40 just west of downtown Asheville by junctioning with I-26 and driving south through Hendersonville and into the outskirts of Saluda. Or you can continue to Tryon and drive northward. From US 74 west of Shelby you exit US 74 in Columbus and junction with NC 108 into Tryon, where you will immediately see signs that direct you to US 176. Or you can reach the area via I-26 out of Spartanburg.

NEARBY ATTRACTIONS:

There are numerous attractions in both Tryon and Saluda as well as in nearby Columbus. In addition you can visit the Carl Sandburg house in Flat Rock, attend the Flat Rock Theatre, and enjoy the attractions in Hendersonville. You are within easy driving distance from Holmes Educational State Forest, Brevard and the many waterfalls surrounding the city, the Blue Ridge Parkway, Asheville and the countless attractions there, Mount Mitchell, and Craggy Gardens. All of these attractions are also described elsewhere in this book.

HOURS OF OPERATION:

The US 176 Scenic Byway is always open, winter weather permitting, but some of the attractions are seasonal and are open only during the warm months of the year. Others operate on an abbreviated schedule, so it is wise to call before planning and starting the trip. Most businesses and restaurants are open from 9 a.m. until 5 or 6 p.m. or later.

ADMISSION:

There are no admission charges for using US 176, but you will pay $2 per person to tour Pearson's Falls, which are just one mile off the scenic byway.

FACILITIES:

There are no facilities along the byway, other than service stations and other commercial establishments and the facilities they offer to the public. You can find public telephones along the way, and at Pearson's Falls you can find picnic tables and a short hiking trail.

WHAT'S THE STORY?

This scenic byway is a two-lane winding stretch of road that extends about 10 miles between the two terrific small towns. The road passes through a valley with steep mountains on either side, and you will encounter trucks, school buses, and other vehicles along the way, so you can expect speed to be somewhat slower than on Piedmont highways. But you don't want to drive fast, anyhow, and miss the scenery. There are passing zones along the way in the event that you get behind vehicles that are too slow even for a scenic tour.

SPECIAL ATTRACTIONS:

Pearson's Falls and hike are the major attraction along the scenic highway.

MAKING THE MOST OF YOUR VISIT:

My suggestion for making the trip is to start at Tryon and drive up the mountain. There are two reasons for this suggestion: first, it is often safer to drive uphill than down, primarily because it is easier to make sudden stops, if necessary. And it is seldom necessary because gravity keeps people and vehicles moving slowly. The second reason is that as you are climbing, you see the mountains starting to take form before you. They seem to grow larger and larger as you climb, and you have wonderful views as you round curve after curve.

The Pacolet River runs alongside the highway for part of the drive, and you can catch views of it as it leaps over boulders and creates tiny cataracts. Within five miles you will reach the turnoff to Pearson's Falls.

Watch your odometer as you drive. You will cross a bridge, and without warning the gate to the waterfall is suddenly before you. You will see a stone gate with a narrow paved road entering the forest. Drive only 100 yards and you will see a sign telling you to wait for the ticket person. Admission, as you learned earlier, is $2 per person for adults. Note that this cost is not per vehicle as is often the case. Cost for children 6-12 is $.50, and children under age six are admitted free.

The waterfall was named for Charles William Pearson, a young engineer who discovered the waterfall while looking for a passage through the mountains for the Southern Railroad line. For years the Pearsons owned the land he bought shortly after discovering it, and the flat rocks at the base of the falls became favorite picnic grounds.

In 1931 the son of Pearson had to sell the property, and he was prepared to sell it to a timber company that wanted the superb forest for lumber. But the falls area was saved by the Tryon Garden Club, which bought the land and set out to preserve the acreage there.

Once you enter the parking area, you will hike one-fourth of a mile to the waterfall, which is a 90-foot cataract pouring over a rock cliff. Along the way you will see thousands of plants that grow in profusion. There are more than 200 species of ferns, moss, algae, and flowering plants.

There are picnic tables scattered around the falls area, with the first ones placed near the start of the trail. There is one table at the end of the trail, only feet from the base of the waterfall. You cannot build any fires here or operate a grill, but you are invited to enjoy a picnic of prepared foods that you bring along.

Once you leave the falls, it is only a short trip to Saluda, which has some fine shops, beautiful churches, and astonishingly beautiful houses. While you are in Saluda (on the steepest main-line railroad grade in the United States), be sure to visit the Church of the Transfiguration, which is a mountain jewel.

Great Smoky Mountains Expressway.

SECTION 6: THE BEST MOUNTAIN DRIVING TOURS
TRIP 7: THE SMOKY MOUNTAIN EXPRESSWAY
THE ROAD TO EVERYWHERE

LOCATION:

As do so many roads in the Great Smokies and the western part of North Carolina, this terrific scenic drive leaves I-40 about 10 miles west of Asheville at Exit 27. You are actually on the following highways: US 19, US 23, and US 64. The drive leads from Clyde to Cherokee. To access the highway from I-26, drive north of the Greenville-Spartanburg area of South Carolina and through the Tryon-Saluda area, past Hendersonville, and into the outskirts of Asheville, where you will junction with I-40 and from there to the Great Smoky Mountain Expressway. US 25 follows much the same path.

NEARBY ATTRACTIONS:

While you are driving the Great Smoky Mountains Expressway, you are within easy driving distance of the attractions in the city of Asheville, Dillsboro, Sylva, Bryson City, Cherokee, and as far southwest as Murphy. You also junction with the Blue Ridge Parkway on a couple of occasions.

HOURS OF OPERATION:

The highway is, of course, open at all times, but the major attractions of the area observe seasonal hours. You should call the attractions for specific details. There are many attractions that operate year-round, while others close at the end of the summer, others at the end of October.

ADMISSION:

This is not a toll road, and there are no costs at any time to use this magnificent highway.

FACILITIES:

Just south of Waynesville you will reach a visitors center with restrooms, travel information, brochures, drinking water, and information for all kinds of water sports, camping, hiking, and river sports.

WHAT'S THE STORY?

This highway was a long time in coming. For years the two-lane highway from the Great Smokies area to Asheville wandered through towns and cities. In more recent years when the highway was widened, bypassing cities, and straightening curves, the road became a sheer joy to drive.

SPECIAL ATTRACTIONS:

The greatest scenes are those of the immense mountains that jut upward on both sides of the highway at you drive through the valleys. The best stops are the many small towns in the area.

MAKING THE MOST OF YOUR VISIT:

First, consider the Great Smoky Mountains Expressway as a bona fide scenic drive, rather than as a traditional commercial highway. While it is true that you will meet and pass (or be passed by) huge trucks and other commercial vehicles, and while you may at times see billboards and advertisements, for the vast majority of the trip the scenery is un-cluttered and the views are nothing less than spectacular. In many ways, the scenery along this highway is as good as, and in many cases better than, the scenic highway through the Great Smokies.

One advantage is that you can drive at a good rate of speed and not have to deal with the timid drivers you often find on the Parkway or on US 441 through the Great Smoky Mountains National Park. For instance, it takes about two full hours to drive the 55 miles from Smokemont to Cades Cove. Much of the way you will be driving, of necessity, at 20 miles an hour. On the Expressway, you can drive 60 to 65 miles per hour and still have a safe and enjoyable trip.

You can take any number of side trips to places like Sylva, where you will find one of the most magnificent courthouses in the United States. The courthouse sits atop a steep hill and has an attractive fountain in front of it. It is said to be the most photographed courthouse in the state. Others claim that it is the most photographed courthouse in the United States.

In nearby Cullowhee you can visit the school where Robert Lee Madison (son of the personal physician of Robert E. Lee) once taught. Cullowhee Academy in 1929 was re-named Western Carolina Teachers College and in 1967 became Western Carolina University.

You can drive to Dillsboro (only about three miles from Sylva) and walk through the town, shop in the many specialty markets, visit Floyd McEachern's railroad museum, and catch the evening dinner train into the Whittier area. The Great Smoky Mountains Railroad excursion leads along the river where the train wreck in the movie *The Fugitive* was filmed. The cars in the wreck still lie on the hillside.

Whittier, incidentally, was started when Clark Whittier moved into the area and settled down. The young man was a cousin of famous Quaker poet John Greenleaf Whittier, who wrote, among other fine po-ems, "Snow-Bound."

The small town of Webster was named in honor of the famous ora-tor and lawmaker Daniel Webster who was celebrated in fiction in the super short story, "The Devil and Daniel Webster." This great speaker said, among other gems, "God grants liberty only to those who love it, and are always ready to guard and defend it."

He also said, "One country, one constitution, one destiny."

Incidentally, if you want to extend your drive to the Great Smoky Mountains National Park, you can add beauty to an already beautiful trip by leaving the Great Smoky Mountain Expressway and taking the Blue Ridge Parkway south to its terminus. The end of the Parkway is in a sense the beginning of the Smoky Mountain park.

If you prefer to visit the attractions of Cherokee, you can drive into town and visit the museum and other tourist favorites in this city. Whatever your destination, you will find that on this highway the old adage holds true that getting there is half the fun.

Laura Foster Memorial.

SECTION 6: THE BEST MOUNTAIN DRIVING TOURS
TRIP 8: THE TOM DULA-LAURA FOSTER DRIVE
FOUR SIDES OF A TRIANGLE

LOCATION:

You can reach the start of this scenic drive just north of Lenoir (off US 321) or in Wilkesboro, in front of the old Wilkes County Courthouse. To reach either area from I-40, exit the interstate at Hickory onto US 321 and drive north through the city of Hickory and across the Catawba River and then to Smiths Crossroads. Continue toward Boone and Blowing Rock, and you will see the highway sign on the right side of the road.

To Wilkesboro, exit I-40 north of Statesville onto NC 18 and drive north, or you can drive to Statesville and exit onto NC 115 north to Wilkesboro.

From the Blue Ridge Parkway you can reach the scenic byway by exiting the Parkway onto US 321 south toward Lenoir. At the foot of the mountain you will see signs directing you to NC 268. You can also exit the Parkway onto NC 18 and drive south to the town of Wilkesboro. Intersect with NC 268 just after you cross the river. Turn west and drive through town to the courthouse.

NEARBY ATTRACTIONS:

You will drive within a few yards of Fort Defiance, and in Wilkesboro you can visit the Old Wilkes Jail Museum and the log house of Captain Robert Cleveland. Also within easy driving distance are the Blue Ridge Parkway, Doughton Park, Boone and Blowing Rock, Julian Price Memorial Park, Moses Cone Memorial Park, and the cities of Morganton and Valdese.

HOURS OF OPERATION:

The scenic byway is always open. Attractions nearby are open from 9 a.m. until 6 p.m. as a rule, although you should call the specific attraction before making your visit.

ADMISSION:

There are no fees charged on the scenic byway. In some of the nearby towns, such as Blowing Rock and Boone, there are some attractions that charge admission. The Parkway attractions are all free.

FACILITIES:

On the scenic highway there are no facilities other than a small pull-off on the north side of the road. You can park here while looking at the Laura Foster grave from the highway. Just off the highway there are campgrounds and picnic areas at the Kerr Scott Reservoir, and there are all types of facilities along the Blue Ridge Parkway.

WHAT'S THE STORY?

The story is indeed an exciting one. The grave site is not open to the public now, but you can see the grave of Laura Foster, which is in a whitewashed fence rectangle, from the roadside. There is now an electric fence that encloses the pasture land and the grave, which is almost on the banks of the Yadkin River.

This is one side of the Tom Dula-Laura Foster-Ann Melton riddle. In the second half of this drive (and at its conclusion in Wilkesboro) you will learn the story of Tom Dula and his role in one of the most infamous and celebrated murder stories in North Carolina history.

SPECIAL ATTRACTIONS:

The grave of Laura Foster is the central attraction on the first half of the drive. On the second half you will see signs directing you along the Tom Dula Road. You cannot visit his grave, either, but you can see photos of the tombstone at the Old Wilkes Jail Museum.

MAKING THE MOST OF YOUR VISIT:

The Laura Foster Story:

As you stand near the grave of Laura Foster, keep an open mind and realize that there are too many questions that have never been answered and, of course, never will be. What is known for a fact is that Laura Foster was murdered, buried in a shallow and hastily dug grave. Beyond that, there are many unanswered and significant problems.

Did Tom Dula murder his lover? The jury said he did, and the appeals courts agreed. Despite the solid defense by one-time Confederate officer, nationally recognized statesman, and former governor of North Carolina, there simply was not a defense that could be mounted. It was, as is the case with many jury trials, a case of contradictory statements and the decisions of the people who heard the arguments.

Read the Tom Dula account in the second half of this trip and you will see that Dula, according to Ann Melton, came to see her and borrowed a mattock from her. If this is true, then it is very possible that Dula premeditated the murder of his mistress. He had gone to the tryst, according to circumstantial arguments, with the plan to kill her. The mattock, of course, was to dig her grave after he murdered the helpless woman.

The question remains, however, of whether the story about the mattock is true. We have Ann Melton's story that Dula had visited her on the day before the assignation (and assassination) meeting with Laura Foster.

It has been argued that Dula needed to be rid of his lover, and the best way to do so would be to present the idea that the two of them were planning to run away together, lure her under false pretenses to the secluded area, and kill her. The fact that she took clothing with her suggests that the elopement was part of the puzzle.

It has also been suggested that Ann Melton, a married woman and another of the many lovers of Tom Dula, knew that her lover was deserting her for the love of another woman, and she made her own plans, waited in secret, and killed Laura Foster. Dula, it would appear in this scenario, thought that Laura had changed her mind about running away with him.

Another side of this impossible triangle is that Ann and Tom conspired together to kill Laura Foster. One argument that at least one student of the tragedy has offered is that Laura Foster transmitted syphilis to Dula who may or may not have infected Ann Melton with the venereal disease, and the murder was their act of revenge against her. But this is all speculation at best, and no one will ever know the full story.

Another thesis is that Laura Foster was pregnant and wanted Tom to marry here, and he could not bear to give up his freedom. Ann, in this theory, also wanted him free to visit her (although she was married) and was willing to help. Or that she persuaded Tom to help her when she killed Laura Foster.

Why did Dula take flight? One argument is that when the body was found, he knew that he would be implicated, and he felt that escaping the area was preferable to standing trial for the murder of the woman, and flight was tantamount to guilt.

As stated earlier, no one will ever know. Like other famous crime cases of more modern times, even with esoteric, elaborate, and highly technical equipment and testing, unanswered questions are among the reasons that we have juries instead of lab analysis as the sole sources of verdicts.

One famous thinker once argued that a jury is a group of 12 men and women whose job is to decide who has the better lawyers.

Using only the arguments at hand, Zeb Vance engaged in a vicious character assassination of Laura Foster. He argued that she was a woman of loose morals, a "wench," who had dragged a good and wholesome man down to her level.

One of Dula's final acts was to write a statement that fully absolved Ann Melton of any part in the murder. Did this mean that Melton was innocent, or did it mean that Dula knew that he was going to die (his appeals had all been denied) and he saw no good reason to cause another person to suffer?

Do not expect answers. Pay your visit and your respects, and then depart, as Thoreau says, into the Walden of your own minds. What else is there to do?

At the pull-off where you parked, there is a marker which reads, in part, as follows: "Laura Foster-Died May 28, 1866-May She Rest in Peace. On the 28th of May, 1866, Laura Foster, a beautiful but frail girl, was decoyed from her father's house at German Hill in Caldwell County to a place in Wilkes County and was murdered. Tom Dula (Tom Dooley) was later hanged for her murder. She was buried on the bank of the Yadkin River on the farm of John Walker Winkler.

"Laura's grave is across the road surrounded by the white-washed locust fence...."

Notice that the message does not state that Dula was the killer, only that he was hanged for the murder.

The Tom Dula Story:

On the remainder of this drive you will cross the Yadkin River on occasion, and on the other side of the large bridge you will see a highway marker that briefly describes the death of Tom Dula.

Tom Dula was hanged in Statesville on May 1, 1868, and his body was taken to Elkville by his sister and buried, according to the tale, on the old Lenoir-Wilkesboro road near the Sam Jones estate. The grave cannot be seen from the road, and the grave itself is on private property. Do not trespass: instead, read the story and hope that someday you will be invited to see the grave. Another tradition says that Dula was perhaps buried near Reedy Branch, near the cabin of Tom's mother.

On this visit you can see not Dula's grave but a photo of his grave. Sorry, but that's the best we can do on this one.

To repeat, no one seems to know what the real story behind the murder of Laura Foster is. We do know what happened to the principals. Laura Foster died of stab wounds in her chest. Ann Melton died in a reported cart accident. And Tom Dula died on the gallows in the foothills town of Statesville, North Carolina. It is the mystery that still lingers that keeps the story alive.

It was this mystery that combined a love story, a vicious triangle (perhaps a rectangle), and the sensational courtroom trial that resulted from the gory murder that prompted the old mountain ballad and the hit song years ago by the Kingston Trio: "Hang Down Your Head, Tom Dooley."

The old jailhouse in Wilkesboro where Dula was held prisoner is one of the major attractions at the end of this trip; the Old Wilkes Jail Museum, behind the courthouse, is a fine place to visit and, if you ask, you can see photos of the grave of Tom Dula.

Tom Dula was more than just another soldier in the Civil War: he was a singer, a banjo-picker, a guitarist, and fiddler.

He was well-known as an entertainer, a fun-loving and handsome man with a rakish attitude and demeanor. In the words of Rudyard Kipling, he took his fun where he found it.

And Tom found love in the company of and in the arms of Laura Foster and in the charms of Ann Foster Melton, who was the cousin of Laura.

When Laura Foster departed from her home, she did not disappear in a cloud of mystery: she packed a bundle of clothes, rode Belle, her brown mare, and apparently left in peace and of her own accord. She had reportedly confided to a friend that she was going to meet Tom Dula.

When her mare wandered home alone, searchers went to look for Laura. They found her body buried in a shallow grave. She had died of a stab wound in her left breast.

Tom Dula had also disappeared, and a posse was formed to find and arrest him. The posse was led, according to one report, by Robert Cummings, a local schoolteacher who may have had his own amorous designs on Laura Foster, who in turn had not been interested in the teacher.

The posse found Dula in Tennessee and brought him back to stand trial. (There are those who contend that Dula was denied his legal rights in that there was no formal extradition.) The grand jury indicted Dula on murder charges, largely on the lurid testimony of Ann Melton.

The trial was moved to Iredell County and to Statesville, where Tom Dula was defended by one of the most influential men in the state: Zeb Vance, whose home you visited in another section of this book and whose grave is near that of Thomas Wolfe and O. Henry (William Sidney Porter) in Asheville's Riverside Cemetery.

Actually, Vance became involved in the trial as a result of a mistaken identity. A man rode to Vance's home one night and told Vance that one of Zeb's former soldiers had been charged with murder and lacked the money to pay for a defense. Vance recalled a musician in his old 26th North Carolina regimental band, a group which had played at Vance's inauguration as the governor of North Carolina. The soldier was identified as Tom Dula.

Vance rushed to the scene only to learn that the man on trial was another Tom Dula, not the one he had once commanded, but Vance nevertheless agreed to defend the man, who had been in the battles at Cold Harbor and Petersburg.

Vance gave the defense his best efforts, and he charged no legal fees at all. He took the line of argument and hinted that it was not Tom Dula who had killed Laura Foster but that Ann Melton was the possibly guilty party. Vance's argument was based on the reported fact that Melton had been engaged for some time in an affair with Dula and that she could not bear to see him marry her cousin and rival, Laura Foster.

But one man who knew Dula allegedly admitted that he had heard Dula make the comment that he would get revenge against Foster for having transmitted to him a venereal disease. Dula denied the allegations, but to no avail. The jury found him guilty, and Vance appealed the verdict, also to no avail.

On the day of execution, Dula rode atop his coffin and played his fiddle as he went to his death. A throng of curious and excited people followed the fiddling victim.

As he waited to die, Dula reportedly held up his hand and said to the crowd, "Gentleman, do you see this hand? Does it tremble? I never hurt a hair on the girl's head."

Tom Dula was, according to Zeb Vance, a soldier who was worth a thousand wenches like Laura Foster. Vance's defense of Dula was essentially that Dula by virtue of his willingness to fight for the South was a good man.

This was a good argument in that Vance had been able to fill many of the jury seats with Confederate veterans, but the verdict was what Vance and Dula had expected-and feared. All of the basic ingredients were there: motive, opportunity, alleged murder weapon, love, lust, and flight.

Dula did not hang down his head, the scholars tell us. He stood erect; his last words were to the hangman: "You have such a nice clean rope, I ought to have washed my neck." His epitaph reads, "Tom Dula-Hanged May 1, 1866, for the Murder of Laura Foster." The death date is incorrect.

Guilty of murder? Perhaps. Guilty of lust? Assuredly. But Tom Dula did not hang down his head.

Don't conclude this trip without stopping at the Old Wilkes Jail Museum, where you can learn a great deal about Tom Dula and Laura Foster and Ann Melton. You can see the cell in which Tom was kept, as well as Ann's cell. The old jail is open for visitors from 9 a.m. until 4 p. m. Monday through Friday.

And after you have learned all that you can, you will leave with the words of Yul Brynner in *The King and I* ringing in your ears: "It is a puzzlement!"

Courthouse in Columbus.

SECTION 6: THE BEST MOUNTAIN DRIVING TOURS
TRIP 9: SHELBY TO COLUMBUS
COURTHOUSE TO COURTHOUSE

LOCATION:

This trip is not a mountain scenic drive in the highest aesthetic sense, partly because it starts in the foothills far away from the mountains. However, unless you live in the North Carolina mountains, you must travel to reach them. The approach here is that it is much better to drive along the most scenic of the highways awaiting you. Why wait until you reach the mountains to see beauty when you can see it along the way?

This trip starts at the old courthouse in downtown Shelby and continues to the old courthouse in downtown Columbus, or you can reverse the direction. And if it sounds dull and unexciting to drive along a commercial highway, try this one before you make rash judgments.

From the Shelby Courthouse, drive south to the second traffic light and then junction with US 74 and turn right. Do not turn until you see the sign outside the delightful town of Columbus indicating NC 108 or the Columbus exit. Once in Columbus drive straight down the main street in town until you see the huge and majestic courthouse on the left side of the street.

NEARBY ATTRACTIONS:

In Shelby there is the Cleveland County Historical Museum in the old courthouse. You are also close to Kings Mountain National Battleground site, and you are within an easy drive of Crowders Mountain, both of which are described in Section 1 of this book.

In Columbus there are many attractions, such as the Sears House, a complete house that was shipped and delivered to the buyer, back when Sears sold nearly everything, including autos, through the mail-order house.

In Tryon there are several historic sites, and you are not far from Pearson's Falls, Hendersonville, Flat Rock, Saluda, and the US 176 Scenic Highway from Tryon to Saluda.

HOURS OF OPERATION:

The attractions on both ends of this drive open around 9 a.m. and close at 5 or 6 p.m. Seasonal hours may vary, so call before making the trip.

ADMISSION:

Most of the attractions you will visit are free, unless you travel to Chimney Rock or similar outstanding area attractions. You can look up admission prices and hours in the appropriate parts of this book.

FACILITIES:

Depending upon where you stop, the facilities may vary. On the actual drive itself there are no facilities, but outlying attractions have nearly everything you would want in travel accommodations. At Gibson Park in Columbus, for example, you can find picnic facilities and restrooms.

WHAT'S THE STORY?

When these two cities were in or near the early stages of their development, there were legendary lawyers and criminals. One lawyer whose fame spread all over the foothills of North Carolina was Clyde Hoey, later governor of North Carolina. O. Max Gardner, whose family home now operates as a bed-and-breakfast establishment, also practiced law in Shelby and later served as governor of this state.

The courthouse in Columbus was made of hand-made brick and was built by slaves in 1857. In front of the courthouse, on the west side, there is an ancient slave block from which human beings were bought and sold. That block remains, but now it is covered by a planter filled with beautiful flowers in warmer weather.

SPECIAL ATTRACTIONS:

In Columbus there is a superb waterfall, and you will find other historical monuments and markers. The Lanier Library is one of the oldest in the state, and the final home of poet Sidney Lanier is on the western outskirts of town.

MAKING THE MOST OF YOUR VISIT:

The legend insists that one day Clyde Hoey was defending a town character who had been charged with stealing chickens. As Hoey lectured to the jury for long minutes on the sterling and highly admirable characteristics of the defendant, the twelve men listened raptly. Later they deliberated for only minutes before returning a verdict of not guilty.

As the defendant was leaving the courthouse, one of the men in the courtroom caught up with him and asked, "Lonnie, did you or did you not steal those chickens?"

Lonnie paused, scratched his head, and answered as honestly as he knew how. "To tell you the truth, I thought I took them birds, but after hearing what that man had to say about me, I just ain't sure any more."

Later, while Max Gardner was governor, the Communist Party of Russia and the American Communist Party laid out plans for a sweeping takeover of the United States. The plan was first for the party's labor union to take over the textile mills, then the transportation, and finally food production.

If this sounds like an insane plot, keep in mind that it came so close to succeeding that no one found it funny. There were countless thousands of communist workers in the textile force of the South, and many others had infiltrated the other industries of the nation.

The immediate plan was to take over the Loray Mill in Gastonia, at the time the largest mill under one roof in the entire world. During a summer of unrest, the Gastonia police chief was murdered, as was a poetess, a woman seven months pregnant. The men found guilty of killing the chief jumped bail and became honorary Russian citizens and were put in charge of building the Russian textile system.

It was O. Max Gardner who called out the North Carolina militia to keep the rioting from spreading across the entire state. You can drive by Gardner's home in Shelby. You can also visit Sunset Cemetery where so many local celebrities were buried.

But the drive between the two towns is the star of the show. Once you leave Shelby, the highway is like riding on a scenic by-way. There are the trucks, of course, and the road is four lanes, but the drive is superb. You'll hate to see it end.

I-26 between Tryon and Asheville.

SECTION 6: THE BEST MOUNTAIN DRIVING TOURS
TRIP 10: I-26 TRYON TO ASHEVILLE
THE TRYON TURNPIKE

LOCATION:

A scenic interstate highway? Yes, indeed. In fact, some of the most scenic drives in the United States are interstates. If you drive on I-40 from Asheville to the Tennessee border, or, for that matter, all the way to California, you will see majestic and scenic mountains, rolling hills, and splendid vistas at every turn. Obviously, you will also pass through many areas that are anything but scenic. The I-40 drives through Oklahoma City, Nashville, and Memphis are not idyllic, but the highway through Arkansas (Did you know that this state has led the nation in the production of rice for the past 15 years?) is wonderful. So is the drive through northern New Mexico: Santa Fe, Albuquerque, Taos, and even Tucumcari and countryside.

So, yes, an interstate can be in rural areas as beautiful as the most scenic highways anywhere. The trick is to pick the places where drives are rewarding. Only the people who must drive the interstate daily will find it displeasing.

Another point: many of the trips in this book are via the best roads available, and I-26 is not only a scenic road but one on which you can make good time to the scenic destinations you are driving to see.

To make the I-26 drive, you can access the interstate in the Greenville-Spartanburg area, or you can leave I-40 at Exit 46A and drive south. Or you can start in Asheville and drive south.

NEARBY ATTRACTIONS:

This drive takes you to or near Asheville with its hundreds of attractions; the Blue Ridge Parkway, which is one continual scenic delight, mile after mile; Hendersonville, which is one of the finest cities in the state; Flat Rock with its Carl Sandburg house and Flat Rock Theater; and the delightful city of Tryon. You are also near the Pacolet River North Carolina Scenic Highway (NC 176) from Tryon to Saluda. If you wish you can drive the short (10 mile) scenic highway and then take other highways back to junction with I-26, or you can make a sort of loop drive of the two highways.

HOURS OF OPERATION:

The highway is always open, and the attractions nearby are usually open from 9 a.m. until 5 p.m. or later. Call specific attractions for hours, especially during the off-season.

ADMISSION:

This is not a toll road, and you can drive it free of charge anytime you wish. Call specific attractions for their fees, or you can consult other chapters in this book for admission fees that were in effect at the time of publication.

FACILITIES:

Along the route of the interstate highway there are exit roads that will provide access to picnic tables, drinking water, campgrounds, hiking, fishing, boating, and other outdoor family recreation.

WHAT'S THE STORY?

You are in the vicinity of the steepest railroad grade in the United States (and trains still occasionally make the run), and Tryon is one of the noted cities in the South because of the fantastic year-round climate and panoramic beauty. I-26 leads you in the scenic drive from I-85 in South Carolina to Interstate 40 in Asheville, one of the great cities in the nation.

SPECIAL ATTRACTIONS:

Saluda's entire business district is listed on the National Historic Register and the town is filled with specialty shops where you can browse and buy gifts, personal items, antiques, books, and other purchases. In 1827 the first toll gate in North Carolina history was installed for the Buncombe Turnpike from Saluda Gap through Asheville and on to the state line in the state of Tennessee. The Buncombe Turnpike connected Greenville, South Carolina, with Greenville, Tennessee. The route led the traveler through Asheville and Hot Springs and into Tennessee. This is also an incredibly beautiful terrain that has brought into the area leading personalities in national entertainment, among them until recently singer Perry Como.

But it is the scenery that is the special attraction, from start to finish of this trip.

MAKING THE MOST OF YOUR VISIT:

If you connect with I-26 in Asheville, you will drive along an uncrowded highway (during the middle of the morning on weekdays) as you have the opportunity to see the French Broad River and the mountains that became one of the greatest literary influences on Thomas Wolfe, who was born in Asheville and spent his younger days there. Before you drive south, you might want to stop in Asheville to visit the home of Wolfe.

You will pass a junction with the Blue Ridge Parkway, and if you want to extend a great drive, you could drive north to Mount Mitchell and Craggy Gardens and then return down the Parkway to rejoin I-26. For a good loop drive, junction with US 64 and drive west to junction with US 276 north of Brevard. Drive north and join the Blue Ridge Parkway and motor north past Mount Pisgah and the Pisgah Inn before you rejoin I-26.

If you want to picnic, camp, hike, or fish, you can find ample opportunities to do so along the Parkway. There are also restrooms on the Parkway.

Heading south again, you will pass near Hendersonville and Flat Rock. Consult other chapters in this book for information about attractions in these two superb cities. When you are in the Saluda-Tryon area, you can visit Pearson Falls, a 268-acre scenic nature and wildlife preserve. The Tryon Garden Club both owns and maintains the preserve. There is a small admission charge, but you will assuredly get your money's worth.

In Tryon you can enjoy shopping, walking around town, and seeing this pretty city with the perfect climate mentioned above. If you are enjoying I-26 greatly, you might want to continue the drive into South Carolina, where the scenery is wonderful and the drive is pleasant. This highway will take you all the way to Columbia, if you want to make the trip as long as possible and still stay in scenic areas. There are great places to eat in Asheville, Brevard, Spartanburg, and Columbia.

Old Kona Church.

SECTION 7: THE BEST OF THE MOUNTAIN CHURCHES
TRIP 1: OLD KONA BAPTIST CHURCH
THREE STONES ON A GRAVE

LOCATION:

The Old Kona Baptist Church is located near Spruce Pine and even closer to Bandana and Loafer's Glory; however, many tourists are not familiar with these latter locations. In order to get to Kona, you have two basic routes. The first of these, starting at I-40, can be made by exiting I-40 at Exit 86 in Marion. You will be on US 226, which you can follow to Spruce Pine. From Spruce Pine follow US 19E west to connect with NC 80. Turn right just outside Micaville and follow NC 80 to Kona.

A second way of reaching Kona is to take the NC 80 exit off I-40 and follow it directly to the community and church. This road winds and curves considerably, and you will make better time if you go through Spruce Pine.

A third (and highly enjoyable) route is to take US 226 from I-40 to just outside Spruce Pine where you will junction with the Blue Ridge Parkway. Drive south on the Parkway until you reach the NC 80 junction. Then, as before, follow NC 80 directly into Kona.

NEARBY ATTRACTIONS:

While you are in the Spruce Pine-Kona area you can drive easily to Penland, to the North Carolina Minerals Museum at the junction of US 226 and the Blue Ridge Parkway, Carolina Hemlock recreation area, and Crossnore, in addition to Parkway stops like Crabtree Meadows.

HOURS OF OPERATION:

The Old Kona Baptist Church is open 24 hours a day, every day of the year. The church is now a small museum that is not staffed and is never locked. You can go in and make yourself at home (actually, at church) any time you are in the vicinity.

ADMISSION:

There are no fees of any sort. Go as often as you wish and stay as long as you like. Donations are accepted.

FACILITIES:

Other than a small parking area, there are no facilities at all. There are no water fountains, restrooms, picnic tables, or any of the other amenities you expect to find at most stops. But the absence of these facilities merely adds to the charm of the beautiful old church and the story you will find there.

WHAT'S THE STORY?

Start your visit in the cemetery behind the church. About mid-way up the hill you will see three tiny grave markers. These stones mark the three graves of Charles Silver, who was buried three different times in three different places and is still buried in all three graves. The fairly recent grave marker tells nothing of the bizarre story other than the basic facts that the deceased was born on October 3, 1812, and died on December 22, 1831. You will read later how Charles Silver was killed by his young wife.

And not just killed! She attacked him with an axe, then sat and watched him die, after which she chopped his body into pieces and burned part of the corpse and hid parts that were not burned.

SPECIAL ATTRACTIONS:

The only two attractions, other than the grave, which should be given the respect required at the burial site of any human being, are the old church itself and the wealth of materials you will find on the walls of the church.

MAKING THE MOST OF YOUR VISIT:

As with any trip you plan to make, learn enough before you start the trip so that you will be prepared for what you find. It is far better to travel prepared than it is to try to learn the basic story once you arrive and, in many cases, have many places to see.

The story is a simple (and always complex) story of tragedy and horror in the loneliness of an isolated mountain cabin where 19-year old Charles Silver and his 18-year old wife Frankie lived with their year-old daughter in the cabin not far from Kona.

A recent novel, written by the very fine author Sharyn McCrumb, is entitled *The Ballad of Frankie Silver*. This book would be good background reading before you make the trip. But if you can't find time to read the book, the story is deceptively simple.

No one knows precisely why Frankie Silver killed her husband or why she waited so long to confess that she had killed him. In the novel McCrumb suggests through the mental process of one of the central characters that Silver may have threatened to kill the couple's child. McCrumb also speculates that Charlie Silver came home drunk and abusive.

But this is only speculation. But, fact or fancy, the story leads to the inescapable conclusion that Frankie Silver was the first white woman ever to be hanged in North Carolina.

During her (and her husband's) last months on earth, they lived in a little cabin at Deyton Bend in the Toe River Valley. (The Toe River is actually the Estatoe River, and the story behind the name is worth researching-or you can read it elsewhere in this book.)

One version of the story is that Charles Silver planned to go on a prolonged hunting trip and Frankie asked him to chop plenty of firewood before he departed. One source reports that Charles, exhausted after a day of wood-cutting, fell asleep on the floor of the cabin. His little daughter was snuggled in his arms while he slept.

Next morning, Frankie walked over the ridge and paid a visit to her in-laws, whom she found washing clothes. She greeted them and told them that she, too, had been hard at work since before daylight. She reportedly said, "I have my cabin all redded up."

Ostensibly, the term 'redded' meant readied, but there is the dreadful irony that she may have, at least in a Freudian slip, been thinking of the blood of her husband all over the floor of the cabin.

Frankie told her in-laws that her husband had gone to visit friends in order to procure his Christmas liquor and had not come back as expected. She asked the family to help look for him. When Charlie Silver did not return after several days, local men formed a search party to be sure that he had not died along the trail.

One of the posse members, identified as Jake Cullis in some narratives, searched the cabin and found the fireplace filled with ashes. He raked through the ashes and reportedly found bones and teeth. Bloodstains were found under the hearth and, at least one source reports, under the house.

Sheriff John Boone, nephew to famed frontiersman Daniel Boone, arrested Frankie and incarcerated her in the jailhouse in Morganton. She was tried, convicted, and sentenced to die by hanging. Once, reportedly using a wooden key carved by one of her family members, she escaped and made her way to Rutherford County before she was recaptured and returned to her cell.

She was hanged on July 12, 1833, and folklore has it that she mounted the scaffold while she carried a poem in one hand and a piece of cake in the other. She reportedly read the poem and then ate her cake.

The poem, which Frankie is said to have written herself, was entitled "I Try That Awful Road" and goes in part:

"The jealous thought that first gave strife
To make me take my husband's life.
For days and months I spent my time
Thinking how to commit this crime.

*   *   *   *   *   *   *

Judge Donnell has my sentence passed;
These prison walls I leave at last;
Nothing to sheer my drooping head
Until I'm numbered with the dead.

The final stanza follows:

"Great God, how shall I be forgiven?
Not fit for earth; not fit for heaven.
But little time to pray to God,
For now I try that awful road."

Frankie Silver's last words are still sung in the mountains of North Carolina. The poem presented in part above was sung in the 1930s in the Toe River valley. And the legacy of the Toe River now includes yet another tragic story.

The tiny community of Kona, incidentally, was named by the dispatcher of the Clinchfield Railroad. The man who labeled the mountain community was an amateur geologist who used the chemical symbols for potassium (K), oxygen (O), and sodium (Na).

In many ways, particularly on a foggy winter morning, the Kona community is desolate; at other times the beauty of the scene is incomparable. When you make your trip, for beauty try crisp October days. If you want to try to understand the tragic circumstances and results, any day is well-suited for your efforts.

Saint John in the Wilderness.

SECTION 7: THE BEST OF THE MOUNTAIN CHURCHES
TRIP 2: SAINT JOHN IN THE WILDERNESS
THE CHARLESTON OF THE MOUNTAINS

LOCATION:

Saint John in the Wilderness is located in a grove of trees, as the name of the church implies, on US 25 in Flat Rock. To reach the church from I-40 in Asheville, junction with I-26 south and drive to the outskirts of Hendersonville, where you will leave the interstate and follow US 64 west into Hendersonville. Then take US 25 south. You will see signs directing you to the church. From I-85 in the Greenville-Spartanburg area of South Carolina leave the interstate onto US 25 north. You will reach Flat Rock within minutes. Look for the church on the left.

NEARBY ATTRACTIONS:

To see the most you can while you are in the area, you can drive quickly to Carl Sandburg's home in Flat Rock and to the Flat Rock Playhouse, both of which are less than a mile away. While in the area you can also visit a number of striking waterfalls in Transylvania County. You are also close to the Cradle of Forestry on US 276 north of Brevard, and on the same highway you will find Looking Glass Falls, Sliding Rock, and the Pink Beds. Farther north you will reach the Blue Ridge Parkway and such attractions as Mount Pisgah, Devil's Courthouse, and Graveyard Fields.

HOURS OF OPERATION:

The church and the graveyard are open to visitors from 9 a.m. until 4 p.m. daily, year-round. Regular church services are held at 9 a.m. and 11 a.m. each Sunday.

ADMISSION:

Admission is free. You may visit the church, which remains open during the hours listed above, and the graveyard, and you may walk around the church grounds and enjoy the tranquility, the beauty, and the reverence that surrounds the church. Please do not litter or in any way deface the beautiful property. Treat it with the respect it so richly deserves. Donations are accepted.

FACILITIES:

There are restrooms inside the church, and you can find drinking water inside. There are no other facilities; however, you can use the sanctuary for your own brief personal and private meditation and worship.

SPECIAL ATTRACTIONS:

The interior and exterior beauty of the church itself are very special attractions, and in the churchyard you can pay your respects at the final resting places of important persons in the history of the state, the South, and the nation.

WHAT'S THE STORY?

Two men in particular built summer homes in Flat Rock between 1825 and 1830. Charles Baring, of London first and of the Charleston area second, bought land and built a house, Mountain Lodge. He found Flat Rock to have the summer climate that he felt his wife needed. Judge Mitchell King of Charleston built his own home, Argyle, as a summer residence, and these two men inspired many others to seek the cool summer climate. So many arrived from the Low Country of South Carolina, in fact, that Flat Rock and its surrounding areas soon became known as the "little Charleston of the mountains."

MAKING THE MOST OF YOUR VISIT:

As you arrive, you will see a parking area inside the gates. Leave your car and walk up to the church first. Notice the dramatic architecture of the church. To photograph the church, a good angle is from the front right corner as you are facing the church. You can take in the stone wall, the wrought iron fence, and the roof lines, as well as the arched windows and entries.

Inside the church notice the box pews with the entries and the ponderously beautiful wood from which the pews were made. You will find that everything inside the church is beautiful and awe-inspiring, from the musical instruments to the stained glass windows.

One plaque in the church contains these words: "We the undersigned inhabitants of Buncombe County, North Carolina, residing near Flat Rock do hereby form ourselves into a congregation under the title of the Church of St. John-in-the-Wilderness, and promise conformity to the doctrines, discipline and worship of the Protestant Episcopal Church in the United States and also to the Constitution and Canons of the same church in North Carolina."

The date on the plaque is August 27, 1836. The church itself had its origins in the estates of Charles and Susan Baring, who built their own private chapel on the estate grounds. The small church burned, and in 1833 the new church was started. Bricks for the church were reportedly made by the Barings' slaves.

In 1836 the Barings relinquished their rights to the church as their own private family chapel and gave the deed to the bishop of the diocese that had been formed only recently.

When worship services were held in the church, slaves and white families attended together and sat together. Space was made available in the churchyard for the burial of the slaves.

As more and more people from Charleston-and elsewhere-continued to arrive, the size of the church was doubled as early as 1852. Many members of the rapidly growing Charleston society moved to the North Carolina mountains. These were followed by men and women from other parts of South Carolina, Georgia, and as far south as Louisiana.

In the burial spaces (inside and outside the church) you can see the names of many highly notable people. Christopher Gustavus Memminger, John Grimke Drayton, and Edward King are among the persons interred in the churchyard.

Memminger was the first secretary of the Confederate treasury, Drayton was the driving force behind the world-famous Magnolia Gardens of Charleston, and King was a World War II general who was one of the commanders in the Bataan Death March.

This historic church is a must-see attraction.

Cool Spring Baptist Church.

SECTION 7: THE BEST OF THE MOUNTAIN CHURCHES
TRIP 3: COOL SPRING BAPTIST CHURCH
WAITING FOR THE MEN IN BLACK

LOCATION:

The Cool Spring Baptist Church can be seen from the Blue Ridge Parkway near Milepost 272, at the E. B. Jeffress area that also has the wonderful Cascades walk and scenic views.

NEARBY ATTRACTIONS:

In addition to the Cascades, you are near Boone and Blowing Rock, a nice drive from Doughton Park, Mount Jefferson State Park, the New River and New River State Park, and the famous frescoes in churches in Glendale Springs and West Jefferson.

HOURS OF OPERATION:

The church is open at all times, year-round, day and night, as long as the Blue Ridge Parkway is passable.

ADMISSION:

There are no charges of any sort.

FACILITIES:

At the nearby E. B. Jeffress Park you will find plenty of parking space, picnic tables, restrooms, drinking water, and two terrific hiking trails, plus one astounding waterfall.

WHAT'S THE STORY?

This very simple, plain, and homespun church is noted only for its antiquity and its place in local history. It is among the churches where the circuit-riding preachers stopped for a few days or a week to deliver sermons to the mountain people.

SPECIAL ATTRACTIONS:

The greatest joys of this trip are the church, the nearby log cabin, the hikes, and the waterfall. This trip is not to the elaborate and luxurious but to the most elemental grassroots forms of religion of ages ago.

MAKING THE MOST OF YOUR VISIT:

The best preparation you can make for this trip is to set your mind right and to inform yourself through reading (if only this chapter) on this most enduring figure in American history and theology. It is helpful if you can visit churches like All Souls in Biltmore Village in Asheville or the Basilica of Saint Lawrence in that same city before you come here.

The purpose is not to show that one is better or more important than the other but to see the two religious structures in a side-by-side mental comparison. Both types of churches are important, and in the past century the homespun form of church service was the only one that some people ever experienced in their entire lives.

One famous circuit-riding preacher that I knew years ago told me on a number of occasions that when he went into some of the mountain communities, often on a once-per-year schedule, the people there told him that they had not heard a sermon of any sort since the last time he had been there.

When I asked if people actually engaged in marriage rituals that involved such incredible forms as jumping over a broomstick, the preacher answered, "That is absolutely true. The young people who wanted to get married in many cases were unwilling or at times unable, from a biological point of view, to wait nine or ten months, perhaps longer, for a real preacher to perform their marriage ceremony. So they used the broomstick and other symbols to demonstrate publicly that they were indeed in their own minds and in the eyes of society married. All that was left was in the mind or eyes of God, and that part came when I arrived to perform the church service."

He went on to say, "In many cases there was no church at all; I found people who had never heard the name of Jesus in their entire lives and who did not have any earthly idea who Mary and Joseph were; they had never heard of Matthew, Mark, Luke, and John. They in many cases could not read and write, so the scriptures remained a mystery to them. Those few who could read and write were essentially unable to interpret the scriptures in any meaningful fashion. So I took my assignment seriously, and I devoted my life to it. I began preaching when I was barely more than a child myself, and I gave it everything I had."

The circuit-riding preacher was, in the beginning, one of the major institutions of the American Methodist Church. The idea originated in England with John Wesley, and it was brought to this country by men like Francis Asbury. Robert Strawbridge had started circuit riding as early as 1764.

Francis Asbury spent 45 years on the circuit and traveled as much as 5,000 miles per year. That, if you stop and think about it, is more mileage than some people put on their modern cars. The ministers like Asbury (who was a great influence in Georgia, South Carolina, and North Carolina and is memorialized in a sense by the Cokesbury church near Greenwood, South Carolina) preached twice a day during the week and three times on Sunday. Their pay was often meals and a place of shelter for the night.

There was an actual salary of $64 dollars per year. That was 17.5 cents per day, or about one cent per hour or less. By 1800 the pay was increased to $80 per year. That amounted to almost 22 cents per day or nearly two cents per hour for a 12-hour day (and it was a rare day that included only 12 hours of preaching and travel, except when the preacher could spend several nights in the same place).

The horse, incidentally, was often furnished by the church. In many cases, however, the preacher had to earn his own mount.

At the Cool Spring Church the preachers held services inside the rustic building and then spent the night with Jesse Brown, whose cabin still stands only a few feet from the church. Circuit riders like Bill Church or Willie Lee saw to it that the people in this part of the mountains heard the Word. Itinerant preachers were responsible for the evenly distributed faith of the Baptist and Methodist churches.

And, so many years later, when people can and do travel more in one day than many people did in a lifetime, it is good to stop and pay respects to those dedicated men of another age.

Basilica of St. Lawrence in Asheville.

SECTION 7: THE BEST OF THE MOUNTAIN CHURCHES
TRIP 4: THE BASILICA OF SAINT LAWRENCE
THE PALM AND THE GRIDIRON

LOCATION:
The Basilica of Saint Lawrence is in the midst of the downtown art and architecture of Asheville, and it stands out as one of the most beautiful buildings in the state, the South, and the nation. To reach the Basilica, exit I-40 onto I-240 in Asheville. If you are driving west on I-240, take the Montford exit; if driving east, take the Downtown Business District and follow signs to the Asheville Civic Center. Otherwise, follow the signs to the Asheville visitors center. The Basilica is only a couple of blocks from the visitor center.

NEARBY ATTRACTIONS:
You are within minutes of Pack Square and the four museums found there, and the Thomas Wolfe boyhood home is within easy walking distance. Downtown Asheville is one of the beautiful cities of the South,

and there are architectural beauties and points of interest at every turn.

HOURS OF OPERATION:

For your own convenience, it is best if you visit the Saint Lawrence Basilica during regular business hours. Do not visit during the regular worship services unless, of course, you are there to worship as well.

ADMISSION:

There is no admission charge to visit the Basilica.

FACILITIES:

The only facilities are restrooms.

WHAT'S THE STORY?

Rafael Guastavino was the architect of the Basilica of Saint Lawrence, and Guastavino himself is encrypted inside the Basilica he designed. The door of the crypt of Guastavino is of lustre-glazed tiles framed in bronze. The lustre-glaze process was the discovery of the architect, who lived from 1842 until 1908. As you visit this extraordinary basilica you will notice that there are no beams of wood or steel in the entire structure. All of the walls, ceilings, floors, and pillars are of either stone, tile, or other masonry materials. The roof is copper-covered tile.

SPECIAL ATTRACTIONS:

Of special interest are the exterior and interior beauty of the architecture and the workmanship, and the artistic beauty of the doors, ceiling, altar, and the windows is spectacular.

MAKING THE MOST OF YOUR VISIT:

Before you go, refresh yourself about some of the saints of the church. Saint Lawrence, who died a martyr's death in 258, was a deacon of Pope Sixtus II, and Saint Lawrence followed the pope to his death during the persecution of Valerian. One story is that when Lawrence was ordered to give up the church goods he was in charge of keeping, he gathered the infirm and the poor and then offered these as the treasures of the church.

While Saint Ambrose and the poet Prudentius affirm that Lawrence died on a red-hot gridiron and said to his tormenters,"I am cooked on that side; turn me over and eat," it is possible that Lawrence was beheaded. He was buried outside the walls of Rome, and the basilica of Saint Lorenzo was built over his burial place. The Feast Day of Saint Lawrence is August 10.

A special note: the Perseid meteor showers that occur each mid-August are sometimes referred to as the Tears of Saint Lawrence.

The story of the death of Saint Lawrence is the reason behind the main facade, which depicts Saint Lawrence holding a palm frond in one hand a gridiron in the other.

As you enter the church proper, notice the massive ceiling, which has a clear span of 58-by-82 feet and is said to be the largest unsupported dome in North America.

At the main altar you will see two archangels, Saint Michael and Saint Raphael, and to the left of Saint Michael there are the images of Matthew and Mark. To the right of Saint Raphael are Luke and John, all four with their symbols at their feet: angel for Saint Matthew, lion for Saint Mark, bull for Saint Luke, and eagle for Saint John.

Stand in the center aisle to study the windows. You will see artistic depictions of the Annunciation, the Visitation, the Nativity, Jesus teaching in the temple, and the Conversion of Saint Paul, all of these on the west wall (the direction of the visitors center). On the east wall are the Marriage Feast of Cana, the raising of the daughter of Jairus, the calming of the wind and waves, the Agony in the garden, and the appearance of the resurrected Jesus to Mary Magdalene.

If you are wondering why this magnificent structure is not called a church or a cathedral, here is a brief explanation. A basilica in its original sense (the word is derived from a Greek word referring to royalty) was a building for public assembly. Today, a basilica is a Roman Catholic church that has been given ceremonial privileges. For a church to merit the title of basilica it must be a place of dignity, antiquity, and of historical importance as a center of worship. The church must also have been consecrated, liturgical rites should be conducted in an exemplary manner, and there must be active participation of the parishioners. These are some of the major considerations.

If you are not absorbed by the majesty of the church, you will be highly impressed by its beauty and its history. Seeing the magnificence of the basilica is like taking a world art tour. The brass doors were handcrafted in India. The architectural motif of the basilica is Spanish Renaissance. There is Italian marble in the center of the altar front. Most of the windows were made in Munich, Germany. At the main altar there is an 1,800-pound block of marble from Tennessee, and the lustre-glaze process originated in Massachusetts.

The visit to the Basilica of Saint Lawrence will leave you in awe and filled with admiration for the art and beauty you see in the church. This is another don't-miss place to visit.

Congregational Church of Christ in Tryon.

SECTION 7: THE BEST OF THE MOUNTAIN CHURCHES
TRIP 5: TRYON-THE CONGREGATIONAL CHURCH OF CHRIST
A HERITAGE AND A PROMISE

LOCATION:

To get to Tryon from I-40, junction in Asheville with I-26 south and drive to the exit to Columbus and Tryon. Drive west on NC 108 into Tryon, and when you are near the center of town, you will see a sign directing you across the street to the visitor information center at 425 North Trade Street. You can stop there and get directions, or you can drive to the immediate corner and turn right (this is the corner of Howard and US 176). Drive to the top of the hill to Lockhart Street, and then turn left. The first road to the right is Embury Street, which leads you to Laurel Avenue, which in turn leads to Melrose Avenue. The church is at 328 Melrose Avenue.

NEARBY ATTRACTIONS:

In Tryon you are within a few minutes drive from three dozen interesting attractions. In the immediate vicinity you can visit Pearson's Falls on US 176; the Saluda Depot and shops; the fifth generation jumbo version of Morris the Tryon Horse (in the center of town); the 1939-era Tryon Theater which once served as a movie house and vaudeville theater and which now still uses its original carbon arc projectors to screen movies four nights each week as well as a Sunday matinee; Warrior Mountain where the Cherokees suffered a devastating defeat; the 200-year old Mimosa Inn in nearby Lynn; the Sidney Lanier house where the noted poet spent his final days (this is now a private residence, so please do not trespass!); the Columbus Courthouse with the statue of the Doughboy (the World War I soldier, not the Pillsbury commercial character) and the stone (now a planter) where slaves were once bought and sold; the original slave chapel at the Good Shepherd Episcopal Church (to be discussed in more detail in another chapter of this book); and many, many other ideal places to visit.

You are close enough to drive, within an hour or so, to Lake Lure, Chimney Rock, Flat Rock, Holmes Educational State Forest, the Blue Ridge Parkway, and Green River Plantation.

HOURS OF OPERATION:

You can visit the church and enjoy an exterior view of the beautiful structure anytime you wish, but if you wish to see the inside of the church you need to visit in mid-morning. The church is open for regular services, and it extends a warm welcome to visitors. The Sunday schedule includes a worship service at 9 a.m. and a fellowship time immediately afterward. Church School is at 10 a.m., and at 11 a.m. there is another worship service to be followed by a fellowship time. Please do not interrupt worship services or other church functions by intruding thoughtlessly. Call (828) 859-9414 before visiting, if you wish to be certain that your timing is appropriate.

ADMISSION:

There are no admission fees.

FACILITIES:

There are parking spaces across the street from the church. Inside you will find the usual conveniences of any church, except that this particular church is even more beautiful on the inside than it is on the outside. No: it is equally beautiful inside and out.

WHAT'S THE STORY?

On May 19, 1991, the Congregational Church of Christ observed its one hundredth anniversary. In 1891 a Sunday School class was formed for people of all denominations. The class was led by Dr. Oscar Missildine and met on Melrose Avenue, the site of the present-day church. The meeting house and property were bought by the First Methodist Church of Tryon for the purpose of starting a church there, but the plans never materialized. The land was again obtained by a group of people interested in forming the Congregational Church, and the land and meeting house became a church and the first worship service was held in 1891.

SPECIAL ATTRACTIONS:

The exterior of the church is a magnificently beautiful stone building with arched windows and delightful architecture that can be enjoyed from all viewpoints. On the inside the church is characterized by elaborate woodwork and stained glass windows.

MAKING THE MOST OF YOUR VISIT:

Learn a little of the history of the church before you make your visit. For instance, when the church was formed, it was known as the United Church of Christ of Tryon, and Dr. Oscar Missildine, according to the published history of the church, may have been the only Congregationalist in the church. The church was bought from the Methodists, many of whom remained with the church body.

The first pastor of the church was the Reverend G. Stanley Pope, who had earlier served as president of Toogaloo College in the state of Mississippi. His salary was $600 a year in 1891.

Other pastors of the church have come from prestigious schools and distant places. The Rev. R. P. Hibbard arrived from Gloucester, Massachusetts, and earlier was in England. Percival Campbell Morgan was the son of a president of an esoteric English college at either Cambridge or Oxford.

The Rev. Will B. O'Neill was a native of Ireland who taught "a liberal rather than literal interpretation of the Bible" and created, along the way, controversy within the church, which now paid its pastors in 1926 the sum of $1,800 per year.

Throughout its century of serving, the church has been the home of many distinguished persons and has been led by pastors who were talented speakers, brilliant theologians, and revered members of the community.

The music in the church is as exemplary as its sermons. One organist, Joseph Erwin, attended the Cincinnati Conservatory of Music, graduated from the Julliard School of Music, and then studied at the Royal School of Church Music in London. He, like others, lived to make their joyful noises to the Lord.

Holy Trinity Church in Glendale Springs.

SECTION 7: THE BEST OF THE MOUNTAIN CHURCHES
TRIP 6: HOLY TRINITY CHURCH
THE CHURCH OF THE FRESCOES

LOCATION:

Holy Trinity Church is one of the major features of the tiny town of Glendale Springs, which is located near New River State Park and Mount Jefferson State Park. The New River itself, the second-oldest river in the world, flows nearby. To get to the town of Glendale Springs from I-40 you can leave the interstate at the Claremont area, near Hickory, or you can exit later at Statesville and take NC 115 to Wilkesboro and then follow NC 16 north from there.

If you are driving the Parkway, drive north of Boone until you see signs to the Glendale Springs exit.

NEARBY ATTRACTIONS:

In addition to those attractions listed above, you are near Boone, Jeffress recreation area and the Cascades, and the towns of Jefferson and West Jefferson. Stone Mountain (the Tar Heel version) is a short drive away.

HOURS OF OPERATION:

There are no scheduled hours of operation. Typically the church is open all day every day, but do not plan to sight-see during worship service times. A good idea is to plan to attend a worship service and then stay to inspect the church.

ADMISSION:

There are no admission charges, but the church will gladly accept donations to help defray the costs of maintaining the beautiful old church.

FACILITIES:

There are restrooms and parking spaces available. There are no picnic grounds or commercial amusements at hand, but you will not need any. The church is far more interesting than secular entertainment is likely to be.

WHAT'S THE STORY?

Many years ago Holy Trinity Church was, as one of the locals said, "dying on the vine." Actually, there were members who were staunch in their faith, but the town is small and so is the church congregation. Then Ben Long, considered by many to be the leading fresco artist in the world, painted the frescoes that made the church famous all over the United States. In fact, there are visitors each year from countries all over the world.

SPECIAL ATTRACTIONS:

The frescoes are the attraction that brings in people from all over the country, and you can find the art of Ben Long and his associates in several areas of the church. But the church, too, is significant and would be interesting even without the art works-but few people want to think in those terms today.

MAKING THE MOST OF YOUR VISIT:

Start by learning what a fresco is.

Fresco painting is a method of painting on freshly applied wet lime plaster walls. The colors are created by the artist's grinding dry powder pigments and mixing with water. As the colors dry, so does the lime-plaster walls, and the fresco painting then becomes a permanent part of the wall. The painting is not only on the wall but in a strict sense is in the wall.

Fresco painting demands experience, time, and money, in one form or another, in addition to talent and the other ingredients of art. A fresco painting is much-desired, but economics will often preclude such work, especially in light of other of the basic requirements in the art form. It has been said that no other art form involves so many technical requirements.

The mural, for example, must be artistically effective from any point in the room. The surface of the painting must be without glare under normal illumination. And the fresco must have an integrated appeal; that is, it must appear to be a part of the wall rather than a picture painted on the wall.

Because the paint is applied to a wet lime-plaster wall, the immediate concern is for the completion of as much as possible of the mural before the plaster sets. Actually, there are generally three coats of plaster troweled onto the wall. The first (often called the scratch coat) and the brown coat are allowed to set completely.

In many cases the artist has made detailed drawings, often called cartoons, and these are complete and ready to use when the fresh lime-plaster is applied. A perforating wheel is used to make the outlines of the drawings, and then the work must begin in deadly earnest, usually in the upper left corner.

Among the most famous fresco art in the world is the ceiling of the Sistine Chapel in the Vatican. Michelangelo worked for four and a half years to complete the work. The finished painting includes 343 figures from the Holy Bible.

The story of the Church of the Frescoes is that the artists virtually lived in the church community and worked incredibly long hours. When the huge fresco that covers the wall behind the altar was completed, the church was almost transformed into an art museum.

Ben Long, who grew up in Statesville, far from the mountains of North Carolina, was obviously a gifted artist even in his very early years. A gifted athlete, Long was an excellent wrestler, in addition to his artistry. He was an accomplished writer and an insightful student of literature.

The fresco work of Holy Trinity Church includes the Last Supper, one of the most magnificent art works you will ever see. Notice the faces of the men seated at the table: many of them are the faces of local citizens or of the artists themselves. Notice the dog, and particularly take notice of the folded letter on the floor of the room. One source has said that this was Long's last farewell to his father, who had died during the work.

Walk around the church and examine the other art works, and then walk around the outside of the church. Feel welcome, because you are. The church is a warm and friendly place, and it offers the perfect setting for a work of art.

St. John's Church in Rutherfordton.

SECTION 7: THE BEST OF THE MOUNTAIN CHURCHES
TRIP 7: ST. JOHN'S CHURCH IN RUTHERFORDTON
A PLACE WORTH A MINT

LOCATION:

St. John's Church in Rutherfordton is located on North Main Street in this attractive town that is near Lake Lure and Forest City. To get to Rutherfordton from I-40, you can take either US 64 off I-40 or US 221, also off the interstate. From I-85 you can exit south of Gastonia onto US 74 and drive to Rutherfordton or take US 221 north from South Carolina.

NEARBY ATTRACTIONS:

You are very close to Lake Lure, Chimney Rock, Brevard, Hendersonville, and Asheville. These trips are within an hour or so from Rutherfordton. Flat Rock and the Blue Ridge Parkway are also within convenient driving distance.

HOURS OF OPERATION:

St. John's Church no longer serves as a church and is not open to the public. The building now houses the historical society, but you can enjoy the exterior views of the church, and you might even be invited inside, if you meet the right people. If you call the Rutherford County Tourism office at (800) 849-5998, you might be able to arrange a visit. You may need to leave your name and number, plus a message, and hope that the personnel will return your call.

ADMISSION:

There are no admission fees.

FACILITIES:

There are no public facilities at the church, but in the main part of town you can find restrooms, restaurants, travel information, and overnight accommodations. Camping and picnic facilities are available in Chimney Rock. If you make a visit to Chimney Rock Park (admission fee is charged) you can enjoy a superior picnic shelter.

WHAT'S THE STORY?

The old and beautiful St. John's Church is but one of several nice attractions in Rutherfordton. You can learn about the old mint that once operated here, see the magnificent and stately courthouse, and enjoy a visit to a pretty town.

SPECIAL ATTRACTIONS:

Notice the murals painted on the walls of some of the downtown buildings. These murals are beautifully done and add a note of interest to the downtown area. There are also some super shops in Rutherfordton and in the countryside surrounding the town, as well as some interesting places to eat.

MAKING THE MOST OF YOUR VISIT:

An ideal plan of action is to include Rutherfordton, Forest City, Chimney Rock, and Lake Lure in one sweeping trip. You can spend a delightful day (or two) enjoying the area's offerings.

Rutherfordton, originally called Rutherford Town, was established in 1787. The town was named for Brigadier General Griffith Rutherford who, like many others during the American Revolution, found himself facing his own older brother during the war. An interesting historical note from the time period is that Colonel Patrick Ferguson, dispatched from Ninety-Six, South Carolina, by Lord Cornwallis, was instructed to destroy the opposition in the area.

Leading about 900 men, Ferguson sent the message that "if they (the rebels) did not desist from their opposition to British arms, he (Ferguson) would march his army over the mountains, hang their leaders, and lay their country waste with fire and sword." Later Ferguson set up his defense lines atop Kings Mountain and announced that "all the Rebels from hell" could not drive him from the mountainside.

Earlier Ferguson had actually pursued the Over-Mountain men from South Carolina into Rutherford County to a place called Gilberttown. If you want to be reminded of the outcome of this historic battle, turn to the chapter on Kings Mountain. In the days previous to the Battle of Kings Mountain, Rutherford, who at the time held the rank of colonel, had led a contingent of troops into South Carolina to aid the needy Palmetto soldiers.

This was the same Griffith Rutherford who, after the victory by the Whigs, campaigned vigorously for a new government that would be uniquely American. He strongly advocated a "simple democracy" in which there would be no established church, complete religious freedom, a weak executive officer who would be held in check by a strong legislature.

While you are in the town named for this Revolutionary War leader, you might want to check out the financial leadership that appeared in the town. Christopher Bechtler and Augustus, his son, operated the first private mint ever sanctioned by the United States government. Rutherford County was the scene of an early gold rush (several years before the famous strike at Sutter's Mill in California in 1849), and between 1831 until 1849 the Bechtler mint turned out more than $2,250,000 in gold dollars.

While you are at the church, which is one of the most delightfully attractive churches in this part of the state, you can admire the simplicity of design, the impeccable neatness of the architecture, and the flawless maintenance of the church, and when you are ready to leave, turn left just across from the church and drive west.

There are some beautiful old houses that look like pages from *House Beautiful*, and on the right side of the road, just in the middle of the block, there is a yellow house where the Bechtler family once lived.

And on the outskirts of town there is an abandoned shaft where the Bechtlers once did part of their business. You will also see highway markers relating the story of the gold in the county. But, as important as gold was-and is-, the real treasure in Rutherfordton is St. John's Church, which is a link in the golden chain of history. It is wonderful that this church has been saved, because, although we cannot live in the past, the past can surely live within us.

Fresco at St. Mary's Church.

SECTION 7: THE BEST OF THE MOUNTAIN CHURCHES
TRIP 8: ST. MARY'S CHURCH IN WEST JEFFERSON
TIMELESS BEAUTY IN A TINY CHURCH

LOCATION:

From I-40 take NC 16 from a point east of Hickory and follow this highway north to cross the Blue Ridge Parkway above the town of Wilkesboro. About 2.5 miles south of Glendale Springs you will intersect with NC 163. Turn right onto NC 163 and drive eight miles, until you come to a stop light. Go through the stop light and turn left immediately on the first road you see. This is the Beaver Creek High School Road. You will see St. Mary's Church about half a mile ahead. It will be on the right side of the road and is almost impossible to miss.

From the Blue Ridge Parkway turn north when you reach the NC 16 intersection north of the E. B. Jeffress Park. The park is at Milepost 273 and the NC 16 junction is near Milepost 260. From this point follow directions above to intersect with NC 163.

NEARBY ATTRACTIONS:

You are near the previously mentioned E. B. Jeffress Park and the delightful waterfall known as the Cascades. You are also near the Cool Spring Baptist Church, which is within an easy walk of the Cascades. You can see the church from the Parkway.

You are also within driving distance of Stone Mountain State Park, Mount Jefferson State Park, and New River State Park. You can drive south to Boone and Blowing Rock and enjoy the many and varied attractions there. The Parkway is, of course, nearby, and you can take this delightful highway south to a point near Boone, and you can drive on to Moses Cone Memorial Park and Julian Price Memorial Park.

HOURS OF OPERATION:

For many months the church remained unlocked at all times, but because of thoughtless vandalism the church office decided, and rightly so, to lock the church at night. Try to make your visit between 8 a.m. and 5 p.m.

ADMISSION:

There are no admission fees. Feel free to make a donation to this church and to the church in Glendale Springs. The money will be put to excellent use.

FACILITIES:

Except for the parking area, which is fairly small because this is a small church, there are no facilities. However, nearby you can find (particularly on the Parkway) facilities that offer restrooms, camping, hiking, picnicking, fishing, nature study, and superb photo opportunities.

WHAT'S THE STORY?

This church, like the one in Glendale Springs, features the masterful fresco art work of Ben Long and those who assisted him in the completion of the sacred art that made both churches well known across the nation.

SPECIAL ATTRACTIONS:

The church, first of all, is wonderfully attractive, with its white picket fence, green roof, and immaculately kept grounds. Inside the church the frescoes are major points of interest. Pay particular attention to the Laughing Christ, Mary with Child, and John the Baptist. The painting of Christ on the Cross with the Spirit rising behind and slightly above him is one of the most dramatic art works you are likely to see anywhere in the state. Or beyond.

MAKING THE MOST OF YOUR VISIT:

"A picture gallery," George Bernard Shaw once wrote, "is a dull place for a blind man." Shaw, like most people, realized that there are many forms of blindness, including that created by those who will not see. Anyone willing to open his eyes, mind, and heart will receive a great aesthetic reward by visiting this church, taking the time to enjoy both interior and exterior, and by reading the question-and-answer material placed in the tiny vestibule.

Don't rush into the church, once you arrive. Walk around the entire structure and enjoy the neatness and the uniqueness of the building. In summer the green grass, the green leaves of the huge trees and shrubs, and the green door and roof of the church add up to a superb picture. The white fence and the white walls, bell tower, and white crosses atop the roof are strikingly beautiful.

Even in winter the green roof and door blend wonderfully with the evergreens surrounding the church and with the grass and the fields beyond. The interior of the church is equally neat and attractive. Everything emits an aura of antique beauty.

The logical question is one of how such world-famed art works came to exist in a tiny mountain church in North Carolina. The story offered by the church is that the artist, Ben Long, who had graduated from Statesville High School in the mid-1960s and later studied in Italy, wanted to create some fresco work in his home state. A student of Pietro Annigoni, Long visited many churches of all sizes and denominations, and everywhere he was rejected. No one wanted the work of an unknown artist, it seemed.

Another problem was that many of the people with whom he talked did not know what a fresco is. So Long, discouraged, was ready to return to Italy. But before he left, he attended a party at the home of well-known artist Phillip Moose in Blowing Rock.

Moose introduced Long to the local priest and immediately the priest accepted Long's offer to create the art work. Only then, the story goes, did the priest ask the question: "What is a fresco?"

When you look at the fresco of the crucified Jesus, you will see, in addition to the Spirit, strange faces in the surrounding clouds. Who are these people? The explanation offered is one that is as remarkable as the art work itself-even more so!

The story is that the concept was rather like formations of clouds, which appear as different symbols to each viewer. When the plaster began to dry, the faces began to emerge, to the surprise of everyone, especially the artist.

Go, make your visit, and then add your own interpretation.

Church of the Good Shepherd, Tryon.

SECTION 7: THE BEST OF THE MOUNTAIN CHURCHES
TRIP 9: GOOD SHEPHERD EPISCOPAL CHURCH OF TRYON
A LINK WITH ANOTHER AGE

LOCATION:

Drive to Tryon via one of two superb highways: US 74 from Shelby area or I-26, which links with NC 108 outside Columbus. Once you are in Tryon, you will need to follow a long, winding road that seemingly leads to nowhere you want to go, but if you will persist, you will reach this historic church.

You can junction with I-26 in Asheville, off I-40, or in South Carolina in Spartanburg. US 74 connects Charlotte and the western part of the state, and you can follow this splendid highway to Columbus and then follow NC 108 west.

You will enter Tryon on US 176, which veers off NC 108 at the outskirts of town. As you proceed toward the middle of town, you will see the Howard Street intersection. Turn left, and then quickly you will reach Grady Street. Turn left again and then turn right when you reach Markham Street. Follow Markham Street (while you drive think of the poet Edwin Markham, author of the depressing but omen-laden poem, "The Man with the Hoe") and as you round curve after curve, keep the faith. Just as you are about to give up and return to downtown Tryon, you will see the point where Markham Street junctions with Jackson Street, and on the corner you will see the Good Shepherd Episcopal Church.

NEARBY ATTRACTIONS:

In the chapter of this book on the Congregational Church of Christ in Tryon you will see a listing of many nearby attractions that you can visit easily. If you want additional places to visit while you are in the area, take I-26 north to junction with US 64 west to Hendersonville and then to Brevard, where you can find an amazing number of waterfalls. Drive on through the small towns of Cashiers, Sapphire, and Highlands to see other magnificent and awesome waterfalls.

HOURS OF OPERATION:

The church is closed except during regular worship hours, but you can enjoy your visit by taking in the beauty of the church exterior. Please do not litter or mar the parking area and the beauty of the church.

ADMISSION:

There are no admission fees.

FACILITIES:

Other than the usual facilities offered by an open church, there are none, except for the small parking lot.

WHAT'S THE STORY?

This church was once the original slave chapel at Coxe Plantation. Known as Saint Francis, this church was moved to its present location in Tryon in 1955.

SPECIAL ATTRACTIONS:

The original furnishings of the church are all still intact, as is the glass throughout the church. These appointments are well worth the time it takes to drive to the church for your visit.

MAKING THE MOST OF YOUR VISIT:

On any of the visits described in this book, you are offered bits of historical information or human interest stories that are intended to add a little spice to your visits. On this particular visit you are encouraged to think of four essential concepts: the western part of North Carolina, the town of Tryon itself, the old Tryon Cemetery that you passed (on the left side of the road as you entered the Markham road mid-point), and the church itself.

A fifth concept is that posited by Edwin Markham himself.

First, the western part of North Carolina is a world unto itself. In this book you have noticed that often all three words in the phrase *Western North Carolina* are capitalized. There is a reason. In North Carolina the Piedmont has only a vague and nebulous resemblance to the mountains. The same is true of the coastal parts of the state. It is not simply the topography that differs: the people differ, as do values and philosophies. This is not to say that one is better than another or more acceptable: all areas of the state have wonderful people and places to visit and enjoy. But in the mountains there is a fierce spirit of freedom and independence that is unequalled elsewhere in the state.

There is also the fact that towns like Tryon are in a large sense retirement places, so there is a laid-back attitude that is rewarding and desirable.

The third ingredient, the Tryon Cemetery, is one of the most interesting burial grounds in Western North Carolina. There are beautiful headstones, ancient and decaying ones, and nostalgia at every turn. Even the engravings on some stones have faded through exposure to sun, wind, and rain until the words can no longer be read. And, as with all large cemeteries, you will find that there are miniature novels contained in family burial plots.

The Good Shepherd Episcopal Church and its original role as a slave chapel is another link to the past, to another age that many of us cannot conceive or understand. The simple beauty of the church is striking and dramatic. The austere grace and charm are arresting. The design of the church is ornate in places and unexpectedly exquisite in others.

The fact that it was a slave chapel tells you something of the age of the building. The fact that it was moved without any significant damage reveals the strength of the chapel. The size of the building tells you volumes about the reasons it was established and why it is presently maintained.

Now, as you look at the church and imagine its past, think of the words of Edwin Markham, who describes the somber physical creature with the hoe. The poet, who lived when the chapel was in its original role, wrote, "Bowed by the weight of centuries he leans/ Upon his hoe and gazes on the ground,/ The emptiness of ages in his face,/ And on his back the burdens of the world."

As you read or remember, you may find this an appropriate time to reflect happily that such times in history are rare.

All Souls Cathedral in Biltmore Village.

SECTION 7: THE BEST OF THE MOUNTAIN CHURCHES
TRIP 10: THE CATHEDRAL OF ALL SOULS
ALL ROADS LEAD TO THE CATHEDRAL OF ALL SOULS

LOCATION:

The Cathedral of All Souls is located at 3 Angle Street in Biltmore Village, Asheville, North Carolina. The mailing address is P. O. Box 5978, Asheville, NC 28813. If you are wondering how to find the cathedral once you have reached the village, have no worries. Just, as the old saying goes, "All roads lead to Rome," in Biltmore Village all roads lead to the Cathedral of All Souls in this picturesque town.

In order to get to Biltmore Village from I-40, leave the interstate highway at the intersection of US 25. This highway leads into Biltmore Village, and, you will notice, the village is laid out so that all roads do in fact lead to the cathedral.

NEARBY ATTRACTIONS:

While you are in the Asheville area, you are very close to Brevard, Hendersonville, Flat Rock, Tryon, Blue Ridge Parkway, the North Carolina Arboretum, Folk Art Center, the Western North Carolina Center, and to all of the numerous attractions in the city that was the home of Thomas Wolfe and William Sidney Porter, better known as O. Henry. You are also within driving distance of Mount Mitchell, Mount Pisgah, Devil's Courthouse, and Graveyard Fields.

HOURS OF OPERATION:

The Cathedral of All Souls holds regular worship services at 8 a.m., 9 a.m., 9:50 a.m., and at 11 a.m. on Sunday mornings. Other services are held at 11:15 a.m. 12:30 p.m., and 5:45 p.m. on Wednesdays. On Monday, Tuesday, Thursday, and Friday there are scheduled services at 12:30 p.m. and 5:45 p.m. The church has extended a welcome to all visitors. Coffee is served in the Parish Hall after the 11 a.m. Sunday morning service. The church may be viewed and enjoyed from the exterior on any day of the week and at any time. It is one of the most beautiful churches anywhere in the nation, and it is unusually attractive from any viewpoint.

ADMISSION:

There are no admission fees of any sort.

FACILITIES:

There are the usual facilities found in virtually any church in the land, but this one has the extra warmth that only superb architectural beauty and warmth of the members can provide.

WHAT'S THE STORY?

The Cathedral of All Souls was formed as a parish church in 1896 as a member of the Diocese of Western North Carolina and is a part of the Episcopal Church in the United States. The church was the result of the generosity and wisdom of George Vanderbilt, who conceived the idea and engaged the services of world-famous architect Richard Morris Hunt to make the idea a reality. The church was completed in 1896 and consecrated on November 8 of that same year. On October 26, 1896, Vanderbilt gave possession of the buildings to the Wardens and Vestry. Vanderbilt himself served as Senior Warden from the time the church was consecrated until his death in 1914.

MAKING THE MOST OF YOUR VISIT:

The church you will visit is delightfully beautiful beyond the power of words to describe. The style is described as being "from the Norman period of transition from Romanesque to Gothic" and the construction is cruciform (shaped like a cross) and was said to have been inspired by the abbey churches in Northern England. The apse is, however, similar to those of churches in southern France.

On January 1, 1995, the church became the Cathedral of the Episcopal Diocese of Western North Carolina. What is the basic difference between a church and a cathedral? According to the brochure used by the church, a cathedral is a parish church in which the bishop has his chair, or seat. As a cathedral, the church is the spiritual center of the diocese.

The windows of the cathedral were designed and constructed by two contemporaries of Tiffany-David Maitland Armstrong and his daughter Helen. Six memorial windows of the transepts (the parts of a cross-shaped church at right angles to the long and main nave, or section) depict scenes from the Bible.

The windows in the east transept portray Jesus and the Doctors in the Temple, Christ before Pilate, and the Entombment. In the west transept the scenes are Solomon and Hiram Building the Temple, Charity, and David Playing the Harp before Saul. In the towers the depictions are Jonathan (left, north side); St. Francis (right, north side); Isaiah (left, south side) and John the Baptist (right, south side); Ruth (left, east side) and St. Peter (right, east side); Daniel (left, west side,) and St. Paul (right, west side).

The organ was installed by Casavant Organ Company of Canada in 1971 and consists of more than 3,000 individual pipes. The two organs in the cathedral have a total of 52 ranks.

The cross rising above the church tower was installed in 1961. Designed by Marianne Zambriskie, the cross consists of two Celtic crosses in which circles represent the eternal nature of God (without beginning or end) and the "interdependence of all the world through Christ."

Visiting the Cathedral of All Souls is a religious and an aesthetic experience that makes the pleasant drive north from Hendersonville or south through Asheville all the more terrific and memorable. Don't miss it!

Zeb Vance home in Weaverville.

SECTION 8: THE BEST OF THE MOUNTAIN HOMES
TRIP 1: THE ZEB VANCE HOME IN WEAVERVILLE
THE FOUNTAIN OF WIT AND WISDOM

LOCATION:
Five miles off the Blue Ridge Parkway at or near Milepost 375 near Asheville you will find the tiny town of Weaverville and, on the outskirts of town, the restored home of Zebulon Vance.

NEARBY ATTRACTIONS:
Within an easy drive from Weaverville you can reach Asheville with its many attractions, including the home of novelist Thomas Wolfe, the Folk Art Center, and fascinatingly beautiful downtown with its unique architecture, great restaurants, and shops. There are also fine museums in Asheville, including the Smith-McDowell Museum and the museums at Pack Square. You are also near Craggy Gardens, Mount Mitchell, the Museum of North Carolina Minerals, Crabtree Meadows, and Old Fort.

HOURS OF OPERATION:
The Zeb Vance home is open 9 a.m. until 5 p.m. Monday through Saturday all year; on Sunday from 1 p.m. until 5 p.m.

ADMISSION:
There is no admission fee.

FACILITIES:
Ample parking, restrooms, and drinking water are available. There are no camping or hiking facilities or the other amenities found at recreational areas.

WHAT'S THE STORY?
Zeb Vance was one of the most fascinating leaders in North Carolina. He served as a United States senator, governor of the state, and as a military officer. He came from humble background but developed a razor-sharp wit that never seemed to fail him, whether in the Congress or in the backwoods.

SPECIAL ATTRACTIONS:
The house and grounds at the Zeb Vance homeplace are the major features. The large house in which Vance spent many of his younger years is only one aspect of the visit: the outbuildings are also worthy of attention. But it is the character of Zeb Vance that is the primary consideration of this trip.

MAKING THE MOST OF YOUR VISIT:
When you leave the Blue Ridge Parkway, you will follow the Weaverville road until it intersects with Ox Creek Road. Turn right and follow signs to Zeb Vance birthplace.

You will probably start your visit by touring the house where Vance lived, after which you can enjoy walks around the home site and see where and how the pioneer family lived, examine the spring house, smoke house, early American tools, and learn about one of the most fascinating men this state ever produced.

To provide some notion of what kind of man Vance was, when he went to Massachusetts to deliver a lecture after the Civil War, he found a portrait of General Robert E. Lee hanging in the men's outhouse. When he returned to join his hosts, one of them asked Vance what he thought of seeing a picture of his beloved South's greatest hero hanging in the privy.

Vance replied, "I thought it was very appropriate. If ever man lived that could scare the dung out of the Yankees, that man was Robert E. Lee."

When Vance was in Congress and a legislator from Rhode Island made a disparaging remark about a river in the Tar Heel state, Vance was on his feet in an instant and proclaiming, "The gentleman who makes that remark comes from a puny little state of Rhode Island. Why, I could stand on one border of Rhode Island and urinate halfway across that state."

(It is doubtful whether Vance ever said "urinate" in his entire life, but he made his point with very direct language.)

"Order!" pleaded the presiding officer. "The gentleman from North Carolina is out of order."

"Yes," said Vance, "and if I wasn't out of order, I could urinate clear across the whole durned state."

Known as one of the quickest wits in the nation, Vance was seldom at a loss for words. You may recall the story, told elsewhere, that Vance once admitted whipping a neighborhood villain because "he was so cussed ugly I couldn't help it."

But Vance was more than a quipster. When he was turning into a young man, he went off in his homespun clothing to become a student at the University of North Carolina at Chapel Hill. There he met and learned to admire Dr. Elisha Mitchell and, much later, when Mitchell became lost on the mountain that now bears his name, Zeb Vance led a search party in an effort to rescue the scholar. Unfortunately, they found Mitchell's body in a plunge pool under a waterfall.

Zeb Vance became a friend to some of the most influential men of his day, and he numbered John C. Calhoun among the men he admired. But no matter who the company was, Vance became the life of the party, whether social or political, with his wit and insights into problems simple and profound.

When asked what kind of currency he would call the practice of selling possum pelts with beaver tails sewn onto them, Vance replied, "A retail currency."

Later, as a prisoner of Federal troops, Vance was brought into the Federal commander's tent. The commander, having heard the rumors that Vance had been degraded by having to ride a mule on the trip, asked Vance if the story was true.

"I never saw a jackass on the entire journey," Vance answered, "until I walked into this tent."

Oddly enough, Zeb Vance, while a staunch member of the South's defenders, put North Carolina's welfare, at least on occasion, ahead of the South's. Vance felt that his home state suffered much from the rigors and hardships of war which the state neither wanted nor caused. He reached out to the people of the state and made his dedicated and sincere efforts to supply arms, clothing, and food for the state's civilians and troops.

The result of his efforts was that he came into direct conflict on more than one occasion with Jefferson Davis. Vance made known his strenuous objections to some of the Confederacy's laws which conflicted with the rights of the state.

For instance, he objected to conscription laws, suspension of the writ of habeas corpus, confiscation of private property of North Carolina citizens, and the use of military officers from the state of Virginia rather than those from North Carolina.

Taking a page from South Carolina's book (the Palmetto State having been the first to secede from the Union), Vance threatened to have North Carolina secede from the Confederacy. Having found an ally in William Holden, newspaper editor, Vance and Holden fought bitterly for Tar Heel rights.

Vance's friend Holden wrote in the *North Carolina Standard* that North Carolina was being treated shabbily by the Confederate government. "She is ignored," Holden wrote. "She has no voice in the Cabinet. She is raked for conscripts as with a fine tooth comb. Her troops are always placed in the forefront of the hottest battles.... A large portion of her people are suspected of being disloyal.... North Carolina must be the equal of the other states of the Confederacy, or she will leave it...."

Small wonder that Vance, aided by Holden, became a symbol of Tar Heel loyalty. Later the two men drifted apart and became more than opponents. They became embittered with each other's policies.

Through it all, however, Vance remained the hero of the people of his state, and it is only fitting that his childhood and boyhood home should be preserved and open for visitors. Here was a mountain lad who became a first-rate student, a more-than-competent officer in the military, governor on two occasions, and senator, as well as a prisoner of war.

It was while he was a prisoner that Vance displayed the wit and courage that made him the hero of the people. When taunted by Northern antagonists, Vance asked his tormentors a riddle: Why is the Southern Confederacy like the Biblical character Lazarus?"

When no one came with an answer, Vance supplied one. "Because it was licked by a set of dogs," he said.

Under Vance's administration as North Carolina governor, the state capital was moved, briefly, from Raleigh to Statesville, and Vance's residence there is known today as the Vance House, a modest dwelling that once served briefly as the state capitol.

But it is Vance's home that deserves your attention. It is not simply a place where a favorite son lived; it is a museum of a way of life. You can examine the outbuildings, as well as the house, carefully and see that the ingenuity of construction, the wisdom of planning, and the execution of the finish work is superlative. You can derive a reasonably good notion of how not just Vance but other mountain people lived, although most mountain families did not live on quite the same level as did the Vances.

When you look at the back side of the house, you will note that the height of the log walls is impressive, and you may wonder how such heavy logs were elevated to such a height. Rest assured that no sophisticated machinery was used. Manpower, coupled with human ingenuity, was nearly always the answer.

Imagine again, as you walk around the home place, how much work was put into the shingles alone. While an expert can use a maul and froe and make up to 1,000 shingles in a day's time, the typical shingle-maker could produce far less. In fact, a novice would be hard pressed to produce a tenth of that amount, especially if he had to secure his own wood in the process.

The chinking of a log house was also a difficult and time-consuming task. Even the outbuildings required a massive amount of work. When you leave the Vance house you will take with you a new respect for the man and for the lifestyle of the mountaineer.

Home of Carl Sandburg in Flat Rock.

SECTION 8: THE BEST OF THE MOUNTAIN HOMES
TRIP 2: CONNEMARA
THE HOME OF THE POET WITH THE BIG SHOULDERS

LOCATION:

The address of the Carl Sandburg Home National Historic Site is 1928 Little River Road, Flat Rock, North Carolina. The phone number is (828) 693-4178. In order to reach Connemara from I-40, junction with I-26 in Asheville and drive south to Hendersonville and then exit I-26 and take US 25 south of Hendersonville about five miles to the small but beautiful town of Flat Rock. As you drive south, you will see the Flat Rock Play-house on the right. Turn right and drive a very short distance down the Little River Road and you will see parking areas for the Carl Sandburg house on the left.

If you are traveling I-85, junction with I-26 in the area of Greenville and Spartanburg and drive north. Then junction with US 25 in Hendersonville, or you can take US 25 off I-85 and drive north to Flat

Rock.

NEARBY ATTRACTIONS:

While you are in Flat Rock, you can visit the Flat Rock Playhouse (during season) for excellent off-Broadway drama and comedy. You are also within a five-minute drive of the historic St. John in the Wilderness Church, and you can find exceptional attractions in nearby Hendersonville and Brevard. You are within easy driving distance of Saluda and Tryon, and Asheville is only a short drive to the north. The Blue Ridge Parkway is nearby to the north.

HOURS OF OPERATION:

The Carl Sandburg Home National Site is open daily (except Christmas) from 9 a.m. until 5 p.m.

ADMISSION:

There is no admission per se to the grounds, but for a guided tour of the house (an absolute must, if you really want to see where one of America's best-known poets lived and if you want to understand more about the man himself) the fee is $3 per adult. Persons 16 and under are admitted free.

FACILITIES:

On the premises there are restrooms, hiking trails, abundant parking spaces, and a gift shop where you can buy souvenirs. The guided tours are thorough and exceptionally interesting, and the guides are well-informed, courteous, and efficient.

WHAT'S THE STORY?

After a hectic youth and early adulthood, Carl Sandburg settled down to a quiet and much-honored life in Connemara, the 264-acre farm in Western North Carolina. At Connemara (he did not name the farm but retained the name given to it by one of the previous owners) Sandburg continued to write, to meet with the leading men and women of letters who came his way, and to enjoy the farm and the goats that made Connemara their home.

SPECIAL ATTRACTIONS:

The people interested in literature will find that the home of Carl Sandburg is the most interesting part of the visit. Such people will be fascinated by the stories about him and by the little touches of the man that are found everywhere. Younger members of the family will be fascinated by the goats and their impeccable environment.

MAKING THE MOST OF YOUR VISIT:

Carl Sandburg was not, in many respects, the man that most people thought he was. He wrote far more than a little poem about fog creeping in on little cat feet. He was a deeply intelligent, energetic, robust, courageous, and dedicated man who compiled one of the greatest biographies ever written by an American, and he had the bravery needed to stick to his beliefs, no matter how unpopular they became. And, like most highly informed people, when he saw that his political beliefs must be reconsidered, he had the integrity to make the changes he felt necessary.

Sandburg was a strong man, both physically and mentally, and his poetry was equally muscular and brawny. He referred to his much-loved city of Chicago as the "Hog butcher for the world" and as the "City of the Big Shoulders" and described it as "fierce as a dog" and like a "savage pitted against the wilderness."

There is little that is cute and pretty in Sandburg's work. He had no difficulty in calling a spade a spade. Born in 1878 in Galesburg, Illinois (not too far in time or distance from another tough American writer, Ernest Hemingway), Sandburg was forced to leave school because of the family economics, and he became for a time a migratory worker at jobs that included stints as a hired hand, dishwasher, milkman, barbershop porter, stage hand, sign painter, and brickmaker. For a while he enjoyed-or endured-the life of a hobo. Returning to Galesburg, he became a house painter before he enlisted in the army during the Spanish-American War.

While in the army he became a correspondent to the Galesburg *Evening Mail*. Home from the war, he enrolled in Lombard College as a provisional student. Only weeks before his graduation, however, Sandburg, who had become a local celebrity as an exceptional basketball player, disappeared from the campus. He never graduated. Sandburg eventually landed in Chicago at the *Daily News* and remained there for years. But he was driven to write poetry, and by 1920 he was recognized nationally as the poet of the common man and as a latter-day Walt Whitman.

Few writers have excelled in so many areas as Sandburg, who was a biographer of Abraham Lincoln, a novelist, autobiographer, political writer, and collector of American songs.

He never minded giving his opinion of anything. Once he and friends were driving through Gastonia, North Carolina, and when the car crossed the bumpy railroad tracks, Sandburg, asleep in the back seat, opened his eyes and asked gruffly, "What in the hell was that?"

"Gastonia," the driver answered, to which Sandburg asked, "Is that a town or a stomach disorder?"

Sandburg fell in love with the North Carolina mountains and spent the final 22 years of his life there. He died in 1967.

Silvermont in Brevard.

SECTION 8: THE BEST OF THE MOUNTAIN HOMES
TRIP 3: SILVERMONT
THE HOME OF SILVERSTEEN

LOCATION:

Silvermont, the home of Joseph and Elizabeth Silversteen, is located on East Main Street in Brevard. To reach Brevard from I-40 the easiest route is to exit the interstate in Asheville onto US 25 south. Follow US 25 to the intersection with US 64 in the terrific town of Hendersonville and then drive on US 64 west to Brevard. Once in town, drive to the courthouse in the middle of town, still on US 64, and turn left at the courthouse onto East Main Street. Four blocks later you will see Silvermont on the right. There is a playground/park adjacent, and you cannot miss the mansion.

NEARBY ATTRACTIONS:

In Brevard you are within quick and easy driving distance of such attractions as Connestee Falls, Whitewater Falls, Looking Glass Falls,

Hendersonville, Holmes State Educational Forest, and the Blue Ridge Parkway, where you will find Mount Pisgah, Devil's Courthouse, and Graveyard Fields only a short drive from Brevard.

HOURS OF OPERATION:

There are no public hours for Silvermont because, at this time, the mansion is used for local government and some social functions. But during daylight hours you can see the exterior of the mansion and, if you call (828) 884-3156, you may be able to see the inside of the house. Be prepared, however; the interior is not fully restored at this writing. Nevertheless, you can gain a real idea of how the mansion once looked.

ADMISSION:

There are no admission charges.

FACILITIES:

There is limited parking, and next door there are park and recreational activities, such as basketball, tennis, and other sports.

WHAT'S THE STORY?

In 1902 the Silversteens moved to Transylvania County and built Silvermont shortly afterward. The 33-room colonial revival mansion is one of the most beautiful houses in Brevard to come out of the early part of this century.

SPECIAL ATTRACTIONS:

The exterior of the house is impressive, beautiful, and astonishing. You will be awed by the size, architecture, and the workmanship that is evident in the house.

MAKING THE MOST OF YOUR VISIT:

In the early part of the twentieth century it was not uncommon for men and women to work for as little as fifty cents per day, often much less. As late as 1929 men, women, and children were working 55 to 60 hours per week for salaries of $12 or less. In light of such low wages, it is even more remarkable that a house like Silvermont could have been built by private citizens.

In many instances, mountain communities fared worse in the economic sense than did people from other parts of the state, although it is obvious that poverty is not necessarily indicated by geography. But the mountains have a colder climate, and the result is that more heat is needed. Poor roads at the turn of the century meant that commuting any distance was impossible, and this remained true even after the advent of the automobile.

The Silvermont mansion, former home of industrialist Joseph Silversteen and his family, is a notable exception to the rules of economy, as the typical person knew them. The family members occupied the mansion until the mid-twentieth century.

Brevard, one of the finest towns in North Carolina, was at the time blessed with better climate year-round than are most places, and the beauty of the surrounding terrain attracted many outsiders with greater affluence to the community. Many of these newcomers to the mountains became strong civic leaders as well as champions of education and culture.

One result, at least in part, was that Brevard blossomed into a city that was the envy of the rest of the state. It was notably lacking in terms of real poverty, crime, low standards of living, and the other problems facing the Piedmont cities of any size. And today Brevard still reflects the values that were part of its origins and growth.

Silversteen, one of the newcomers-in this case from up north (in Pennsylvania, which was far north to many people at the time) was at first a tanner and he established the Toxaway Tanning Company shortly before he started the Gloucester Lumber Company, the first of several lumber businesses he would originate in Western North Carolina. In 1972 Dorothy Bjerg, the last surviving member of the family, willed the mansion and its grounds to Transylvania County. A trust fund for the upkeep of the mansion was included in the bequest.

Having survived many years of neglect, Silvermont benefitted from the work of Friends of Silvermont, now chartered by the state of North Carolina. The Friends saved the mansion, and today it is used by several government, business, and community groups and it also serves as a recreation center with adjoining playgrounds and park space. The first floor of the mansion is now open for public use, and the second story houses the Silversteen Room, an area furnished in accordance with the Silversteen will.

The house has served as location for parties and dinners as well as for weddings and other celebrations. The house is locked when not used for special occasions, so you may have to search for a time when you can see the inside. Even if you cannot go into the house, you can enjoy seeing the grandeur of the outside and the public use of the surrounding grounds.

The park located on the grounds is open from 8 a. m. until 10 p. m. For more information about Silvermont, call (828) 877-3939. For details about the park call (828) 884-3156.

Home of Thomas Wolfe in Asheville.

SECTION 8: THE BEST OF THE MOUNTAIN HOMES
TRIP 4: THE THOMAS WOLFE MEMORIAL
WOLFE'S OLD KENTUCKY HOME AND DIXIELAND

LOCATION:

The Thomas Wolfe Memorial sits inside an oblong city block in Asheville, a block bounded by North Market Street, Woodfin Street, College Street, and Oak Street. The Thomas Wolfe Memorial is located at 52 Market Street. To get to the house, take I-40 into Asheville and leave the interstate onto I-240. Leave I-240 at Exit 5B onto North Market Street, which intersects with Woodfin Street. Write to the Memorial at Post Office Box 7143 in Asheville, NC 28802, or call (828) 253-8304.

NEARBY ATTRACTIONS:

While you are at the Thomas Wolfe Memorial you will be near Pack Square and the terrific museums there, and you are within easy driving distance from Craggy Gardens, the North Carolina Arboretum, the Western North Carolina Center, the Folk Art Center, the Blue Ridge Parkway, and Mount Mitchell State Park.

HOURS OF OPERATION:

Hours for the Thomas Wolfe Memorial are seasonal. From April through October, hours are, Monday through Saturday, 9 a.m. until 5 p.m. and on Sunday from 1 p.m. until 5 p.m. During November through March the hours are, Tuesday through Saturday, from 10 a.m. until 4 p.m. and on Sunday from 1 p.m. until 4 p.m. The Wolfe house is closed on Mondays during the winter.

Note: In late July 1998 fire damaged the Thomas Wolfe Memorial badly, necessitating the closing of the memorial until the damage is repaired. Authorities ruled that the fire was the result of arson, and obviously many changes will be made in the near future. At this writing there is no date given for the re-opening of the house.

ADMISSION:

Admission fees are very low. The Thomas Wolfe Memorial, one of the North Carolina Historic Sites, Division of Archives and History, costs $1 for adults and $.50 for children.

FACILITIES:

There is ample parking outside, and inside you will find restrooms and a book store as well as a souvenir shop.

WHAT'S THE STORY?

When Thomas Wolfe was growing up in Asheville, his mother operated a boarding house for people who came to Asheville for the climate. The constant comings and goings of the array of people into My Old Kentucky Home, or Dixieland, provided fuel for the imaginative and creative mind of Thomas Wolfe. However, the house, as much as any of the temporary (or permanent) residents, became an integral part of Wolfe's fiction, which at one time placed him among the leaders in fiction in the early years of the twentieth century. Wolfe, a contemporary of Hemingway, Faulkner, Steinbeck, T. S. Eliot, Sherwood Anderson, Theodore Dreiser, and similar notables, was one of the strongest voices of the age. The house is the Wolfe fan's best introduction to the writings of one of the literary masters of this nation.

SPECIAL ATTRACTIONS:

While it is impossible at this time to speculate reasonably on what the contents of the house will be once repairs are made, it is easy to state that the contents of Dixieland that relate to Julia, the fictional Luke, and Wolfe himself are of primary interest to the visitor.

MAKING THE MOST OF YOUR VISIT:

The best way to prepare for this visit is to obtain a copy of *Look Homeward, Angel, You Can't Go Home Again,* and *Of Time and the*

River and read these books carefully in order to derive the best image of the larger-than-life Thomas Wolfe, whose mind (and his ego) were at least as large as his massive body.

When Nobel Prize-winning novelist William Faulkner was asked to rate writers who were his contemporaries, Faulkner immediately responded that Thomas Wolfe's name must be placed at the head of any such list because, since the extent of greatness can be at best measured by the extent of failure, Wolfe was unquestionably the major writer in America. Faulkner added that Wolfe failed the most because he attempted the most.

You can benefit from this trip greatly if you will also find and read a biography of Wolfe. You can read the marital conflict of Wolfe's father and mother, the financial-minded mother who was at odds with the free-wheeling occasional attitudes of the father of the family, and the loves and tragedies in the family.

Several characters in *Look Homeward, Angel* (originally named *O Lost* and mercifully changed when editor Maxwell Perkins took Wolfe in hand and attempted to discipline him at least to a degree) had in fact died before the novel was written, so Wolfe used their real names. Among these were W.O., the stonecutting father, Grover, the brilliant and lovable child who died in 1904 at age 12, and Ben, with whom Wolfe enjoyed a warm, affectionate, and wonderfully close relationship, who worked for a local paper and who died shortly after Wolfe went off to Pulpit Hill (quite obviously Chapel Hill).

Not only was Ben's death the climax of the novel (the title of which came from line 163 of Milton's "Lycidas"), the death was also the climax of Wolfe's own life, in a strong sense.

"The Asheville I knew died for me when Ben died," Wolfe said later. He added that it was the death of his brother that caused Wolfe to believe that he could never again call Asheville his home in the future. In *Look Homeward, Angel* Eugene Gant, the real Tom Wolfe, tells the ghost of Ben that Gant would never again be able to return permanently to his hometown.

Wolfe was born on October 3, 1900, in Asheville; he entered the University of North Carolina at age 16, and when Wolfe was 29 years old, he published his monumental *Look Homeward, Angel*. By age 35 Wolfe had published *Of Time and the River* and *From Death to Morning*. At age 38 this giant of American literature was dead. Cause of death was listed as tuberculosis of the brain. And Tom Wolfe died in Baltimore, far from the mountains he loved.

The house in which Wolfe grew up had been built in 1883, and at the time it consisted of about six rooms and a front and back porch. By 1889 the house had been modified greatly and now had doubled the original size. By the time Wolfe was ready to enroll in the University of North Carolina, Tom's mother had brought the house into the 20th century by adding electricity and plumbing of the indoor variety. The house was now an 11-room structure.

Today the house contains original Wolfe family furnishings or belongings, arranged by family members so that the house would reflect the environment of Wolfe himself. After reading the novels of Wolfe, you can spot locations in the house easily. They are described with usually unerring accuracy by the author, who also documented his townspeople with equal accuracy.

So detailed were the characterizations that for seven years *Look Homeward, Angel* was banned from the Asheville public library. And if Thomas Wolfe felt that he could not go back to his home again, you certainly can go to his home. And you will not likely leave without feeling the strong presence of Wolfe in the spacious house.

Fort Defiance near Lenoir.

SECTION 8: THE BEST OF THE MOUNTAIN HOMES
TRIP 5: FORT DEFIANCE
THE WINDOW TO THE FRONTIER

LOCATION:

Fort Defiance is located on the Yadkin River between Lenoir and North Wilkesboro. From I-40 take US 321 out of Hickory north to the Lenoir area. You will bypass Lenoir and drive on north to the tiny town of Patterson, where you will turn right on NC 268. Watch carefully for signs. After you drive five minutes, you will turn right and cross a bridge. Three minutes later you will come to a fork in the road. Turn right, and you will find the house of General William Lenoir only a few hundred yards away. From the Blue Ridge Parkway you should take the US 321 exit and drive south to Patterson. Turn left and follow instructions given above.

NEARBY ATTRACTIONS:

You are near the Blue Ridge Parkway, Valdese and the Trail of Faith and Waldensian Museum, Morganton and its attractions, Blowing Rock, and Boone.

HOURS OF OPERATION:

Fort Defiance is open from April through October on the first and third Sundays of each month from 2 p.m. until 5 p.m. You can arrange special tours by appointment. Call (828) 726-0323, or you can write to Fort Defiance, Inc., P. O,. Box 686, Lenoir, NC 28645. The telephone number is for the Caldwell County Chamber of Commerce.

ADMISSION:

The admission charge is $2 for adults. Children under age 12 are admitted free.

FACILITIES:

There is ample parking space, and you have access to restrooms. You can also buy souvenirs. A picnic shelter is also available for your use.

WHAT'S THE STORY?

Fort Defiance is the historic home of General William Lenoir, one of the leading citizens of North Carolina in fields of the military, education, politics, and law. The house was built in 1792 and today houses more than 300 pieces of original clothing and furnishings that are displayed to the public.

SPECIAL ATTRACTIONS:

It is difficult to select only one or two items that are special: the entire house is highly interesting; however, the furniture, dishes, and clothing are of special social and historic interest.

MAKING THE MOST OF YOUR VISIT:

To appreciate General William Lenoir, you should first read a thorough account of the battle of Kings Mountain. Better yet, make a visit to the Kings Mountain National Battleground park and make a tour of the battlefield.

If you cannot do either of the above, turn to the chapter of this book on the visit to the Kings Mountain battleground and read the account. As you have made your way through this book, you have noticed an emphasis on the historical as well as the scenic. The reason for this emphasis is that as a teacher for more than 30 years I have witnessed an awareness-or lack of it-of American history that is deplorable. It is entirely too easy to forget how many people fought, suffered, and devoted their lives and property to the United States. And many college students do not recognize that Harry Truman was President of the United States. We must wonder how many could identify Millard Fillmore, Franklin Pierce, or James Buchanan.

General Lenoir was never President, but he was the kind of man who became a strong and positive leader in local and regional politics and military endeavors. He was a member of the Council of State, a member of both houses of the Legislature of North Carolina, president of the Senate, and a member of the Convention of 1788 which laid claim to fame by rejecting the first proposed Constitution of the United States. Having served as president of the first Board of Trustees of the University of North Carolina, he was also a successful surveyor, a justice of the peace for more than half a century, and a militiaman who fought against both the Native Americans on the frontier and against British troops. He also wrote one of the most accurate accounts of the Battle of Kings Mountain.

At the Battle of Kings Mountain, the famous Over-Mountain men made their historic march from the highlands to the small ridge on the North Carolina-South Carolina border where they met the forces of the British commanded by Major Ferguson, one of the classical military men of his day. The Over-Mountain men soundly defeated the British and prevented Ferguson from joining forces with Lord Cornwallis for their march northward.

It is difficult to realize that the Lenoir area was many years ago the frontier between civilization and wilderness. The Lenoir house stood on the actual frontier and effectively bridged the gap between the opulence of the Charleston region and the almost primitive lifestyles of the western part of the state. Over a period of decades the house was occupied by seven family generations of the Lenoir family. It was only in 1965 when the house was turned over for restoration and conversion into a public and historic attraction.

Inside the house, in addition to the beautiful and authentic furniture, you will find teacups, bowls, plates, and utensils that date back to the original time of the house. The massive bedsteads are in themselves worth making the trip to see.

When you go outside, you have five acres of woodland, the family cemetery, and English boxwoods. Some of the shrubs and trees were brought from the Charleston area to the mountains of North Carolina as part of an effort to link the two cultures.

When you make your visit, plan to allot enough time for you to take the tour of the house and have enough left for the slow and thorough inspection of the grounds. It's one of the few places where you can actually walk back in history.

Cleveland Cabin in Wilkesboro.

SECTION 8: THE BEST OF THE MOUNTAIN HOMES
TRIP 6: THE ROBERT CLEVELAND HOUSE
RESTORING A MOMENT IN HISTORY

LOCATION:

The Robert Cleveland log house can be seen behind the Old Wilkes Jail Museum in Wilkesboro. To get to Wilkesboro, exit I-40 at Statesville onto NC 115 and drive north to Wilkesboro, or exit the interstate at Hickory onto US 321 and drive north to Smith Crossroads at Lenoir. Turn right a few minutes past the crossroads and take NC 268 into Wilkesboro.

From the Blue Ridge Parkway drive south on NC 18, which you can reach near Doughton Park. You can also follow NC 16 south from the Parkway.

NEARBY ATTRACTIONS:

You are close to Fort Defiance on the outskirts of Lenoir, to the Parkway, and to Boone-Blowing Rock areas where you can find Tweetsie, several museums, Julian Price Memorial Park, and Moses Cone Memorial

Park.

HOURS OF OPERATION:

The Cleveland House is open from 9 a.m. until 4 p.m. Monday through Friday.

ADMISSION:

There is no admission charge.

FACILITIES:

You can park on the street in front of the Old Wilkes Jail Museum, on the north side of the building, or behind the old jail. There are no picnic tables or campgrounds in the immediate vicinity, but you can camp, picnic, fish, hike, or enjoy nature study at nearby Kerr Scott Reservoir parks or on the Parkway.

WHAT'S THE STORY?

Robert Cleveland was a captain in the military forces that engaged Colonel Patrick Ferguson and the British Tories at the battle of Kings Mountain. He served under the command of his brother Benjamin, who held the rank of colonel. Shortly after the Revolution, Cleveland built his house in western Wilkes County, and after his death the house went into disrepair until local organizations bought the house and had it moved to the present location. The house today is a shining example of what can be done in the area of conservation if the spirit is willing and the funds can be found. The house is also a superb place for people of all ages to learn about the way of life two centuries ago in this country.

SPECIAL ATTRACTIONS:

In a log house nearly everything is an attraction, because this type of house is rather uncommon in many parts of the United States and in many foreign countries. But some of the furniture in the house is highly interesting, and the fireplaces are objects of interest and admiration. But perhaps the best part of the attraction is the guided tour of the house. You will see and learn of myriads of interesting objects or information, all of which will add up to a superior trip.

MAKING THE MOST OF YOUR VISIT:

Start by reconsidering your notion of what a log house really is. Start by reflecting on what one is not. A real log house is not one of the many kits offered on the market today, kits that include all of the logs cut to exact lengths and milled to precision so that the owner has actually little or nothing to do with the actual wood itself, other than placing each log in its predetermined position.

This is not to say that there is anything wrong with the log house kits; they can be beautiful, unique, and comfortable beyond description. But they are not typical of the log houses of an older period of time.

Neither are log houses the lean-tos or shanties that people threw together centuries ago to offer a semblance of protection against the elements. Such houses were intended to last for only a few months before the occupants moved on.

A real log cabin is much closer to the authentic model. The log cabin can be neat, tight, precision-built, and durable as any type of natural material you are likely to find in common use. The cabin, by tradition, was usually small, with rough logs spaced an inch or two apart and with a chinking substance, which was often clay or mud, packed between the logs to insulate the house and protect it from invasion by insects, snakes, and other unwelcome visitors.

A log house is a permanent structure, some of which have stood for more than 200 years. The logs are shaped with an adz or similar instrument, and the sides of the logs are flat and nearly smooth.

Don't leap to the conclusion that log houses were unique to the American frontiersman. They were, of course, common in Canada and a few other parts of the world. The Norse traditional log house could be and often was an imposing structure, with several floors or stories in one building. Early Germanic people also built strong and enduring log houses.

Robert Cleveland built his Wilkes County house in 1779. When it was purchased by the Old Wilkes organization, the house was taken apart log by log, rock by rock, and moved to its present site where it was reconstructed as meticulously as possible.

Such houses are usually built along the plan of two large rooms on the ground floor and a sleeping loft overhead. The idea is a good one, in that in winter heat rises and the upstairs part of the house will be warmer than the lower part. In the event of an intrusion by a bear or other foe, the higher part of the house is more protected.

Notice the froe-split shingles, and pay particular attention to the construction of the chimney. These represent exceptional workmanship, both in the original and the restored version of the house. Even the few new timbers in the house were cut from the Cleveland property of ages ago.

The house you will visit is thought to be the oldest house in Wilkes County, and you are visiting not a house, but history.

Caudill Cabin near Doughton Park.

SECTION 8: THE BEST OF THE MOUNTAIN HOMES
TRIP 7: THE CAUDILL CABIN
THE BOTTOM OF THE TOP OF THE WORLD

LOCATION:

Laurel Spring is a tiny mountain community located at the base of a beautiful mountain miles above Wilkesboro. To reach the area from I-40, you have several possible routes. If you want the most scenic tour, drive to Statesville and junction with I-77 to Elkin. There take US 21 north to junction with the Blue Ridge Parkway. Drive south on the Parkway through Doughton Park (at Milepost 238 through 244) to junction with NC 18. Follow NC 18 south for 6.2 miles and turn left to junction with Longbottom Road (State Road 1728), and remain on this road for four miles to State Road 1730. Drive three miles, cross a neat bridge over a trout stream, and park on the right side of the road, then walk across the road to a trail that leads past a gate and up Grassy Gap Road.

A second way to the Caudill Cabin is to drive to Statesville and take NC 115 north to Wilkesboro, then junction with NC 18 and drive north to Longbottom Road. At this point follow directions given above.

A third option, if you have plenty of time and a desire to see the Blue Ridge Parkway and its surrounding beauty, is to leave I-40 at Asheville, Marion, Morganton, or Hickory and drive north to junction with the Parkway. Then drive north to junction with NC 18.

The above routes will then require a hike of 10.9 miles, but if you want to see the house without walking, then simply drive to Doughton Park, walk up to Wildcat Rock, and look down at the cabin, almost a mile below, in the deep cove which is almost like an ice cream cone.

NEARBY ATTRACTIONS:

You are near Stone Mountain, the Blue Ridge Parkway, and the towns of Jefferson and West Jefferson. You are within driving distance of Glendale Springs and the Church of the Frescoes. And, if you have abundant time, you are within a delightful drive from Boone and Blowing Rock, although these trips will take more than an hour each way.

HOURS OF OPERATION:

The park and the trail to the cabin are open every hour of every day, year round, unless the roads are closed by snow, ice, or other forms of bad weather.

ADMISSION:

There are no fees of any sort.

FACILITIES:

You have a small parking area, a fantastic hiking trail, a superb park, and some of the most wonderful scenery you will ever find in the South. There are no other facilities, except up at the park, where you will find campgrounds, picnic tables, gas, food, restrooms, and information.

WHAT'S THE STORY?

Decades ago a pioneering family moved into the mountains of northern North Carolina, built a cabin in the tiny cove at the base of the mountain, and reared children there-17 of them. A relative had a cabin a short distance away, and, all told, the families consisted of 35 persons.

SPECIAL ATTRACTIONS:

Along the hike to the cabin you will find a wonderful series of small waterfalls, gigantic trees, remnants of old homes that were destroyed in the devastating flood of 1916, and beautiful flowers in season.

MAKING THE MOST OF YOUR VISIT:

Start by driving to Wildcat Rock and looking down at the Caudill cabin. Spend a little time pondering why anyone would live in such a deserted, desolate place, and then reconsider: the place is neither desolated nor deserted: it is filled with life of all sorts, and the vegetation is overwhelming in its beauty and sheer mass.

There is a makeshift trail leading down the slope of the hill straight to the Caudill cabin. I do not suggest that you take this trail, although you may see others attempting it. This is not only a highly strenuous trek; it is also a dangerous one.

If you want to see the cabin close-up, your best bet is to hike to it. Follow the directions given above. If you hike this trail, you will ford Basin Creek several times, so be prepared to carry along dry socks, to wade barefoot, or hike in soggy socks. As you hike you will pass a series of old chimneys, a millstone lying in the creek, and other evidence of a once-vital village. The houses in this area were washed away by the tragic flood of 1916. The Caudill Cabin is one of the few that survived one of the most devastating floods in the history of North Carolina.

If you are not familiar with the flood, the rising waters followed day after day of torrential rains, and small trickles and quiet rills became raging rivers. As incredible as it may seem, there were wells left above ground as the waters washed away all the soil and left the chimney or stacks of rocks standing high above the new surface of the soil.

In other areas railroads were undermined by the raging water and left stretches of tracks hundreds of feet long with nothing but space under them, and down in the Piedmont there were bridges and houses washed away, and in one tragedy a group of men were on a bridge where they hacked at trees and other debris that had washed against the supports. The bridge gave way and all the men were swept downstream. A few were saved, but the majority of them died in the waters.

Martin Caudill's cabin is at the end of the trail, in the highest part of the cove. There was little water except surface water behind him, and his house was not severely threatened. When you reach the cabin you will see that the residence, where Caudill and his wife reared their 17 children, is little more than a hut. There are cracks in the walls and in the floor, and there is very little room inside the cabin. The cabin would not have lasted five minutes in the flood.

You can imagine the family huddled around the tiny wood stove as the high winds and sub-zero temperatures chilled the valley and clearing where deer, bear, foxes, and other animals once roamed the forests. Or imagine the family sleeping in the tiny loft or in the family part of the structure.

Far more dramatic, in a sense, is to imagine the family as they made the trek you just completed whenever they wanted to buy or trade for flour, coffee, or other staples. Any time any member of the family wanted to visit "civilization," that person had to make the 10.9 mile hike and cross the same creek you crossed about a dozen times on your trip in.

If you visit in winter, you will have the park nearly all to yourself. One one winter day my family and I saw 18 deer, one fox, one skunk, numerous hawks, owls, and many other animals in one visit to the park.

Better yet, visit the park and hike the trails in winter and in warmer weather, and make a motor visit to the park in October and then in July. It's a fabulous trip!

Richmond Hill in Asheville.

SECTION 8: THE BEST OF THE MOUNTAIN HOMES
TRIP 8: RICHMOND HILL
THE DREAM OF RICHMOND PEARSON

LOCATION:

Richmond Hill is situated atop a lush green hill outside Asheville, a half-hour's carriage ride in the old days and a 15-minute automobile drive in the present day. To reach the mansion from Interstate 40, drive into Asheville from either direction and exit onto I-240. Then exit I-240 onto the Weaverville Road (US 19/23). Watch for Exit 251 (the road signs will indicate UNC-Asheville). You will drive down a ramp and then turn left as soon as you reach the intersection. Start watching for traffic lights, and at the first one turn left onto Riverside Drive. Your next move is slightly tricky, unless you know the area. You must watch carefully for Pearson Bridge Road, and then turn right and cross the river. Next you will round a very sharp curve and you will then immediately turn right onto the drive up the hill to Richmond Hill.

NEARBY ATTRACTIONS:

While you are in the area you might also wish to visit the famous Riverside Cemetery, where authors Thomas Wolfe and William Sidney Porter (O. Henry) are buried. Zebulon Vance is buried not far from the two authors. You are close to the Blue Ridge Parkway and the North Carolina Arboretum. You are also within an easy drive of the Western North Carolina Center, the Folk Art Center, and the wonderful attractions of downtown Asheville.

HOURS OF OPERATION:

The estate is open during regular business hours. If you wish to inquire about overnight accommodations or reservations at Gabrielle's Restaurant, call (828) 252-7313.

ADMISSION:

There is no admission charge to enjoy the grounds and to take a look at the mansion. There are two restaurants, both with excellent menus and with varying prices. Call for information.

FACILITIES:

At Richmond Hill everything is upscale. There are 12 guest rooms in the mansion and all are decorated in the style of the 1890s. There are also nine Victorian style cottage rooms near the inn. The cottages feature a fireplace with gas coals, huge bathrooms, and a front porch with rocking chairs.

WHAT'S THE STORY?

Richmond Hill was built in 1889 as the private residence of Richmond Pearson, ambassador and congressman. The mansion was designed by James G. Hill and was one of the most beautiful, innovative, and fascinating private homes in North Carolina at the time of construction. The Queen Anne style mansion was once the social center of Asheville's best society.

SPECIAL ATTRACTIONS:

As with many attractions, it is difficult to isolate one beauty out of so many. At Richmond Hill the dining is elegant and sophisticated, the gardens are large and fascinating, and the grounds are beautifully maintained. Inside the mansion the oak staircase, the astoundingly great furnishings, and the paintings command special interest.

MAKING THE MOST OF YOUR VISIT:

Richmond Hill Inn is on the National Register of Historic Places, and within seconds of your arrival you will understand why. The common rooms and Oak Hall offer large and beautifully dark atmosphere, the result of the subdued lighting, massive fireplaces, richly dark wood, and tasteful furnishings. It is rare to see a room with such good taste and total absence of pretentiousness.

In the Oak Hall you will see exposed beams and paneling of oak throughout. Just off the Oak Hall is the library where you will see a rather large collection of books about Western North Carolina as well as books owned by the Pearsons.

In addition, there is a large ballroom, a front parlor, and more splendid decorations and furnishings. The two restaurants are Gabrielle's and the Arbor Grille. Gabrielle's is the original dining room of the mansion and offers formal dining enjoyment. The Arbor Grille, in the Garden Pavilion, features casual dining. In the Garden Pavilion you will also have an opportunity to visit the gift shop which features the artistic productions of a number of local artists. Fifteen guest rooms overlook the garden. A man-made waterfall accentuates the garden beauty.

Moses Cone mansion near Blowing Rock.

SECTION 8: THE BEST OF THE MOUNTAIN HOMES
TRIP 9: THE MOSES CONE MANSION
THE ESTATE OF THE DENIM KING

LOCATION:

The easiest way to reach the Moses Cone Memorial Park is via US 321 off Interstate 40 in the Hickory area. Drive north on US 321 through the Lenoir bypass and to slightly beyond Blowing Rock where you will intersect with the Blue Ridge Parkway. Drive south on the Parkway to Milepost 294 and turn left on the paved road leading from the Parkway to the mansion.

You can also leave I-40 at Asheville and drive north on the Parkway. This route will take considerably more time, but the drive is one of exceptional beauty. Along the way you will pass through Craggy Gardens area, Mount Mitchell, Crabtree Meadows, and through a series of tunnels near Little Switzerland.

NEARBY ATTRACTIONS:

At the Moses Cone Memorial Park you are very near one of the most beautiful mountain lakes you will find anywhere. Drive five miles south to Price Lake for a wonderfully beautiful experience. You are also near Grandfather Mountain, Blowing Rock, Boone, the Tweetsie railroad experience, and Linville Falls.

HOURS OF OPERATION:

The Moses Cone Memorial Park observes the same hours as do the other Parkway attractions. Usually the mansion is open from 9 a.m. until 5 p.m., but seasonal hours vary. When the Parkway is hit by winter storms, the Parkway and all its attractions in the afflicted area are closed.

ADMISSION:

There are no fees to see the Moses Cone Memorial Park.

FACILITIES:

There are hiking trails, a gift shop, abundant parking spaces, and information brochures here, as well as restrooms. Camping and picnicking can be enjoyed at nearby Price Lake.

WHAT'S THE STORY?

In 1897 Moses Cone, the textile magnate whose economic prowess and business acumen earned him the title of "the denim king," took his wife to Blowing Rock to see the land where they would build their dream house. The Moses Cone Memorial Park is where the Cones, Moses and his wife Bertha, enjoyed the mountain air and scenery.

SPECIAL ATTRACTIONS:

The house is one of the most beautiful in Western North Carolina. The 20-room manor sits atop a hill and overlooks a lake, a vast meadow, orchards, and mountains. The hiking and carriage trails are also highly interesting.

MAKING THE MOST OF YOUR VISIT:

When Moses and Bertha Cone lived at the manor you will be visiting, they also owned 3,516 acres of scenic mountain land where, Cone thought, his health might be improved. A man of delicate physical condition even as a rather young man, Moses Cone experienced a decline in health even as he built his vast textile empire, and he felt that the mountain climate might be helpful to him.

If you want to see the land that Cone owned, or at least a good portion of it, try the hiking trails. When Moses Cone wanted to give Bertha a gift that would allow her to enjoy the outdoors and at the same time be insulated against the public, he "gave" her a present of 25 miles of carriage trails that traversed much of the estate. Today these carriage trails have been converted into bridle trails and hiking trails.

For a strenuous or at least a thorough workout, try one or two of the trails north of the Blue Ridge Parkway. Rich Mountain Trail and Watkins Trail are now one with the Mountains-to-Sea Trail. If you add Flat Top Mountain Trail to the other two, you have a combined length of slightly more than 11 miles. If you want to hike only one of the trails, the Rich Mountain hike is 4.3 miles; Flat Top is 3 miles, and Watkins is 4 miles.

If you want to hike south of the Parkway, you can combine several trails for a 5.7 mile hike that will take you past the orchard, around the bass lake, and through a considerable part of the forest. The trails are wide, smooth, and moderately easy.

In 1950 the Moses Cone estate in the mountains was donated to the National Park Service. What you see today is much as it was when the Cones lived there, but, obviously, time has made its own changes.

The small orchard once contained 40,000 trees, and the Cone trees bore prize-winning fruit. Your walk will take you around to the apple packing house where the fruit was prepared for shipment around the country.

One of the unusual trees you will see in the forest, in addition to the hemlocks, pines, oaks, and service-berry trees, is the sugar maple, a rare tree in the North Carolina mountains. The trees are not native to the area. Cone had the trees shipped in from New England and added them to his own woodlands.

The forest hills also include cherry trees, which were then (as now) valued for their fruit as well as for the beautiful and valuable wood. The bass lake you will pass has 20 acres of water surface, and the lake is open for public fishing. Check with local rangers to be sure that you have the proper license and equipment.

The carriage barn still stands near the manor house, and you can enjoy inspecting it and the craft shop. But the real star of the visit is the awesome manor house. You can look through some of the downstairs rooms and browse through the gift shop. Part of the house is occupied by the Southern Highlands Handicraft Guild and its offerings.

You can also enjoy the spacious porch and, if you are there at the right time, you can hear a lecture or two on the house and its history. But if you miss the lecture, you can buy books that will fill you in on the background of the estate. Failing in that, you can simply sit on the porch, revel in the view, and be grateful that the property is now open to the public.

Oconalufree Village crafts near Cherokee (photo courtesy of Cherokee Tribal Travel & Promotion).

SECTION 8: THE BEST OF THE MOUNTAIN HOMES
TRIP 10: OCONOLUFTEE VILLAGE
THE HOME OF THE FIRST AMERICANS

LOCATION:
You can drive to the Oconoluftee Village from I-40 by exiting the interstate at Clyde, west of Asheville. Take US 19 south of the interstate southwest to Cherokee, at which point you will junction with US 441. The Oconoluftee Village is on Drama Road. Call (828) 497-2111.

NEARBY ATTRACTIONS:
Within convenient driving distance from the Oconoluftee Village is the Great Smoky Mountains National Park, the most visited national park in the United States. You are also close to Bryson City, the Blue Ridge Parkway, Maggie Valley, Dillsboro, and Sylva. Without driving more than a few minutes you can also visit the Museum of the Cherokee Indian, Qualla Arts and Crafts, and the drama *Unto These Hills.*

HOURS OF OPERATION:

The village is open from 9 a.m. until 5:30 p.m. daily from May 15 through October 25. *Unto These Hills* runs from June 13 until August 23 each summer and plays every night but Sunday during the period. The Qualla Arts and Crafts attractions is open daily during regular business hours, as is the Museum of the Cherokee Indian.

ADMISSION:

Admission to the Oconoluftee Village is $10 for adults, $5 for ages 6-13, and children under age 5 are admitted free. There is no admission fee charged at Qualla Arts and Crafts. Call (828) 497-3103. At the Museum of the Cherokee Indian admission is $4 for adults and $2 for children 6-12. Children under 6 years are admitted free. Call (828) 497-3481. For *Unto These Hills* the regular admission cost is $10 for adults, $5 for children under 12. Reserved seats are $12. Call (828) 497-2111.

FACILITIES:

Restrooms are available, and there is plenty of parking space. Gift shops are located in Qualla Arts and Crafts and in the Museum of the Cherokee Indian.

WHAT'S THE STORY?

The Oconoluftee Village is on the Qualla Boundary, the home of the Eastern Band of Cherokees. It is a full-size replica of an 18th century Cherokee town. The residents appear in native dress.

SPECIAL ATTRACTIONS:

Be sure to spend time at the Cherokee Botanical Garden and Nature Trail, where you can enjoy more than 150 species of plants native to the region. Pay particular attention to the seven-sided Council House, the Sweat House, and the Square-ground, which form the hub of ceremonial village life.

MAKING THE MOST OF YOUR VISIT:

First, you may be surprised to see that an entire Native American village is included in a section of this book about the best mountain homes. But why not? The homes in this village are not singled out as the private residences of particular Native Americans known because of their roles in history; instead, these homes symbolize some of the most famous people in the history of this state and this nation. Here you can see the dwellings of the Native Americans who are, without doubt, among the noblest and most admirable people this country ever produced.

The Cherokee people were well-established Americans before any European settler ever saw the land or, for that matter, did little more than dream of a New World. Cherokee history dates to 10,000 years ago. What better mountain homes could you visit?

When Hernando DeSoto and his followers explored the area of Western North Carolina, they met in 1540 a nation of 25,000 hard-working and peaceful people. When Europeans entered the area in search of gold, land, and trapping opportunities, the Cherokees welcomed the people and accepted them as neighbors. But it was the European's hunger for gold that caused the agreements with the Cherokees-the original owners of the land-to disintegrate.

As more and more Cherokee land was stripped away, Henry Clay, Davy Crockett, and Daniel Webster spoke emotionally and intelligently on behalf of the Cherokees. But such men as Andrew Jackson (who may have owed his life to Chief Junaluska during the War of 1812) decreed that the Cherokees must be relocated. It was Jackson as President who signed the Removal Treaty which led to the infamous Trail of Tears, a 1,200 mile journey to a new part of the nation for the Cherokees. During the trek, at least 4,000 of the Cherokees perished.

As you visit the village you can see Native Americans as they demonstrate their artistry in basket making, finger weaving, bead work, flint chipping, making dugouts, carving wooden spoons, creating combs and bowls, and pounding Indian corn into meal. The crafts are performed without benefit of metals, machines, or wheels.

You can experience primitive life in log cabins chinked with clay and roofed with bark or wood shingles. The village is a basic lifestyle of 250 years ago

As you visit the village, you may be mildly surprised to learn that the Cherokees lived in log cabins. Keep in mind that the log cabin was in Europe and America the home for so many people in so many countries of the world.

From an historic point of view, many Cherokees hid among the hills and were not removed to Oklahoma. These became the Eastern Band of Cherokees, while those who were removed became the Western Band. Today there about 11,000 members of the Eastern tribe. The communities within the Eastern Band are Yellowhill, Birdtown, Painttown, Snowbird, Big Cove, and Wolftown. These communities expand into five North Carolina counties, and the "Land of the Blue Mist" is an educational and spiritual place to visit and to honor a noble people.

Lake Lure.

SECTION 9: THE BEST MOUNTAIN LAKES AND STREAMS
TRIP 1: LAKE LURE
THE JEWEL AT THE END OF THE GORGE

LOCATION:

Lake Lure is one of the most beautiful lakes in the state, and you can reach it from I-40 by exiting from the interstate in Asheville onto US 74A and driving south through Bat Cave and Chimney Rock. Lake Lure is two miles past Chimney Rock. You can also exit I-40 in Marion and take US 221 south to Rutherfordton and from there take US 64 18 miles west to Lake Lure.

From I-85 you can exit the interstate in the Greenville-Spartanburg area and drive north on I-26 to Hendersonville and then follow US 64 east to Lake Lure. You can also take US 221 north of Spartanburg to Rutherfordton and follow US 64 to the lake.

NEARBY ATTRACTIONS:

While you are in Lake Lure you are within a very short drive to Chimney Rock, Hendersonville, and Brevard. You can also drive to Asheville and to the Blue Ridge Parkway. In Brevard and the surrounding countryside you can find gorgeous waterfalls as well as urban attractions.

HOURS OF OPERATION:

Most of the businesses in the town of Lake Lure are open from 9 a.m. until 5 to 6 p.m. In summer the hours are somewhat longer. In winter some of the attractions close or observe fewer hours of operation. The lake itself remains open year round every day of the year.

ADMISSION:

There is no charge for using the lake. The fees you will pay are for boat tours of the lake and for the meals you enjoy while you are in the area. The costs of a boat tour are $8.50 for adults and $5 for children ages 6-15. Seniors can take the tour for $8. If you want to buy a season ticket or pass you can take the tour as often as you like for $25 per person.

Dinner cruises are available for $14 for adults and $8 for children, plus the cost of the meal. The dinner cruises and twilight cruises or special charters require advance reservations. The dinner tours usually start at 6 p.m. or 7 p.m. Part of the cruise is eating at either Jimmy's Steak and Seafood or Lakeview Restaurant at the Fairfield Mountain Resort.

FACILITIES:

There are no facilities on board the boats, other than the flotation devices. Restrooms are available at the restaurants or, if you take the daytime cruise, in the town of Lake Lure. You can also picnic in the area but there are no picnic grounds as such. Neither are there campgrounds on the lake, but you can camp two miles west at Chimney Rock.

WHAT'S THE STORY?

Back in the 1920s the Rocky Broad River was dammed, and the lake was formed. National Geographic Magazine, according to one report, named Lake Lure as one of the top 10 man-made lakes in the world. And there is ample reason for the popularity of the body of water. There is the scenic lake made more picturesque by the mountains that surround it, the wide variety of song birds and accipiters that live on or near the water, the birds like ducks and geese that make the water their home, and the animal life in the forests around the lake.

SPECIAL ATTRACTIONS:

The best part of the trip is, for many people, the narrated tours the guides offer, and these narrations are filled with many human-interest stories and legends that grew along with the lake and its popularity.

MAKING THE MOST OF YOUR VISIT:

You can, of course, drive around much of the lake, and you are urged to do so, so that you can see the lake from as many perspectives as possible. When you arrive from Rutherfordton you first see the lake through the trees and only as a neck or cove apart from the major channel of the river. As you continue around the lake, you will see the main channel and the tall mountains in the background, and finally you see the Lake Lure Inn, made famous by such movies as *Dirty Dancing*.

You can also park the car and walk along the shoreline of some of the lake. There is a walking area that leads along the shore of part of the lake, and there is also a small beach for swimming and sunbathing.

But the boat tours are superb. First, you get to see the lake at its very best, with huge peaks rising from the range of smaller mountains and the setting sun reflecting in the water. You will hear facts and figures about the dimensions of the lake. The lake, incidentally, is 127 feet deep at its deepest point, and the story is that there are houses, a church or two, and a regular town under the water. Legend holds that some huge or even enormous fish live in the lake, in addition to the fish the anglers regularly pull from the clear waters.

One of the best stories is that when the dam was built and the waters began to rise, rattlesnakes and other reptiles took refuge on the higher rises of land that eventually were left as islands. One land owner offered a sizeable amount of money to anyone who would rid the island of the rattlers.

One enterprising farmer took the job and simply rowed some hogs to the island and released them. Within a few days the hogs, which hate reptiles and are deadly enemies of them, had killed all of the rattlers.

Another terrific story is that of Rumbling Bald Mountain, which continues to rumble like thunder, even today, decades after the earthquake that in legend-or fact-toppled the boulders into the river, which was called Broad River at the time but is now the Rocky Broad River. Locals say that when the rumbling, which sounds like thunder, is heard, the sound means that rocks and caves are constantly being re-shaped. There are many more stories. Don't miss out on them. It's a great trip!

Fontana Lake as seen from Great Smoky Mountains Railroad.

SECTION 9: THE BEST MOUNTAIN LAKES AND STREAMS
TRIP 2: FONTANA LAKE
THE BIGGEST DAM EAST OF BIG MUDDY

LOCATION:

Fontana Lake and Fontana Dam are located in the extreme western part of North Carolina, near Bryson City. To get to Fontana Lake and Dam from Interstate 40, leave I-40 at Clyde and follow US 19 past Bryson City to the intersection with NC 28. Follow this winding road to Fontana Dam and Lake.

NEARBY ATTRACTIONS:

You are close to Fontana Village, Bryson City, Robbinsville, the Cherohala Skyway, and the Great Smoky Mountains National Park. Keep in mind that in this territory being close means a drive of an hour or so, sometimes more.

HOURS OF OPERATION:

The village itself is always open, as is the lake, but the offices and shops in the area observe traditional business hours.

ADMISSION:

There is no fee for entering the visitors area at the dam, but if you wish to take the Incline Tram there is a fee of $2 per person. If you want to stay at the Fontana Inn rooms rent for $79 per night down to $49 per night, during the off-season.

Cottages rent for $139 in the off-season up to $189 for the peak season. Camp sites with hook-ups are $15 nightly, and tent camping spaces cost $8 per night.

Keep in mind that these prices were in effect several months prior to the publication of this book and may well have changed upward in the intervening months.

FACILITIES:

Here you can find restrooms, abundant parking, hiking trails (in fact, the Appalachian Trail crosses the dam), loads of tourist information, campgrounds not far away, and a wonderful introduction to Fontana Lake and Fontana Dam.

WHAT'S THE STORY?

No matter what the travel brochures tell you about this area, there are three terrific attractions: the lake, the dam, and the mountains. In the fall the peaks and valleys are one vast artist's easel of colors and designs, and in winter the stark beauty is, if possible, even greater. In late October the leaves are still magnificent, even in the higher elevations.

And if the colors fade, the mountains do not, and their eternal beauty will last until you get there. If you need a specific attraction, it would have to be the impressive Fontana Dam and the history of the engineering feat.

SPECIAL ATTRACTIONS:

The drive there is terrific, all the way from I-40 to the dam itself. The dam is one of the marvels of engineering you will find in the East, and the lake is always spectacular.

MAKING THE MOST OF YOUR VISIT:

At the dam itself you have two immediate options. You can drive across the bridge and take an immediate left out to a pair of overlooks. From these vantage points you can enjoy a superior view of the lake above the dam and the dam itself. This is a special spot to watch the Incline Tram that transports visitors from the welcome center above to the powerhouse below. And back, of course.

If you wish to stop at the visitors center first, you can find persons on duty who can tell you about the history of the dam and area. You will learn, if you ask the right people, that at 480 feet the Fontana Dam is the highest concrete dam east of the Rocky Mountains. The dam is 2,365 feet long and has three generating units with a total capacity of 225,000 kilowatts.

Construction started on the dam on New Years Day 1942 and the first electricity was generated on January 20, 1945. Total cost of the project was $74.7 million.

The lake has a shoreline of 240 miles and the reservoir with its 11,685 acres has a drainage area of 1,571 square miles. The construction of the dam provided 6,340 jobs and the project required 34.5 million man hours.

One interesting aspect of the dam is that it required 2.8 million cubic yards of concrete to complete.

One of the major purposes behind the construction of the dam was flood control. The area receives 75 to 80 inches of rain each year, and in the past the Little Tennessee River flooded to such an extent that nearby towns (and even far-away towns) were in danger. Cities as far away as Chattanooga were flooded.

Before the dam could be built there had to be a railroad constructed into the area, and near the construction site a village for the workers and their families was constructed. The workers toiled in three shifts 24 hours a day and the hills were brilliantly lighted by spotlights all night long. Because of the importance of the dam and its hydroelectric power, workers were urged to work faster and faster in order to complete the massive project in record time.

Visitors to the area can find dozens of good places to eat and a wide range of outdoor activities ranging from hiking and fishing to shopping and touring the mountains. What had once been first a tent city (in 1890) and later a construction village is now a tourist resort, and fishermen can try their luck at landing rainbow, brook, and brown trout, large and small-mouth bass, walleye, pike, perch, sunfish, and crappie.

Nearby are interpretive trails, swimming in warmer months, picnic facilities, hot showers for hikers who have dubbed the visitors center and its comfort station the Fontana Hilton, tennis, and other outdoor activities.

The tram from the top of the dam to the bottom runs from May 3 until November 2 and from 10 a.m. until 6:30 p.m. It has a capacity of 40 passengers and takes three minutes to travel the 666 feet from top to bottom.

There is also a pioneer cabin and museum at Fontana Village and here you can catch a glimpse of the past that makes the present even more remarkable and enjoyable.

Catawba River near Morganton.

SECTION 9: THE BEST MOUNTAIN LAKES AND STREAMS
TRIP 3: THE CATAWBA RIVER
FROM A TRICKLE TO A TORRENT

LOCATION:

The Catawba River originates in the mountains slightly to the south-west of Old Fort, near Asheville. Before it completes its run to the sea, the Catawba flows through several mountain counties, into the foot-hills, and finally to the ocean. The part of the river visited in this chapter flows through mountains only, and you can reach it by driving I-40 east of Asheville to the exit for Old Fort. But if you wish to trace the river as it flows through North and South Carolina, you can do so easily, just as you can follow it through a series of dams that form lakes along the course of the river. These lakes include Lake Hickory and Lake Norman, the latter the largest man-made body of water in North Carolina.

NEARBY ATTRACTIONS:

In Old Fort you can find the Mountain Gateway Museum and a series of other attractions. You are also near Asheville, the Blue Ridge Parkway, Mount Mitchell, and Lake James. You are also within reason-able driving distance of Linville Falls, Chimney Rock, Lake Lure, and Little Switzerland.

HOURS OF OPERATION:

The river can be fished or canoed at virtually all times, except during flood stages, but if you want to hike to the two waterfalls near the origin of the river, it is best to do so in midday hours, out of courtesy to the people who live nearby and who own the land where you will be walk-ing part of the way.

ADMISSION:

There are no fees of any sort.

FACILITIES:

There are, as a rule, no facilities along the river in its early stages; however, as you follow the river as it grows larger and larger, you will find nearly any kind of facility you wish to take advantage of. There are restrooms, campgrounds, picnic tables, gift shops, and river-run outfit-ters along the river.

WHAT'S THE STORY?

The Catawba River is at the same time an inconsequential stream and a mighty waterway, depending upon the area in which you explore it. While not nearly as large as the Mississippi, the river reaches far into the mountains, just as Big Muddy flows through Minnesota, to the surprise of some people, on its way to becoming the Father of Waters.

SPECIAL ATTRACTIONS:

The best attractions are the two waterfalls along the small stream that eventually becomes the Catawba River that most people in Western North Carolina know. Some of the dams and lakes in the lower reaches of the Carolinas are awesome, too, and offer much in the way of fishing and water recreation, if you care to follow the river that far.

MAKING THE MOST OF YOUR VISIT:

Getting to the place where it starts is part of the joy of exploring the Catawba River. You get a sampling of the influence of the river when you realize that in Old Fort you take Exit 73 off I-40 and enter town limits on Catawba Avenue.

You are then in a place once known as Catawba Vale, which soon was changed to Old Fort. Catawba Vale stood near the headwaters of the Catawba River, and near the town visitors can park their cars and hike up a two-mile trail to two beautiful waterfalls on the tiny Catawba River.

To get to Catawba Falls, drive back out to I-40 but do not take the access lane. Instead, drive under the Interstate, and as you emerge you will see a road immediately to your right. Only a few yards up the road a side road known as Catawba River Road veers off the highway. Follow this road to its terminus.

In order to see the falls, you must park on the left side of the road, pass across a bridge and through a gateway, and then follow the trail that leads alongside the river, which at this point is narrow and very shallow in most places. The hike is at times strenuous, but the waterfalls are worth the trek.

You may recall the story of early explorers who sailed up the Mississippi until they reached the point beyond which none of the vessels could maneuver. The explorers walked the rest of the way until one man stood, one foot on either side of the tiny rill that was the origin of the river, and boasted that he was able to straddle the Mississippi River.

You can do the same with the Catawba River, or nearly so. The tern *Catawba* is from a Choctaw word meaning "divided" or "separated." The word, while it applies to the river, was first intended to describe the Native Americans who lived along the banks of the river. The "Katawpa" or Catawba Indians considered the river channel their home.

Another part of the nature scene that is more familiar with many people is the Catawba grape, a variety of *Vitis labrusca*. This grape grew (and in many places still grows) in profusion, and because of the many wonderful characteristics of the grape, it was cultivated into the far northern parts of the United States. By 1807 it had reached Washington, D. C., and in later years reached the Finger Lakes area of New York, portions of Ohio, and even into Ontario, Canada. The grapes are still used for making a champagne base and a variety of sweet wines.

As you follow the Catawba River southward and eastward, it grows rapidly into a modest-sized stream suitable for river-riding in canoes, tubes, and kayaks. As the river flows through the Old Fort area, it is still small enough that it is almost impossible to see as you cross the bridges along the river. But by the time the Catawba reaches Morganton, it has become a true river and can accommodate larger types of crafts.

Though lacking in white-water rapids like those of some of the other mountain rivers, the Catawba has much to recommend it, including beauty, tranquility, and many fish ranging from panfish to huge bass as the river flows serenely into the foothills.

Lake James near Marion.

SECTION 9: THE BEST MOUNTAIN LAKES AND STREAMS
TRIP 4: LAKE JAMES
THE END OF LINVILLE GORGE

LOCATION:

Lake James lies slightly north of and between Morganton and Shelby, with the westernmost tip of the lake reaching to the little town of Nebo. To reach Lake James State Park, the most public area on the body of water, leave I-40 at Exit 90 and drive north until you cross US 70. Here you will see signs directing you to the park. You can reach other points of the lake by taking NC 126.

NEARBY ATTRACTIONS:

Centrally located among some of the most beautiful terrain in North Carolina's magnificent mountains, Lake James is near Table Rock, Linville Gorge, Linville Falls, Little Switzerland, Spruce Pine, and Mount Mitchell. You are also within an easy drive of Asheville.

HOURS OF OPERATION:

The lake is open at all times and you can launch a boat and fish all night, if you wish. If you want to spend your time at the state park, the hours are as follows: from November through February, 8 a.m. until 6 p.m.; during March and October, from 8 a.m. until 7 p.m.; during April, May, and September, from 8 a.m. until 8 p.m.; in June through August, from 8 a.m. until 9 p.m.

ADMISSION:

There are no fees for visiting Lake James State Park, but if you wish to camp, there is a fee. You can call (828) 652-5047 for updated information, but at this writing the costs for camping were $12 per campsite. The campground is open from March through November, and the swimming area, which is roped off, is open all year, if you can take the frigid waters, which actually are delightful on a warm summer day.

FACILITIES:

There are abundant parking spaces, restrooms, picnic tables and grounds, a concession stand, hiking trails, wash house, and public telephones. Restrooms are handicap accessible.

WHAT'S THE STORY?

Lake James lies 1,200 feet above sea level, and the lake surface covers 6,510 acres. The lake was formed between 1916 and 1923 by the impoundment of the Catawba River, the Linville River, and Paddy Creek. Lake James State Park was established in 1987 when the State of North Carolina used a purchase of 565 acres of land along the lakeshore for public recreation. Today the lake and the park are among the favorite recreation sites for the state's outdoor enthusiasts.

SPECIAL ATTRACTIONS:

In addition to the beauty of the lake and the mountains on nearly all sides of the water, there are two superb hiking trails for those who want to stretch their legs, see the forests, catch a glimpse of wild life, and enjoy an unparalleled view of Table Rock and other peaks across the lake. The trails are short and easy enough for nearly anyone in reasonably good health to make the trips without difficulty.

MAKING THE MOST OF YOUR VISIT:

By all means, bring along a picnic lunch or evening meal. Even in the cooler months, the lake is pleasant and temperatures are bracing in spring and autumn and seldom frigid in all but the coldest days of winter. There are 20 picnic tables, complete with grills, garbage receptacles, and exceptional views of the lake and mountains. There is no fee for the use of these facilities. If you need drinking water, there are faucets and fountains nearby.

If the weather is bad, there is a picnic shelter with 12 tables for public use. The shelter is free, unless the shelter has been previously reserved.

If camping is your interest, there are no auto-accessible campsites; however, this is a definite plus, not negative in any sense. There are 20 backpack campsites a short walk from the parking lot. The nearest campsites are about 150 yards off the pavement, and the most distant sites are only 300 yards away.

This is, as stated above, a plus, because if you are able and willing to carry your gear a short distance, you are assured of privacy and peace and quiet. Your rest will not be disturbed by motorists driving too close to you. Each campsite has a picnic table, fireplace, grill, and tent space. There is no water at the campsites, but you can get it from faucets scattered about the camping area. You are never more than a few feet from fresh and safe water. Campsites are available on a first-come, first-served basis.

The two hiking trails are the Sandy Cliff Overlook and the Lake Channel Overlook. The first trail is half a mile long, and the other is three-fourths of a mile. At the end of the trails there are overlooks that afford you wonderful views of the lake and forests. You can see Linville Gorge as it opens onto the lake, and along the way you might see nesting Canadian geese that have made the park their home for years.

Animal life in the park includes rabbits, squirrels, flying squirrels (becoming increasingly difficult to find in most rural areas), red and gray foxes, muskrats, minks, herons, kingfishers, pileated woodpeckers (sometimes known as raincrows), mallards, geese, hawks, owls, turtles, lizards, and an occasional snake.

Park rangers offer guided tours of the woodland, and there are interpretive programs for those interested in learning more about their state or area.

Fishing has for years remained popular at Lake James. In the lake you might hook largemouth bass, walleyes, perch, catfish, muskellunge, crappie, white bass, bluegill, and other fresh-water delicacies. If you have never eaten freshly caught and cooked bream or crappie, you have missed a culinary delight. And if you have never caught bream and crappie on a fly rod, you have missed a great experience. You must have a valid fishing license, so check with rangers before starting to fish.

New River near Jefferson.

SECTION 9: THE BEST MOUNTAIN LAKES AND STREAMS
TRIP 5: THE NEW RIVER
THE GREAT SPIRIT'S FIRST RIVER

LOCATION:

The New River is in the northwest corner of North Carolina and is most easily reached from Interstate 40 by taking the exit to NC 16 near Claremont and Hickory. You can also drive from the Blue Ridge Parkway by exiting at US 421 and then to US 221, or you can leave the Parkway at NC 16 exit.

NEARBY ATTRACTIONS:

Close to the New River are Mount Jefferson, New River State Park, Boone and Blowing Rock, Doughton Park, Stone Mountain, the Church of the Frescoes at Glendale Springs, and the Cascades. You can drive to any of these attractions in an hour or so.

HOURS OF OPERATION:

While the New River is obviously open all the time, some of the attractions nearby are not. Call or check other sections of this book for details. Some of the New River area outfitters are also closed except during business hours; others are closed on a seasonal basis.

ADMISSION:

There are no fees for using the New River, but you must pay a fee to camp at New River State Park or to rent canoes or other water-craft at any of the outfitters.

FACILITIES:

Along the New River you can find picnic areas, campgrounds, restrooms, parking areas, and outfitters who will rent to you the vessels you need for a canoe trip down the New River.

WHAT'S THE STORY?

Stated simply, the New River is the oldest river in the United States or in North or South America. As difficult as it is to believe, the New River is older than the Mississippi, Amazon, Ohio, Ganges, or any of the other major rivers of the world-with one exception. The New River is the second oldest river in the world, with only the Nile being older. And, if you want to take the information plaques and boards in the area seriously, as so many geologists do, the Nile and the New River once flowed nearly side by side, and both in a northward direction.

MAKING THE MOST OF YOUR VISIT:

On July 30, 1998, when President Bill Clinton designated the New River as an American Heritage River, the President told the crowd attending the ceremonies at West Jefferson that "this ancient river has flowed through this land for hundreds of millions of years longer than blood has flowed through any human heart."

The President added, "The Cherokees say that this is the very first river created by the Great Spirit's hand. Who are we-such brief visitors on Earth-to disturb it? But when we cherish it and save it and we can hand it on to our children, we have done what we are charged to do."

At the ceremony, the President signed the official document on a tabletop made of Balm of Gilead, a local growth called by some "gilly bud." A local resident named Tom Sternal made the table from a 40-foot log that came from a tree that a beaver gnawed and dropped into the New River.

"This feels so fitting," Sternal said. He added that a beaver had dropped the tree into the river and it got stuck against a bridge. Sternal pulled it out, chainsawed it, and carved the pieces for a table where the President signed the official documents.

"It has come full circle," Sternal said.

The American Heritage River program includes money to be used to protect the river from commercial exploitation. Money will also be appropriated for bringing a "river navigator" into the area for the purpose of helping river communities to become involved in federal resources to protect the river.

The 250-mile long river flows through the mountains of North Carolina, into Virginia and West Virginia, and empties into the Ohio River. Daniel Boone once trapped on the river, and the father of Thomas Jefferson surveyed the area.

At the New River State Park you can canoe more than 25 miles of the New River, which was earlier designated a National Wild and Scenic River. There are actually three parks along the river, each one a day's canoe ride away from the others. You can enjoy primitive riverside camping after you have spent a day on the river that is generally clean, shallow, and relatively smooth. Farther north there are rougher rapids and genuine whitewater challenges, but in the North Carolina mountains the trip is a smooth one.

While there are exceptions to this (and you should by all means exert caution anytime you are on water, and this is even more crucial for the young ones on the trip) if your canoe should capsize, you could walk to shore. To repeat: this is not always the case, so don't be lulled into a false sense of security.

As you canoe the river, you can pull the canoe out along the way and enjoy a picnic on the banks. The river flows through some of the most tranquil mountain valleys in the state, and you can have a trip of almost uninterrupted beauty.

If you want to rent a canoe, you can call one of three major rental agencies: New River Outfitters (800-982-9190), Wahoo's Adventures (800-444-7238), or Zaloo's Canoes (800-535-4027).

And, since the end of July, 1998, the trip you make will be on a National Heritage River. Because of the designation, the water will be a little cleaner, the scenery a little more beautiful, and the Great Spirit will undoubtedly be a great deal happier.

Price Lake on Parkway.

SECTION 9: THE BEST MOUNTAIN LAKES AND STREAMS
TRIP 6: PRICE LAKE AT JULIAN PRICE MEMORIAL PARK
A NEARLY PERFECT LAKE, HIKE, AND WALK

LOCATION:

Price Lake is without doubt one of the most beautiful lakes in the state, and, being located on what this author considers to be the most wonderful scenic drive in the South, the combination is a perfect place to visit. The lake is found at Parkway Milepost 297.1. From Interstate 40 there are several ways to reach the lake, and almost any of the major highways leading north off the Parkway between Hickory and Asheville will get you into the vicinity. You can take the Parkway from Asheville, US 221 from Marion, US 226 from Marion, NC 181 from Morganton, and US 321 from Hickory. For the most direct access, in order for you to stay on the interstate as long as possible, take US 321 north. Then when you reach the Parkway, drive south for 10 minutes.

NEARBY ATTRACTIONS:

From Price Lake it is an easy drive to the attractions in or near Boone, Blowing Rock, Little Switzerland, Linville Falls, Grandfather Mountain, Morganton, Spruce Pine, and Asheville.

HOURS OF OPERATION:

The lake itself has no gates and is therefore open all day every day, but the campground and nearby picnic grounds observe seasonal hours. The campground is usually open virtually all year, except when snow or ice forces the closing of the Blue Ridge Parkway. Picnic grounds are usually open from early morning until sunset. Call (828) 298-0398 for camping information.

ADMISSION:

There is no fee to use the picnic tables or lake, but there is a $10 per day per site fee for camping.

FACILITIES:

In addition to picnic grounds and campgrounds, there are restrooms, hiking trails, cold shower area, drinking water, and abundant parking. There are also campfire or amphitheater night programs in season at the campground.

WHAT'S THE STORY?

Julian Price Memorial Park consists of more than 4,000 acres of superb forests, rolling hills, clear and beautiful creeks, a great lake, space for 129 tent sites, 68 RV-trailer sites, and large numbers of deer, beaver, foxes, owls, hawks, and numerous other mammals and birds, as well as the occasional reptile.

The park area was originally purchased by Jefferson Standard Life Insurance Company, but when Julian Price died in 1946 the land was donated to the National Park Service. The territory was the hunting and trapping grounds, much earlier, for frontiersman and explorer Daniel Boone.

Today the property is available for public enjoyment, and thousands of people, from in-state and out, come regularly to the lake to fish, picnic, camp, or just enjoy nature.

SPECIAL ATTRACTIONS:

The lake is picturesque, the picnic area is unsurpassed, and the gentle walk around the lake is both exciting and calming at the same time. For a longer walk, the Boone Fork Trail is one of the finest trails you will find in North Carolina. Not only do you get to enjoy the forest and the streams, but you also get an up-close look at some majestic waterfalls that most people, even those who come to the park regularly, never see.

MAKING THE MOST OF YOUR VISIT:

The Boone Fork Trail is 4.9 miles long and takes 3 hours to hike at a comfortable pace. The trail is easy most of the way and moderately difficult in a few places. It leads from the campground at Price Lake through forests, meadows, along a series of beautiful streams, and returns in a loop to the starting point.

The best place to start is at the amphitheater parking lot on the southern end of Price Lake. To get to the parking area, drive along the Blue Ridge Parkway to Milepost 297.1. From the south, you will see the campground on your left and the parking lot for the amphitheater across the road from the campground. Turn right on the first paved road into the Price Lake area. If you arrive from the north, pass a picnic area on your right at Milepost 296.6. Cross a bridge over the Price Lake spillway and pass the parking area on the left. In .5 mile you will see a campground office on the right and another paved entrance on the left. The road to the left leads into the campground and will take you to the parking area, but you have a more direct entrance if you will drive to the next paved road to your left.

At the lakefront there is a large information board that shows the lake shoreline as well as three hiking trails: Price Lake Loop Trail, the Green Knob Loop Trail, and Boone Fork Loop Trail that starts at the information board.

Start the hike by walking along the paved parking area until you see a paved walk that leads through a small laurel and rhododendron thicket into the forest along the lake. Inside the forest you will see the amphitheater ahead of you. The trail leads along the back of the amphitheater and toward the Parkway. You will see trail markers depicting the Boone Fork and Tanawha Trails, the latter also a great trail.

Cross the Parkway and enter the southern edge of the campground on the opposite side of the Parkway. A narrow trail leads through a tangle of ground cover and to the edge of a hardwood forest and then bends sharply to the left as you enter a heavy growth of pines. The trail descends a gentle slope toward an open meadow.

You will be hiking a portion of the Tanawha Trail, along with the Boone Fork Trail, for about .8 mile before the Tanawha Trail continues to the left and the Boone Fork Trail veers to the right. At this point you will merge with the Mountains-To-Sea Trail and the two trails overlap for much of the way.

When you leave the pine growth the trail opens into a wide and beautiful area of meadow and green rolling hills. The hike is easy along this stretch and remains so until you cross two hills and descend sharply into a forest. You will arrive at a stile that permits hikers free access in and out of the pasture land but keeps cattle from leaving the pasture.

From this point the trail becomes rougher and steeper, but it is easy if you walk at a comfortable pace. Soon you arrive at a trickle of a stream that becomes Bee Tree Creek, which grows larger and larger as it is joined by springs and run-off from the mountainside.

As the creek grows in size and volume, you will need to cross the stream either by wading (the stream is not deep along these crossings), by rock-hopping, or by walking a foot log. The trail continues through dense and moist woodland, with laurel and rhododendron on both sides of the trail. You will also see hemlock, spruce, and fir mixed in with the poplars, hickories, and birch.

If you are hiking in the colder months, the branches of the laurel and rhododendron are often coated with ice from the spray from the stream. At 2.4 miles you will hear a loud roar to your left. Bee Tree Creek has left the trail temporarily and, out of your vision, there is a large cascade. Almost immediately you will reach the Boone Fork Creek which is more deserving of the title of river at this point.

The trail climbs along up the slope and you get a great view of one of the many waterfalls along the creek. The waterfalls are among the most spectacular sights along the trail. At times huge cascades roar across rocks and crash into the pools below, or the swift current of the stream strikes the huge boulders and sends spray flying into the air.

At 3.5 miles you will arrive at a series of huge flat rocks spaced two feet or so apart across the width of the Boone Fork Creek. The Mountains-to-Sea Trail leaves the Boone Fork Trail at this point and crosses the stream via the stepping stones. The Boone Fork Trail continues up the side of the stream and leads to an open meadow that was for centuries a favorite gathering place for Indians who lived in the mountains.

At the end of the meadow you will see a bridge that crosses the stream and leads into a picnic area. Do not cross the bridge; follow the trail to the right and enter the forest again. The trail from this point leads into the north side of the campground from which you started.

Plan to visit the picnic area, which is dissected by two streams where you can see medium-sized trout swimming casually despite the numbers of people around. The picnic grounds are very crowded on summer weekends, particularly on Sunday. In early spring and late fall the place is virtually deserted.

Don't neglect the walk around the lake. You will follow a trail that in turn follows the shoreline of the lake, and you can see huge fish near the bridges and an array of trees and flowers that is rewarding, especially in spring and early summer. You can spend hours on this one-mile walk and never run out of pleasant scenes to enjoy. And you can spend days at Price Lake. There are many visitors who spend a week at a time here, and they continue to find relaxation and rewarding beauty at the lake.

Bradley Fork in Great Smokies.

SECTION 9: THE BEST MOUNTAIN LAKES AND STREAMS
TRIP 7: BRADLEY FORK CREEK
THE FOREST REBORN

LOCATION:

Bradley Fork Creek is located in and around the Smokemont section of the Great Smoky Mountains National Park. In order to drive to Smokemont from Interstate 40, drive to a point 10 miles west of Asheville and take the exit connecting you with US 19 south to Cherokee, where you will junction with US 441, the only highway leading through the Great Smoky Mountains National Park. You will arrive at Smokemont within 15 minutes or so after you enter the park.

NEARBY ATTRACTIONS:

While in the national park, you are close enough to several attractions to make the drive to them worthwhile. Attractions in the area include Cherokee, Oconaluftee Indian Village, Qualla, the Cyclorama, Bryson City, Maggie Valley, and Cades Cove, a great drive away, still on US 441.

HOURS OF OPERATION:

The Smokemont campground is open from May 15 through October 31. You can visit Bradley Fork Creek any time of the day or night or throughout the year, as long as roads are not closed by ice and snow. However, the hours between 7 a.m. and 6 p.m. are super for a visit to this delightful creek.

ADMISSION:

There is no admission fee.

FACILITIES:

At Smokemont there are campsites, tables at the sites, fireplaces or fire circles, restrooms, and parking areas. You will find here essentially what you can expect to find in any federal campground. There are 142 campsites at Smokemont, and the fee per night (per site) is $15. For information call (423) 436-1200.

WHAT'S THE STORY?

There are many hiking trails in the area, some of them long and rather difficult, others short and easy. And one trail in particular continues alongside Bradley Fork Creek for long and delightful stretches at a time. One of these trails is six miles long, but it is easy enough that you can hike it without severe difficulty. And, if you tire, you can always turn around and go back. Or you can just sit and enjoy the creek, which in autumn is especially beautiful.

The Smokemont campground is one of the most popular in the Great Smokies National Park. The area is quiet, serene, and bounded on three sides by tall peaks. In the spring and early summer, the rhododendron and laurel and other flowering plants are in bloom, and the creekside is a place of pure tranquility.

Bradley Fork Creek flows through the Smokemont campground, and other creeks feed into the Bradley Fork in the forests outside the campground. The Oconaluftee River flows in front of the campground, which is on US 441, three miles from Cherokee Indian Reservation.

SPECIAL ATTRACTIONS:

One of the most interesting points is the 1921 bridge that spans the creek at the end of the Smokemont Loop Trail. The bridge was built during the time lumber operations were in full swing in the Smokies. Up the creek you will reach cascades that are attractive and impressive, although they are not extremely large and powerful.

MAKING THE MOST OF YOUR VISIT:

Bradley Fork Creek, Chasteen Creek, and the Oconaluftee River are all within a short walk. These are not whitewater streams with roaring torrents and majestic waterfalls, such as those you visited on the

Horsepasture River outing. Nor can they compare with the Nantahala River or the Whitewater River.

But while Nature is sometimes at her most beautiful and awesome when she produces cataracts and mist-shrouded waterfalls, she is also immensely beautiful in her quiet moments, too. This trip is in a large sense for the people who, for various reasons, are not able or inclined to trek through the forests to the huge and gorgeous chasms and raging rivers.

This is a quiet, peaceful, even tranquil trip--unless you happen to encounter a bear (and there are large numbers of them in the forests nearby, but they are shy creatures who prefer not to visit with people as a rule).

To hike the Smokemont Loop Trail drive to the extreme northeast end of the campground, past D Loop, and enter a maintenance road blocked to vehicle traffic. There are parking spaces near the road. Other parking spaces are labeled as parking for scenic trails. Do not park in spaces numbered for campsites.

As you start up the maintenance road, at no time is the climb steep or difficult. The maintenance road leads into the forest and continues to the junction with the Chasteen Creek Trail.

As you hike the Smokemont Loop, you will parallel nearly at all times with Bradley Fork Creek, which is clear, broad, rocky, and impressively scenic at all times. It varies from a smooth flow to deep pools and wider boulder-strewn expanses.

The trail along the Bradley Fork is bounded by a series of ridges on the right. These wooded mountains are the homes of deer and bears, and it is advisable to stay on or near the trail at all times.

Continue and you will junction with the Smokemont Loop. The area you now enter is part of what was once a huge lumbering process. Around 1918 the Champion Fibre Company purchased a series of smaller wood-cutting operations which were combined into one giant logging operation that made Smokemont the central location for the corporation's entire logging work.

In the area were constructed a boarding house, or hotel, and the commissary or company store. Today, however, nearly all the evidence of the lumbering operation has disappeared. But effects of the operation will remain in the Smokemont area for decades. The Smokemont Loop Trail wends around the lower slopes of Richland Mountain as the trail leaves the Chasteen Creek Trail. The final three miles of the trail lead down from the slopes of Richland Mountain and back toward Bradley Fork. The trail ends at the bridge over the Bradley Fork. From the bridge you can hike up the campground exit loop road to the parking space in the B loop. You will see huge stands of yellow poplar, which was often used for log cabins for the mountain folk. These are often the first trees that invade cut or burned-over areas.

The poplars along the trail are about 50 years old, which means that the trees sprouted about 1940 to 1943, around the time that President Franklin D. Roosevelt dedicated the Great Smoky Mountains National Park.

The terrain around Bradley Fork and other streams in the area hosts relatively new forest growth. Here the railroad system penetrated the forest for miles upstream in order to haul the logs from the forest to the mills.

Between 1918 and 1925 more than 115 million board feet of lumber was cut and shipped from the area. The new forest growth is a tribute to the wisdom and foresight of government and park leaders who wanted to see the forest re-born, not desecrated. If you camp in the Smokemont Campground you will be warned by park rangers that you *must* extinguish campfires at night (or any other time). Even though the Smokies receive lots of rain, there are also long dry spells, which help to create severe fire hazards. Imagine the Bradley Fork, Chasteen, and Oconaluftee sans trees and you will be even more grateful for the forest beauty.

Chain of Lakes near Robbinsville.

SECTION 9: THE BEST MOUNTAIN LAKES AND STREAMS
TRIP 8: HIWASSEE, CHATUGE, SANTEELAH, AND APPALACHIA LAKES
FOUR LINKS IN A SUPERB CHAIN

LOCATION:

All of these beautiful lakes are located in the Nantahala National Forest, and all are within a short distance of each other. Hiwassee and Appalachia are especially close, and you can drive to all of the lakes easily from points in the western part of the state. To get to Lake Hiwassee from I-40, at ten miles west of Asheville exit onto US 19 and keep on this highway all the way to Murphy. The southern tip of Lake Hiwassee is just outside Murphy.

To reach the northern part of Lake Chatuge, drive to Murphy as before and then just outside Murphy's main part of town you can junction with US 64 east. Lake Chatuge is about halfway between Murphy and Franklin.

Appalachia Lake is northwest of Lake Hiwassee and is the smallest of the four. This lake and Lake Hiwassee are so close that you are within a stone's throw of one when you are at the extreme reaches of another. Outside Murphy on US 19, watch for NC 294 leading off to the right. You will pass through Suit as you approach Oak Park and Hiwassee.

To get to Santeelah Lake, follow US 19 as before, but when you reach US 129 near the Nantahala Gorge, turn right and drive north to Robbinsville and on to Lake Santeelah.

NEARBY ATTRACTIONS:

You are amid some of the finest lake and river territory in North Carolina. This state is blessed with clear and usually clean rivers, lakes, and all the recreational activities we tend to associate with water. Fishing is good in all of the lakes, and nearby there are the cities of Murphy, Hayesville, and, if you don't mind a little longer drive, Franklin, where the wonderful Scottish Tartans museum is located. In Robbinsville you can visit the grave of the Great Chief Junaluska. The Great Smoky Mountains National Park is not far away.

HOURS OF OPERATION:

The lakes are, of course, open to the public all the time, year-round unless weather is prohibitive, but the restaurants, rental businesses, and sports shops observe their own hours. You can call Yellow Page listings for details.

ADMISSION:

There are no admission charges for using the lakes, but there are fees for using campgrounds. Typical costs per night for a camp site in the Nantahala National Forest are $5 to $15.

FACILITIES:

Depending upon where you visit, the facilities will vary. You can find boating opportunities, restrooms, canoeing and fishing opportunities, hiking trails, picnicking, drinking water, sanitary facilities, water skiing, swimming, trailer dump stations, trailer spaces, and sight-seeing and nature study opportunities. Some of the campgrounds are open year-round, while others operate seasonally.

WHAT'S THE STORY?

These lakes are meccas for hunting, fishing, sightseeing, camping, hiking, boating, and nearly all other forms of outdoor recreation. The mountains and the lakes in the valleys produce an unbeatable combination of scenic wonders.

SPECIAL ATTRACTIONS:

At Chatuge Lake you can visit Chatuge State Park if you want to drive south across the state line into Georgia, and in North Carolina you can visit Jackrabbit Mountain. At Santeelah Lake one point of interest is

Cheoah Point. Hanging Dog and Hiwassee Village are some places to visit at Lake Hiwassee, and at nearby Appalachian Lake you can visit the small town of Hiwassee.

MAKING THE MOST OF YOUR VISIT:

On your way to the lakes, you might want to stop and pay a visit to Standing Indian or Standing Indian Basin, which is off US 64 between Franklin and Hayesville. You can combine this trip with a visit to the world-famous Appalachian Trail. The Standing Indian Basin has some of the finest trout streams in the nation, and you can hike to waterfalls or visit the Wasilik Poplar, the second-largest yellow poplar tree ever discovered in the United States. This tree, with its 8-foot diameter (folks, that is the *diameter* of the tree, not its circumference, and seeing is, unless you are watching David Copperfield, believing!), is one of the marvels of nature.

Another marvel of nature is the Standing Indian "himself." This, according to legend, is what's left of the Indian brave who refused to meet the responsibilities and duties of his tribe. If you are reminded of a story in the Bible, that's understandable. The fee for camping here is $10 per day per site. Call (828) 524-6441 for details. There are 84 campsites in the campground and you can also find drinking water, picnic tables, sanitary facilities, fishing, and hiking trails. You must call ahead for reservations. Look for Rainbow Springs on Forest Road 67.

Adjacent to Standing Indian is the Coweeta Experimental Forest, established in 1934, where you can learn about such topics as silviculture, hydrology, and other work at the Forest. You can find the office on US 441 south of Franklin.

On Hiwassee Lake you can visit Hanging Dog, where there is a large campground-with 67 campsites at $5 per site per day. Call (828) 837-5152. You can also take advantage of hiking trails, drinking water, fishing, and hiking trails.

Jackrabbit Mountain (828) 837-5152 has 100 campsites at $12 per day per site, a swimming beach with showers, hiking trails, picnic areas, and launching ramp for boats. Fishing is also one of the popular sports here.

The Cheoah Ranger Station is the place to get brochures and information as well as the chance to enjoy picnicking, hiking, jogging trails, and educational trails devoted to the management of forests. Hours for the Ranger Station are 8 a.m. until 4:30 p.m. Monday through Friday. And this is just the beginning!

Snowbird area near Robbinsville.

SECTION 9: THE BEST MOUNTAIN LAKES AND STREAMS
TRIP 9: SNOWBIRD CREEK
THE LAND OF TSALI

LOCATION:

Snowbird Creek is located in the northwest corner of North Carolina in the Snowbird area of the Nantahala National Forest. To reach the Snowbird Creek part of the forest, drive from Asheville and I-40 to the Clyde exit and head southwest on US 19 or US 23/74 to Bryson City. Follow US 19 south of Bryson City toward Murphy. Watch for US 129 which leads off to the right of US 19 and takes you into Robbinsville. On US 129 you will junction with Kilmer Road (State Road 1127). Drive a little more than three miles along SR 1127/1116 and turn left onto SR 1115 (Little Snowbird Road) and from there to Hard Slate Road (SR 1121). In one mile you will cross the bridge over Little Snowbird Creek. Turn right onto Big Snowbird Road (SR 1120), which in turn becomes Forest Road 75. Six miles later you are at the parking area.

NEARBY ATTRACTIONS:

Other than the beauties of the forest and streams, there are no other attractions within the immediate area. However, you can drive back to Robbinsville and from there to Murphy, or to the Cherohala Skyway, or to any of several other nearby sites where you can enjoy museums or outdoor recreation.

HOURS OF OPERATION:

There are no hours posted. The area is open night and day, every day of the year except when closed by heavy snows or ice.

ADMISSION:

There are no admission fees of any sort.

FACILITIES:

You are now in a primitive part of the state when you enter these woods, and there are no facilities of any sort. You are on your own, and you must be completely self-sufficient while you are in the forest. There are no shelters, camping areas, fresh water (and do not drink water from the springs or streams, no matter how clean and pure it looks: there are microorganisms in the water that can cause severe problems) or trail networks. The trails are blazed, but you are responsible for your welfare while you are in the forest. There are, you must remember, bears and other dangerous animals, including rattlesnakes.

WHAT'S THE STORY?

Snowbird Creek flows through the area where the Unicoi and Snowbird Mountains meet. This is the one-time home of such men as Chief Junaluska and Tsali. The latter Cherokee killed a man who had attacked a family member, and as a result he was a man hunted by the law. A group of Cherokees had hidden out in the Snowbird area, and the law enforcement agencies set out to flush out these Cherokees and send them, along with other Cherokees, along the Trail of Tears to Oklahoma. Tsali agreed to surrender, if the agencies would spare the others in his group. He was executed, but the pocket of Cherokees remained in the Snowbird region.

The story on record is that Tsali was an old man with grown sons when the soldiers came. Tsali, his sons Alonzo, Jake, and George, as well as their wives, had already agreed that they would stay on their land. The soldiers chose to take the men and women to a stockade several miles away, and en route they had to camp in the forest.

The women had feigned illnesses and said they could not walk, so they were given horses to ride. When the procession entered a dense thicket, the women threw weapons they had hidden inside their clothing to Tsali and the men, who fought off the soldiers while the women fled down the trail. Three soldiers died in the battle, and later another group of soldiers came to find the Indians and bring them to what they considered justice.

A traitorous friend betrayed Tsali's sons, and they were captured and then shot near the Little Tennessee River. A friend of Tsali promised the old man that if he surrendered, the Indians found not guilty of the earlier crimes would be permitted to stay on their lands. He agreed, surrendered, and was quickly tried, found guilty, and shot.

The only positive part of the story is that Tsali's people were allowed to remain in the North Carolina mountains. The noble Native American died as bravely as he had lived, and his death exemplified the idea of "greater love hath no man, than to lay down his life for his friends."

SPECIAL ATTRACTIONS:

You are entering some of the most primitive, beautiful, and interesting parts of North Carolina and the United States. The land is wild and savage, and you will follow, part of the way, at least, a creek that is more than a bold rill; at times it looks more like a river. There are waterfalls, cascades, trout pools, and outcroppings, all of which are seldom seen except by the most adventurous members of the outdoor enthusiasts.

MAKING THE MOST OF YOUR VISIT:

This part of the countryside was one of the last wilderness areas to be settled by people of European descent. It was in the 1830s when the settlers arrived. In 1908 George Moore developed a hunting preserve in the Snowbird territory, and he imported such animals as buffalo (or bison), Russian wild boars, elk, mule deer from Colorado, native and Russian brown bears, and wild turkeys.

But long before Moore the Native Americans known as the Snowbird Indians inhabited and were friends to the area.

Remember as you explore the area that some of the boars still live in the forests, and it is hard to imagine an animal more terrifying to meet on a trail. The boar can be ferocious and deadly, as can the bear.

If you want to hike the Big Snowbird Trail, you must ford the creek a number of times. Carry along fresh and dry socks and other items of clothing. In fact, if the weather is warm, you may decide eventually that it is too much trouble to keep changing shoes and socks and just wade through the creek.

Take along the basics of outdoor adventure. These include the following: whistle, compass, flashlight, knife, matches or cigarette lighter (or both), plenty of fresh water, food, a first aid kit, extra clothing, topo map and trail map, and a can opener, if you are carrying canned foods. Be sure to take along rainwear in case of bad weather.

You will find that good shoes are an absolute necessity. Do not try to do any walking in this area if you are wearing loafers or street shoes. Boots or high-top shoes are essential. Remember that you are not taking a stroll through the mall: this is rugged terrain, and you are the invader, not the resident.

Do not make this visit alone, unless you are supremely able to handle yourself in the wilderness. Even the hardiest and the most competent sooner or later encounter circumstances that they cannot control.

The Big Snowbird Trail is 12.7 miles long and at times it can be difficult. Snowbird Mountain Trail is extremely difficult even though it is only 9.4 miles.

You do not need to hike the trails to their completion. You may simply want to see Snowbird Creek and some of the other wild and beautiful streams in the forest. You can, of course, fish for trout, but be sure you have the necessary license. Be sure, too, that you are equipped with the proper gear. Check to see what the season dates are and what kind of bait or lures can or must be used. You will see relatively little of the creek in many areas, but what you do see makes the trip worthwhile.

Nantahala River.

SECTION 9: THE BEST MOUNTAIN LAKES AND STREAMS
TRIP 10: THE NANTAHALA RIVER
THE LAND OF THE MIDDAY SUN

LOCATION:

The Nantahala River, with special emphasis on the gorge, flows through miles of rugged terrain, extends from Beechertown to Fontana Lake. To get to the gorge from I-40, exit at Clyde and take US 19 all the way to Bryson City and beyond. Keep driving south until you pass through a series of small communities and you reach the junction of NC 28. You are actually in the gorge in this area, but it becomes deeper and rougher as you move south toward Beechertown. Actually, US 19 runs all the way to Beechertown and on down to Andrews.

NEARBY ATTRACTIONS:

You are near Fontana Lake and Fontana Dam and Village, all of which are worthy of a visit. You are also near Bryson City, Robbinsville, Cherokee, the Blue Ridge Parkway, Dillard, and Sylva. There are many opportunities for camping, picnicking, fishing, rafting, canoeing, and hiking.

HOURS OF OPERATION:

Many of the outfitters along the highway through the gorge operate from 9 a.m. until 6 p.m. or perhaps later. You can, of course, drive the gorge anytime you wish, day or night, all year long, if the roads are open.

ADMISSION:

No fees are required, unless you plan to camp or run the river. You must rent the equipment and pay a deposit.

FACILITIES:

This is a gorge with a highway running through it, so you will find no facilities except an occasional service station and restroom before you reach the gorge and after you leave it.

WHAT'S THE STORY?

Nantahala Gorge is, it almost goes without saying, a rare and beautiful place to spend a few hours or days. The nine-mile gorge contains a world-class whitewater river that challenges the best. There are continuous rapids and, with spring and summer rains aided by melting snow or run-off from the many feeder streams, the water level is usually high. This is heavy rainfall territory, and the water level is seldom down to the point that the whitewater fun is missing.

SPECIAL ATTRACTIONS:

If you don't want whitewater rapids as a sports arena, you can always enjoy the river from a spectator's viewpoint. If you want smoother water, you can have it, too. But it is the gorge that attracts the whitewater crowd, and you may want to watch them rather than take on the river itself.

MAKING THE MOST OF YOUR VISIT:

The drive is beautiful from the time you leave I-40 via Exit 27 ten miles past Asheville. Follow US 19 and US 23 southwest and when the two highways split, remain on US 19 through Bryson City. You will enter the Nantahala Gorge within 15 miles after leaving Bryson City.

To enjoy Linville Gorge you must drive down a dirt and gravel road, park, and hike a considerable distance to get into the gorge itself. To explore the Cullasaja Gorge you must struggle down through the thick undergrowth and then follow uncertain trails along the river. The gorges formed by the Whitewater River and Horse Pasture River are almost inaccessible for all but the most experienced hikers.

The Nantahala Gorge, on the other hand, offers the ultimate in comfortable exploration. You can drive through and enjoy major parts of the gorge and never leave your car, unless you want to get out and enjoy some of the at-hand points of interest.

The name of the Gorge is a Native American word literally meaning "middle sun," and the area is fittingly called "the land of the midday sun." When you are in the gorge you will see that the high cliffs prevent the sun from shining directly into the gorge until the middle part of the day, and you will realize just how accurate the name of the gorge is.

The highway through the gorge is not new. Prior to the appearance of the Europeans into the area it is probable that the Native Americans created a trail to be used for trading purposes, and in the 1830s a crude road was built through the lower part of the gorge and to the main United States Army installation known at the time as Fort Butler. The present-day name of the settlement is Murphy.

One of the points of interest in the gorge is that of the Indian caves. To get to the caves, drive west along US 19 until you reach the 150-foot swinging bridge. Park at the bridge and on the other side of the river hike half a mile along the railroad. Half the length of a football field north of the railroad you will find a series of caves that are connected. These caves were the homes of the little people of Cherokee myth, and in more recent times the convicts used to build the railroad through the gorge used the caves as shelters. Sunday morning church services were held in the caves.

The major outdoor activity in the gorge, other than sight-seeing, may be rafting. In summer months you can see not just hundreds but literally thousands of people enjoying the river and the gorge in canoes, kayaks, tubes, and other forms of floating transportation. It is estimated that 150,000 persons float the river each year.

The water, depending upon the area, may be perfect for the family that wants to float along peacefully, with occasional mild whitewater thrills, and it is also swift and turbulent enough in other areas to satisfy the whitewater enthusiasts.

There are many outfitters in the area, and you can rent the needed equipment, or you can provide your own. Fishing is also a popular sport in the area, and the photo opportunities are great. Wild life is abundant, and your chances of seeing larger animals are greater in the early spring or fall before the whitewater sportsmen arrive.

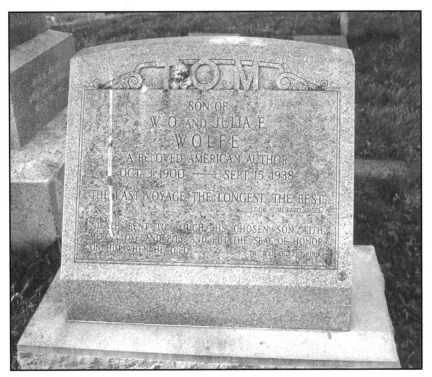

Thomas Wolfe grave in Asheville.

SECTION 10: THE BEST MOUNTAIN GRAVEYARDS
TRIP 1: RIVERSIDE CEMETERY
THE WEB, THE ROCK, AND THE MAGI

LOCATION:

Riverside Cemetery is located at 53 Birch Street in downtown Asheville. To reach the final resting places of novelist Thomas Wolfe, short story master William Sidney Porter (O. Henry), and statesman, legislator, soldier, and wit Zebulon Vance, exit I-40 in downtown Asheville to I-240. From I-240 exit onto Montford Street and then turn left onto Courtland Street, then right onto Pearson Street, and then left onto Birch Street and into the cemetery,

NEARBY ATTRACTIONS:

While you are in the Asheville area, you might want to stop by Pack Square and tour the art museum, Health Fair, and the other museums in the complex. Then you might want to take a tour of downtown Asheville-a walking tour that will take you to many of the city's manifold land-marks. Just on the edge of town you will find the Western North Carolina Center, the North Carolina Arboretum, the Blue Ridge Parkway, Craggy Gardens (about 18 miles north of Asheville on the Parkway), Mount Mitchell (which can also be reached via the Parkway), Wolfe's home down-town in the city, Zeb Vance's home in nearby Weaverville (just off the Blue Ridge Parkway), and, south of the city, the home of historian-poet-novelist Carl Sandburg at Flat Rock.

HOURS OF OPERATION:

Riverside Cemetery is open from 8 a.m. until 8 p.m.

ADMISSION:

There are no admission fees.

FACILITIES:

In the Riverside Cemetery you will find sparse parking area except alongside the road. There are no public facilities here, but in and around nearby Asheville you can find nearly anything you would like in the way of gas, food, overnight lodging, picnic tables, campgrounds, hiking, and enjoyment of historic sites.

WHAT'S THE STORY?

In the latter part of the 19th century and the early years of the 20th century, Asheville attracted thousands of people who wanted to enjoy the exceptional scenery and wonderful climate. These people included novelist F. Scott Fitzgerald, his wife Zelda, Douglas Fairbanks and Mary Pickford, presidents, and leading persons from all walks of life. Among the people who came and remained for significant periods of time (or people who were born in the area) were novelist Thomas Wolfe, short story writer William Sidney Porter (O. Henry), and Civil War officer Zeb Vance, member of Congress and governor of North Carolina. These lat-ter three persons are buried in Riverside Cemetery.

SPECIAL ATTRACTIONS:

Other than the three graves, you will enjoy the winding road that moves like a giant serpent around the hills of the cemetery, and you will also be fascinated by the amazing array of ornaments and elaborate gravestones throughout the cemetery.

MAKING THE MOST OF YOUR VISIT:

Much has been written in this book about novelist Thomas Wolfe, and Zeb Vance has been covered fairly completely in the allotted space, but to this point nothing has been said about the master of the surprise-ending short story, O. Henry, who was born on September 11, 1862-during the Civil War-and died on June 5, 1910. Although he did not live half a century, O. Henry turned out several volumes of short stories.

While he seemed to lack the romantic idealism and poetic vision of Wolfe, O. Henry had a marvelous literary style of his own that in many ways equalled Wolfe's emotional outpourings. The difference was that O. Henry did it with wit, humor, and irony.

It has been observed that virtually all real romantic poets and novelists are almost totally devoid of a sense of humor, and there may be more than a germ of truth in the idea. Wordsworth, Shelley, Keats, and others of their school seldom if ever penned a line intended to convey a smile. Byron was one of the few of his age who dared to write humorous and satiric poetry that also contained genuine insights and beauty.

Similarly, Wolfe rarely engaged in humor. Many have noted that an unhappy and often unstable life influenced the emotional style of Wolfe, but O. Henry's life was anything but an Horatio Alger story.

Born William Sidney Porter in Greensboro, North Carolina, young Porter essentially had no father. His biological father was a medical doctor who was obsessed with the idea of perpetual motion and devoted endless hours to his pursuit. Porter was never close to his father, and when his mother died when Porter was only three years old, the child was virtually an orphan.

A pale, anemic-looking child, he was sickly as a young adult when he moved to Texas to seek his fortune. Instead, he found a job as a sheepman and a calling to write fiction.

He married a young Texas girl and their first child died in less than a year. Debt-ridden, Porter started a magazine called *The Rolling Stone*, which failed almost immediately. Porter then accepted a job in an Austin bank where he apparently embezzled $1,000 to help meet expenses. Forced to leave his wife and their second child, Porter crossed the border into Mexico, and there he managed to secure money to send to his family.

Some say, although this has never been proven, that the money came from a bank robbery. When Porter's wife became deathly ill, he returned to Texas shortly before her death, after which he was arrested, convicted, and sentenced to three years in a Texas prison.

Years later he was in New York, where he wrote stories at a manic pace. He once said, "I've got some of my best yarns from park benches, lamp posts, and newspaper stands.... There are stories in everything."

O. Henry's best-known stories include "The Gift of the Magi," "The Last Leaf," "The Ransom of Red Chief," "The Cop and the Anthem," "Black Bart," and "An Afternoon Miracle." It was O. Henry who introduced one of the most memorable characters in the annals of western fiction: the

Cisco Kid.

O. Henry opens "The Gift of the Magi" with these lines: "One dollar and eighty-seven cents. That was all. And sixty cents of it was in pennies."

And for decades people have read the story without wondering how there could be $1.87 and only sixty cents in pennies. And no doubt somewhere at this moment O. Henry is still chuckling over his little joke. But don't leave the story with only the sad tale of two people in love who bought each other impractical gifts.

O. Henry did not think they were foolish children. He wrote, "But in a last word to the wise of these days let it be said that of all who give gifts these two were the wisest. Of all who give and receive gifts, such as they are wisest. Everywhere they are the wisest. They are the magi."

As you drive through Riverside Cemetery, you will see road signs directing you to the burial places of Zeb Vance, William Sidney Porter, and Thomas Wolfe. Be sure to read carefully and perhaps make a copy of Wolfe's epitaph, taken from two of Wolfe's best works: "The Last Voyage, the Longest, the Best" (from *Look Homeward, Angel*) and from *The Web and the Rock*, "Death Bent to touch his chosen son with mercy, love, and pity, and put the seal of honor on him when he died."

Wolfe, at age 38, died even younger than O. Henry.

Wolfe's Angel at Hendersonville Cemetery.

SECTION 10: THE BEST MOUNTAIN GRAVEYARDS
TRIP 2: HENDERSONVILLE
LOOK HOMEWARD, ANGEL

LOCATION:

Hendersonville is directly west of Chimney Rock and Lake Lure, east of Brevard, south of Asheville, and north of the South Carolina cities of Greenville and Spartanburg. From I-40, take US 25 south from Asheville and intersect with US 64. From I-85 take I-26 or US 25 north to Hendersonville and then again intersect with US 64. From Lake Lure and Chimney Rock, follow US 64 west to Hendersonville. No matter how you arrive, when you reach the city of Hendersonville, drive west through the city. As you reach the city limits on the west side of town, look for the Hendersonville Cemetery (Oakdale) on the left side of the highway.

NEARBY ATTRACTIONS:

In addition to the attractions inside Hendersonville, you are very near Flat Rock, Asheville, the Blue Ridge Parkway, Lake Lure, Brevard, Saluda, and Tryon. All these locations have fine attractions in them.

HOURS OF OPERATION:

The cemetery is open from morning until sundown every day of the year.

ADMISSION:

There are no admission fees at any time.

FACILITIES:

The only facility is parking space, and this is at a premium except alongside the roads that dissect the cemetery.

WHAT'S THE STORY?

The cemetery is both old and new, with graves dating back for several decades and others only days old. The interest in the cemetery, other than its beauty, lies in its connection with the famed Asheville novelist Thomas Wolfe. See Section 8, Trip 4 for more detailed information on Wolfe. In this section and in Trip 1 there is additional information about Wolfe.

SPECIAL ATTRACTIONS:

The angel that once stood at the stonecutter's shop of Tom Wolfe's father and which now reportedly decorates the grave of the wife of a minister is the major reason for the typical person's decision to stop at the cemetery.

MAKING THE MOST OF YOUR VISIT:

You've read this before, several times, and here it comes again. Prepare yourself before you make the visit. Know the story of the angel and the book by Wolfe, if only through reading the material in this brief chapter.

The angel here is not a replica or copy of the angel that Wolfe wrote about; this is, we are told, the original, as far as anyone can determine. In the Bryson City cemetery there is another angel, and the people there claim that it is the original. The vast majority of people with educated opinions seem to feel very strongly both ways, as Billy Martin said.

What's more important is the story of the angel. If you read Wolfe's masterful short story, "An Angel on the Porch," you will receive two distinct impressions: one true, one blatantly false.

In the story a customer comes to buy the angel on the porch for the grave of a recently deceased woman. When she announced her intentions to purchase the angel, the stonecutter's face was "startled and unwilling." Wolfe writes that W. O. Gant (the real man was, of course, Wolfe's own father) "...gnawed the corner of his thin lip" with anxiety. No one, Wolfe tells the reader, knew how much the angel had meant to the stonecutter.

In public, Gant told people that the angel was "his white elephant." He cursed it and admitted that he had been a fool ever to order it. The angel had stood, unsold, for six years on the porch in heat and cold, rain and snow and sleet, and now it looked stained and fly-specked.

The angel had made the trip from Carrera, Italy. It held in one hand a stone lily; the other hand was lifted heavenward "in benediction." The angel stood, clumsily, Wolfe said, upon the ball "of one phthisic foot. The expression on the angel's "stupid" face was one of "soft stone idiocy." Don't spend a lot of time wondering about Wolfe's use of the word "phthisic."

In his rages, drunken and otherwise, Gant the stonecutter had raged against the angel, verbally abusing it, accusing it of having impoverished him, ruining him, cursing his declining years, and now threatening to crush him beneath its weight.

Sometimes, when he was drunk enough, the stonecutter fell on his knees before the Angel, which he had secretly named Cynthia, and begged its forgiveness and pleaded with it to love and bless him.

In Greek mythology, incidentally, Cynthia was sometimes used in place of Artemis (or Diana), the goddess of the moon. The name was often used to personify the moon and its powers.

When the woman paid Gant, he walked with her to the front door and onto the porch. The moon (Cynthia) already shone "like its own phantom" in the evening sky. The questions plaguing Gant were "Where now? Where after? Where then?"

And so, according to the Wolfe story, the angel was sold-but not for the grave of the Methodist minister's wife. The woman who bought the angel was Elizabeth (whose name means "God is my oath"), a madame in a local brothel and former lover of W. O. Gant, the stonecutter.

And the angel was for the grave of one of her prostitutes.

How the story of the angel on the prostitute's grave came into being is uncertain, but the highly probable truth is that people who read Wolfe's short story also knew of his tendency to be autobiographical and assumed that he had told the truth in the story. But Wolfe was too creative to be totally factual.

In any event, visit the cemetery, examine the angel and you decide if the look is one of stone idiocy and if the foot appears phthisic. Admire the work, contemplate its role in Wolfe's life, and let your own imagination soar. Perhaps you, too, can see the angel standing on the porch of the stonecutter's shop.

Wolfe's Angel in Bryson City Cemetery.

SECTION 10: THE BEST MOUNTAIN GRAVEYARDS
TRIP 3: BRYSON CITY CEMETERY
ANOTHER ANGEL FROM THE PORCH

LOCATION:
You reach Bryson City the same way you get to so many of the Western North Carolina attractions: drive on I-40 for 10 miles west of Asheville and take the Clyde exit on US 19. This highway, which is wide and uncrowded (except during the leaf season in October) is a great pleasure to drive. It will take you into downtown Bryson City. To get to the cemetery drive to the courthouse square on Main Street and then take Arlington Avenue to the cemetery turn-off on the right. This one-mile drive leads along a fenced area to the top of a knoll. Bryson City Cemetery is near the top of this gentle hill that overlooks Bryson City.

NEARBY ATTRACTIONS:
While you are in Bryson City, the closest attractions are the Great Smoky Mountains Railroad, just down the street from the courthouse; nearby Dillsboro, where you can catch another of the Great Smoky Mountains Railroad excursions and where you can see the terrific railroad museum of Floyd McEachern; the Great Smoky Mountains National Park, with emphasis on the nearby Cherokee Indian Reservation, the Qualla attractions, the Cyclorama, the Mountain Farm Museum at the Visitor Center; Sylva, with one of the most beautiful courthouses in the country; Fontana Lake, Dam, and Village, located only a short distance away; Maggie Valley with all of its attractions; nearby Robbinsville, where the Great Chief Junaluska is buried; and the Cherohala Skyway.

HOURS OF OPERATION:
While the Bryson City Cemetery does not keep posted hours as such, the times to visit are from about 8 a.m. until dusk. In the summertime 6 p.m. is a good time to leave.

ADMISSION:
There is no admission fee. But please show utmost respect and consideration for the cemetery and the memory of those who are resting there. Please do not litter, deface, or in any other way damage the property.

FACILITIES:
There are no public facilities here.

WHAT'S THE STORY?
As with nearly every old cemetery, this one is the final resting place of some of the leading citizens of the area. In fact, some of the people

409

interred here made their lasting marks on the mountains, and their contributions will long be remembered by those who know their stories.

SPECIAL ATTRACTIONS:

Check out the angel, described in another part of this book, that is, according to local lore, the angel that stood on the porch of the stonecutter's shop owned and operated by the father of novelist Thomas Wolfe. And visit two other interesting graves.

MAKING THE MOST OF YOUR VISIT:

When you enter the cemetery, look north past the maintenance shed where you will see an angel holding lilies. This angel marks the grave of Fannie Everett Clancy (1884-1904), whose burial place is marked by a marble angel that some local people insist is the same angel that novelist Thomas Wolfe immortalized in his most famous novel, *Look Homeward, Angel.*

The local story is that the angel was imported from Italy, specifically from the famous Carrera. The angel was shipped by rail, you will be told, in 1907 from the stonecutter's shop owned by W. O. Wolfe. The local legend (or factual story) holds that the angel in Hendersonville, reputed to be Wolfe's angel, holds a sheaf of wheat rather than lilies. A publication originating in the Bryson City area insists that the Hendersonville angel is on the grave of a 71-year old woman, but the local people who saw the angel in Wolfe's shop described it as holding lilies and that the man who bought the angel purchased it for the grave of his young daughter. The story concludes that the local angel better fits the one described in Wolfe's famous novel.

For the record, the highway marker in Hendersonville states without hesitation that the angel is a "marble statue from the Asheville shop of W. O. Wolfe." It "inspired title of son Thomas Wolfe's *Look Homeward, Angel.*"

Who is correct? If you look at the Hendersonville photo carefully, you will see that the angel is standing with both feet firmly on the pedestal, not poised as Wolfe describes it in the book. The angel in the Hendersonville graveyard is not holding lilies, as Wolfe described the angel in his father's shop. So you are invited to read the book, visit both graveyards, and make your own choices.

The Kephart grave is hard to find, unless you follow these directions: stand with your back to the maintenance shed and face Bryson City. Straight ahead is 12 o'clock, and at one o'clock you will see the Kephart stone (a huge stone!) almost at the bottom of the hill. His epitaph reads, "He loved his neighbors and pictured them in 'Our Southern Highlanders.' His vision helped create the Great Smoky Mountains National Park."

The Cathey grave is just above the Hillside Baptist Church, and his epitaph reads, if I made it out correctly, "Mark Cathey 1871-1944. Beloved Hunter and Fisherman. Was Himself Caught by the Gospel Hook Just Before the Season Closed for Good."

William Marcus Cathey, famed as the greatest of all trout fishermen and story-teller, was a living legend. One of his yarns is that, he said, it was once so cold that when he hung the thermometer outside the mercury dropped so fast that it jerked the nail out of the post.

Kephart died in an automobile accident in 1931, but he left a legacy behind him that will last about as long as the mountains stand. And that promises to be a long, long time. The Mark Cathey legend will have a continuous following, and the debate about the angel on the porch will endure as long as *Look Homeward, Angel* is read, which may be for decades to come.

Old Field Cemetery near Sylva.

SECTION 10: THE BEST MOUNTAIN GRAVEYARDS
TRIP 4: OLD FIELD CEMETERY
PSALMS IN STONE

LOCATION:

Start this trip from I-40 west of Asheville at Exit 27 where you will take the Great Smoky Mountains Expressway. Drive south around Waynesville and to a point just outside Sylva. From the Great Smoky Mountains Expressway take Exit 85 near Sylva. Turn off the Expressway onto Cope Creek Road. As you leave the Expressway, turn left immediately onto Cope Creek Road. Drive .5 mile or so along a winding road and then turn sharply to the left. You are on the cemetery road, and instantly you will see the old Scotts Creek Church and the hillside covered with gravestones.

NEARBY ATTRACTIONS:

You are near not only Sylva with its exceptional courthouse but also Dillsboro, Bryson City, Cherokee, Blue Ridge Parkway, and Great Smoky Mountains National Park.

HOURS OF OPERATION:

While there are no gates, common courtesy and respect would dictate that you limit your respectful visit to this old church graveyard to the hours from about 8 a.m. until dusk.

ADMISSION:

The only payment you will make is that of paying your sincere respects to the loved ones of many mountain families: men, women, and children who departed this life decades and even centuries ago.

FACILITIES:

Other than limited parking space, there are no facilities available here.

WHAT'S THE STORY?

The old Scotts church, which has neither electrical power nor drinking water, served the Cope Creek Community for hundreds of years. The members of the church for the most part lived their lives of dignity, respect, and honor within their community. Most never strayed far from the place of their birth and the origin of their social awareness. These people knew hard work, hardships, and hard lives. But they were in their way noble, courageous, and upright people who knew the value of a home, a home church, and a quiet place in the sun for their time on earth.

SPECIAL ATTRACTIONS:

For one of the most interesting portions of the Old Field Cemetery, look to the immediate west of the church where you will see an enclosed area with many pointed stones, all white and all symmetrical, mounted on the top of the wall.

MAKING THE MOST OF YOUR VISIT:

As with old churchyards generally, you can read an unwritten history of the area by making a study of the stones in the graveyard. And also by making a study of the church, which is wooden and, by today's standards, might be regarded as primitive.

But please keep in mind that the primitive churches were not necessarily crude, unattractive, or lacking in dignity and self-esteem or image. The word *primitive* has many definitions, among them "original, existing from earlier times, basic, primary, and not derivative."

As you study the stones, keep the select definitions in mind. The people who attended the church and are buried in the graveyard were, by definition, of an early age, and they did not seek to imitate thoughtlessly the standards or levels of others. These people were strong, determined, and characteristically bold and straightforward.

Extend the etymological derivation of the term *primitive*. The root words include terms such as "prime, prim, primary, primer, primacy, primogeniture."

You will be impressed favorably with the neatness and the loving care that is evident in the cemetery. And you will read the lessons of the past-the unrelenting and often agonizing ordeals that marked any social existence.

For example, you can see many stones marking the final resting places of women who, despite their decades of toil, the ravages of time, and the rigors of their time in life, lived to ripe old ages. These people maintained a healthy life by working ceaselessly, tirelessly (or they kept working despite their total exhaustion), and happily, at least much of the time.

You will see graves of infants whose life span was only a matter of days, and you will realize again the deepest pains of infant mortality. You can pinpoint the outbreaks of deadly and merciless diseases for which there were, at the time, no forms of effective prevention or treatment. This was a day when the sudden shout of "Typhoid" or "Smallpox" could send chills through the entire community-chills that were greater than those in any of the horror movies Hollywood could produce in a later day.

The oldest gravestones are found at the top of the hill to the east of the church and to the south side of the slope. If you stand with your back to the front door, these stones will be to your left (at ten o'clock) and straight ahead.

You will see tombstones that reveal tragic stories from all walks of life. Some stones are elaborate and obviously at the time of their purchase were expensive. Others were essentially fieldstones.

A word of caution: if you drive up the hill past the front of the church, you will come quickly to a dead end, and you be faced with the slight problem of backing down the hill and to the intersection of cemetery roads below the church.

Remember the stones here as you make your way to other stops in the mountains. You will see the side-by-side graves of seven children in one graveyard, and you will see the unique epitaph of a master fisherman and storyteller. As you visit these ancient cemeteries, remember the strengths and determination of the people who rest there. There truly were giants in the earth in earlier days, and they helped make our culture possible.

Quaker Meadows Cemetery outside Morganton.

SECTION 10: THE BEST MOUNTAIN GRAVEYARDS
TRIP 5: QUAKER MEADOWS CEMETERY
A LONG ETERNITY

LOCATION:

There are several ways to reach the Quaker Meadows Cemetery, and the easiest of these ways are all from Interstate 40, which runs along the south side of Morganton. You can drive via US 64, US 70, or NC 18 and NC 181. Of these three, the easiest route is NC 18 and NC 181.

Exit I-40 at the NC 18 junction and drive north into the town of Morganton. As you pass under the railroad tracks, keep right on Green Street. You will pass the old Burke County Courthouse on your left, and you notice the road signs directing you to NC 181. All you need to do, in fact, is keep driving straight north.

As you pass through town, you will intersect with US 64/70, but keep straight. Cross the Catawba River and stay on the road that is still marked Green Street. Quaker Meadows Cemetery is on the left side of NC 181, almost directly across the highway from Quaker Meadows Plantation House. Turn left, then turn back right as you follow the signs to the cemetery.

NEARBY ATTRACTIONS:

In addition to the attractions in downtown Morganton, there are other superb places to visit nearby. These locations include Valdese, South Mountains State Park, Linville Falls, Table Rock, the Blue Ridge Parkway, Linville Gorge, Lake James and Lake James State Park, and Little Switzerland.

HOURS OF OPERATION:

Your easiest way to visit Quaker Meadows Cemetery is to stop by the old Burke County Courthouse (you can stop in as you drive through town) and ask one of the staff members to accompany you to the cemetery. In fact, if you will call ahead of time, you will not need to worry about making spur-of-the-moment plans.

ADMISSION:

There are no admission fees.

FACILITIES:

There are no facilities of any sort.

WHAT'S THE STORY?

Here in this tiny cemetery are buried some of the most famous leaders of Burke County. You can buy a small book that provides details on many of the people buried there, or you can let the gravestones tell you their stories. In many cases, you can learn an enormous amount from the brief inscriptions.

SPECIAL ATTRACTIONS:

Pay particular attention to the huge gates to the cemetery and to the wall around it. And look for the tales on the stones that you see in the circular pattern of the cemetery.

MAKING THE MOST OF YOUR VISIT:

As I have suggested repeatedly in this book, the best way to get the most out of a visit is to go prepared. For this reason, you may want to obtain one of the historical publications about the cemetery. You can read the printed matter and thereby make your visit much more rewarding.

One particular stone reads simply: William C. Butler-Died Apr. 10, 1841. Ag'd 39 y's, 25 d's.

Admittedly, there is not much of a story on the surface here. But William Butler became sheriff of Burke County when he was only 28 years old, and the county, which is a large one, stretches from the flatlands east of Morganton to and through the South Mountains, the site of a modern state park, and to Linville Gorge, or at least part of it.

So, in a day when travel was difficult even on good roads and with a fine team of horses and a carriage, moving from place to place was almost agony when the weather was cold and the roads were rutted and muddy.

The most famous prisoner Butler was responsible for keeping was Frankie Silver, an 18-year old wife who was charged with the killing of her husband, Charles. See the Kona Church chapter for more details on this sensational crime, trial, and execution.

One of the most famous sons of the territory was General Charles McDowell, whose gravestone says that he lived from 1743 until 1815. His epitaph proclaims that he died as he had lived, a patriot. Notice the birth date. He was in his thirties when the Revolutionary War broke out.

McDowell and his brother were military men who served during the war and distinguished themselves. Both men signed petitions urging the formation of Burke County.

But it was not only the British that threatened their area; the Cherokees and other Native Americans were at times hostile and dangerous, and keeping the peace meant at times dealing with highly inflammatory situations that might at any moment break into open warfare. In fact, after the county was established, Charles McDowell joined General Griffith Rutherfordton and in 1776 the forces defeated the Cherokees and led to peace in the territory.

One of the major accomplishments of General McDowell was that he, after the defeat of the American patriots at Camden, fled into the mountains, reorganized, and marched southward to engage the British at the Battle of Kings Mountain.

You will see what is almost a social register of the day when you look at the names on the gravestones. There are 16 Tates buried here, and 12 McDowells, making a total of 28 burial plots occupied by two families. That is almost half of the total graves in the cemetery.

There are two Unknown gravesites, and one that is marked only MMG. Unquestionably there are stories that would rival fiction behind any of the stones in the cemetery.

One recommendation, also made elsewhere in this book: Take along a copy of Gray's "Elegy Written in a Country Churchyard" and pause in the shade of a huge oak tree and read stanzas from this most famous of all graveyard poems. The poet pays a great and much-deserved tribute to the residents there.

Entrance to Chief Junaluska's Grave.

SECTION 10: THE BEST MOUNTAIN GRAVEYARDS
TRIP 6: ROBBINSVILLE
THE SAVIOR OF OLD HICKORY

LOCATION:

Robbinsville is a small town nestled among the mountains of far western North Carolina. To get there from I-40, exit, as you have often done, at Clyde and follow US 19 all the way across the state in a southward direction until you have passed through Bryson City. On the south side of Bryson City be on the lookout for US 129 that leads westward to Robbinsville. The graveyard is on the west side of town, close to NC 143.

NEARBY ATTRACTIONS:

You are within easy driving distance of Bryson City and the Great Smoky Mountains Railroad, the Nantahala Gorge, Fontana Lake and Fontana Village, the Cherohala Skyway, and Santeelah Lake. You can find many enjoyable attractions in these locations.

HOURS OF OPERATION:

The Robbinsville cemetery is open every day from morning until sundown.

FACILITIES:

There are no facilities, other than a small parking area just off the highway.

WHAT'S THE STORY?

During the War of 1812 at the Battle of Horseshoe Bend, it is said that Andrew Jackson was in danger of losing his life to Creek Indian warriors when Chief Junaluska of the Cherokee Nation came to the rescue of Old Hickory. As a way of recognizing the chief's contributions to the nation, he was given land in western North Carolina, and years later he and his wife Nicie were buried in the cemetery at Robbinsville.

SPECIAL ATTRACTIONS:

The major reason for the typical tourist's decision to visit the cemetery is to pay his respects to the great Cherokee man of war and peace and to honor his memory.

MAKING THE MOST OF YOUR VISIT:

First of all, the story persists that Chief Junaluska later remarked, after having saved Andrew Jackson's life, that he wished he had never done so. Whether the story is true or not, there are many who would have agreed with what he may have said. During and after the infamous Trail of Tears ordeal, many who had championed Jackson vilified him for his role in one of the blackest periods of American history.

Here is how the Battle of Horseshoe Bend developed, in the long view of history. Andrew Jackson was born on the North Carolina-South Carolina border, and to this day the exact location is disputed. One scholar has even said that Jackson was actually born at sea and not on United States land at all.

At the close of the American Revolution young Jackson, who had been slashed across the face by a sword-wielding British soldier who attacked because Jackson refused to shine the soldier's boots, began the study of law in Salisbury. By the time the War of 1812 had broken out, Jackson became an officer in the American army and was sent to Alabama to end the Creek uprising.

Here's a bit of historical trivia. The old expression that says, to this effect, "We'll see you on Sunday if the creek don't rise," is not an ungrammatical statement, but the capitalization is incorrect. What is meant is that we'll see you on Sunday unless the Creek Indians don't rise-or attack.

On August 30, 1813, the Creeks did in fact rise and they attacked

Fort Mims near Mobile. The Creeks killed almost half the people in the fort, and Jackson, who was in bed recovering from a street brawl he had fought against Thomas Hart Benton, was sent to crush the Creeks.

On March 27, 1814, at the Battle of Horseshoe Bend on the Tallapoosa River, the Creek resistance was ended and their help to the British was over. It was during this battle that, so the story goes, Jackson was in danger of losing not only the battle but his life when Chief Junaluska and some of his men swam across the Tallapoosa River and took the canoes the Creeks were planning to use to cross the river and attack the out-numbered and out-gunned men under Jackson's command.

Another detail from the story includes the encounter when a Creek warrior had Jackson at his mercy and was preparing to kill Old Hickory when Junaluska drove his tomahawk through the skull of the Creek warrior and saved Jackson's life.

The sad denouement of that story is that later, when Chief John Ross sent Junaluska to plead with Jackson to save the lives and the property of the Cherokees, Jackson listened for a few minutes, then said sternly, "Sir, your audience is ended; there is nothing I can do for you."

Another story is that in the tragic Trail of Tears episode Junaluska witnessed the deaths of his people and lifted his face to Heaven and said in an anguished voice, "Oh, God! If I had known at the Battle of Horseshoe what I know now, American history would have been written differently."

It is assumed that Junaluska meant that he would have allowed the Creeks to slay Jackson on the spot.

It was at the Battle of Horseshoe Bend that Jackson won national recognition as a military leader, and shortly thereafter he was commissioned as a major general in the United States Army. As a direct result of the battle, he was put in charge of the defense of New Orleans and later won the bloody battle there, a battle which, as it turned out, need not have been fought because the war had already ended officially. And, in a strong sense, it was Junaluska who deserves an immense amount of credit.

The Creeks, by the way, had a novel way of making political decisions. The two "parties" in the nation were the red (war) and white (peace) divisions. When it was time to decide whether to go to war or to remain at peace, the opposing factions held a series of four ball games, and the losers had to accept the views of the winners.

Junaluska's role in the Battle of Horseshoe Bend and his role as a leader in peace and war is commendable in all aspects. He was, from all reports, a magnificent man whose physical stamina, courage, intelligence, and integrity are commendable. His name meant "He who tries repeatedly and fails." The reference is to the vow Junaluska made to wipe out all the Creeks. But after the Creek wars Junaluska admitted ruefully that there were a few Creeks left alive.

After he was forced to leave his land in what is now Graham County and was sent to Oklahoma, Junaluska left the reservation and walked all the way back to North Carolina, we are told. And in Graham County he was deeded 337 acres of land where he and his wife spent the remainder of their lives. He died in this state in 1858.

The land grant was a fitting and much-deserved tribute. And those of us who know Graham County can understand why Junaluska acted as he did. It is well worth the walk from Oklahoma to live in one of the finest parts of the United States. The tragedy is that he had to make the walk in the first place. But you cannot travel the North Carolina mountains without encountering numerous references to the tragic story of the Trail of Tears. What you can do is resolve to make a determined effort that his type of tragedy can never happen again in this country.

Mount Harmony Cemetery near Polkville.

SECTION 10: THE BEST MOUNTAIN GRAVEYARDS
TRIP 7: MOUNT HARMONY METHODIST CHURCH GRAVEYARD
BROKEN STONES AND LIVES

LOCATION:

There are two easy ways to drive to Mount Harmony Methodist Church (established before the United Methodist Church had come into being as a label). The easy way from I-40 is to junction with US 226 in Marion and drive south through Rutherford County and to the very outskirts of Cleveland County. On the left or east side of the road you will see a highway historical marker describing Mount Harmony Methodist Church. Turn left and drive one mile west. The road is paved for the first quarter or half of a mile and is gravel from that point on, but the road is good and you can drive it easily.

The second way to reach the Mount Harmony graveyard is to junction with US 226 off I-85 south of Shelby. Drive north on US 226 through

Polkville. On the outskirts of Polkville you will see the road fork, just past the only traffic light in Polkville. Resist former New York Yankee superstar Yogi Berra's advice: When you come to a fork in the road, take it!

In this case, take the left fork, drive until you have crossed two bridges, and take the next road to your left.

NEARBY ATTRACTIONS:

You are in the rolling hills south of Asheville and Marion, and there are few area locations that could be classified as real travel destinations. You can drive to South Mountains State Park, which is a 15-minute drive away, or to the towns of Morganton and Valdese, both of which are described earlier in this book. You are also within a reasonable driving distance from Asheville and Old Fort, both of which have fine attractions. You can also drive to the Blue Ridge Parkway, Mount Mitchell, and Craggy Gardens on or just off the Parkway.

HOURS OF OPERATION:

The graveyard is open all the time and you can visit any hour of the day, any day of the year. Courtesy and respect for the burial ground and the people interred there suggests that the best times to visit are between the hours of 8 a.m. and dusk.

ADMISSION:

There are no admission fees.

FACILITIES:

There are no facilities of any sort, other than a small parking area. This church was established before the automobile let people travel rather long distances in a single day.

WHAT'S THE STORY?

The Mount Harmony Methodist Church was established in 1791. This date meant that the American Revolution had ended some years earlier and that adult members of the church could well have been soldiers in the Over-Mountain Men militia, or they could have been veterans of other area battles.

Some of the area young men served in the bloodiest conflict in American history. This war claimed the lives of more Americans than did World War I and World War II combined. The grave of one Civil War soldier is especially striking.

In historical perspective, there could also have been men buried there who fought in the War of 1812, the Spanish-American War, World War I, and World War II. The Mount Harmony church is one of the few in this part of the country that could have had men in every war this country ever fought except the French and Indian War and those fought after 1942.

SPECIAL ATTRACTIONS:

You might want to bring along the paper and other materials needed for gravestone rubbing. Some of the dates and epitaphs are so dim that they cannot be read otherwise. Look particularly for the grave of Lewis M. Wells, son of J. K, and M. Y. Wells, who was born June 12, 1840, and was killed on May 2, 1863, in the Battle of Chancellorsville.

When you travel, I remind you to take along a collection of a dozen or so books, among them books of poetry (especially that of Thomas Gray and his "Elegy Written in a Country Church-yard"), Thorton Wilder's *Our Town*, a history of North Carolina, and books or pamphlets on regional history.

This is a good place to take out one of your books, as you stand at the grave of the young man (he was only 23 years old when he was killed in this battle that also included the death of one of the most famous men in the Civil War: Stonewall Jackson.) The Battle of Chancellorsville was fought from May 1 through May 4, and young Wells was killed on the second day of fighting.

The Union leader of the Army of the Potomac was General Joseph Hooker, whose camp followers were believed to have been the origin of the term "hooker." However, the slang term was in use as early as 1567 and did not originate with the "friends" of Hooker's army. The Southern army was led by General Robert E. Lee.

MAKING THE MOST OF YOUR VISIT:

One bizarre note relative to this graveyard is that only a five-minute drive from where you stand there lived a man who reportedly had a collection of letters written by an ancestor who fought in the Civil War. One of the letters is said to concern itself with a soldier from the Polkville-Casar area who admits that when a general made the soldiers march for days without boots, the soldier waited his chance and then shot the general from his place of concealment behind a tree. That was on May 2, the same day that Wells was killed. Stonewall Jackson died on May 10.

Is it possible that the neighbor of Wells actually killed Stonewall Jackson?

This is a great place to read the first part of Act III of Wilder's *Our Town*, where the stage manager speaks of young men who "had a notion that the Union ought to be kept together" though they had never in their lives seen more than 50 miles of it. All they knew was the name, the United States of America, and, as Wilder said, "they went out and died about it."

It's a thought worth remembering.

Cemetery at Cades Cove in the Great Smokies.

SECTION 10: THE BEST MOUNTAIN GRAVEYARDS
TRIP 8: CADES COVE METHODIST CHURCH
THE LENGTHENED SHADOW OF ONE MAN

LOCATION:

This trip is one of the few that lap over into another state. This book is essentially about the best mountain trips in North Carolina, but we in the Tar Heel State are bounded by four terrific neighbors, and I did not think you'd mind stopping over to spend a few minutes in the neighbors' yard.

To get to this graveyard (and still-standing but not active church), drive west of Asheville on I-40 and take Exit 27 to the Great Smoky Mountains Expressway. This magnificent highway takes you to Waynesville, Sylva, Dillsboro, and Cherokee, where you can hit US 441 north into the Great Smokies National Park.

Here's a hint: Cherokee is very crowded at times and the traffic moves at a snail's pace. If you will junction with the Blue Ridge Parkway north of Cherokee you can drive comfortably into the Great Smokies National Park. Once you are inside the park, you will pass the Visitors Center and Smokemont, both on the right side of the highway. Continue north and you will reach the road leading to Clingman's Dome (the road is on the left) and almost immediately you will reach the Tennessee State Line and Newfound Gap.

Keep driving, and soon you will reach the road to Cades Cove. This trip is described in another chapter, but for now you need to know that the Cades Cove Loop is slow driving. Unless the Cove is almost deserted, it will take you about two hours to make the eleven-mile trip; however, there are lanes that cut through the Cove and if you wish you can cut across and eliminate some of the loop.

NEARBY ATTRACTIONS:

If you want to drive a few miles more, you will arrive in Gatlinburg, Tennessee. This is a favorite city for many mountain travelers, and you may enjoy touring it. Back in North Carolina you can reach Clingman's Dome easily, and at the entrance to the Great Smokies National Park you will find the Mountain Farm Museum and its attractions. The Mingus Mill is near Smokemont.

Outside the park you can visit the attractions in Cherokee, Sylva, Bryson City, and Dillsboro. You are also near the Blue Ridge Parkway.

HOURS OF OPERATION:

The Great Smoky Mountains National Park is open day and night, but you will need to complete your tour of Cades Cove by eight o'clock in the evening in summer and by 5 p.m. in winter.

ADMISSION:

There are no admission fees to the Great Smoky Mountains National Park, despite published reports to the contrary. In the past months there have been articles in large newspapers to the effect that there is now a $10 entry fee. This was not true at the time of this writing. There are fees to camp inside the park, but you can call the park and secure this information. Call (423) 436-1200.

At Cades Cove there are donation boxes with the message that the Great Smokies need your help. You can drop in whatever money you feel like giving. Don't give what it's worth! You'd go home broke. It's a superb trip from start to finish.

There are also booklets at the entrance to Cades Cove. These cost $2, and the purchase is an honor-system basis. You can put your money into the waiting containers.

FACILITIES:

In the park you can fish, hike, ride horseback, canoe, tube, picnic, camp, and engage in other outdoor activities. There are restrooms, picnic tables, and campgrounds in Cades Cove.

WHAT'S THE STORY?

This graveyard trip is to an old Methodist Church that was built by one man for an incredibly low price. As you visit the church, notice the workmanship that this one man demonstrated, and take particular notice of the man's dedication to his faith and to his work.

SPECIAL ATTRACTIONS:

The entire trip is special, but you will likely enjoy the church and the graveyard equally; both are important links in the chain of history.

MAKING THE MOST OF YOUR VISIT:

Ralph Waldo Emerson once wrote, "An institution is but the lengthened shadow of one man." And this Methodist Church is the lengthened shadow of J. D. McCampbell.

Here is his story, and this is also the story of the church.

McCampbell, a blacksmith and carpenter working alone, did all the work on the entire church in 115 days at a cost of $115. In those days it simply was not possible for the country church to receive donations from wealthy church members, and if there was to be a church, someone had to take the initiative.

There was also the matter of necessary funding for the building materials, the manual labor, and the dedication and desire to serve one's faith in a tangible way. McCampbell was a one-man band in more than one way: he also served as pastor of the church for many years.

Notice the double doors of the church. In that day and in that area, men, women, and children did not enter or exit by the same door. The men used the right door; women and children used the left door and sat on the left side of the church. It was only when a boy reached manhood that he could sit with the men of the community.

The cemetery is behind the church. As you tour it, notice the ancient stones, some of them simple, almost primitive. There are few expensive or elaborate stones in the graveyard, because the people of Cades Cove were a hands-on society: they made what they needed, and there was neither opportunity nor real desire for luxury. The graveyard reflects not only a final resting place but also an entire way of life. Study the dates and inscriptions on the stones, and you can read the legacy of an isolated people.

General Gordon's Grave in Wilkesboro.

SECTION 10: THE BEST MOUNTAIN GRAVEYARDS
TRIP 9: THE GRAVE OF GENERAL JAMES B. GORDON
THE LAST OF THE FREEMEN?

LOCATION:

Located in Wilkesboro, as is the final graveyard visit in this book, the grave of Brigadier General James B. Gordon can be found at the Wilkesboro Episcopal Church. See directions in the next trip to Wilkesboro from I-40 and the Blue Ridge Parkway. Once you are in Wilkesboro, drive west of the old Wilkes County Courthouse to West Street. Turn right and climb the hill to the intersection. You will see a sign directing you to the Wilkesboro Episcopal Church. The grave of General Gordon is near the west side of the church. It is very easy to find.

SPECIAL ATTRACTIONS:

See the attractions listed in the next trip. In addition, you are within easy driving distance of Boone, Blowing Rock, Jefferson, West Jefferson, and Lenoir, where you will find one of the best private homes in the state: Fort Defiance.

HOURS OF OPERATION:

Plan to visit the churchyard during week days between the hours of 8 a.m. and dusk. On Sunday plan to visit after the morning church services have ended.

ADMISSION:

There are no admission charges.

FACILITIES:

There are no facilities, other than parking spaces, at the church. See the listing in the next trip of nearby facilities.

WHAT'S THE STORY?

During the UnCivil War, General James B. Gordon died on May 18 as a result of wounds received on May 12, 1864. No matter how you feel about the Civil War, it is hard to be indifferent to the hundreds of thousands of deaths of Americans killed by yet other Americans in the most tragic clash of ideals and values in the history of this nation.

While the exact number of deaths in the various wars this country has fought can never be accurately determined, take a moment to examine the readily available figures. In the American Revolution there were 4,435 deaths; in the War of 1812 there were 2,260 killed in action; in the Mexican War 13,283 perished; in the Spanish-American War there were 2,446 deaths; in World War I this nation lost 116,708 Americans; in World War II this country lost 407,316 of its best young men and women in battle; in the Korean War there were 36,916 American deaths; in the Vietnam War there were 58,193 deaths. During the Persian Gulf War this nation lost 299 Americans.

The staggering total of battle deaths is 641,856 Americans who died in battle or of infections and illnesses as a result of the armed conflict.

And in the Civil War there were more than 617,512 American deaths: almost as many deaths in the one war as there were in all the other wars in American history. There is a very strong message contained in those figures. It is true that in the Civil War Americans were strongly divided against each other, but in the Vietnam War and in the earlier Korean War American sentiment was also bitterly divided.

Even during the American Revolution there was bitter and prolonged disagreement and dissension. And, in a moment of pure editorializing, ideals are one thing; deaths of hundreds of thousands are quite another. As Oliver Wendell Holmes once wrote, "This is a moral that runs at large; take it, you're welcome, no extra charge."

The reason for the above statements of statistics and ideals can best be summarized by Carl Sandburg's poem "Buttons," in which the author describes the buttons and pins used to mark the war map and show whose army had conquered what city or territory. Sandburg softly asks who would have guessed what it cost in the lives of thousands of men and boys in order to move two buttons one inch on the war map.

SPECIAL ATTRACTIONS:

In addition to the grave of General Gordon, you will find the Episcopal Church to be a beautiful and serene place. You can also enjoy paying an exterior visit to the old Wilkes County courthouse. Downtown you can see the site of the Tory Oak, where several tories were "swung off" for their roles in the American Revolution. The original tree is gone now, the victim of time and the elements, and a new (and tiny) tree has replaced it. But adjacent to the original tree is a second oak, this one called Tory, Junior. At the site you are very close to the Old Wilkes Jail Museum.

MAKING THE MOST OF YOUR VISIT:

The inscription on the tombstone of General James B. Gordon, who died at age 44, is a poem that is both lovely and tragic. The poem says:

And thus perished with the last of freemen,
Last of all that dauntless race
Who had rather die unsullied
Than outlive the Land's disgrace.
O, thou noble-hearted soldier
Reck not of the after-time.
Honor may be esteemed dishonor,

Loyalty be called a crime.
Sleep in peace with kindred ashes
Of the noble and the true.
Hands that never failed their country
Hearts that never baseness knew.

Who could have guessed, to remind you again of the lines by Carl Sandburg, that it would cost more than half a million lives to move a button a couple of inches on a war map?

Don't contemplate the question too long, or you may join Ernest Hemingway in his bitterly ironic statement to the effect that if we talked about World War I too long we might decide that it was a bad thing that maybe shouldn't have happened.

When you have studied the churchyard to your satisfaction, you can drive around the town of Wilkesboro and see the many old houses, historic sites, and perhaps tour the home of Captain Robert Cleveland, an officer who served under his brother, Colonel Benjamin Cleveland, at the Battle of Kings Mountain.

The house is old, rustic, and beautiful. It is a fitting place to end your visit to Wilkesboro.

Martha Lenoir grave in Wilkesboro.

SECTION 10: THE BEST MOUNTAIN GRAVEYARDS
TRIP 10: THE GRAVE OF MARTHA LENOIR
THE INNOCENCE AND POWER OF A CHILD

LOCATION:

This grave is in the mountain town of Wilkesboro. The actual grave-yard is behind the Wilkesboro Presbyterian Church and is a little difficult to find, unless you know the area.

To get to the graveyard, you can exit I-40 in Statesville and drive NC 115 to Wilkesboro, or you can exit I-40 near Hickory and follow NC 18 into Wilkesboro. From the Blue Ridge Parkway take the NC 18 exit south to Wilkesboro.

Once inside Wilkesboro, drive down the main street through the center of the town. From the west you will pass the old Wilkes County Courthouse; from the east if you reach the courthouse you have gone too far. Heading east from the courthouse, watch carefully on the right side of the road for the Wilkesboro Presbyterian Church, which is back off the road 200 feet or so. There are two ways to get to the graveyard. The easier is to take East Street, which you will see on the west side of the church. Drive down a modest hill and you will see the graveyard on the left. There is a gate near the northeast corner of the cemetery and the grave of Martha Lenoir is near the gate, just west of the wrought iron enclosure.

NEARBY ATTRACTIONS:

In Wilkesboro you can visit the Old Wilkes Jail Museum from 9 a.m. until 4 p.m. The museum is behind the old courthouse and across the street from the police station. There you can see the Robert Cleveland log house, the cells in which Tom Dula and Ann Melton were incarcerated, and see an interesting video of the tragic story of Dula, Foster, and Melton. Read more about these lovers/haters who crossed their own stars and created their own earthly misfortunes and tragedies.

It is a 45-minute drive from Wilkesboro to the Blue Ridge Parkway via NC 18 and an hour's drive to Doughton Park. You can also drive easily to Stone Mountain and other area attractions. The Kerr Scott Dam and Reservoir are just west of town on NC 268, and there you can visit the several parks along the impoundment.

HOURS OF OPERATION:

The graveyard is open from 8 a.m. until dusk. Please do not show any form of disrespect to the final resting places of the people who are interred there.

ADMISSION:

There is no admission fee. There is no admission to the Old Wilkes Jail Museum, to Doughton Park, or Stone Mountain. If you visit the Kerr Scott parks, you will pay $1 per adult in order to tour the parks, use picnic tables and restrooms. Not all of the parks have picnic tables, but the Berry Mountain park has some.

FACILITIES:

At the graveyard there are no facilities. You must park on the side of the road. But there are opportunities to picnic, hike, fish, swim, and enjoy nature study at other attractions in the area. At Doughton Park (See the chapter in the Get-Out-and-Go section) you can have a world of great fun an no cost, unless you choose to camp.

WHAT'S THE STORY?

The Martha Lenoir story is that of a child, incredibly determined and resolute, who insisted on seeing her father, who was a prisoner of war at Camden, South Carolina, during the American Revolution. What she accomplished is remarkable.

SPECIAL ATTRACTIONS:

In addition to the Martha Lenoir grave site, you can also visit the graves of others in the cemetery. Some are ancient, some are highly interesting, and others are fascinating in the bucolic setting. This is another place to have Gray's "Elegy Written in a Country Churchyard" handy.

MAKING THE MOST OF YOUR VISIT:

As you enter the gate on the north side of the graveyard, turn left toward the tall trees in the corner. You will see the gravestone of Martha Lenoir, with the inscription facing east. Her epitaph reads: "Martha Lenoir-Wife of Richard Gwyn, Daughter of Col. Thomas and Martha Lenoir. Born in Kershau District, SC Born September 16, 1767-Died February 23, 1829.

The story is that Martha Lenoir was only a child when her father, Colonel Thomas Lenoir, was held prisoner by the forces of Lord Cornwallis in Camden, South Carolina. Stories came back to the child that her father was being poorly fed, that he was near starvation.

With the optimism of a child, she asked the family cook (she lived in the care of the cook and a second servant) to prepare a huge basket of food (she specifically requested fried chicken, one source says), and then she asked the servant to accompany her on the trip to Camden.

The old man reluctantly agreed, and somehow they made their way to the beautiful town of Camden, which was then held by the British army. The story goes on to say that the two unlikely and innocent travelers gained entrance into the headquarters of Lord Cornwallis, and the commander himself asked the purpose of their visit.

When the girl told why she was there, Cornwallis reportedly took the girl to her father so that she could give him the food, and it was only a short time later that the family was reunited, thanks to the courage of a child, the gentle guidance of the old servant, and the sometimes hard heart of a military man who could not bear the sadness of the child.

Leaving the grave of Martha Lenoir, you can wander about the graveyard and witness the other links with antiquity. Or you can go to the Old Wilkes Jail Museum and learn more about Tom Dula, Laura Foster, and Ann Melton. See in the scenic drives section of this book the narration of the Dula-Foster-Melton story.

This trip concludes the *100 Practically Perfect Places in the North Carolina Mountains*. Making these trips myself enriched me greatly. I sincerely hope you, the reader, can say the same.

Overlook at Blowing Rock.